Shaman or Sherlock?

Shaman or Sherlock?

The Native American Detective

Gina Macdonald and
Andrew Macdonald

With MaryAnn Sheridan

CONTRIBUTIONS TO THE STUDY OF
POPULAR CULTURE, NUMBER 74
Kathleen Gregory Klein, Series Editor

GREENWOOD PRESS
Westport, Connecticut • London

Library of Congress Cataloging-in-Publication Data

Macdonald, Gina.
    Shaman or Sherlock? : the Native American detective / Gina Macdonald and Andrew
Macdonald ; with MaryAnn Sheridan.
        p.   cm. (Contributions to the study of popular culture, ISSN 0198–9871 ; no. 74)
    Includes bibliographical references (p.   ) and index.
    ISBN 0–313–30841–1 (alk. paper)
    1. Detective and mystery stories, American—History and criticism.   2. Indians in
literature.   I. Macdonald, Andrew, 1942–   II. Sheridan, MaryAnn.   III. Title.
IV. Series.
PS173.I6M28   2002
813'.0872093520397—dc21   2001023335

British Library Cataloguing in Publication Data is available.

Library of Congress Catalog Card Number: 2001023335
ISBN: 0–313–30841–1
ISSN: 0198–9871

First published in 2002

Greenwood Press, 88 Post Road West, Westport, CT 06881
An imprint of Greenwood Publishing Group, Inc.
www.greenwood.com

Printed in the United States of America

The paper used in this book complies with the
Permanent Paper Standard issued by the National
Information Standards Organization (Z39.48–1984).

10 9 8 7 6 5 4 3 2 1

"Indians are big right now," said Rupert, the [literary] agent. "Publishers are looking for that shaman thing, you know? The New Age stuff, after death experiences, the healing arts, talking animals, sacred vortexes, that kind of thing. And you've got all that, plus a murder mystery. That's perfect."
—Sherman Alexie, *Indian Killer*

Contents

Acknowledgments

Our thanks must go to Kathleen Klein, without whose vision this book would never have come to fruition; Brian Garfield, who shared with us his experiences creating the Sam Watchman books and transferring them to film; and Margaret Coel, whose advice about the Wind River Mission and Reservation Band and whose comments about her purpose and characters brought her books to life for us in new ways.

We also deeply appreciate the support of colleagues and friends like David Estes, Andrew Horton, Paulette Richards, Suzanne Moore, and Ellen and Paul Plaisaunce, and the Language and Literature Department at Nicholls State University, Thibodaux.

All artwork is the conceptualization and creation of Jeanie Kay Duvall.

1

Introduction

20 to 22 percent of all books sold in the United States are . . . mystery or detective fiction . . . enjoyed equally by male and female readers from age seven to adults. . . . And . . . much contemporary detective fiction explores issues of cultural interaction . . . through the investigation of serious crime.

—Klein, *Diversity and Detective Fiction*, 2

When this project began, a recurrent objection by colleagues was, "Native American detectives? A *whole* book about them?" The incredulity of these questioners, many of them avid consumers of popular fiction in general, is easily understood: in their view, the project lacked a subject matter. This puzzlement was usually followed by, "Well, there's Tony Hillerman, of course, but does anyone else write about Indian detectives?"

The answer, as the bibliography of primary sources shows, is, "Yes, lots of writers." In fact, indigenous "detectives" (known by other names but functioning similarly to contemporary urban investigators) have a long, honorable history in American culture. As Lisbeth Paravisini-Gebert observes in *The Oxford Companion to Crime and Mystery Writing* entry

"Native American Sleuth," there were Native American detectives as early as the dime novels of the 1880s, with heroes who crossed cultures easily and spoke English and several native languages: Judson R. Taylor's *Phil Scott, the Indian Detective: A Tale of Startling Mysteries* (1882); T. C. Harbaugh's *Velvet Foot, the Indian Detective, or The Taos Tiger* (1884); Buffalo Bill Cody's *Red Renard, the Indian Detective, or The Gold Buzzards of Colorado: A Romance of the Mines and Dead Trails* (1886); and Harlan Page Halsley's (Old Sleuth's) *Pawnee Tom, or, Adrift in New York: A Story of an Indian Boy Detective* (1896) (307). These stories exploited Eastern interest in Western themes and tied their concept of detection directly to abilities for which Native Americans were renowned: tracking skills involving close observation of nature, the "reading" of forest and trail, and survival in the wilderness.

However, the twentieth-century decline of the Old West led to waning interest in native detectives. Not until 1946 did another native detective appear, and then only in a short story: Manly Wade Wellman's "A Star for a Warrior" (*EQMM*, April 1946) introduced David Return, a tribal policeman from an imaginary tribe (a Cheyenne-Pawnee mix), whose insights into local crimes came from his knowledge of tribal ways, ceremonies, and religious beliefs (307). Then, suddenly, the 1970s rediscovered the figure, and the revival of the Native American detective began with Brian Garfield's Arizona state trooper, Navajo Sam Watchman, Richard Martin Stern's mixed-blood Apache police chief, Johnny Ortiz, and Tony Hillerman's tribal policemen, Joe Leaphorn and Jim Chee. Since then, the revival has led to a new subgenre of the modern detective story. Our bibliography includes well over 60 modern authors with Native American detectives either as the central detective or as a significant co-detective.

Despite these historical precursors, the phrase "Native American detective" makes most modern readers think first of Hillerman's detectives, because his multivolume series established and popularized the subgenre's modern image, moving detection from the metaphorical canyons of the big city, in a memorable critical phrase, to the literal ones of New Mexico and Arizona. But for all that Hillerman remains the gold standard of present-day Native American detective fiction. One of the best of its practitioners, he did not invent the figure of the Indian detective, nor does he now still hold a monopoly on such fiction. Hillerman's genius lay in resituating the detective, allowing others to spin out the diverse roles and possibilities of the new setting. In fact, the Native American detective's present popularity with dozens of writers of greater and lesser talent is simply another manifestation of an old American theme: the Indian as a marginal figure on the border of civilization, a guide, an escort, or a companion into a darker and freer world, and sometimes a mentor or a guru who teaches a secret wisdom.

Today's Indian detective may be a gun for hire who helps the threatened disappear into a new identity; a hunter whose companions are being killed off one by one; an archaeologist caught in the netherworld of stolen artifacts, pottery, and petroglyphs; an artist worried about the exploitation of native artists; or an FBI agent caught up in a family battle against skinwalkers. Today's Indian detective may be a returnee to traditional life on the reservation, an escapee from modernism and all that it implies. Today's Indian detective may also be a native princess with a flair for fashion, a lesbian pushing feminist theories and attitudes, or a computer whiz using high-tech means to skirt the law and assist the weak, impoverished, innocent, and not-so-innocent stand against big government, big corporations, the Mafia, dirty banks, greedy trustees, or any large organization that treads roughshod over the individual. Today's Indian detective may be a New Age spiritualist who crosses time and space through ancient native arts that open windows into other dimensions; an Eskimo guided by visionary children who "see" the crimes he detects; a shaman who calls on animal and earth spirits for guidance, who flies above the crime scene with the eye of a crow, or who journeys to the land of the dead to defeat a sorceress; or a ghost from the past who aids a modern detective in order to right old wrongs and free itself from the trap of a space-time warp. That such figures are now termed *detectives* suggests the changed attitudes toward assimilation and otherness in American culture.

HISTORICAL MODELS

Native Americans served as scouts and guides for European explorers and settlers from the earliest encounters with the invaders from the east. Their motives were as varied and complex as their tribes and circumstances, sometimes the honorable ones of desiring peace and friendship with strangers in their land, sometimes the less admirable wish for revenge on or advantage over rival tribes. As the initial trickles of immigrants turned into waves and floods, serving the enemy clearly became a *modus vivendi*, a way of negotiating survival by playing both ends against the middle. Working for whites for private gain must have seemed little different from making temporary alliances with other tribes against mutual enemies, a common enough Native American phenomenon in pre-European eras. The Algonquin and the Huron, for example, made common cause with the French against their traditional enemies, the Iroquois. The Navajo worked as military scouts to revenge themselves on the Apache, as did the Crow to undermine the Sioux.

Apart from some commentary on James Fenimore Cooper's characters as "early detectives," little notice has been taken of the similarities in function between Indian scouts and the prototypical modern American detective figure. Both put themselves out for hire, usually to people who consider themselves their social superiors. Both work in potentially compromising situations, sometimes against the interests of the people from whom they sprang (in the classic detective story, the working classes, the common folk) and in favor of employers far more wealthy and powerful. Both scout and detective interpret alien cultures, ways, and in the case of Indians, languages. Both are classic middlemen, reconciling different cultural agendas.

Although scouts may simply show the physical way through a wilderness, they often also protect and guard against unseen or unpredictable dangers, using their superior knowledge to shield their employers both physically and psychically. As sidekicks, Indian scouts have lent frontier authenticity and exoticism to any number of mainstream heroes. Like detectives, scouts often deal with problems of theft, violence, kidnapping and ransom, and murder and its consequences. As Thomas Perry's modern-day Seneca guide, Jane Whitefield, says of her ancestors, their special role as guides for refugees from other tribes was to save people "from the horrible things that could happen," to remove victims from threats and hide them in new locations among strangers (*Vanishing Act*, 18). Clearly, America's varied cultures, its social checkerboard of conflicting ways and lifestyles, long necessitated guides and scouts to steer the innocent past trouble.

Brian Moore's *Black Robe*, a dramatization of conflicts between various Indian tribes and French Jesuit missionaries in seventeenth-century Canada, captures this conflict superbly. All participants are constantly on guard when an Algonquian group leads a priest into territory controlled by hostile Iroquois. Based on historical accounts in the Jesuit *Relations* (17), a compendium of letters from missionaries to their superiors in France detailing their successes and problems, the novel illustrates its protagonist, Father Laforgue, struggling with the theft of his personal property and trade goods, death threats from within and outside his group, torture, mutilation, and kidnapping. Chomina, Laforgue's Algonquian guide, keeps his promise to protect the priest from harm and to lead him to a Jesuit mission to the Hurons, even though he is convinced the French will bring no good to his people. Like any good Southern California private eye, he acts according to a private code of honorable conduct, even when it alienates him from his tribe and leads to his family's destruction.

Labeling Chomina a detective may seem to torture the term more brutally than the Iroquois do their enemies; Chomina simply shows the priest the way and guards his person rather than solving crimes. Yet, although the term *detective* was coined 200 years after the time period of the novel, the social role played is very similar. Focusing on the part played by the modern detective rather than on his urban surroundings and the trappings of modern technology shows any number of early U.S. scouts fitting the mold. These include such famous white scouts as Daniel Boone, Davy Crockett, Bat Masterson, and William (Buffalo Bill) Cody, as well as William Sherley Williams, who lived among the Osage, and Thomas Jeffords, a friend of the Chiracahua Apache. Also included are such native scouts as the Shoshone Sacajawea, who guided the Lewis and Clark expedition; Chief Washaskie, who led U.S. troops against the Shoshone's traditional enemies, the Sioux and the Cheyenne; Northern Paiute Sarah Winnemucca Hopkins, who used her position as scout and interpreter to rescue her father and grandfather (tribal chieftains) from the Bannocks; and Buffalo Horn, a former scout who led the uprising known as the Bannock War. The detective figure has too often been defined by the cliches of setting and "beat" rather than by how the figure operated in social and cultural terms in a given environment.

This perceptual shift in imagining the detective in new territory was precisely Garfield's and Hillerman's achievement and has been the paradigm shift that has revived the genre. Garfield's Watchman and Hillerman's Chee and Leaphorn neither look nor behave like traditional urban mainstream detectives, police-affiliated or private, and they play out their investigations in settings seemingly nonconducive to genre conventions. More importantly, they reason in ways that Philip Marlowe, Lew Archer, and the Continental Op might find quite alien. Nevertheless, Watchman, Chee, and Leaphorn are undeniably detectives working in the fictional genre and, in the tradition of the hard-boiled, organizational detective of police procedurals, they are, in their way, trying to set the world right. The question of definition is thus foregrounded: What is detection, and how should the form of investigation—the approaches to finding the truth about malfeasance—define how we see the detective? Although the investigator figure is apparently fluid in the new millennium, some stable elements remain, mainly the detective/investigator's appeal to readers and the methods by which the detective reasons out solutions.

Interestingly, the modern Native American detective figure developed from the ethnic detective (see Klein). Classical early-twentieth-century British detective stories equated ethnicity with the sinister and suspect. The Charley Chan stories marked a major departure from this convention, one that since the 1970s has blossomed into a plethora of ethnic detectives with myriad agendas. Kathleen Klein's *Diversity and Detective Fiction* confirms their diversity: Native Americans from 24 different tribes, African Americans, and Americans of Armenian, Basque, Chinese, Cuban, French, German, Gypsy, Indian, Irish, Italian, Japanese, Jewish, Mexican, Norwegian, Polish, Portuguese, Puerto Rican, Russian, Scots, Slovenic, Tibetan, and Vietnamese descent (this list could easily be extended with recently published works). Such ethnic detectives have provided a sympathetic voice for often ignored populations, have pushed social, political, and sexual agendas, and, in crossroads cultural encounters, have served as guides to cultures new to American readers and as interpreters of cultural difference. They make the alien and suspect familiar by perceiving new experiences through the eyes of the Other. These functions are especially true of the Native American detective subgenre.

THE APPEAL OF THE DETECTIVE

If the origins of a genre lie in the material its precursors dealt with, the crime "novel" in English may be said to begin with the prose fiction narratives of writers such as Robert Greene, whose coney-catching pamphlets described the purportedly true-to-life activities of the Elizabethan underworld, or Ben Jonson, whose plays *Bartholomew Fair, The Alchemist*, and *Volpone* hinge entirely on activities of criminal intent. These tales of marginal members of society duping their betters and often being duped in return were clearly meant to titillate as much as to inform or warn; Greene and his compatriots knew how to sell their prose to the emerging middle-class readers of London, and Jonson's plays were highly popular. However, these sensational turn-of-the-sixteenth-century crime stories eventually led to the more ambitious goal of using underworld settings and detective fiction as uniquely appropriate mediums for social criticism, especially critiques of the abuses of marginal or ignored groups. While elements of the crime story survived with works such as Daniel Defoe's *Moll Flanders*, it found a much wider audience in the middle-class readers of the nineteenth century.

Curiosity about forbidden lifestyles in prohibited districts of big cities has always been an important part of the appeal of detective stories, as have the secret sins of the wealthy and powerful as they trample over the poor and weak. As a means of consciousness-raising about the social failings of a community, the detective story is made to order. Pathologies such as delinquency, drug abuse, violence against self, family, and others, and of course the mechanics of crime itself, are the stuff of its existence, whether as the events that drive the plot or as background in the milieu in which the investigator must operate. The hard-boiled American genre has usually illuminated social justice questions, directly or indirectly.

The Native American as a detective or an important player in a detective story is thus ideally situated by long tradition to foreground the many injustices plaguing Indian communities. Since most detectives or investigators are trained in mainstream law and forensic science, there is a natural link to the mainstream audience familiar with the genre and a unique opportunity to cast a sympathetic light on issues otherwise left obscure, exotic, or impenetrable. Social and cultural issues in detective fiction featuring Native American detectives can be broadly outlined in a number of categories: religious conflicts, political struggles for control of land and resources, theft/fraud committed against Native Americans, manipulation of law, eradication of culture, degradation of ecology, and so on. The following represents issues and particular situations covered in the novels discussed in this text; all reflect, at worst, varying degrees of cultural and sometimes literal genocide, of cultural hegemony at best.

- *Religion*: forced conversions; the destruction of native religious items (such as sacred masks/totems); banned religious practices (potlatches; Sun, Ghost, and Snake Dances; peyote rites); the institutionalization into insane asylums of practitioners of native religions; the dismissal of native spiritual beliefs and funeral practices as irrelevant for "scientific" collectors (museum collections of Native American body parts—strings of ears, bones, scalps, and pouches made of scrotums or breasts); the continued conflicting influence of Christianity on native cultures (attacks on Mormons, Catholics, and Baptists for proselytizing and imposing religious hegemony balanced with praise for the social services of Catholic and Protestant missions); fear of witchcraft/skinwalkers; the offenses of New Age groupies and New Age hoaxes.

- *Politics*: historical disenfranchisement as late as the 1940s/1950s; intertribal disputes over reservation land (for example, Hopi versus Navajo); intertribal conflicts over the granting of federal funds; legal conflicts between tribes that were historically enemies; age-old conflicts between Pueblo Indians and the descendants of the Spanish conquistadors; Bureau of Indian Affairs meddling; heavy-handed FBI responses to Native American political activism.

- *Law*: questions of jurisdiction (federal or tribal?); oral versus written tradition; tokenism in representation and disenfranchisement; denial of social benefits to Native Americans whose tribal associations did not appear on eighteenth- or nineteenth-century documents; fishing rights disputes; attempts to regain tribal lands; legal conflicts concerning compensation for losses.

- *Theft/Fraud*: illegal real estate deals, including theft of land through declarations of insanity; corrupt institutions receiving government funds for services and goods not delivered; Bureau of Indian Affairs' approval of the looting of Indian resources (such as reservation oil or uranium); theft of/illegal trade in artifacts and petroglyphs, depriving the community/tribe of its heritage, of its religious items, and possibly of its ancestors; defacement of petroglyphs and ancient ruins; graverobbing; legal theft by companies with monopolies on native-produced goods, bought for low prices and sold for exorbitant prices; construction fraud; cattle rustling, horse theft, dinosaur bone theft.

- *Culture*: turn-of-the-century institutionalization for speaking native languages; conflicting ideas about etiquette (not meeting eyes directly; no tradition of polite conversation; tradition of waiting outside a residence until invited in); conflicting ideas about private property (mainstream versus native); the negative effects of gambling and alcohol on a native community; cultural acceptance of drug use for religious purposes resulting in unchecked drug smuggling across barren stretches of reservation land; generational differences related to degree of assimilation to mainstream culture (reservation youth gangs); the economic depression of reservations—poverty, unemployment, despair; reservation problems of wife beating, child abuse, incest, and gratuitous cruelty; conflicts over purity of blood (pure bloods versus half-breeds and mixed bloods); questionable adoptions of native infants; racial conflicts between reservation dwellers and nearby whites erupting into vigilantism and violence.

- *Ecology*: illegal logging of old growth forests on reservation land; illegal wildcraft harvesting from tribal lands of plants used for herbal medicine or of animal parts in demand in Asia (e.g., the pituitary glands of bears); reservation land as a dumping ground for nuclear and chemical waste; strip mining/open-pit mining of minerals on reservation land, with no follow-up, cleanup, or safety precautions; industrial and organic pollution of reservation rivers; flea and tick infestations carrying plague and other diseases.

The above classification amply demonstrates why the frustrated hopes and dreams, anger, and disappointment that characterize crime and mystery stories and often create radical authorial worldviews also characterize the Native American detective story. The native detective is not only identifying a wrongdoer but is stopping large-scale cultural injustices—theft of a heritage, destruction of a way of life, decimation of a population. In the case of the Native American detective, doing right by clients might sometimes mean acting outside the strictures of the law (a law imposed by force) or providing street justice (or canyon justice) when justice can be obtained by no other means. Other questions raised, particularly by the shamanistic detectives, relate to ways of knowledge, or epistemology: How can a criminal be identified, the crime laid bare?

Hillerman's Leaphorn and Chee, representing the ratiocinative Western and the intuitive native traditions, respectively, bridge the cultural chasms that separate mainstream and native cultures. Leaphorn is very much in the Sherlock Holmes school of ratiocinative deduction, while Chee, as a shaman, follows traditional Navajo ways to knowledge. Chee does not carry his shamanism as far, however, as do most modern native detectives, and instead sees it as a cultural counter to evil to restore harmony. This text will explore this division between a mainstream outlook on crime and a native viewpoint, for herein lies the deepest, most divisive gulf between the cultures. In the most extreme cases, the essential differences are:

Sherlock	Shaman
relies on deductive reasoning, observation, and ratiocination	relies on intuition, spirit guides, and spiritual tools
goes to real places and interviews suspects; checks police records	travels to the spirit world and battles skinwalkers, witches, and sorcerers
has a sense of present time and present events	ties present events to historical ones; envisions past, present, and future times overlapping and interlocking
dreams may reflect how the subconscious mind helps one interpret facts gathered by the conscious mind	dreams are more real than the everyday world; battles can be fought and won in dream-worlds; visions foretell events

villains are flesh and blood and vulnerable	villains exist in a spiritual dimension and may be invulnerable except through the spirit world
tools include forensic evidence (from autopsies, DNA tests, fingerprinting, shoe and tire tracks); computer files; police records; close observation of crime scene; ratiocination/deductive reasoning	tools may be chants, rituals, sand paintings, shadow catchers, sacred masks, spirit boats, cedar smoke, carved cedar boards, corn pollen, purification by fire.

Clearly, writers with shamanistic detectives push the envelope of the detective genre and verge on what has in the past been the domain of the horror story or of science fiction. While shamans are somewhat in the psychic sleuth tradition of scientists, philosophers, or magicians with special psychological/extrasensory powers and a knowledge of occult practices that make them more speculative and intuitive than deductive, psychic sleuths traditionally have used the power of the spirit world to exact retribution for guilt unpunished on earth rather than to detect.

Writers more interested in justice than detection show both the advantages and hazards of pushing the genre to its social criticism limits. By setting his mysteries just after World War II, Richard Parrish makes the genre face questions of legal rights and protections for isolated minorities who could die for their country in war but not vote in a national election, much less a local one. The huge irony of the World War II generation sacrificing itself for civil rights abroad while denying them at home has not usually been confronted. Through Senecan guide Jane Whitefield, Thomas Perry examines the cracks through which the innocent may fall in the justice system and their need for protection beyond what the law provides. Native American feminist detectives naturally highlight the frequently invisible lives of Indian women, sometimes the limitations imposed on them, other times presenting them as tough feminist models of taking control of one's own life and beating men in the male workplace. Detective stories in Native American settings inevitably raise issues of poverty, exclusion, racism, and assimilation, even if their central focus is elsewhere. When such stories depict shamanism and the supernatural, the contrast with mainstream religions and ways of seeing the world comes into focus, and the general reader may suddenly become aware of how deeply forensic detection and standardized procedures are rooted in Western crime-solving.

FINDING ANSWERS: APPROACHES TO REASONING IN DETECTIVE FICTION

Apart from its often forbidden milieu and the human dramas demanding consideration, one key appeal of the detective story in its modern incar-

nations—that is, since the end of the nineteenth century—has been the
reasoning process itself. How does the investigator work? What contrasts
with everyday reasoning are evident? What methodology informs the detective's crime-busting? From procedure-driven police to the most free-
wheeling private eye, the one predictable element is that there *will* be a
methodology; it will be tested against wily villains and/or difficult
circumstances, and readers will learn the minute details of a distinct crime-
solving approach. Every detective has one; many are self-conscious about
their approach, explaining it in first-person addresses to the reader or
through the omniscient voice of third-person narration. The detection system may be abstract and distant from messy realities, as in the self-
conscious cerebrations of a Sherlock Holmes or the abstract ponderings of
Hercules Poirot or Nero Wolfe, or they may be as physical and brutal as
the methods of Sam Spade, Philip Marlowe, or Mike Hammer. In police
procedurals the approach is that of a police service located in a city or
region, or perhaps of a particular precinct or team. More often than not,
the unique, even eccentric, approach of the investigator hero is played off
against the plodding conventionality of commonplace thinking or of the
established authorities, as in the Holmes-Watson and Poirot-Japp relationships, allowing readers the double pleasure of indulging offbeat superiority
while simultaneously siding with orthodoxy against true criminal aberration. When the approach is somewhat bizarre, as in the imaginative processes of Sherlock Holmes, there is the appeal of sharing in secret knowledge,
of discovering what others never suspect. Even the most pedestrian police
procedural offers some of this pleasure, the thrill of being taught how
things really work under inherently dramatic circumstances. As readers, we
are set apart by this knowledge and by our new understanding of events
invisible to the mere average citizen.

Even the most ham-handed, hard-boiled detectives have an approach to
crime beyond the beatings and torture they may inflict to suppress it. Mike
Hammer may live up to his name, but his mayhem makes a larger ideo-
logical point as well: the prissy conventionalisms of the law promote injustice, not the rough equity that Mike hammers out. The Continental Op,
in turn, stirs up trouble as frequently as he can in *Red Harvest*, because in
a corrupt, decadent society, any change might turn out for the better. Part
of our fascination with the various approaches to detection lies in just these
assumptions by the detectives and their creators, assumptions about the
nature of humankind and what stimuli of language or behavior will force
the issue and reveal what *really* happened, what hidden springs of motive
have been at work. Just as when speculative gossip reveals how the gossiper
thinks the world works, so we construct from the ruminations of detectives
a particular theory of human behavior. All detectives have such theories
about how humans work and share the supposition that their own method
best uncovers truth. These inherently interesting theories of human nature,

manifested either indirectly in the methods of detection or made explicit and exhaustive, are a large part of the detective story's appeal.

If theories of human nature lie behind every detective's methodology, then some of the appeal of the Native American detective story becomes evident as well. The nature of the Indian has been one of the most problematic questions in American history, a definition made impossibly complex by the existence of hundreds of different tribes, cultures, and ways, and by the multiplicity of agendas inherent in all European descriptions of Indians. Present-day mainstream observers of Native Americans are, hopefully, more sophisticated than the Europeans who shared the first encounters, but also authentic Native Americans are more distant than they have ever been, set apart on usually isolated reservations or hidden behind layers of assimilation. Modern mainstream curiosity about native peoples can be partly satisfied through the familiar conventions of the detective story, which will inevitably also highlight human nature, whether with sensitivity, knowledge, and intelligence, as Hillerman does with the Navajo, or with generic "Indian" traits, as do some of his imitators. Some writers do underscore social problems in native communities and their causes, but oftentimes the Native American detective is as much a fantasy figure as some of his predecessors, the nineteenth-century scouts and guides—fictional human nature, not sociological fact, dominates most of the writers we will discuss.

If detective fiction at the very least always implies a theory of human behavior in the investigative methodology, then Native American culture provides an enormous challenge. As with any cross-cultural encounter, observers may ignore difference and act as if the Others are identical to themselves. An early example is of Spanish conquistadors giving due notice to their Indian antagonists that they were officially Spanish subjects and must cease all resistance or be decimated; the fact that such notices were read aloud in Latin or Spanish, languages the Indians could not understand, from distances of up to a mile, seemed not to offend the conquistadorian sense of propriety. (Any European would have understood their intentions!) Many recent works of detective fiction with Native American topics do in fact presume that indigenous values systems, psychology, and sense of self are identical to mainstream ones but, as with the Spanish conquerors, this denial of obvious difference clearly serves other agendas.

While it is easy to mock the motives of conquerors intent on exploitation, addressing difference is nevertheless always complex; wide variations between tribes and even subgroups such as bands make generalizations hazardous, with stark contrasts between even neighboring peoples quite possible. A typical mainstream investigator reading behavior or hearing explanations intent on detecting guilt presumes that an individual's knowledge of personal culpability will express itself through unconscious, uncontrollable signs, a notion central to Western ideas about establishing guilt. Even untrained jurors are presumed to have this capacity to detect untruth, which will inevitably come out, at least in the popular imagination. (Professional gamblers, an unsentimental lot, agree that bluffs can be read by "tells," unconscious gestures such as an ear tug or a twist of a ring.)

Such signals of falsity may not be universal, however. In *Deep Valley Malice*, Kirk Mitchell's Paiute Dwight Rainwater, hired to guide Los Angeles SWAT teams around Owens Valley, simply walks off the job when SWAT team members misunderstand his reticence and squeeze him for intelligence about the trustworthiness of fellow Indians working for the Department of Water and Power. The more they push, the more uncomfortable he becomes, and the more they suspect his involvement in terrorist bombings of the Los Angeles aqueduct system. Mitchell observes that the urban outsiders do not understand that "Indian-style democracy, clan consensus," depends on "subtle gestures, approving or disapproving silences," not "posturing and opinionating" (100). Raintree finds the SWAT team's behavior and queries mystifying and embarrassing, their manner rude and intrusive. Paiutes traditionally deplore direct confrontation, so walking away is the only way he knows to avoid a worsening situation. Richard Parrish likewise notes the quick assumptions of guilt Arizona lawmen frequently made about Papagos, taking their traditional politeness form of not meeting the eyes directly and purposely turning away their gaze as a "tell" indicating guilt. In other words, telltale signs law officers rely on in mainstream culture serve them poorly in native cultures.

Furthermore, in what anthropologists call "shame" cultures, no familiar dynamic of guilt is in operation, and a suspect will be broken down not by the supposedly intolerable stress of a guilty conscience—deep inner feelings struggling for release—but by the suspicion that peers are aware of his disgrace, a very different kind of inevitable conclusion to an interrogation. An Inuit story tells of an old Chugach woman whose meal is interrupted by a thief. She sings to him, "Old Shit, Old Shit. He makes me ashamed. He was looking at me when I was eating. Old Shit, Old Shit." He feels no guilt, but after the verse spreads through the village, the thief is cured of his criminality (Farb, *Man's Rise to Civilization*, 45, 151). Among the Northwest coastal tribes, the shame totem pole serves the same function, reminding individuals and families of past wrongs yet to be righted. In shame cultures, the Western detective might be excused for thinking all suspects are psychopaths, unencumbered by guilt but chastened severely by public disapproval.

Motive as well can be culture-specific and sometimes actually invisible to an outside detective with a limited understanding of those being investigated. For example, traditional Native American attitudes about sexuality varied dramatically, as the historical record shows. The Algonquians tolerated open affairs between their young girls and French trappers, a license unthinkable for other tribes. The Sioux and other Plains Indian groups had the custom of the *berdache*, a "man-woman" who serviced the sexual needs of single males and of married braves whose wives were unavailable due to childbearing or other reasons. The Inuit famously lent out wives to men in need and played a sex game called "putting out the lamp," in which married couples chose partners randomly. In Scott Young's series featuring Inuk Matteesie Kitologitak, Kitologitak has married a white wife whose mere existence has enabled him to be promoted far beyond the rank attained by other native investigators, but his most comfortable relationship is his ongoing affair with a native woman who shares his traditions and values—neither he nor his mistress feels any guilt about this relationship. Clearly, adultery has a very different definition among the Eskimos (Farb, 43). The Navajo revel in double and triple sexual puns, and their Sacred Clowns engage publicly in sexual behavior meant to be humorous but often seen as scandalous by outsiders, white and Indian. In contrast, the Apaches cut off the nose of an unfaithful woman, and the Kiowa denounced infidelity. As a result of such diverse values, sexual jealousy or revenge for what might be seen as a sexual transgression in one tribe, a killing offense, might be meaningless in another.

Obviously, travel to distant places frequently changes what constitutes motive, but few casual observers appreciate how much variation exists even among native groups sharing the same reservations. In particular, voluntary and forced migration has juxtaposed widely differing values. Hopi and Zuñi ideas about witchcraft and the supernatural differ from those of their Navajo neighbors, with the latter believing wholeheartedly that skinwalker-witches pay back enemies for old grievances. The Hopi have little innate fear of dead bodies, but the Navajos believe the living can be contaminated, made ill, or even killed by contact with not only the body but the dwelling where a person died. Naturally, behavior of the respective groups at a crime scene should be read accordingly. In consequence, generalizations about the "Indian way" are perilous. The Cherokee in their original home in Georgia were highly successful accumulators of property (including African slaves) and fought for the Confederacy during the Civil War, while many Oklahoma Cherokees fought for the Union to protect their new farms and towns; the Navajo disapprove of conspicuous wealth as divisive of their community, while some Pacific Northwest tribe members actually give away their property in regular potlatches. Other measures of status may be at work (including, for example, giving the potlatch itself), but they are unlikely to be readily apparent to an outsider. Thus the materialistic and utilitarian definitions of wealth and status so prominent in mainstream American tracings of motive ("Follow the money trail") may mean little in Indian culture. Wayne Ude's youthful thieves in *Becoming Coyote* simply want to hunt one lone buffalo in the old way in traditional attire with traditional weapons stolen from the local museum; selling these valuable items for personal profit has no part in their thinking, but using them to regain a lost part of their heritage does.

The other two legs of the prosecutorial stool, means and opportunity, may also be shaped differently in cultures unfamiliar to the mainstream investigator. Societies that believe firmly in supernatural forces may not demand empirical causes for illness or death, believing with complete consistency that non-material means may be at work. This is in no way unique to Native American societies; people of many cultures, even well-developed Westernized ones, acknowledge such spiritual forces. The Greeks and Turks, for example, believe in the force the evil eye has to do damage, and even the most skeptical Western rationalist will acknowledge the power of suggestion coupled with deeply held beliefs, like the force of voodoo cults in Haiti and in other Caribbean cultures. Thus, Navajo skinwalkers or witches may have profound effects even at great physical or temporal distance from their victims, laying waste to Western detective theories of means and opportunity. In *The Visitant*, Kathleen and Michael Gear depict modern archaeologists contaminated by corpse dust from a 900-year-old Anasazi/Katsina grave site and a modern Hopi convinced that they must be purified with fire, cedar smoke, chants, and prayers to protect against evil spirits that defy time. Rodney Barker's non-fiction work, *The Broken Circle: A True Story of Murder and Magic in Indian Country*, shows how the Navajo belief in skinwalker power recasts "random" accidents as deserved retribution on the tormentors of Navajos freed by white law. The obverse may also confound: what might seem perfect opportunities to steal from the dead might be psychologically/culturally impossible for an Arapaho who shares his tribe's fear of corpses.

Such cultural distortions of the "science" of criminal investigation become all the more complicated in the face of assimilation into the mainstream culture. The vast majority of the more than 2 million present-day Native Americans participate in the general American culture to some degree, whatever their involvement in traditional practices. The cultural mix of old and new confuses even participants, as Barbara Tedlock's amusing, insightful ethnographic narrative about the Zuñi, *The Beautiful and the Dangerous*, confirms in the lists of foods served at a Shalako celebration: "Breads included Hopi blue-corn piki, Zuñi sunflower and wheat, Navajo fry, Pueblo sourdough, and Rainbow from the store"; dessert is "apple, peach and pumpkin pie, corn pudding, cattail-flour muffins, and Oreo Creme Cookies" (251). Understanding the degree of assimilation of a suspect involves a tolerance for a highly fluid state of being since a wide range of behavior may be possible, even on the part of a single individual. Hosteen Joseph Joe, in Hillerman's *The Ghostway*, witnesses an execution-style murder in front of the local washateria, but walks away because "this was white man's business"; that is, the dead Navajo was an outsider, unable to answer a question asked him in the Navajo language (5). Modern technology has brought mainstream ways to the most remote reservations and wilderness areas, but has also enabled many tribal members to rediscover old customs and folkways that might have died out in the absence of ethnology's recording devices and the information media (such as websites) that have made cultural practices readily available. Tedlock's role as an ethnographer among the Zuñi is to observe and record, but as a scholarly participant in Zuñi culture, she and her husband Dennis also inevitably validate and inform as well. Ironically, the technology that has encouraged conformity to national standards has also permitted highly idiosyncratic ways to survive, muddling the cultural "purity" that less complex periods enjoyed. Criminal investigations conducted outside the mainstream should be rife with exceptions to the "science" of forensic understanding.

Because of this cultural variation, a long, sometimes contradictory, list of silent assumptions may underlie the interpretation of evidence, or the testimony and behavior of any given suspect. Such premises tend to inhabit the back areas of the brain without examination unless challenged by irreconcilable evidence or a culturally aware opponent.

1. Anyone is capable of anything.
2. Suspects can be identified by their M.O. (method of operation); they do not change.
3. Women do not commit suicide with a gun.
4. Cherchez la femme (search for the woman).
5. Follow the money trail.
6. Occam's Razor (the simplest explanation is the most likely) explains this.
7. When the impossible has been eliminated, what remains, no matter how improbable, must be the answer.
8. "Murder will out!"
9. Follow the evidence trail.
10. People who explain too much have something to hide.
11. People who remain silent have something to hide.
12. People who avoid direct eye contact have something to hide.
13. "The butler did it!"

This list could be extended indefinitely, confirming that each culture (and the many subcultures within each culture) has innumerable ways of interpreting "normal" human behavior and supporting the premises listed above. Whether people differ radically in essential nature regarding guilt and innocence or whether different cultures simply highlight different facets of universal human behavior is not the question. What matters is that different cultures undeniably assume varying "normal" responses concerning motives and reasoning patterns.

A further complication in setting forth Native American motives in detective fiction relates not to the nature of indigenous people themselves but rather to the uses to which the mainstream puts Indian culture. Robert Berkhofer, in *The White Man's Indian: Images of the American Indian from Columbus to the Present*, argues that white culture has been unable to see Native Americans as whole, but rather has made a construct serve white agendas and white interests by reshaping the many cultures and indigenous identities into one generic Indian figure, a simplified stereotype easy to view as coherent and consistent. Philip J. Deloria, in *Playing Indian*, proposes that much of the fascination with Indians in American culture can be explained as a need to find cultural authenticity in a blended European culture transplanted to the New World, a bland, constrictive culture which offered few releases. Playing Indian serves as a safety valve, allowing mainstream Americans an escape into a free way of life, even if only temporarily, as when children and adults adorn themselves in purportedly Indian garb and "go native," whether at summer camps, fraternal organization meetings, or other quintessentially American gatherings. Playing Indian serves as a marker of a common (if synthetic) American experience in an immigrant nation potentially riven with cultural differences. Playing Indian also inoculates against guilt about cultural and literal genocide. This activity addresses deep emotional needs unrelated to bloodlines or attempts to recapture true ethnic heritage: most of the players are Indian only in their imaginations.

Given that so many mainstream Americans feel that Indian culture is somehow built into their personal American experience, their perspective on the nature of Indian culture is severely compromised. As Deloria observes, playing Indian is just that, playing, and while some play builds on authentic cultural and sociological fact, authenticity is not the point of the exercise. Consequently, the nature of native life and ways becomes an infinitely variable commodity, a set of plastic lifeways and mores that can be shaped to meet the wishes and needs of the mainstream player. Since ideas about Indian ways are rooted in emotional needs rather than intellectual understanding, they can be highly resistant to correction by historical or present-day fact, as any number of wilderness myths attest:

- Indians are grim, serious, and humorless;
- Indians can talk to animals;
- Indians have a sixth sense;
- Indians had no culture before the Europeans came;
- Indians lived to go on the warpath and to attack their neighbors.

Devon A. Mihesuah's *American Indians: Stereotypes and Realities* delineates more such myths.

When a mainstream majority with vested interests in singular Indian practices, real and imaginary, and in an "Indian" cultural nature that accords with its own need to play Indian in its own way interprets a community composed of scores of tribes and cultural ways, mutual incomprehension is inevitable. Particular tribes and subgroups clearly want to be acknowledged and celebrated for their particular virtues, while mass culture America deeply needs a generic Indian Other, one lacking messy details. Encyclopedic knowledge about a given tribe satisfies enthusiasts both within and outside that tribe, but surly fact travels poorly from tribe to tribe, and an intimate knowledge of Hopi ways may mean little in Cherokee country. The worst of the books we will examine founder on these shoals of difference; the best find deeper channels of behavior that reflect verities of human nature, acknowledging how the geographic constraints of region shape culture. These channels are most often reflected in and shaped by spiritual views of the world, what Westerners call religion, but which may require a broader understanding in native cultures that see no necessary lines of division between ways of worship, healing, acknowledging the passages of social status, and creating art—the entire fabric of life.

Why should we look to religion to understand the behavior of detectives, of all people? If our assertion that all investigators bring with them a theory of human nature is correct, then the sources of their assumptions can be found in their ideas about the place of human life on the face of the earth, notions established by what might be called the background map of spiritual instruction. Naturally, not all religious systems, native or other, address human motive and behavior directly and fully, but the presuppositions of even the most arcane creation myths can find their way into very practical understandings of the behavior of a particular group. We have based our discussion of the detective in Native America on just this foundation, that deep-seated assumptions about how humans behave normally come to the foreground in any analysis of aberrant behavior. The special role of the criminal investigator, established after the European Enlightenment to further the search for forensic and judicial truth through scientific rationalism, both complements and clashes with the broader role of the scout and tracker in native culture, and when assimilation is brought to bear, some reconciliation between Western empiricism and ancient intuitive ways of knowing and exploring must take place. When the rational meets the intuitive, we are forced to consider what drives human behavior, and whether science, which purports to exist beyond any particular culture as a universal standard, truly can provide final answers.

It may be objected that the true difference between Native America and Euro-American culture lies not in spirituality or rationalism but rather in attitudes toward technological change, the ready acceptance of new ways by modern Western societies, ways which have clearly brought them wealth and power. Certainly opposing steel and gunpowder with Stone Age weapons was part of the Indian downfall, and even when modern weapons could be acquired, the natives always lost the arms race. Martin Cruz Smith's first novel, *The Indians Won*, postulates that the Plains tribes might have united for the common purpose of defeating the U.S. Army and, by putting aside differences, could have purchased modern weaponry from European suppliers. One scene has the U.S. cavalry racing into a village to extermi-nate the women, children, and old people they expect to find there, only to see tepee sides lifted to reveal—modern machine guns! However, as Smith's narrative acknowledges, political unification itself reflects a will-ingness to change deeply rooted definitions of tribal identity, or at least to accommodate the lifeways of other groups. Such willingness derives from sources far deeper than simple preferences for new or old, and in fact is a function of how a group defines its place in the world, a question of spir-itual identity, in other words.

Other shaping forces on human nature are economic and environmental, and we will equate the power of the land to supply or withhold sustenance to the spiritual systems that evolved in different regions of the country. The people of the Southwestern deserts, for example, survived by means of agrarian and herding economies and developed sets of beliefs appropriate to a stable, settled society. The nomads of the Plains, in contrast, had mark-edly different beliefs established by their way of life. The rational-material beliefs of the white Europeans, of course, were predicated on dominating the natural world rather than adapting to it, and thus were little affected by region.

Our goal, however, is not to construct a unified field theory of culture, but rather to highlight through the very concrete and practical circum-stances of crime and its detection in popular fiction how a much larger drama is still being played out. The drama is the still unfinished debate between European and Native American about nothing less than the nature of the world: a place limited to the material and physical, or parallel re-alities moved by invisible forces and influences? The success of science and technology in controlling nature and transforming the physical environ-ment seems to suggest that the material argument has won the day, yet the recurrent malaise that afflicts so many Western industrialized societies may reveal a hunger for older, less materialistic, more spiritual ways of living. The enormous popularity of so-called New Age products and lifestyles, alternative medicines and ways of healing, and religious and psychic dis-ciplines testifies to the yearning for solutions beyond the technical and sci-entific. The huge sales of escapist fiction is a sign of needs unmet by material culture. Certainly, the case for cultural diversity is being made with increasing frequency. Intellectual cover has been provided by postmodernist attacks on the primacy of reason, and especially on claims for the univer-sality of what might simply be termed *cultural practice* in fields from law to medicine and science itself. For example, cultures from the Middle East to the Far East have fiercely resisted the encroachment of Western ideas about "universal" human rights, especially rights for women, arguing that they are based on definitions of humanity not shared by all cultures.

Thus, in both the popular and the scholarly mind, the jury may still be out about the efficacy of non-empirical ways of knowing and of solving problems: even committed rationalists may feel a nostalgic hunger for figures such as Carlos Castañeda's Don Juan, shamans in touch with simple, ancient, and authentic ways of living. The detective fiction we will discuss works just this territory, from fairly straightforward assimilated sheriffs, police officers, and investigators who just happen to be Native Americans to full-blown shamans whose ways of tracing crime owe nothing to the Old World. All writers creating such detectives must deal with the problems delineated here in general and explored in depth in the next chapter: How should a non-mainstream investigator approach crime? What constitutes aberrant behavior by someone not completely assimilated to empirical/materialist ways? What views of human nature do non-assimilated groups hold, and how do these views relate to definitions of aberrancy or criminality?

Chapter 2 will trace the broad assumptions that underlie Western criminal investigation, comparing them to other ways of knowing among Native American groups. Chapter 3 will examine eight Native American crime and detective fiction authors from different geographical regions to establish the very different ways in which tribal affiliation and region determine outlook.

The chapters that follow will build on the Native American premise that life is inextricably bound to the land and that understanding the nature of the crime means understanding the land from which it sprang. These stories of Native American detectives feature rural settings, not urban, and consequently, instead of being played out in bars, restaurants, shopping malls, theaters, department stores, libraries, and urban workplaces, they take place in deserts and mountains, on open plains, amid forests or tundra, with threats from nature, not just man: death by bear, rattlesnake, scorpion, dehydration, blizzard, and flash flood. The antithesis of closed-world settings like the cozy village mysteries of Agatha Christie and Ruth Rendall, they have open-world settings, like those of Arthur W. Upfield, who casts his tales in the wide open spaces of the Australian outback. Distances are huge, and geography plays a vital role in the detection. Their detectives must know the highways and byways of Northwest coastal shipping lanes, Sangre de Cristo mountain trails, desert water holes, and Alaskan rivers. Yet, at the same time, the cast of characters remains limited, and locals immediately recognize outsiders as intruders. The characters of Peter Bowen, Dana Stabenow, and Christopher Lane, for example, immediately recognize a "flatlander," a "cheechako," or an "outsider," because they are inappropriately dressed for the weather conditions, they talk too much and say too little, they fail to mind their own business, and they take stupid risks that no local would.

The focus on the natural world is not a unique Native American detective story premise, since many traditional mysteries have turned on the conditions of weather, climate, and topography, for example, coastal conditions in Erskine Childers' *The Riddle of the Sands* (1903), the ebb and flow of local tides in Dorothy Sayer's *Have His Carcase* (1932), or Florida's inland swamps and coastal islands in John D. MacDonald's Travis McGee novels. Sherlock Holmes, in "The Adventure of the Copper Beeches" (*Strand*, June 1892), observed that "the lowest and vilest alleys in London do not present a more dreadful record of sin than does the smiling and beautiful country-side." However, the Native American concept of the spirits of the land affecting human affairs adds a dimension that the traditional outdoor stories lack, and the turns of mind unique to particular tribal perspectives widen that sense of difference. They also provide new forms of evil, not simply greed, jealousy, envy, pride, lust, or revenge, but an evil that destroys the land, pollutes the water, decimates a people's pride and heritage, steals their gods, mocks their way of life, disparages, demoralizes, strikes down with disease, and dehumanizes.

Our middle chapters (4 through 9) progress geographically from the Southwest in a very rough circle counterclockwise to the Plains and Mountains, the Northwest, then Alaska and the Canadian Northwestern Territories, and finally the Great Lakes and East Coast regions. They begin with an overview of the land: its geography and weather, animal inhabitants, and fictive representation. Then they examine the indigenous peoples from the region and their beliefs and culture, as these impinge on the crime and detective stories of the area, and the representation of regional history in detective fiction. The major sections of each chapter contrast stories dominated by native spiritualism and shamanistic approaches to detection with stories dominated by the more assimilated outlook of ratiocinative detectives, the Native American Sherlocks of our title. Our title, *Shaman or Sherlock: The Native American Detective*, encapsulates the key distinction between Native American detectives and assimilated investigators. By these approaches we hope to capture the unique perspectives that Native American detectives add to the general detective genre. Since close to 80 detective novels feature Native American detectives in the Southwest, we devote two chapters to this region.

We will not discuss books which fail to link Native American detectives with culture, region, or way of life. Surprisingly, in a number of works, the Indian detective is only one of a group of ethnically unique characters with no real diversity except their racial/ethnic labels. His/her presence presumes the open-mindedness of the writer or a general awareness of diversity, but no attempt is made to show differences in perspective or in attitudes that impinge directly on how cases are solved and how justice is rendered.

Typical of this category are the Dave Cannon detective series of Michael Delving and the Jeremiah St. John series of William Babula, both of which feature totally assimilated native detectives as associates of their main detective.

In Delving's series, the native amateur detective is Bob Eddison, an Oklahoma Cherokee, who, despite Cherokee features and skin color, knows little about his tribe and less about the Cherokee language; he simply invents reports of Indian cultural practices to amuse acquaintances or escape compromising situations. He translates his Cherokee name *Ahuludegi*, He Throws Away the Drum, as Big Hawk, or whatever comes to mind, to satisfy those who expect the exotic. A dealer in old books and art who travels regularly to England seeking merchandise and who in *A Shadow of Himself* marries the English girl with whom he fell in love in *The Devil Finds Work*, Eddison occasionally suffers nostalgia for a past he knows little about ("I should have been born two hundred years ago, when I could have followed the trail or made pemmican, or whatever we noble redmen did when we weren't sleeping off our liquor"—*A Shadow of Himself*, 25); though no activist and no tribal representative, he jokes: "You white faces . . . took my country away from me a few hundred years ago. Now I'll see whether I can't do the same for you" (192). Despite an antiquarian's turn of mind, he seems out of place in these British-style cozy mysteries, set in small villages with stereotyped characters (the village parson; the elderly spinster; the unruly yob) and featuring thefts of antiques from village churches, disputed twelfth-century manuscripts, village witchcraft, and long-standing class grievances.

In Babula's St. John series, the native professional detective is a partner. At six feet, seven inches and 300 pounds, "Chief Moses" towers above any real Seminoles (a tribe distinguished by short, wiry men) and, though clearly Native American (dark eyes and skin, straight black hair, Indian nose), reflects other bloodlines. In a few lines, Babula provides him a history of wrestling alligators for tourists in the Everglades, acting as a casino bouncer in Las Vegas, and consulting for reservation gambling operations before joining the San Francisco investigative team. However, except for infrequent jokes about his being "a raw force of nature," saving this or that "squaw," or loving oil, firewater, and "the Great White Father in Washington" (*St. John's Baptism*, 17), Chief Moses is indistinguishable from the other characters. His Native American ethnicity serves no real function except as an excuse for offensive wisecracks. Like the racial, ethnic, and religious diversity featured in the frontline platoons of old war movies, the Native American substance of Delving and Babula's characters is so superficial and so clearly manipulative that it deserves no attention. The continued existence of such works, however, reflects a need among some readerships to see Indians played as cultural non-entities, as cartoon figures of feathers and furs in a stereotypical shorthand empty of meaning.

This text will investigate only genuine attempts to capture the Other in detective fiction, legitimate efforts to show the difference in personal perspective and worldview between the Native American and mainstream communities about the most important issues of life, about what constitutes criminal or aberrant behavior, and how it can be brought to light and rooted out.

2

Two Ways of Knowing:
Mainstream and Native American

For the people of Turtle Island, spirituality was not a part of life, but informed all of life. In no Native American language is there a single term that can be translated as "religion," because all acts are . . . religious acts. Likewise, Native Americans do not have the concept of "art." The practical design and decorative embellishment of artifacts, dwellings, clothing, . . . are spiritual symbols reflecting . . . the harmony of life. The natural materials used in the designs . . . [are] manifestations of sacred natural powers or *energies*, giving the . . . artifact its own medicine power through the synthesis of all these energies . . . ; an object . . . created in "spiritual balance" . . . will bring balance to all who touch it.

—Wa'na'nee'che' (Dennis Renault) and Timothy Frere,
Native American Spirituality, 4

If I make the connections that [the evidence] automatically suggests to me, join up the myths with the facts, it changes everything. . . . Nothing will make sense anymore. . . . This cup might not be a cup anymore. That window might not look onto your yard anymore. The sun might not necessarily rise in two hours.

—Muriel Gray, *The Trickster*, 75

PERCEIVING CULTURAL DIFFERENCES

The deep gulf separating European-based white culture and unassimilated Native American society often seems a mere minor impediment to mainstream observers. Why make so much of a shallow gap to be crossed, at worst a gully which can be traversed with little effort? After all, so much of the world has adopted "modern" European-American ways, such as the business uniform of coat and tie or dressy suit, that so-called ethnic clothing can look like an affectation even when worn by heads of government. U.S.-style processed and standardized fast foods, produced by assembly line, have traveled around the world, sometimes supplanting local cuisines, a seemingly irresistible "modern" movement. Around the world, what are termed "lifestyles" (itself a modern word; there is no other way to convey the notion) are increasingly shaped by European-American models. In general, the economic systems of corporate capitalism and the governmental infrastructures of European-American liberal democracies are promoted as the new world order, the way of the new millennial future. History is history, claim some observers; new eras of material prosperity and cultural congruence await us. All that is needed is the shrugging off of some resistant old ways, old languages, old religions.

The movement for a standardized world culture—"McWorld," it has been called—tends to be promoted in two ways, firstly that it is self-evidently "modern" and as such requires no further defense, and secondly on utilitarian grounds, that modern ways bring enormous benefits to large numbers of people. Sadly, old cultures must give way to new, but the imperatives of change demand it, and change is irresistible. Besides, how well have the old ways worked?

The problem with the first argument is that while the definition of "modern" keeps moving forward with each generation, in general terms, modernity has been mostly based on the assumptions of reason and rationality of the European Enlightenment. Whether modern ways have met Jeremy Bentham's test by consistently improving the lot of the greatest number is precisely the question, a seemingly simple judgment complicated by modernity's most profound and most indisputable effect: multiplying population numbers in geometric progressions. The good promised is being shared among increasing numbers, and the very increase dilutes the good and causes new, unanticipated miseries; the promise is that technology and standardized approaches will "catch up" with population increases and deliver the goods and services that will bring happiness. The second argument thus pushes the benefits for the many into the future, claiming that the privileges enjoyed by the few will trickle down to everyone else, transforming traditional societies. This promise is oddly similar to those made by religions and ideologies about perfect future lives—the proof rests on faith in the future.

Such global questions might not seem important in a study of the Native American detective, but unfortunately they involve the bedrock beliefs of the promise of the modern. The near eradication of native peoples from the American West was almost always rationalized with the need to move forward, to replace "primitive" and "savage" ways with those of "civilization" and "the future." To these oppositions Paula Gunn Allen adds "childlike" and "pagan" as opposed to "adult" and "Christian" ("The Sacred Hoop," 3); the polar contrasts frame the need for change as inevitable, as the demand of the future. The European conquest of North America was accomplished by sheer force of numbers, and the swelling multitudes who supplanted the original owners of the land and wiped out older ways of life found legitimacy in a deep faith in their modernity, in their representing the wave of an irresistible future. While some changes were inevitable given the exploding immigrant population on the Plains, which killed off and displaced the buffalo and other foundations of nomadic culture, some of the most damaging behavior of white Americans in their dealings with the Indians often derived from a shallow understanding of culture, both of their own European-originated ways and of the Native American cultures they encountered. Like the proverbial fish that cannot perceive the water in which it lives, the settlers of the American West seemed to suffer little doubt about the rightness of their conduct toward the indigenous population.

The reasons for this certitude are evident. Settlers often moved in cultural bubbles that allowed no accommodation to older ways, and by the time of the settling of the Plains, earlier amalgams of Indian and white ways in the settled East must have seemed dated and irrelevant. Even today, the elements defining Indian culture for the mainstream tend to be the most superficial: ceremonial ethnic clothing, regional food, overt social and family structures. Even native religion is frequently finessed into a proto-Christian abstraction that provides a framework to accommodate Christian beliefs comfortably, a vague deism that allows one-to-one equivalents of Western religious notions: the Happy Hunting grounds are a primitive heaven, the Great Father a patriarchical God. That Christianity is "modern" in this formulation is evident.

American civil religion replaces traditional religious observance with broad generalities, suggesting that little is lost with the demise of tradition and detail (e.g., Robert Bellah's canon on civil religion). Margot Edmonds and Ella E. Clark, who, in *Voices of the Winds: Native American Legends* (1989), have collected over 130 oral narratives from six regions (many of them creation stories) are struck by the depth of Native American belief in the power of the spirit in nature—"in every river, waterfall, echo, thunder, and even the changing positions of stars in the sky"—and ask, "Is it possible that both the Great Spirit and the Chief of the Sky Spirits was [*sic*] the Indians' interpretation of the white man's God or Supreme Being?"

(xv). That is, are our deep-seated beliefs not very much alike beneath "superficial" differences of culture? In fact, the real patterns of culture are often invisible even to participants and must be teased out carefully to become evident.

The surface features of standard U.S. clothing, cuisine, and general behavior shroud the reality of difference, creating the illusion of assimilation where in fact it may not exist. In the popular imagination, "Indian" tends to be equated with Hopi snake dances, Zuñi Shalako celebrations, the Koshari Boy Scout dancers, trading post sales of Navajo jewelry and blankets, Plains reenactments, powwows throughout the nation, and the like, all events of varying authenticity but generally taken to be "real" according to their degree of exoticism, of surface difference from mainstream ways. It is no secret that Native American culture was commodified from its earliest days, with everything from wampum belts to weaponry finding ready buyers on the American East Coast and around the world, and even scalps and other ghastly "trophies" becoming a currency for trade. Commodities, even authentic ones, provide no guarantees of the authenticity of the people involved, for true culture lies elsewhere than in the material. In fact, culture may find its expression through any number of physical features but cannot be located in any mix of them alone; rather, people's ways inhabit deeper, usually invisible matrixes, the participants' assumptions about how the world works and how humankind fits into those workings. The essential element of human identity is not how one looks or what one buys, mainstream culture notwithstanding, but rather how one behaves in any number of situations, trivial and significant. Such behavior, of course, is associated with appearances but responds to far deeper codes, both explicit and unexamined, embedded by cultural upbringing. The behavior involved, sometimes even behavior explicitly recognized as culturally meaningful, will also frequently be labeled as "normal," the way all human beings behave under similar circumstances.

Two common areas of cultural difference may serve to illustrate these generalizations. Edward Hall demonstrates how cultural attitudes about time and space vary. "Politeness time," the length of time one may be late for a formal appointment without having to offer more than a casual apology, may range from a few minutes to the better part of an hour or more in different parts of the world; in some cultures, any lateness at all is looked upon with disfavor (Hall, *The Silent Language*, 1–19). Notions about the comfortable distance between speakers, what Hall calls "proxemics," vary from twelve inches or closer in some Mediterranean and North African cultures to as much as 24 inches in northern Europe (162–85). Unexpressed feelings that one has been shown disrespect by a latecomer or inchoate unease at what is perceived as another in too close proximity (or the opposite, being kept at a rude distance) are made all the worse by the lack of vocabulary with which to examine such behaviors. After all, definitions of normal behavior begin with the perceiver's understanding of his or her culture's norms, and extend outward from the personal only given the benefit of travel and study. Politeness time and comfort space are, of course, only trivial examples of the elaborate complexities involved in encounters between practitioners of different religions, different social systems, or different general worldviews. It is not simply the natural tendency of every culture toward ethnocentricity; in addition to seeing our norms as "natural" and "right," we are likely to bring legions of unexamined premises to our dealings with those who are truly different.

It is thus difficult to explain these deep underpinnings to people who have never contemplated the cultural springs of their actions, and it is particularly difficult in the United States, with its heavy bias toward the practical and the utilitarian, even about non-utilitarian matters. Many Americans, perhaps understandably in a far-flung though interconnected society that has embraced standardization in goods, dwellings, and life practices as have few other cultures, seem to think fairly superficially about cultural differences, as garments to be put on or discarded, as roles to be played but then dropped, as hobbies and avocations indulged in in spare moments. Deloria builds an interpretation of American culture around the act of playing Indian. We often are ready to accept profound difference in places and cultures far away and obscure (the natives of New Guinea, for example, or the aborigines of the Brazilian jungle) but are much less willing to entertain more than cosmetic dissimilarity among residents of the North American continent. No doubt, proximity and huge numbers of stereotypes, myths, children's adventure tales, and the like create a false confidence in our understanding of real people who often share few premises with mainstream culture. In fact, Paula Gunn Allen's "Introduction" to her *Studies in American Indian Literature* notes that the standard division of human experience into fact or fancy cannot be safely applied to the study of American Indian literature, whether traditional or modern, because for many Native Americans, "Statements that stem from the 'imagination' are taken to be literally true, even though they are not based on sociological or historical 'facts' " (ix). Gunn goes on to add that even Native American ideas about "intellectual harmony, structural balance, thematic or symbolic unity," function, significance, end goal, reader expectation, and so on differ from those of European-American cultures (ix–x).

REASON AND INTUITION: DETECTION'S TWO WORLDVIEWS

Perceiving the depth of cultural difference thus requires practical models of how diversity works in practice, and popular literature—literature in general, for that matter—offers scant examples. Where Native Americans are concerned, popular fiction has primarily depicted surface features, particularly the dramatic appearances and ways of life of the Plains Indians, even though Native Americans practiced a wide variety of ways of life, many of them neither nomadic nor hunting based. What did unify Indians were common assumptions about the goals and purposes of life. Two works that capture difference effectively and dramatically, showing the depths of the division between the European material-rationalist way of thinking and the spiritual-intuitive way of Native Americans, are by white mainstream authors but nevertheless are excellent examples of how to render the demarcations between white and native cultures: Brian Moore's *Black Robe* and Oliver LaFarge's *Laughing Boy*. Neither is a detective story as the genre is defined in this study, though both novels include "crimes," mysteries of a sort, problem-solving strategies, violence, and judgments about culpability. Since one is set in an early, pre-European time and the other in an isolated location before the effects of assimilation, the conventions of the modern crime genre do not apply, but its elements are all present for examination.

Brian Moore's *Black Robe*

Brian Moore's *Black Robe* (1985; filmed in 1991 by director Bruce Beresford) is a carefully researched, serious novel about the triangle of relationships between the French Jesuits, the French fur trappers and explorers under Champlain, and the Native American tribes of what is now Canada: the Algonquin, Iroquois, and Huron. Set in the seventeenth century, the novel establishes a culturally level playing field on which no one group can dominate. Extensive French incursions have had relatively little impact on tribes such as the Iroquois, who recognize the threat to their culture and respond with ferocious violence. The Hurons in the story have capitulated by allowing Jesuits missions in their villages, and by novel's end have desperately traded their religious identity for hoped-for protection from the plague, probably brought by white traders. The Algonquin occupy a middle ground, trading with the French and guiding the Jesuits to their Huron mission, yet maintaining their independence.

The Native American responses to the Europeans thus establish three possible recourses: hostility, submission, and wary cooperation. At this point in history, however, all groups need each other, for the French demand the fur trade, the Jesuits require conversions to Christianity, and all the Indian groups, even the proud Iroquois, lust after iron knives, tomahawk heads, and muskets with the same fervor that the fur traders desire Indian maidens. The novel nicely dramatizes how trade goods corrupted independent cultures: the Iroquois leaders debate the virtues of French muskets over bows and arrows, understanding that the superior firepower will come at the price of independence. The situation is emblematic of a larger historical truth: once a preference for manufactured goods is estab-

lished, crafts are quickly supplanted and the laborious methods of man-
ufacturing stone weapons forgotten; the economic self-sufficiency of
hunter-gatherers becomes a relationship dependent on trade, linking North
America to Europe as a colony, with raw materials exchanged for French
manufacture.

Moore's novel is historical in other ways as well. Francis Parkman's history, *The Jesuits in North America*, led the novelist to the Jesuit *Relations*,
the extensive archives containing correspondence by missionaries back to
their Jesuit superiors in France, a treasure trove of practical anthropology
as well as descriptions of the practical problems of wilderness life and suggestions for future missionaries. As Moore notes in his introduction, the
Relations are the only reliable record of the Native Americans of this period
and place (viii); later descriptions came after far more extensive contacts
with European culture and with all the changes, subtle and dramatic, that
those contacts stimulated. (What oral histories survive from this distant
past would reflect the points of view of competing tribes and the inevitable
mutability of unwritten history.) Moore sums up the three tribes he deals
with in the novel as "handsome, brave, incredibly cruel people who, at that
early stage, were in no way dependent on the white man and, in fact, judged
him to be their physical and mental inferior" (ix). He confirms how little
these tribes had in common with later stereotypes of "Red Indians," and
how both Jesuits and later anthropologists and historians record native
contempt for the white man's "stupidity" in not understanding that "the
land, the rivers, the animals, were all possessed of a living spirit and subject
to laws that must be respected" (ix). He argues that the Native Americans
suffered a "strange and gripping tragedy" when their "belief in a world of
night and in the power of dreams clashed with the Jesuits' preachments of
Christianity and a paradise after death" (ix). The novel records the historical failure of Jesuit missions to the Huron and the conquest of the latter
by their traditional enemies, the Iroquois, a fate dictated, says Moore, by
the introduction of an alien faith ill adapted to the brutal realities of the
Canadian physical and human landscape. *Black Robe* is a wonderful cor-
rective to sentimental views of Indians, and especially to the easy, comforting assumption that because many tribes had a "great father" god figure
and a notion of an afterlife, American Indian spirituality in general was a
Christian prototype, a primitive form of the European religion that validates Christian beliefs as elemental. The novel courageously argues the contrary, risking reader unhappiness with its gloomy (though entirely
historical) ending and the disapproval of readers seeking an affirmation of
Christianity in this confrontation of cultures. Moore uses the term *tragedy*
correctly, a situation that in its very terms can come to no good end; Jesuit
and Indian ways can find no common ground.

The plot traces the journey of Father Laforgue, a young Jesuit assigned
to the order's Huron mission 1,500 miles west of the tiny settlement

of Quebec. As Laforgue endures the physical discomforts of paddling for
over twelve hours daily, sleeping in temporary habitations and eating half-
cooked meat and sour sagamité (corn gruel), he contemplates a lonely future: the rest of his life spent with the Hurons. Unfortunately, the Algonquin have received a sign, a dream that the Blackrobe, as they call him
because of his clerical garb, brings them danger. They delay action against
Laforgue since the dream is ambiguous, but "A dream is more real than
death or battle," so it must be obeyed (46). Annuka, the Indian girl who
has begun an affair with Daniel, Laforgue's only European companion on
the trip, reacts as no young French woman would to the common suspicions about Blackrobe, for the Algonquin believe that animals have souls
and intelligence and that trees are alive and watch what humans do:

But tonight she feared the forest. The forest would be angry because the Blackrobe
had cast a spell on it. . . . The forest might revenge itself on . . . Iwanchou [the Indian name for her lover Daniel]—and on her, if she were with him. (78)

Her father would say, "How can I give you as wife to a Norman [Frenchman]?
Everyone knows they are stupid as a blind elk. They do not know that the animals
and fish are possessed of reason and will revenge themselves on us if we do not
respect their dead. These stupid Normans feed the bones of beaver to dogs. The
beaver does not forgive them." (81)

Night was the time of the dead. In the forest all around them, they walked and
talked and watched what was happening here. (85)

The Algonquin believe in the She-Manitou, a great demon of the forest,
whose call (like the rustling of leaves) names those destined to die. Laforgue, beginning to fully appreciate the great distance between their understanding of the universe and his own, speculates that perhaps the
wilderness is the polar opposite of Europe, a Manichean opposition to
God's rule: "Daniel, listen to me. I am afraid . . . of this country. . . . I don't
mean the ordinary dangers: starvation, capture, death. I mean the other,
the greater danger. . . . Belial rules here. . . . the devil infects their minds—"
(100–102). Daniel answers that the Indians have their own afterworld and
do not need Christianity; they believe in a world of the dead connected to
the living, where "the souls of men hunt the souls of animals," through
night forests composed of "the souls of trees which have died" (102). The
"dead Savages," says Daniel, sit on the ground, crouched with elbows on
knees and heads between hands, but with nightfall "they rise up" and "go
to the chase" (102). Given such beliefs, Daniel concludes that Laforgue will
never truly convert the Indians to his teachings (103). By the novel's end,
Laforgue has learned the wisdom of Daniel's warnings and has toyed with
the possibility that the Indians are right, that life is a dream and dreams

are reality. The death of Annuka's father in particular challenges the Black-robe's trust in God, and Daniel chooses Annuka and her tribe over staying with the priest, in spite of the young man's incomplete understanding of her: "He looked into her brilliant dark eyes and, as always, saw there the self she had not given, that unpredictable Savage self, which judged him by rules and signs he did not understand" (201).

The Hurons ultimately accept conversion to Christianity but only in hopes of saving their lives from the plague, not to save their souls from perdition. "The dream," as the novel calls it, becomes a shorthand for the whole "savage" life, of sexual license in youth, easy divorce for men and drudgery and near slavery for wives, gluttonous feast and frequent famine, ritual cannibalism practiced on enemies, and finally the belief in dreams themselves: a fatalistic acceptance that seems to Laforgue like drifting through life without planning for the future or struggling against inevitable reverses (Chomina, Annuka's father, insists that he be abandoned when he becomes weak, since he feels ready to meet the She-Manitou). Yet the Algonquin work and play furiously, accepting the flow of nature rather than trying to change it, and in every significant way are far better adapted to the northern forests than is Blackrobe. The most significant difference is "the dream," the dramatically different way of understanding the spiritual and material worlds.

For Laforgue, religion is not simply the Sunday activity it might be for some of the French fur traders in Quebec, for as a Jesuit he has dedicated his life to serving God and to expressing his faith through service to others. However, despite this commitment, religion still does not infuse his understanding of reality completely; it is one of many levers he uses to manipulate his psychic world; though the most important, it is not the only one. Laforgue remains a man, desiring Annuka and suffering doubt and weaknesses. When he sees a soaring eagle, he takes it as a sign, a symbol, but not a reality itself. For the Indians, in contrast, the spirit world infuses every material part of their world, and every action has spiritual causes and consequences. Though in Laforgue's view they lack formal faith, they exist in a supernatural world. There can be no reconciliation between these two views, one rational-materialist, the other spiritual-supernatural. This is the great divide that stands between the European and the Native American views of the world.

Though fiction, *Black Robe* reflects accurately and forcefully the underpinnings of scores of trivial and important differences between Western and Indian outlooks, a difference confirmed in the horrified, contemptuous words of Pierre de Charlevoix's *Journal of Voyage to North-America* (1761):

There is nothing in which these barbarians carry their superstition to a more extravagant length, than in what regards dreams . . . [for] in whatever manner the dream is conceived, it is always looked upon as . . . sacred, . . . the most ordinary way in which the gods make known their will to men.

For the most part, they look upon them either as a desire of the soul inspired by some genius, or an order from him; and in consequence of this principle, they hold it a religious duty to obey them; and an Indian having dreamed of having a finger cut off, had it really cut off as soon as he awoke. (quoted by Perry, *Vanishing Act*)

The idea that dreams are real was, of course, not held exclusively by Native Americans; any number of cultures shared this notion, including de Charlevoix's Medieval countrywoman Joan of Arc. We should look past de Charlevoix's righteous indignation at a practice he considers virtually inhuman to see a measure of how deeply the French, like their compatriots in Europe and white America, had been influenced by modernist and Enlightenment ideas and how culturally blind they were to this influence. The Frenchman is unaware that for most cultures and periods dreams did have profound consequences, and his materialist denial of a dream-vision's significance is a sign of his own modernity. A further measure is that most present-day readers would probably agree with him.

Oliver LaFarge's *Laughing Boy*

Another dramatic example of how native views of the world differ from those of European rationalists comes from the other end of the continent, the American Southwest, and from the end of the historical period of the frontier. Oliver LaFarge wrote *Laughing Boy* (1929) between 1926 and 1928, but he set the story in 1915, the year the first automobile made it into the northern Navajo country, an intrusion, he says in the Foreword, that marked a turning point (5–6). La Farge felt that the early 1930s were the beginning of the end for traditional Navajo culture, and that within 30 years, the people described in the book and what the author calls their "wholeness" of life was gone (6). *Laughing Boy* won a Pulitzer Prize in 1930, enjoyed widespread acclaim, and remains in print, yet it has been vilified by Native American critics for distorting Navajo life, a perhaps inevitable fate for a novel written by an outsider. However, as an outsider's look at the devastating impact of modern mainstream life on a traditional native culture, *Laughing Boy* has few rivals, and LaFarge, a Harvard-trained anthropologist who lived among the people he wrote about, was ideally situated to write the book. Still innocent of highways and freeways, the Southwest was linked to the majority culture only by the railroad, so LaFarge had a perfect laboratory for his study of the effects of assimilation before the floodgates of modern transportation opened.

In 1915, the Navajo were still a people on horseback, their main encounters with whites at trading posts or railheads. While towns on the tracks in Arizona and New Mexico offered easy opportunities for interaction with "Americans," the Indians in the hinterlands lived much as they always had. The novel examines the effects of assimilation on a Navajo known as Slim Girl, a young woman of about eighteen who was taken from her family as a child and sent to a Bureau of Indian Affairs school in California. Placement with girls from other tribes forced Slim Girl to learn English and give up Navajo ways. After leaving the school, she was seduced by a white man and abandoned when pregnant. Her baby was born dead, and after being shown kindness by prostitutes, she took up prostitution briefly before deciding, given her experiences with whites, to rejoin her own culture. To do so requires relearning her native language and the culture's myriad traditional ways, all the while enduring the hostility of traditional Navajos who see her as an outsider who betrayed her culture and did "bad things" (traditional Navajos had no words for prostitution, since the practice did not exist). After meeting Laughing Boy, a completely traditional Navajo, she chooses him as her route back to cultural authenticity.

Their romance and exploration of each other's cultures, as well as their touching attempt to define a middle way which would incorporate the best of both worlds, is handled with restraint and finesse. LaFarge's skill lies in allowing us to see and understand the lovers' dilemmas with a minimum of condemnatory judgment, even when Laughing Boy and Slim Girl violate both Navajo and white cultural codes. While Native American critics may be right about the novel's failures at seeing from inside the culture, its true goal is to show these two Navajos trying to survive rapid, utterly dislocating change, the shift from a spiritual and an intuitive culture to a materialist, rational one.

Laughing Boy's eponymic hero is a carefree young man as relaxed as his name, riding cross-country on his pony, *hozoji nashad*, traveling in beauty. Laughing Boy is in his early 20s, strong and handsome, a talented maker of Navajo silver and turquoise jewelry, at one with himself and his natural environment. Though penniless, he is happy and full of life. Coming from the trackless north, he is blissfully unaware of the ways of white Americans and feels only mild social embarrassment around relatively assimilated Navajos, who know about the American Chief's jails and who wear hats like white Westerners. (The American president is conceived of as a tribal chief in Washington.) Laughing Boy meets Slim Girl at a dance and is shocked but intrigued by her uniqueness: she is heavily laden with silver, coral, turquoise, and white shell, more wealth than he has seen on any Navajo woman, but when he dances with her, she treats him with calculated contempt. She also dances with another man, American-style, close to her partner and face to face. When they meet again, seemingly by accident, her difference fascinates him: she is a familiar practitioner of Navajo culture but also more sophisticated and set apart. He quickly decides to marry her, but when he asks permission of his uncle, he is told that Slim Girl is a "school-girl" who was taken to "that place," a Bureau of Indian

Affairs Indian school, and Americanized over her six-year stay (33). She
has been lost to the Navajo community because she lives near the railroad
and "does bad things for the Americans": "She is not of the People any
more" (33). Laughing Boy, unconvinced, leaves with her. She promises him
a new life, enriched by her knowledge of American ways but still set apart
from both communities.

Slim Girl's agenda in enticing Laughing Boy is, as the narrator explains,
to make him "an axe with which to hew down the past," "a light with
which to see her way back to . . . the good things of her people" (45–46).
For her, "going back to the blanket" means returning to some worthwhile
things, but "all the rest was hideous" (46). However, she thinks her knowledge, experience, and lessons from Americans will help her guide her man
and create for the two of them "the most perfect life . . . with an Indian, a
long-haired, heathen Indian, a blanket Indian, a Navajo, the names thrown
out like an insult in the faces of . . . her own people, Denné, The People,
proud as she was proud, and clear of her heart as she could never be" (46).
Slim Girl is determined to reinvent herself, to conquer herself and circumstance, to emerge from the struggle "not American, not Indian, mistress of
herself" (46). Taking the means to recreate herself from the Americans and
the end from the Indians, she would make a home in the wild northern
desert where the white agent's men would never come to snatch her children for Indian school as she was. Her children would be "Navajo, all
Navajo"; Laughing Boy, all Navajo himself, would teach her "*bik'é hojoni*,
the trail of beauty" (46).

This reinvented self would be totally new, partaking of the best of Navajo and white. She would let no other wife share their hogan (46). Nor
would she slave "away her youth in . . . hard labour, herding sheep, hoeing
corn, packing firewood, growing square across the hips and flat in the face
and heavy in the legs" (47). Instead, she had learned from American
women. Going on to the formal ending of the ritual song ("In beauty it is
finished"), she then changed it to, "In beauty it is begun. In beauty it is
begun. In beauty it is begun. Thanks," and wondered if she could learn to
believe in this creed: "That is a good religion, as good as Christianity. . . .
One needs some religion. At least, I can get some good out of its ideas. . . .
I am not a Navajo, nor am I an American, but the Navajos are my people"
(47). Slim Girl *is* an American in the larger sense of the word, for her
California Indian school experiences have taught her to believe in the second chance, the possibility of starting over, constructing a new self by
picking and choosing from the models of living she has experienced. In this
way she has become quintessentially American, even as she rejects the material and social aspects of mainstream life, but she remains unaware of
just how far her embrace of self-actualization has moved her from the
People, if only in her thinking.

Nevertheless, Slim Girl and Laughing Boy make a life for themselves in her adobe (that is, Mexican-style) house near Los Palos. They marry in the traditional Navajo way but maintain no contact with relatives or the whites of the Anglo community; she is careful to keep Laughing Boy busy with his jewelry making, his horse trading with other Navajos far from town, and other agrarian enterprises that will be profitable but distant from white civilization. She doles out whiskey to him in small doses so he will avoid addiction. In turn, Slim Girl learns to weave traditional Navajo rugs but also maintains a secret sexual relationship with an Anglo lover in town, a young rancher who is fascinated by her and who lavishes her with money and gifts. With these sources of wealth, the couple amasses thousands of dollars, a fortune for Navajos of the time. A trip to meet Laughing Boy's family in northern Arizona turns out better than expected, and their relationship survives, even after he discovers her white lover. Her past catches up with her, however, when a former would-be lover, a Navajo named Red Man, kills her with a random rifle shot. Laughing Boy buries her with a full four-day Navajo ceremony, and then returns to his people in the north.

Laughing Boy is usually regarded as a love story—"the greatest Indian love story of all time," according to the Signet Classic back-cover blurb— and it is hard to fault any reader for being touched by the sensitive portrayal of two needy souls, one crippled by a brutal theft of her language and culture, and other fascinated by his lover's artful attempt to walk a tightrope between cultures. The love story is reason enough to read the novel. Yet *Laughing Boy* is also about economics, the way the Navajo, a pastoral-agrarian people, reacted to the incursion of whites with a new economic system. The Navajo had by this point perfected means of amassing wealth and storing food, a stage that hunter-gatherers such as the Algonquin of *Black Robe* or the Plains buffalo hunters had not managed. The Navajo keep sheep, create jewelry of silver, turquoise, coral, and other stones, and have workable means of exchanging value: trading horses, for example, or bartering animals for jewelry, or vice versa, activities visible throughout the novel. Even Laughing Boy, who has never encountered paper money, manages to trade his silver handicrafts with whites. But Slim Girl's attempt to amass capital as an "investment" which she and Laughing Boy will live on in luxury in the primitive north of Arizona is doomed to failure as a violation of the Navajo ethos: she is attempting to bring a form of capitalism to a culture blithely and happily free of material obsessions. In fact, the true Navajo Way looks askance at setting one's self apart from one's neighbors by building up wealth. Laughing Boy loses all his horse racing winnings to gambling but is unrepentant and undisturbed by again being penniless; this is simply the way life works: goods come and go, while the real goal is the Trail of Beauty.

Although the plot does not carry through Slim Girl's capitalist experiment (she dies before we can see its end result), the ethos of the Navajo is so entirely opposed to such a way of regarding wealth that we can predict a tragic failure to her plans, and by extension, authentic Navajo culture when it is impacted by the larger American economic system. Traveling the path of beauty cannot correspond with keeping track of gains in dollars, silver, blankets, or head of stock; the value of the silver or the rug lies in the labor invested and in its authentic vision, not in its exchange value. The Trail of Beauty is intimately connected to personal identity and cultural convention, as is confirmed when Laughing Boy's family discusses his worth as a man, and therefore his status as one of the People, after he links up with Slim Girl:

"We have all seen his silver, her blankets. We have seen him dance. We know, therefore, how he is now . . . [that] all is well with him."

"A man makes a design well because he feels it. When he makes someone else's design, you can tell . . . [No one can be told] 'make heat-lightning clouds with tracks-meeting under them [as a jewelry design], and make it beautiful'."

"My son is thinking about a design for his life. Let him tell us, and if it is not good, perhaps we can show him." (115)

The temptation for Westerners is to read these comments as metaphor, a comparison between two inherently different elements to elucidate how one informs our understanding of the other. LaFarge, however, is at pains to show the Navajo Way of Beauty as unitary, a way of life so interconnected that Enlightenment compartmentalization into discrete domains ("religion," "art," "philosophy," "choice of spouse") is completely meaningless.

The economic conflict between Navajo and white ways of measuring value makes manifest the novel's central focus, the philosophical conflict between living on the Trail of Beauty and living to secure a safe, prosperous material future. Slim Girl believes she has found a way to combine the two through a form of primitive banking that stores their fortune in "things of beauty" and that thereby wins "his astonished admiration," carefully appraising the jewelry and "checking it against their mutual profits, his sales and horse trades, her blankets, and what she brought from the town" (85); a traditional Navajo, he fails to understand her system of profit. Laughing Boy gives her some of the best pieces of jewelry he has made, telling her it would be a waste to sell it to the Americans, since they will not understand what it means (85). While the trading of horses is "meat and drink" to the Navajo (86), it is simply part of the pastoral life (87), and the fact that Laughing Boy is a superior trader (indicated by no one believing a word he says when he is trading horses) has nothing to do with the entrepreneurial spirit manifested in Slim Girl. Trading is like watching free-range horses graze endlessly, always in motion but free of the restlessness of animals penned in a corral; similarly Laughing Boy whiles away time by tricking a white trading post owner into treating his party to free coffee and snacks, a way of showing one's cleverness and putting one over on a deserving target, not a means to profit.

The Trail of Beauty

Hozoji, Beauty, is a difficult concept for mainstream readers, not just because it is a Navajo term and lifeway, but because the very means of thinking about it is so tainted by the Enlightenment tendency to classify and compartmentalize all such terms. The unitary pastoral life of traditional Navajos has no such tendency. While an aesthetic meaning is clearly at work in *hozoji*, the very word *aesthetic* sets the notion apart, evoking the idea of finer artistic responses to a designated art object quite different from a total response, a gestalt, a design for life. Calling *hozoji* a *philosophy* has a similar effect, eliciting meanings ranging from abstruse academic theorizing to practical strategies for accomplishing a pragmatic result, as in *business philosophy*. A frequent mainstream solution is to lump all such ideas under the general category of religion, a catchall including abstract philosophy, aesthetic pleasures, and moral/ethical guidance, but calling the Way of Beauty a religious idea severely distorts Navajo culture, which has no indigenous religious beliefs in the Western sense. Rodney Barker, in *The Broken Circle: A True Story of Murder and Magic in Indian Country*, sums up the notion clearly and succinctly:

Finally, he [the Navajo informant] wanted to make sure I knew that the categories of good and evil, as personified by God and Satan, were not viewed the same way by the Navajo. Evil was not negative in a moral or ethical sense. Rather, there was harmony and order on one side and chaos and confusion, which produced premature death, illness, and misfortune, on the other, and almost all the Navajo deities had both inclinations. They could punish as well as reward, be helpful as well as hurtful. No god was wholly good and wholly bad, but a mix. Just like human beings. (312)

The Way of Beauty is just that, a road combining elements which European-influenced readers would see as byways leading in very different directions, some minor (aesthetic paths), others major (philosophical and religious avenues). An equivalent would be Asian religions that promise an enlightened way of living rather than belief systems, ethical guidance, and manifestations of ultimate justice and order.

Thus, the sad attempt of Slim Girl to find a way between the Navajo and American economic systems is ultimately doomed, not by technical problems of amassing wealth but by the contrasting foundations of each culture's approach to life. The Navajo economic system, beyond being a way of sustaining life, has no connection to the goals and purposes of the capitalist one she mimics. For practitioners of Navajo culture, economic

behavior is just one seamless manifestation of a self-evident goal, that being
a unified sense of harmony, an extinguishing of the stress of life in a harsh
environment, a totally integrated experience whose very point is its wholeness. The notion has been described by any number of commentators,
scholarly and popular, but Peter Farb, in *Man's Rise to Civilization*, says
it well:

[The Navajo] visualizes himself as living in an eternal and unchanging universe
made up of physical, social, and supernatural forces, among which he tries to maintain a balance. Any accidental failure to observe rules or rituals can disturb this
balance and result in some misfortune. Navajo curing ceremonies [such as sand-
painting] are designed to put the individual back in harmony with the universe. . . .
the good life consists of maintaining intact all the complex relationships of the
universe. (38)

The Way is distant from the crude capitalism Slim Girl tries to practice;
maintaining balance and harmony through nurturing "intact all the complex relationships of the universe" is about as far as one can get from
leveraging capital to maximize return on investments. It is this perception
that *Laughing Boy* conveys so artfully and that makes it an ideal reference
point for a contrast with the Way of Europe, the road of reason, classification, and compartmentalization. While different tribes practiced different
spiritual ways, and generalizations are hazardous, that the general Navajo
attitude toward nature has much in common with other native groups is
generally accepted. Tom Bahti, in *Southwestern Indian Ceremonials*, observes:

The most striking difference between the philosophies of the Southwestern Indian
and Western man is the manner in which each views his role in the universe. The
prevailing non-Indian view is that man is superior to all other forms of life and
that the universe is his to be used as he sees fit. The value placed on every other
life form is determined only by its usefulness to man, an attitude justified as "the
mastery of nature for the benefit of man."
  The Indian view is that man is part of a delicately balanced universe in which
all components—all life forms and natural elements—interrelate and interact, with
no part being more or less important than another. Further, it is believed that only
man can upset this balance. (Preface)

  A measure of the competence and seriousness of the works of detective
fiction discussed in the chapters that follow is the degree to which they at
least acknowledge the dramatically different worldviews delineated in our
discussions of *Black Robe* and *Laughing Boy*. Stories that ignore this difference or that reduce it to minor questions of etiquette or "lifestyle" are
usually simply exploiting the popularity of the genre. The best works, those
of writers like Tony Hillerman, Margaret Coel, Muriel Gray, and Thomas

Perry, make these differences the key to plot, character, the detection itself. Mark Sullivan's *The Purification Ceremony* captures this defining element of the Native American detective story in two speeches by Diana "Little Crow" Jackman:

But I ran through that fractured terrain, a rising sea of snow billowing about knees, with a growing sense of my place in it. My ancestors believed that nearly everything could change both its shape and its mind. From my perspective—a 1990s woman with an MIT degree in computer engineering—their universe was unpredictable, unreliable, frightening. They had survived in what must have been a psychologically brutal environment, where nothing was as it seemed. . . . I was learning. (254)

I have come to believe, like my Micmac and Penobscot ancestors, that we live more than the sum of the present moments in this visible world; we exist within layers of reincarnated, reinvented memories that shape-change and prod us across invisible boundaries into the many worlds of the mind. Until we gather unto us the Power to navigate there with confidence, we are lost and alone, savages in a dark forest. (292)

Little Crow has come a long way from Sherlock Holmes, Poirot, and even the American hard-boiled private eye. At its best, the Native American detective story gives readers a new way of perceiving the universe.

THE WAY OF REASON

For all that Native American spiritual ways may seem exotic to mainstream readers, they are in fact in accordance with traditional ways of viewing the world in a wide variety of different cultures. Instead, it is the European-rationalist way that, at least historically, is the anomaly. What brought about this systematic, highly successful (though often destructive) way of dealing with nature as antagonist to human existence? How did it develop in Europe and in the United States?

Origins and Development

The Renaissance in Europe, and especially in England, in addition to opening a window on the glories of Greek and Roman civilization also lifted the lid on a Pandora's box of trouble. The relaxation and then destruction of medieval class roles and relationships, the social glue binding disparate groups together, unleashed passions and possibilities of all kinds. The struggles of the European nations to find new identities as organized nation-states were aided by an innovative new way of looking at the relationship of man and nature, one that still touches every aspect of our daily life. The significance of this study is that modern notions of what constitutes crime, punishment, and the control of aberrant behavior derive directly from the new way of defining the human relationship to nature, the place of men and women in the world.

It is sometimes difficult to appreciate the struggle contemporary rationalist approaches had in gaining primacy. With modern management methods distant future developments, kings and queens ruled as they always had, by instinct and intuition. Machiavelli's *The Prince* (1532), the modern world's first political handbook advocating rationality and rigorous analysis of technique, was so attacked for being manipulative and immoral that its writer's name became a catchword for evil. Even the cunning and coldly manipulative Elizabeth the First of England, the model of a calculating ruler, nevertheless relied on John Dee, an astrologer and alchemist of dubious scientific credentials whose pronouncements now sound ludicrously irrational. Another century of revolution and civil war would pass before England enjoyed the stability brought by the philosophy of reason.

The Neoclassical Age of Reason

The exhaustion with chaos in England and Europe makes sense of the period which followed it. The second rediscovery of the ancient European past—the Renaissance was the first—is variously known as the "Neoclassic" period for its dependence on Greek and especially Roman models of stylistically coherent art, as the "Age of Reason" for its philosophical foundation, and as the "Enlightenment" for its openness to new ideas and its sometimes merciless examination of old practices with the scalpels of reason and scientific method. Reason was the hoped-for guide and governor of the unruly passions threatening to tear apart European culture. From the mid-seventeenth century to the end of the eighteenth century, the struggle to curb and rein in the emotions and the irrational behavior of extremist groups these passions drove informed great literature and great thinkers, from Moliere and Voltaire in France to Swift, Pope, and Samuel Johnson in England. Just as Voltaire's *Candide* formally opposes the chaotic events of real life with the aphorisms of a rational philosopher, Dr. Pangloss, a parody of Leibnitz, so the contest between passion and reason was also a running theme in the newly developed English novels of the period, from *Tom Jones* to *Pamela*.

Naturally, politics provided the most dramatic arena for this struggle, and it is tempting, given the neat rationalist theories of the period, to frame the beginnings of the rationalist movement in terms of its dramatic culminations, the American Revolution (a successful application of reason which ended in order) and the French Revolution (an ultimate failure which descended into runaway passion). Certainly, the American Deist thinkers, from Thomas Jefferson to Thomas Paine, consciously and unconsciously drew on the ideas of earlier European rationalists. Thomas Hobbes (*Leviathan*, 1651) proclaimed that the social contract is secular rather than sacred in its inception, a rational means of controlling universal open warfare rather than a God-given model for society. Descartes and Leibnitz in Europe and John Locke and David Hume in Britain threw doubt on the certainty of human understanding of reality, which might simply involve the mechanics of the outside world imposing itself through limited perceptions to impinge on consciousness; mechanistic theories of how we know were paralleled by conjectures about similarly machine-like operations in the natural universe. In the famous chestnut, God is the eternal Clockmaker who devised the universe and therefore all of its contents; a unified field theory of how all of nature worked seemed to be emerging.

In England, the Royal Society formed in 1662 marked a new method of investigating nature and reporting the results. A fascination developed with the similarity between mechanical inventions such as clocks, pumps, fountains, and navigation instruments, all being perfected at the time, and new understandings about the organic "mechanisms" that sustained life. Harvey, who discovered the circulation of the blood in 1628, also sought order and logic in English grammar; like later eighteenth-century grammarians Joseph Priestley and George Campbell, Harvey attempted to reduce the language to almost mathematical exactitude, parsing sentences with the same expectation of finding God-given order as surgeons exploring the human body and astronomers examining the heavens, prohibiting such forms as the double negative due to its illogical self-cancellation. This apparent coherence among very different domains of existence validated the idea that human problems as well should be dealt with on a rational basis. Thus, the U.S. founding fathers found rights to life, liberty, and the pursuit of happiness as self-evident principles of existence, not as boons granted by the state or some other authority; reason dictated that, at least in principle, rights enjoyed by a few should not be withheld from the many.

The French, famously rational as a people, attempted to apply reason as a curb on passion and a guide to human behavior. (Much later, the French led criminology and the scientific investigation of crime, though the best French literary detectives were created by English-speaking writers.) The Universal Rights of Man was a blueprint for egalitarianism, but the Revolution lurched away from hammering out consensus on the American model and instead unleashed passions long suppressed, ending with the bloody payback of the guillotine and Napoleon's dictatorship. In *Sister Revolutions: French Lightning, American Light*, Susan Dunn quotes Gouverneur Morris, the American Minister to France, writing in 1790: the French "have taken Genius instead of Reason for their Guide, adopted Experiment instead of Experience, and wander in the Dark because they prefer Lightning to Light" (39). Perhaps America did indeed take reason for its guide in the wonderful balance of the Constitution and in the carefully contrived checks and balances that govern our political and governmental life. It is in other areas, however, that reason governs our less obvious attitudes and beliefs, in particular, our attitudes toward the natural world and toward human nature itself.

Exploring Nature through Reason

The underlying attitude toward nature in the Age of Reason can be summed up in the key metaphor of exploration and discovery, an appropriate intellectual and scientific figure for a period wherein European sailors and travelers laid open and recorded much of the world's geography. Nature provided the matter for intellect to dissect and classify; finding the patterns in the confusion of disparate appearances was the intellectual challenge. One can only imagine the excitement involved in reducing the multiplicity of the natural world to rule, in seeing for the first time the economy and elegance of organic systems, with, for example, the physiology of respiration and the oxygenation of the blood repeated in mammals of all shapes, sizes, and types, huge differences in appearance giving way to overriding principles of biology, chemistry, and physics. For the first time, unifying principles could be teased out through exploration and the application of classification and taxonomy, the new tools of intellect. The human form might no longer be divine, sharing as much as it did with lower animals, but it certainly revealed a Divine Hand, an Intellect capable of planning and shaping these amazingly efficient principles.

The Emergence of Cultural Universals and Commonalities

When attention turned toward human nature, a similar optimism about discovering common forms and practices prevailed. In 1786, Sir William Jones, a British official in India, postulated a hypothetical language as a metaphorical parent to Sanskrit, the ancient language of the north of the subcontinent; this "proto-Indo-European" language would have been the ancestor to all the branches of the Indo-European language family, including the German, Italic, Slavic, and other important divisions of the family "tree." Jones' proto-language, though long dead, would explain why the Sanskrit Indian *Vedas* and other sacred works predating Greek, Latin, and German would include word roots (*diva* for *divine, deiw* for *deus* or *God*) and recurring grammatical forms (verb conjugations and noun declensions) inherent in the European branch languages of the Indo-European tree: derivation from the same source. The evidence was ultimately compelling: beneath the utter dissimilarity of surface features, the people of dozens of cultures and religions shared similar basic linguistic forms, and therefore, in the historical absence of loaning and borrowing, must have had a common cultural-linguistic origin. As with the claims of Darwin and his fellow biologists, that all life evolved from a common origin, an idea so initially counter-intuitive as to be ludicrous, science was unearthing commonalities undreamed of by earlier scholars. The earthworm, the whale, human beings, horses, and elephants, all evolving from a common biological parent? Persians, Russians, Anglo-Saxons, East Indians, and Italians all speaking related languages, derived from a common source? The enormous explanatory power of scientific exploration, description, classification, and experiment overcame the resistance of tradition, religion, and common sense to establish a new ideology, one which sought for similarity in orderly patterns of development.

VIEWS IN CONFLICT

The notion that all humankind is unitary—that there is one human way beneath surface difference—is still not accepted universally, though it is the underlying premise for much of the European-American outlook on the world. The accelerating "globalism" or "modernism" of the millennium has raised consciousness about this notion, though there is still no accepted term to describe the movement. (Francis Fukuyama's *The End of History* and "Will Socialism Make a Comeback?" helped promote "globalization" over the older "modernism.") Globalism is not new; essentially it means living with Enlightenment Reason as the governing schema or outlook on life, and thus thinking that most (perhaps all) human ways are universal, with local practices simply variations on a common theme. Anthropologists, the mop-up troops of the social sciences, sort out the classification of different Ways, consigning them to this or that category, one or another means of expression of the common human spirit. Human culture might have infinite means of expression, but the forces of taxonomy are not intimidated, finding a niche and label for every imaginable behavior. The contrasting view is that the intuitive/spiritual varies drastically according to culture, place, religion, and circumstance. Not all psychic visions are the same; they would be subject to rules if they were, and would simply be manifestations of universal psychological states. In the Western view, different regions shape common possibilities in economics, social structures, and lifeways; in the intuitive/spiritual, people are the unique creation of their land and have their own creation stories to describe their special place in their region. Tribe after Native American tribe calls itself "The People"; no wonder anthropologists who deny this uniqueness and classify creation stories as cosmogonic theories or myths are resented and even maligned by Indians who perceive the threat to their special status.

Cultural Singularity versus Generic Consistency

This notion of cultural and even racial singularity opposed by a unitary view of human nature and culture is sufficiently important to require illustration. Devon A. Mihesuah's *American Indians: Stereotypes and Realities* pairs a key generalization against a view of reality:

STEREOTYPE
Indians arrived in this hemisphere via the Siberian land bridge.

REALITY
Indians believe that they were created in this hemisphere. (46–47)

In fact, the two statements should not even be put into conflict, since the first is a statement of fact to be proven or disproven, and the second is a question of belief, which, if reported accurately, is by definition true no matter the factual underpinning. The conflict, however, is absolutely central to the underlying disagreement between Western rationalism and Native American intuition. As Mihesuah rightly observes, only fairly recently has science challenged Christian creationism (and other Western creation narratives), thus making the far earlier attacks on native creationism seem gratuitous, tendentious, or politically motivated (for example, to justify archaeologists removing Indian remains from burial sites). We have no stake in either side of this argument other than to identify just how completely the two worldviews conflict, and thus how unresolvable the conflict truly is, no matter how good intentions might be. With creationism comes singularity; with science comes the notion of the common run of humanity. Thus, a generally unappreciated consequence of seeing through the eyes of Reason is this reduction of all human activity to formulaic responses: a given group's "religious" rituals and ceremonies constitute attempts to propitiate supernatural forces and reduce stress. This or that particular ritual is no more than a manifestation of a general human response to uncertainty. (Mihesuah correctly suggests a certain hypocrisy in parts of the scientific world: mainstream religious organizations usually escape the reduction of their practices to anthropological data; this special treatment of powerful groups looks like capitulation to the majority, while vulnerable "sects" or "cults" may be bullied at will.) While Western classification systems do much to further intellectual understanding, they shortchange the need to feel special and important, a deeply felt requirement of a satisfying identity. Certainly the European-American establishment has applied unsentimental analytical tools inconsistently to its own practices.

The phenomenal success of Western technology in accomplishing material goals has advanced the claims to universality of less objective Western ways. For example, to many observers, Western medicine reigns supreme over folk and herbal remedies, in spite of recent enthusiasm for Chinese treatments such as acupuncture, organic medicines, and Asian religio-therapeutic philosophies such as *qi gong*. Yet even physicians completely committed to Western rationalism and the scientific method acknowledge that as many as 50 percent of doctor-patient contacts involve psychosomatic complaints, and that even illnesses firmly grounded in known organic causes often respond to psychological or "spiritual" therapy. The triumph of capitalism over socialism (itself a European invention) is another example of one-world ideology, the substitution of myriads of ways and means of organizing economic relations with a single, "rationalized" standard, just as so-called "Arabic" numerals triumphed over most other mathematical notation systems. The process of standardization initiated in the trade relations described in *Black Robe* (acquiring standardized guns, knives, and iron tomahawk heads necessitates becoming part of the capitalist world order) comes to completion in *Laughing Boy* (with American dollars the favored currency, and amassing capital, Slim Girl's strategy). A frequently articulated premise of free-market enthusiasts, that all economic relations obey the "laws" of their economic philosophy, though not necessarily meriting denial, requires some skepticism, for until quite recently believers in socialism made exactly the same claims about their own theories of capital and labor.

Another arena in which cultural differences have been rolled over by Western definitions is the law. All the features of Western law—the grand and petit jury system, disinterested judges, advocates pro and con, rules of evidence, public proceedings, meticulous records, controls on emotion and rhetoric—have been extended around the world. This is not to disparage these elements of our legal system, nor to make counter-claims for opposing methods but simply to assert that other approaches to finding truth and establishing justice have long-standing and oftentimes respectable records, and their supplantation in favor of the European-American model is often seen by those supplanted as high-handed. Certainly, the record of the American legal and governmental system in finding the truth and establishing justice in relation to Native Americans is a sorry one. In both *Black Robe* and *Laughing Boy*, the Native American sense of what constitutes a "contract" in the civil law sense or a "crime" in the justice system differs distinctly from that of the whites with whom they deal. Moreover, even present-day defenders of our legal system caution against the automatic expectation of justice; procedure rules here, just as it has in courts around the world.

The insistence of the West that its social, economic, legal, and even spiritual arrangements partake of the essential nature of all human nature may simply annoy non-believers, may seem a manifestation of the arrogance of the wealthy, powerful, and temporarily transcendent, or may even be taken as a death sentence for weak, isolated, or "obsolete" cultural ways. Scores of venerable languages and cultures die out across the world every year, and the rate of this onslaught is accelerating due to improvements in transportation and communications, and due to the crush of population growth which pushes cultures into proximity. For Native American ways of knowing, the problem of extinction is most pressing, with the argument against standardization complex and frequently skewed, distorted by the insecurity and defensiveness of minority status, the perceived weakness of being on the wrong side of modernism, and, most significantly, the inability to frame the terms of the discussion. Both *Black Robe* and *Laughing Boy* describe their respective native cultures just before the forces of Western rationality and standardization overcome them; both novels, however, set up a level playing field on which the players compete in equal numbers, according to fair rules (as fair as possible: the books are European-style novels, written in English by whites, however sympathetic). Because of its thematic focus on aberrant behavior, crime, and punishment, and its inherent foregrounding of ways of knowing (detection is practical epistemology, after all), the Native American detective novel can set up a similarly flush arena in which a plane surface provides equity.

The Detective Story: A Window on How We Think

What is it about the detective story that allows such claims for its importance, its potential as a window on how we think, how we regard the thinking of others, and what values our system privileges? Why are 20 percent to 22 percent of all U.S. books sold detective or mystery fiction, and why is the proportion of these books that is Native American in setting, theme, or character growing larger? As Klein notes, the familiarity of the detective genre's conventions creates a comfortable context for the exploration and contemplation of larger issues which might never be confronted otherwise. The two most significant issues raised by Indian detective stories and thus the encounter between reason and intuition are the relationship of humans to the natural world they inhabit and the actual nature of human nature itself.

American detectives of the classic, hard-boiled kind tend to see society as corrupt, with the "civilization" of the modern world corrupting innocence. Raymond Chandler's unforgettable description of Los Angeles in *The Long Goodbye* (1953) is the best statement of this attitude:

Out there in the night of a thousand crimes people were dying, being maimed, cut by flying glass, crushed against steering wheels or under heavy car tyres . . . beaten, robbed, strangled, raped, and murdered. People were hungry, sick, bored, desperate with loneliness or remorse or fear, angry, cruel, feverish, shaken by sobs. A city no worse than others, a city rich and vigorous and full of pride, a city lost and beaten and full of emptiness. (69)

Chandler's image of the modern American metropolis as a malignancy was conventional wisdom; Dashiell Hammet's Continental Op stories, Ross Macdonald's novels of California degeneracy, and John D. Macdonald's

Florida stories all find perversity behind the glossy exteriors of modern American urban life. The pulp fiction of the 1920s, 1930s, and 1940s and the *film noir* which spun out of it made the corrupt city with its million stories of depravity and degradation a modern cliche, perhaps best summed up in the caricatures of the *Batman* films: a *noir* Metropolis, literally and metaphorically dark, with every alley and nook sheltering a lunatic villain. In part, this cliche has worked in synergy with conservative visions of a utopian American past corrupted by the modern; the frontier villages so dear to the set designers of the American western became urban centers of balefulness, fallen societies in which people tumbled quickly from states of innocence if they ever enjoyed such a state to begin with.

Indian detective stories have changed this cliche, if only by moving locations and settings. Evil is no longer automatically located in urban or city life, though the Los Angeles seen by Hillerman's Jim Chee is a spiritual wasteland where assimilated Indians lead empty, deadened lives of despair. When Hillerman moved the detective from the metaphorical canyons of the city to the real ones of the Southwest, he necessarily reinvented the causal equations of corruption: the city may be evil (it certainly affects many Indians, literary and real, negatively) but, given the usually rural setting of the Native American detective story, it cannot be the immediate and necessary cause of crime. Individuals must be at fault, either because of social role (skinwalkers, for example), pathology, or traditional sins (greed, pride, lust, or the like).

The change in setting thus affected the nature of the literary social order, which in the city involved the turbulence of social relations, class relations, and domestic human drama. Traditional detective stories, British and classic hard-boiled American, are all about human rules, social class strictures, aberration, and authority, whether in the classic English village or the U.S. metropolis. Some of this remains when the story setting goes rural or primitive, but the physical geography becomes a significant player as opposed to the social structures of the complex human culture of traditional stories. Climate and weather, the handmaidens of landscape, become important elements. The landscape is typically uninscribed by human forces, not "written down" like the streets of Los Angeles or New York, but left open to interpretation and possibility, to inventiveness and freedom from human definition. Characters can escape into the wilds of the desert, the emptiness of the Great Plains, the skirts of the Rockies, the mysterious forests of the Pacific Southwest, and even, in a return to Native American origins, the virgin forests of Vermont. The old maps of North America sometimes carried the inscription, "There be monsters out there," and the movement to Native American settings, often still wild and unknown to the mainstream, has reopened this possibility of new terrors. As in Thomas Perry's Jane Whitefield novel *Vanishing Act*, the forest, though no longer all primeval, becomes a locale evocative of pre-European life, a wild, challenging place of new mysteries and possibilities. In a way, these new settings are infusing the detective story with archetypal American myths about escape, freedom, self-definition, and rebellion, all of the values that spurred early scouts, explorers, mountain men, and other European-Indian amalgams to escape the bounds of "civilized" society.

Along with the setting, the nature of human possibility changes. Detectives from Jane Whitefield and Jim Chee to Vicky Holden and Jordan Tidewater work for very different motivations than the daily fee plus expenses of the classic private eye or the minimal salary of a government employee in a police station. Whitefield, for example, works for nothing, asking simply for a gift when the spirit moves the person she has saved; in fact, she truly works to realize a traditional role in the modern world, to make the past speak in the present. The classic detective motivations of money, protecting the community, and working for the abstraction of justice are complemented and supplanted by new reasons to seek truth or to return stability to a subset of society at large.

The Native American detective story, unpacked, thus points toward any number of unresolved issues in American society: homogeneity versus diversity, the claims of the past versus the demands of the present, and the very nature of crime, aberrancy, and justice. Most important is the never-settled question that begins as epistemology—how we confirm the truth of this occurrence, what really happened—but which ultimately questions our view of the world at large, as a material universe linked by "scientific" chains of cause and effect, or as a spiritual world rich with unseen forces and powers, some psychological, perhaps, but others quite real and sometimes terrifying.

3

Native American Crime and Detection Novels: Earth and Spirit Power

The river had always flowed through the canyon, cutting the sandstone and granite, carving motion into the rock the same way it had carved the people into its own shape. Over generations they had learned the seasons and motions of the water, the blood that coursed through them beginning with the river and returning like water to earth and sky. He looked down at the brown, sloping backs of his hands, the rise of branching veins beneath smooth skin, and he felt the current of the river in his body.

—Louis Owens, *Nightland*, 202

Although crime and its consequences are a broad topic in Native American culture, the number of Native American authors employing the conventions of the crime/detective fiction genre is more limited. This chapter will focus on eight such representative native writers with common themes: Louis Owens, Ron Querry, Anna Lee Walters, Robert Conley, Mardi Oakley Medawar, Sherman Alexie, James Welch, and Linda Hogan. Interestingly enough, particularly when writing about spirit power, these authors prefer to illustrate general principles through the religious beliefs of tribes other

Regions of Native American detection: (1) Southwest; (2) Plains and Mountains; (3) The Northwest; (4) Alaska and Canadian Northwest Territories; (5) The Northeast and Great Lakes.

than their own, as does Choctaw Ron Querry, who writes about Apaches, Hopis, and, more particularly, Navajos and their conception of witchcraft, or Pawnee/Otoe Anna Lee Walters, who describes Navajo beliefs. Cherokee Mardi Oakley Medawar sets her mysteries amid the Kiowa, while Chickasaw Linda Hogan depicts an infamous period of Osage history.

Author	Detective	Tribal Affiliation
Robert Conley	Go-Ahead Rider	Cherokee
Linda Hogan	State Red Hawk	Lakota Sioux
Mardi Oakley Medawar	Tay Bodal	Kiowa
Louis Owens	Siquani	Cherokee
Anna Lee Walters	Johnnie Navaho	Navajo
	Wilbur and Anna Snake	Pawnee
James Welch	Sylvester Yellow Calf	Blackfeet

Two concerns recur in these authors' novels: the Native American sense of identity with the physical environment, the earth, and all of its life forms, and the simultaneous sense of connection to the spirit world or the sources of spiritual power.

Native American respect for the natural world is well known, but speaking of a sense of identity with the physical world clarifies the philosophical sources of that respect. As Louis Owens observes in the opening quote, the human body and the features of the earth's surface share a structural identity. That is, the human body reflects the plan the Creator used to shape and define the earth. This congruence between the great and the particular is also evident in the shaping forces of nature on human culture, economics, and psyche, the various Indian Ways, as later chapters show. While individual Native American tribes may describe this identity differently, they concur that human beings and the earth share similar physical structures.

The mythology of each tribe constantly reinforces this physical connection to the earth. For the Hopis, an open channel runs through the earth's center—a passageway providing the primary mode of communication between the Creator and all points on earth. Similarly, a channel through the center of each human body links it to the spirit world and spirit power. For the Navajo, ancestors' bodies returned to the earth from which they emerged constitute the four sacred mountains protectively ringing the Navajo people. Both the Crow and the Apache affirm that the land the Creator gave them was specific in its location and physical dimensions, a particular, unique bequest in perfect accordance with tribal identity:

The Crow country is a good country. The Great Spirit put it in exactly the right place; while you are in it, you fare well; whenever you are out of it, whichever way you travel, you fare worse. . . . The Crow country is exactly in the right place. It is good to be found there. There is no place like the Crow country. (Virginia Armstrong, 67)

For each tribe of men Usen [Apache for the creation deity] created, He also made a home. In the land created for any particular tribe He placed whatever would be best for the welfare of that tribe. Thus it was in the beginning: The Apaches and their homes each created by Usen himself. When they are taken from these homes, they sicken and die. (Barrett, *Geronimo*, 69)

Each of the tribe's rituals was aligned to its mythology. The four sacred mountains of the Navajo appear in the sandpaintings of their healing ceremonies. The Plains Indians offer back to the earth a piece of flesh (their physical substance) when they are connected to a sacred pole that forms the axis of the physical universe, the place where the physical and the spiritual converge. Thus, sacred history recounting the creation story, the oral tradition of each succeeding generation, and sacred geography all point to an inescapable identity with the land, the physical structures of human life.

A second theme our eight authors address is spiritual power: the Native American premise that spirit power runs through all things animate and inanimate on the earth and in the sky. Every physical object and each living person has some basic connection to spirit power. However, tribal roles lead certain individuals to seek specialized powers. Hunters seek animal guardians who can bestow success in the hunt; warriors seek specialized powers to enhance their war shields and weapons. Also, spirits or ancestors call some tribal members to devote themselves entirely to gaining and dispensing spiritual power. While the almost generic title "shaman" covers all types of tribal spiritual specialists, each tribe had its own specific understanding of what constituted a person of spirit power. Thus, this chapter's consideration of the eight representative authors will determine exactly how spiritual power manifests itself in their novels and with what emphasis. All eight consistently depict spirit power through the traditional tribal elder, one who has never lost his connection to the tribal heritage and so is able to "see" and "act" in ways that combine ordinary and spiritual ways of "knowing." A chart at the end of this chapter summarizes the particular focal points of each author.

LOUIS OWENS (CHOCTAW, CHEROKEE)

Louis Owens' crime novel *Nightland*, set in New Mexico, exemplifies the intricate ways that geography, history, and religious beliefs weave tightly into a single storytelling fabric. The drama begins with a man falling out of an airplane, desperately clutching a suitcase with almost $1 million in drug money. The body is impaled on a tall cedar, a type of tree common throughout the Southwest. Thus, the opening moments of the story strike a jarring note, for traditionally in Native American ceremonies, cedar in its perpetually green state is the creator/protector of strength in living. The tree's original identity has been twisted into an instrument of death; holding the man's body aloft, it waves a grim death flag over the entire area. That is exactly the note that Owens intends to strike—climactic changes locally have extinguished the very vitality of the land:

[L] and . . . worth three dollars an acre in the thirties was virtually worthless sixty years later—too far from civilization to be developed, too dried-up and dead for ranching or farming. And it wasn't just the water. It was as though a force had gone out of the very earth. The scrubby prickly pear, piñon, and juniper hung on, scorched and brittle with a kind of resignation he felt in the dry air, but about their roots the earth turned gray and hard, showing ribs of hot granite. . . . The land was dying and the people were beginning to turn on one another like grim survivors. (43)

Drought has devastated land once usable for raising corn or cattle, its surface waters have dried up, and even such extraordinary means as the expensive sinking of a deep well are fruitless.

Into this physical environment of exhausted resources come Billy Keene and Will Striker, two Native Americans, raised almost as half-brothers on adjoining parcels of land that their parents purchased when they left Oklahoma Indian Territory seeking a better life. Many years have elapsed since the move to New Mexico. Both sets of parents have died in tragic accidents, and the two men are now well into middle age, with lives as arid and desperate as the geography around them. With the drug "money from the sky," both men believe that their lives and land will flourish again.

Owens, a Cherokee, regularly incorporates traditional Cherokee cultural elements into his novels. Keene and Striker, Owens' main characters, are also Cherokee, though far from the original Southeastern landscape of the Cherokee nation, in a New Mexico area influenced by Pueblos. Thus, the novel's references to the traditional Native American religious perspectives, storytelling, and ritual curiously blend what these displaced individuals bring with them with what they encounter in a setting very different from their own. However, mixed cultures are common in Native American society, and Owens provides an authentic Native American perspective here, one to which most non-natives would be blind. The Cherokee, originally from the Southeast coastal region and then the mountains and hills of Georgia and southern Tennessee, were removed forcibly to Oklahoma; consequently, multiple past experiences inform their outlook on geography and culture. A mix of indigenous cultures characterized New Mexico and the entire Southwest long before whites came, so placing multicultural Cherokee characters in this blended atmosphere provides complex resonances of which mainstream readers, whose concept of generic "Indian" is often stereotypically simple, are unlikely to be aware.

Another authentic note is Owens' integration of tribal lore. The role of the creation story in tribal storytelling cannot be overestimated. Even a few references to a creation story are enough to anchor a story unfolding in present time. Owens anchors *Nightland* in the stories of Selu the Corn Mother, Kanati, her husband, and their sons (later the Thunder Boys); Awi Usdi, or the Little Deer; and finally Buzzard and his role in shaping dry land as the earth emerges from a watery domain. These traditional mythological references enrich the novel's setting.

However, Owens' most consistent use of Cherokee materials lies in the role of old man Siquani Kaneequayokee, who lives in a trailer adjacent to his grandson Billy's home and is the wisdom-bearer of the traditional Cherokee way. Though addressed as grandfather, he is not the direct in-line grandfather of either man but rather a time traveler from a more remote time. Siquani is the storyteller, the ritualist who finally releases the soul of the man impaled on the cedar tree, the seer who "speaks" with the crows, "reads" the thunder in the west, recognizes witch power, and hears the cries of the massacred indigenous peoples. He foresees that one of his grandsons will not survive the ever-deepening crisis in which they are embroiled.

Owens frequently incorporates characters with identities linked to mysterious spiritual powers beyond everyday experience. Siquani is the male elder who carries spirit power in its positive mode, whereas Odessa Whitehawk, his female antagonist, is linked to witchcraft, a negative dimension of power. The mistress of hidden motives and false appearances, she affects victims almost hypnotically. Owens provides a clue to her dangerous nature—her allergy to cedar, a traditional medicine for exorcising evil—and thereby alerts readers to watch for further indications of her true nature and intent. His murder mysteries *The Sharpest Sight* and *The Bone Game* also feature this classic confrontation of dual spirit powers, life-preserving versus life-destroying.

If the Siquani figure can access positive spirit powers, then he is the center point at which geography, history, and religious perception intersect. He was with the Cherokee people before their removal from the Southeastern United States (early nineteenth century) and later experienced the Trail of Tears (1838–1839), noting with horror the desecration of the dead—fallen men, women, and children not properly buried, their souls' journeys forever incomplete:

Mourning cries rose from the mass of old and young, men and women, in a single, woven song, and the fog hovered like smoke from a hundred campfires. As he wove his way among them, the People began to fall, mothers curling around the shriveled forms of children, husbands lying beside wives. The ground beneath his moccasins was cold and hard, and he saw a woman's hair frozen in ice as she strove to rise from the blue earth, the captive hair pulling her face tight so that it was bone that beseeched him as he passed. (*Nightland*, 253)

Though removed to present-day New Mexico, Siquani sees the land there harboring a similar experience: the murder of numerous native peoples and the desecration of the dead. Indeed, he alone understands that the dead have withdrawn the surface waters and control the resulting drought. Siquani and the ghost of the cedar-impaled man discuss the possible redemption of the wrongful death lodged beneath the earth's surface:

"Maybe they can use the money to help this land," Arturo said. "Maybe if they put it into the earth here somehow it will break the evil power of that money. . . . For my people the dead have an important job," Arturo said as they walked together down the hill, Siquani bent over by the weight of the sheet. "The dead bring rain to the people." (329)

The proper offerings will appease the dead and free the land from the death curse that holds all in its grip.

This story does not employ the traditional mainstream figure of the detective rationally and methodically solving a major crime. Rather, the major crime sorted out by Siquani, the shaman-like character, is the historical one against the native peoples and their land. The more contemporary crime of the stolen drug money and the extreme measures used to retrieve it plays out against this significant backdrop. For Native American readers, however, the historical crime will loom far larger than for a mainstream audience, providing a context for current violations of the law.

Each author discussed in this chapter uses Native American materials in a variety of ways. Owens employs the archetypal tribal elder, who reads the present world in ways that link multiple time frames—past, present, and future—and multiple dimensions of existence—the earth's surface, the spirit realm, and the world of the dead. Thus, the elder holds information unavailable to the ordinary person. In the tribal context, however, knowledge does not always equal the power to change the course of events, for example, to stop the process of an unfolding crime. At times the images the tribal elder receives from his spirit sources may be fragmentary or unclear, thus complicating the puzzle to be unlocked before the power of the message is manifested. Owens' tribal-wisdom figure stands in the background, always watchful, ever ready to help younger characters cope with the consequences of destruction unleashed by the story's antagonists.

As in *Nightland*, Owens' *The Sharpest Sight* and *The Bone Game*, a family saga of Choctaws displaced in the California coastal mountain region, require the intervention of ancestral spirits and the aid of a Choctaw elder or elders (like Uncle Luther from Mississippi) to combat the forces of sorcery. In the first, Hoey McCurtain's son, Cole, must return to Mississippi for spiritual guidance in locating the bones of his murdered brother Attis, whose body has disappeared in the churning waves of river flood waters; in the second, the college-age daughter of the remaining son, Cole, needs spirit protection from a brutal serial murderer. Though set in the present, like *Nightland*, both novels depend on the tribal ways and tribal histories to overcome evil arising from ancient causes. *The Sharpest Sight* features Choctaw burial rites for the dead (displaying remains on an open-air platform, and later "picking the bones" to remove the flesh from the skeleton) and Choctaw beliefs about the nature of the soul, the realm of the dead, and the black panther or "soul eater," which stalks outside shadows ("wandering souls") to prevent their passage to the realm of the dead. Identifying Attis' killer turns on clues from the sheriff's dead grandfather and Uncle Luther's warnings about a *bruja* (female witch). In the second novel, *The Bone Game*, a malevolent spirit presence springs from the bloody Spanish abuse of the Pueblo population 180 years earlier but stimulates similar murders and dismemberments in the present.

Thus Owens mingles traditional spirit powers with contemporary crime stories to suggest the ongoing struggle between creation/destruction. This blend differentiates him from most mainstream detective/crime story writers with Native American characters, for only an author steeped in a native culture would see past and present linked so intimately, a defining cultural characteristic for many authentic native writers.

RON QUERRY (CHOCTAW)

Choctaw Ron Querry and Pawnee/Otoe Anna Lee Walters share a second focus of Native American materials: a healthy respect for the dark side of spirit power, the negative, threatening features, such as witchcraft or an attack by wronged "ghosts," sometimes strongly connected to spirit power. Again, the tribal elders or medicine men cannot always deflect or defuse these negative forces once set in motion.

Ron Querry's *The Death of Bernadette Lefthand* and Anna Lee Walters' *Ghost Singer* raise the problem of understanding the dimensions of spirit power. In both, a tribal elder or seer intimately connected with the "old ways" must guide the skeptical current generation. Faced with a crisis, the modern generation is inadequately equipped to deal with life-and-death matters. Out of touch with traditions judged of little value in present-day settings, they must come to understand the limits of science and technology, accept the intervention of a seer, medicine man, or shaman, and realize that rather than easy solutions, a whole new series of challenges and responsibilities confronts them. Most of the information that a seer receives is in images to be deciphered, usually by the one who has petitioned for help in the first place. The petitioner must use the information he gains to get in touch with his own spirit knowing—a process requiring time and discipline. If the petitioner needs physical healing or a release from witchcraft, again, he must approach a tribal specialist.

The success of the cure, however, rests not only on the expertise of the medicine man, but equally on the disposition of the patient and his immediate family. For example, in *The Death of Bernadette Lefthand*, when Anderson George's grandfather performs a healing for him in a ceremonial hogan, there seated beside him is his wife Bernadette, and nearby are her father and sister, the few close family members available to him. Their presence is critical for his successful cure. Of course, any system which identifies witchcraft as the cause of illness has ready explanations for a ceremony failing to win release for the patient. The power of the ceremony itself is unquestioned, but failures are blamed on the ceremony having been held too late in the witching process, or the true cause of the witching remaining undiscovered, making the choice of corresponding ritual healing erroneous.

The Death of Bernadette Lefthand provides ample opportunity to observe traditional Navajo attitudes toward disease and appropriate ritual remedies. The brutal slashing murder of a young woman almost universally admired for her qualities of character as well as for her skills as a traditional dancer suggests witchcraft. Told from the perspective of the two women who spent the most time with Bernadette, her sister Gracie and her white employer Starr Stubbs, the story sets no investigative process in motion. Rather, the evidence presented in the first and final pages points to Bernadette's husband Anderson George, who is thought to have committed the heinous crime while in a drunken rage. Yet, the body of the novel depicts Anderson George being framed and explains his entire descent into drunkenness and malaise as the result of the evil witchcraft of a trusted clan relative.

The opening time frame shifts from Bernadette's tragic death to three years earlier, when Anderson George and Bernadette meet at the Indian boarding school in Santa Fe. As the story unfolds, the witch insinuates his presence into Anderson's life and begins his destructive deeds. Even though Anderson's grandmother is a "hand trembler" or diagnostician of sources of evil, and his grandfather is a trained "singer" of healing ceremonies, neither can stop the destructive forces set in motion by the witch. The novel confirms Clyde Kluckhohn's landmark ethnographic studies of Navajo witchcraft, particularly *Navaho Witchcraft* (1944). While a half-century has passed since these studies, the beliefs and practices described therein remain very much in evidence among the Navajos. According to traditional lore, the witch "pays" for his training in power with both money and tainted artifacts stolen from the dead and studies with someone who has given ample evidence of his own abilities to manipulate forces of destruction and death. Witching power is thus transmitted in a type of apprenticeship, and certain ritual steps must be followed for a curse to be successful:

"I do have somethin' in my mind," the old man went on. "I know how this witchery business is done. But just knowin' the right prayin' to do, it ain't all it takes neither—you gotta have some certain things to make something bad happen," he said, becoming more and more agitated as he spoke. "First you gotta know the person you're aimin' to witch. You gotta know that person's secret name and sometimes that's hard to find out since even their family don't hardly ever call them by that name outside of their hogan. And then you gotta have somethin' private of theirs—like maybe some part of their clothes that ain't been washed or some of their hair or fingernails, or even some of their shit or somethin' that they spit out from their mouth." (125)

The Christian belief system posits a "Prince of Darkness," a Satan, responsible for the existence of evil. In contrast, the belief system of most Native Americans asserts the duality of power, life-giving versus life-destroying, inherent in the very structures of earthly existence. Witches claim no power from a god-like being, but rather expertly manipulate the powers inherent in all physical objects. Thus, a simple stone, taken from the sleeping place of one who has died, easily becomes a source of "corpse poison." Eventually a witch's power even invades his victim's dreams, as in this episode from one of Anderson's continuing nightmares:

And then it was like the hole was a gorge or a canyon and I was running as hard as I could and that place was getting narrower and narrower and I was more scared than I've ever been. And then it came to me that I was running because there was something following me. And I could hear whatever it was back there and I could feel it. . . . And when I turned around I noticed that the thing that had been followin' me was a coyote and that it had these bright yellow eyes and its tongue was hanging way out and I could see its teeth and smell its terrible stinkin' breath even. But just then it disappeared behind a bush. (*The Death of Bernadette Lefthand*, 155)

Coyote, one of the Holy People in the Navajo creation story, is not the divine source of the witches' power. Instead, the Coyote figure's appearance, either in dreams or in the shadowy form of a man wrapped in a coyote skin, is a powerful warning to a Navajo that evil is close at hand. Whether or not an individual heeds the warning in time will determine his or her chances for survival. Anderson George's brother dies on a lonely road, a victim not simply of the witch's craft but also of his direct action; Bernadette and her faithful dog Chaco are literally cut down by the witch, and Anderson George, who has been framed for his wife's murder, is driven to despair and suicide as the witch intends. Thus, behind the overt crimes in *The Death of Bernadette Lefthand* are the covert acts of witchcraft that destroy a man's spirit, acts that result from jealousy and a will to evil. Querry's ending, however, suggests that the forces of nature will provide a final retribution that restores balance; the witch has noted the strange flashes of lightning that seem out of place for the time of year, and Querry's very next and final chapter opens with a quote from Kluckhohn about "a diffuse supernatural sanction against witches" existing in the belief that "a witch who escapes human detection will nevertheless eventually be struck down by lightning" (215).

ANNA LEE WALTERS (PAWNEE, OTOE)

The Navajo belief system concerning the sources of evil and the physical consequences of contact with evil is essential to Anna Lee Walters' *Ghost Singer*. However, Walters emphasizes less the role of witchcraft than the power of the spirits of the dead to influence the living, even in a twenty-first century urban environment. Like Querry, Walters explores the theme of spirit power. She also draws on a major thematic strategy from *Nightland*: that honoring the Native American perspective in fiction necessitates multiple layers of storytelling in which past and present coincide. For Owens, the bloody history of the native peoples and their lands explains *Nightland's* present-day setting, which is marked by buzzards, crows, and drought—all signals that the realm of the dead demands recognition.

In *Ghost Singer*, two layers of crime similarly unfold. First are the historical crimes against the Navajo people: 1830s slave raiders decimating traditional Navajo small family groups, abducting the younger women and children, murdering the rest, and cutting off the ears of the dead in order to collect a bounty. Evidence of this brutal activity surfaced in 1969 in the Natural History Department of the Smithsonian Museum and marks what Native Americans consider a second, ongoing crime against the native peoples: horrifying museum "holdings" that few Native Americans are allowed to view. Locked away in an attic office, along with more traditional tribal artifacts, are boxes of human remains: Navajo skulls, mummified bodies, and three strings of ears, each four yards long, ears that garnered a considerable bounty. These bones are irrevocably connected to the spirits of their owners, and because they have been denied proper burial, these spirits cannot complete their journey to the afterworld. In effect, the Smithsonian attic is alive with spirit people, one of whom, a dead warrior, is a particularly menacing, powerful spirit presence. However, these historical abuses are not the only criminal dimensions the novel explores. Past crimes are inextricably linked to present crimes, and this tangible evil continues to impact on those who unwittingly enter its sphere. Three unexplained deaths or supposed suicides over an eighteen-month period all involve museum staff members who had contact with the "artifacts" lodged in the attic.

Three tribal elders join the dramatic action, the only ones capable of containing the powerful negative forces that continue to claim new victims. Wilbur and Anna Snake, two traditional Pawnee healers once invited to Washington to help identify the museum's Native American holdings, return in 1969 to visit their grandson. A formerly skeptical museum employee now ready to link the suicides and the ghostly apparitions seeks their guidance. He has been physically assaulted by the warrior spirit in the attic office and has no desire to follow his predecessors to an untimely death.

Concurrent with the Washington arrival of the Pawnee elders is that of another tribal elder, Jonnie Navaho, and his granddaughter Nasbah, who come to help their hospitalized relative Willie Begay overcome hallucinations and seizures. The hospital staff has no medical explanation for Willie's physical difficulties, but the old man, well respected for his healing knowledge among the Navajo community, invokes traditional Navajo healing methods. After a lengthy talk with Willie about his museum archive research, the grandfather visits the attic archives along with Anna and Wilbur Snake. Shown the contents of a single archive drawer, he draws back and shields his eyes from the evil. The grandfather now clearly understands the cause of Begay's spirit-illness and quickly leaves the dangerous attic room. The mysterious ghosts do not appear while the three elders—Jonnie Navaho, Wilbur Snake, and Anna Snake—are present.

Nonetheless, Wilbur had seen the warrior spirit on his previous visit to the museum, and his earlier advice to his grandson was:

I seen what you up against, and you ain't no match for it. Don't take it personal, but it's bigger than you. . . . In this place where you saw those three peoples is a giant man. He's naked, Sonny. He's crazy, too. But his craziness ain't his own doing. Someone or something made him that way. Still, this one ain't to be trusted. When he's around, Sonny, leave right away! His heart is all black. (*Ghost Singer*, 76–77)

Wilbur himself does not feel threatened by his visit to the museum attic, because his spiritual powers are much stronger than those of his nephew. All three Indian elders know that their identity and power come from their unbroken connection to the land. Jonnie Navaho explains:

Navaholand—is where the People belong. My uncle told me of the beginning of our people, of the Five Worlds . . . , and of our four sacred mountains by which we are protected in this world. He told me that this place was created for us by the Holy People . . . all the sacred mountains, . . . out of sacred soil brought from a lower world by the Holy People. The northern mountain had been fastened to the earth with a rainbow and . . . decorated with various plants, animals, and birds. Each mountain had been similarly created. (136–137)

Only within this sacred environment can any Navajo find well-being. Thus, after performing a protection ceremony as a temporary remedy for his grandson, Jonnie Navaho warns Willie that to complete his recovery he must return to his homeland and the lifestyle established by the Holy People, the powerful Navajo spirit beings. Wilbur Snake also holds a ceremony to mollify the destructive spirits roaming the museum attic, a ceremony cut short when the non-Indian participants cannot handle such a direct confrontation with the spirit world. Wilbur and Anna Snake return home, and Wilbur renews his own spirit and power by reaffirming his intimate connection with the land:

[T]he out-of-doors brought much comfort and knowledge to Wilbur, and an awareness of the delicate relationship of all things to one another out there. . . . And out here, there was nothing to block his connection with other life surrounding him. He became an extension of the wind, . . . trees, . . . land, and . . . sun. . . . His relationship to the universe, to the world, was for infinity. (230)

ROBERT CONLEY (CHEROKEE)

The next two authors downplay supernatural influences on crimes to emphasize the bedrock foundation of the detective fiction genre, the methodical ratiocination with which a skilled detective analyzes a crime, establishing the means, motive, and opportunity and, ultimately, the identity of the guilty. Prolific long-time novelist Robert Conley and newcomer Mardi Oakley Medawar both use this standard detective format. Both set their novel series in the second half of the nineteenth century, and both feature central characters who rival Sherlock Holmes in their powers of observation and deduction. Conley's numerous historical novels featuring crime, however, are somewhat more varied than Medawar's. Of five representative works, one captures the Cherokee just as white contact has begun to affect tribal life, and four convey a vivid picture of the Cherokee people after removal from the Southeastern United States to reservation lands in Oklahoma.

Conley's *The Peace Chief* dramatizes the more distant history of his tribe in the Southeast and illustrates the Cherokee's historical outlook on crime and retribution through a telling incident. During a fight with the enemy Ofos tribe, a sixteenth-century Cherokee named Young Puppy accidentally kills his best friend, Asquani, in the heat of battle. Modern courts would call the death an accident of war, but for the Cherokee, the accident is more serious. As a Long Hair Clan member, Young Puppy has killed a Wolf Clan member, creating an imbalance between clans. By Cherokee tradition, a Wolf Clan member should kill Young Puppy in retribution. However, Young Puppy flees to Kituwah, a Mother town, a refuge wherein no one may be killed. By custom, if he leaves, Asquani's relatives may kill him; if he stays until the new year, he may be pardoned. While self-confined in Kituway, Conley's criminal/hero Young Puppy is spiritually reborn as "Comes Back to Life" and becomes his people's ceremonial leader. The novel is purposely set at a time of uneasy relations with the French, an incursion from the Spanish, and trouble with the Seneca to provide a dramatic background for this "crime" story. Thus, unlike Conley's Go-Ahead Rider series, the perceptions of crime and justice in *The Peace Chief* are far afield from the mainstream detective fiction tradition.

In contrast, the attitudes toward crime and retribution in Conley's four novels, *Zeke Proctor: Cherokee Outlaw, Go-Ahead Rider, Outside the Law*, and *To Make a Killing*, all set in Oklahoma Indian Territory, are much closer to mainstream perspectives. *Zeke Proctor* dramatizes the behind-the-scenes politics in territorial conflicts fought between the Cherokee reservation leadership and federal authorities, as a Cherokee court acquits Zeke Proctor of accidentally killing his sister when she leaped into his line of fire to protect her lay-about white husband, while federal officers try to arrest Proctor for attempting to murder a white man; in this instance, the judicial conflict is more important than the ambiguous crime.

The politics of the three series novels are equally convoluted. Their central character, Go-Ahead Rider, has been named High Sheriff of the Cherokee nation after distinguished service in the Indian Home Guard, the native troops who fought on the Union side during the Civil War. Accounts of the suffering and loss endured by the Cherokees as they walked the "Trail of Tears" (1838–1839) from their homes in Georgia and North Carolina to their uncertain futures in Oklahoma do not prepare readers for these novels. Despite material wealth lost in the forced passage, the Cherokees carried with them qualities of mind and spirit that helped them reestablish the highly structured, orderly, prosperous existence they once had. Sheriff Rider's prison is in Tahlequah, a bustling stagecoach town and the new capital of the Cherokee nation. The reservation land has been divided into districts, and council members from each district regularly meet in the two-story brick capital building at the town's center. Business before the council includes matters with serious consequences for the well-being and continued stability of the whole Cherokee nation, such as the railroad's encroachment on Indian lands and its ensuing uncontrolled development, or the U.S. government's forced sale of 6 million acres of Cherokee land to the Pawnee for yet another "reserve."

The makeup of his staff mirrors the complexity of Sheriff Rider's situation. Beehunter, the most traditional group member, speaks no English, is a superb hunter/tracker, and consults a Cherokee conjurer when witchcraft may affect a criminal investigation, as in the locked-room mystery *To Make a Killing*. Therein, Beehunter, as the lone guard on night duty when the prisoner died, is the prime murder suspect. White Tobacco, a Cherokee conjurer, listens patiently as Beehunter describes the crime scene: the prisoner in a locked cell on the second floor of a locked jailhouse shot dead, with no rational explanation of how the crime was committed. White Tobacco then consults a crystal for reading the past, present, and future, and presents Beehunter with two packets and the cryptic instructions to wash with the soap, "smoke the tobacco four times a day for protection, and look for the whiskey man" (91). Apparently, witchcraft was not at work, and exposure to the crime scene evidence had not fatally contaminated Beehunter, though he needed purification. Clearly, this investigation is distant from ratiocinative detection.

Worlds apart from Beehunter is George Tanner, Rider's new deputy sheriff, a recent Harvard graduate in Latin and Greek classical studies. Tanner has lost much of his traditional heritage, including the Cherokee language, but he returns to the reservation intending to use his professional training to prepare the future doctors and lawyers of the Cherokee. Upon his arrival in Tahlequah, he is immediately deputized by Sheriff Rider as an emergency erupts on the town's main street. Tanner's studied, logical approach is to mentally work out all possible combinations of motives and suspects in a crime, followed by action-oriented investigation. For example, in *Outside the Law*, when the new classics teacher at the Cherokee Boys School is murdered in his office, Tanner hypothesizes three probable motives for the crime and four suspects, considers the possible guilt of each suspect, and deduces the possibility of a fourth, as yet hidden, motive and a corresponding suspect who may emerge only as the investigation proceeds.

The centerpiece of the law enforcement team, however, is Rider himself, a man who easily bridges traditional and present Cherokee worlds. Rider's strength is his intimate knowledge of the area's citizens and the thoroughness of his investigative procedure. When an influential member of the Cherokee High Council is murdered right before a critical vote on railroad concessions, Rider's relentless posing of uncomfortable questions brings him most reliably to the truth:

We're going to question everyone between the capitol and Al's place, . . . then east and west from Al's. We're going to ask them to recall everything they saw last evening. Who was out on the street? Did they see anything unusual?. . . . We find out who else was out on the street, then we track them down and ask them the same questions. Somewhere along the line someone's going to tell us where Mix went to. (*Go-Ahead Rider*, 41)

Rider has already carefully examined the crime scene, so questioning all of those in the general area is the next logical investigative step. Action-oriented, he puts into play his staff members' intuitive and rational insights.

Either the political intrigues of the railroad interests or schemes to circumvent the strict prohibition of alcohol anywhere on Cherokee land drive the murders in the three *Go-Ahead Rider* novels. Rider's official status as

High Sheriff for the Cherokee nation limits his jurisdiction in his search for the guilty parties. He cannot charge a white man with a crime committed on Cherokee land; similarly, a white man's murder on the reservation does not fall under his jurisdiction, and he cannot officially pursue criminals who seek refuge beyond the reservation borders. Thus, he often depends on the goodwill and cooperation of the U.S. marshals with whom he shares jurisdiction. While Rider's reputation for integrity and skilled investigation is renowned, his success in the detection process often hinges on his ability to integrate the insights and talents of a widely diverse group of people—Beehunter, George Tanner, and Elwood Lovely, the U.S. marshal. He explains: "We're just going to have to think this whole thing through again, . . . from the beginning. . . . Sometimes you have to clear a whole bunch of stuff out of your way before you can start to get at the truth" (*Outside the Law*, 174). Hence, Go-Ahead Rider's use of experience, logic, observation, and deduction fits easily into the classic detective fiction genre. He does not rely on spirit powers to provide missing pieces of information or to facilitate his investigations in any other way. Conley, as a historian interested in Cherokee adaptation and in the preservation of tribal tradition and culture, reflects these concerns in his range of detectives, from purely tribal to highly assimilated.

MARDI OAKLEY MEDAWAR (EASTERN BAND CHEROKEE)

All set in approximately the same time frame, Mardi Oakley Medawar's three novels, *Murder at Medicine Lodge, The Witch of the Palo Duro*, and *Death at Rainy Mountain*, detail a period when the relations between the Kiowa nation and the white community are increasingly strained. The Kiowa, who identify their original homeland as the Black Hills of South Dakota, by 1866 are located above the Red River in Texas, and they still experience relative freedom as they continue their traditional patterns of movement from summer to winter camps. The Kiowa narrator of the stories, Tay Bodal, or Meat Carrier, describes the events of these years almost wistfully as they mark the final era when his people could sustain their traditional lifestyle. In a period of ten years, major change will impact the Kiowa: reservation confinement.

Murder at Medicine Lodge records the events which open this ten-year period. The Kiowa, Comanche, Arapaho, Apache, and Cheyenne tribes travel to Kansas to negotiate a peace treaty with the U.S. government. Shortly after they have gathered, an army sergeant's decomposing body is found some distance from the encampment, a Kiowa sub-chief is charged with the murder, and Tay Bodal has five days to clear his nation of dishonor.

What makes Tay Bodal so highly trusted that he is regularly called upon when crisis confronts the Kiowa? How can he operate in a nineteenth-century tribal culture, yet fit the mold of the twenty-first century medical detective? Not a skilled hunter, tracker, or warrior, he fits no traditional roles within the highly organized Kiowa social structure. Their complex system of clans, bands, and classes provides some degree of upward mobility in reward for extraordinary deeds, as well as downward mobility, when a family unit is partially destroyed. However, in general, an individual is born or marries into a clan and a class and is free to join and change membership in a band, age-related society, or specialized group such as the Bear Women society, whose members make the moral rules, or the Keepers of the Ten Grandmothers, who provide sanctuary for the endangered. Yet, the circumstances of Tay Bodal's life have conspired to place him outside of Kiowa traditional structures. He passes through the Rabbit and the Herder societies for children and boys, but no adult warrior society claims him because of his lack of skill and interest. The healing societies (the Owl Doctor spiritualists and the Buffalo Doctor bleeders) have also not offered membership. The deaths of his parents and wife from smallpox have freed him to pursue his own identity, one which emerges from his childhood days and is characterized by the minute examination of nature:

Plants and their uses had always fascinated me. So too, did the anatomy of animals and people. I regarded every life form as something miraculous, and I burned with a deep hunger to understand just what made these forms so different yet so uniquely the same. Which was why I dissected the first rabbit I ever killed instead of skinning it out and presenting it to my mother as a good son ought to do. (*Murder at Medicine Lodge*, 5)

Having gained knowledge of organic structures, he concentrated on healing wounds and curing illness with remedies unknown to his people, like using maggots to eat away the dead tissue of an infected wound and afterwards tallow to seal the wound from further infection. To enhance his knowledge of the healing arts, Tay Bodal often travels to Fort Bent, Colorado, a gathering place where healers of many nations exchange their accumulated wisdom. His friendship with a U.S. Army doctor stationed nearby also enhances his training. Whenever possible, Tay Bodal observes the doctor's medical practice and barters for medical instruments, such as a tool to remove bullets embedded in the flesh. Until age 30, Tay Bodal enjoys an unusual amount of freedom to create an entirely new role for himself, that of practical doctor, a role very close to that of the modern scientist.

However, much of this freedom is forfeited upon his second marriage to Crying Wind, a member of the Ondes, or the highest class of the Kiowa. This marriage propels him into the inner circle of the highest-ranking Kiowa, and into the complicated network of their loyalties, disputes, and intrigues. All three of Medawar's novels feature the same major cast of characters with the inner circle of the Kiowa as the focus: White Bear, a principal Kiowa sub-chief, the Cheyenne Robber, one of their finest warriors, and Skywalker, the only Owl Doctor thought powerful enough to work on his own. All of these become Tay Bodal's close associates. Thus the man who stood on the fringes of his people while gathering knowledge and perfecting his skills moves to the very center of the Kiowa nation to utilize his learning.

In *Murder at Medicine Lodge*, Tay Bodal's investigations occur primarily within a huge army encampment set up for a peace treaty signing, an unfamiliar environment in which to interview witnesses or suspects and examine material evidence and cadavers. His friend, the army doctor, guides him, and a mixed-breed Kiowa translates, for Tay Bodal neither speaks nor reads English. However, his acute powers of observation and deduction enable him to surmount these cultural differences.

The Witch of the Palo Duro shifts to a murder investigation within the Kiowa nation. The Kiowa are encamped for the winter in Palo Duro Canyon, a place thought by some to be cursed by the ghosts of those massacred in 1864, when Kit Carson led an assault on the canyon. General uneasiness quickly escalates to hysteria when two horses penned for the night have their throats cut. The boys guarding the horses believe that they have sighted a witch, a human shape transformed into a raven on a rock ledge near the horse pens. Coming in quick succession, the horses' slaughter, the raven's appearance, and the mysterious death of a young woman are all attributed to witchcraft. Upon examining the young woman's corpse, Tay Bodal rejects witchcraft as a cause of death and suspects non-witchcraft explanations for the other unusual events. White Bear, one of two principal sub-chiefs, impresses upon him the urgent need to resolve the murder mystery:

"The gossips . . . [blame] Kicking Bird . . . for sending the witch against me. If this trouble isn't sorted out before we leave this canyon, . . . the next time Kicking Bird and I meet, I will have no choice but to kill him". . . . If White Bear killed Kicking Bird, the council would . . . demand White Bear's death. That would mean the loss of not one but two of our strongest leaders. (91)

The situation reaches a personal crisis for Tay Bodal when his wife Crying Wind is named the witch who must be destroyed.

Finally, in *Death at Rainy Mountain*, The Cheyenne Robber, White Bear's nephew, is accused of murder, and Tay Bodal again must quickly resolve a situation which threatens not only The Cheyenne Robber's life, but also the well-being of every member of White Bear's band:

I say to your face that if The Cheyenne Robber killed the nephew of Kicking Bird, he will be banished, his name spoken no more, just as we are no longer allowed to say the name of Kicking Bird's nephew. Also I say that every member of White Bear's family clan will serve for the rest of their days the family clan of Kicking Bird. White Bear will no longer be chief. He will be a servant, the leader of the servants. (20)

In each novel, Tay Bodal's analytical mind, astute observation, and thorough questioning of all connected even slightly to the crime bring him success. This last quality, his intensive questioning of friends, relatives, and enemies, underscores his unique position, for Kiowa tribal etiquette makes it rude and insulting to ask questions. However, Tay Bodal is not limited by traditional roles and mores, nor gifted by spirit helpers or a spiritual vision to help him penetrate hidden mysteries. Instead, he is a man of science, systematically working his way ratiocinatively through the puzzles set before him.

SHERMAN ALEXIE (SPOKANE, COEUR D'ALENE)

The themes of our final books are quite distinct from those examined earlier. Sherman Alexie's *Indian Killer*, James Welch's *The Indian Lawyer*, and Linda Hogan's *Mean Spirit* all describe dramatic crime scenarios but downplay or eliminate the role of the detective. Their message is the victimization of the Indian peoples, with the "crime" only the latest addition to a long-standing series of crimes against the Native American community. Crimes begun in the historical past shape and impact the historical present. Far from traditional mainstream models, the "detective" here does little formal investigation, acting instead as an unreliable narrative voice which presents possibilities to misdirect readers (*Indian Killer*), as a competent lawyer potentially compromised (*The Indian Lawyer*), or as a trained FBI investigator increasingly disillusioned by high-level conspiracies against Indians and thus, to some degree, rejecting assimilation in favor of traditional ways (*Mean Spirit*).

The mystery at the core of Sherman Alexie's *Indian Killer* is who is murdering and scalping a series of victims, leaving two white owl feathers as a signature at the crime scene. Despite the nature of the crime, there is no detective to unlock the mystery, only a cast of characters whose personal histories intersect in urban Seattle in the late 1980s. Each character (Indian and white) is a candidate for the title "Indian Killer"—if not as the one responsible for the "owl feather murders," then certainly as the one responsible for the ongoing destruction of Indian identity. Thus, the book's title, *Indian Killer*, is intentionally ambiguous. The murderer may be a white who hates Native Americans so much as to implicate them in the crimes, or the murderer may be a Native American whose rage at historical injustices and the present dislocation of his people has erupted into physical attacks.

In addition to these two options, Alexie exposes a wide variety of ways in which the title *Indian Killer* is appropriate to a highly disparate group of people. There are Daniel and Olivia Smith, a well-to-do white couple who have adopted a newborn Indian baby; Truck Schultz, an incendiary white radio talk show host who stokes the fires of racial hatred; Dr. Mathers, a white anthropology professor at the University of Washington, who fancies himself the local expert on Native American literature; Jack Wilson, an ex-cop who believes his own vague claim to Indian ancestry sufficient to legitimize a book series featuring a Native American detective hero; Buck Rogers, a white rancher who uses as target practice the Indians who come at night to dig sacred camas root on his land; and finally Bird Lawrence, a white man who beats his half-breed son until he has memorized a history of Native American heroes and events that twists the details into a sordid depravity.

Of this long list of potential Indian Killers, Daniel and Olivia Smith occupy prime roles in the novel, since much of the action unfolds from the point of view of their full-blood Indian son John Smith. The couple adopted a newborn whose fourteen-year-old Indian mother signed the adoption papers prior to her child's birth. Immediately after the birth, the mother is sedated, the child is whisked away to a waiting helicopter, and the adoption agency refuses to release the child's tribal affiliation. The result is a simultaneous birth-death, with the child's link to his specific Native American community forever severed. He may be Navajo, Sioux, Spokane, or any of a long list of native tribes. His new parents' attempts to surround him with a generic "Native American experience" via books and music, powwows, and intertribal basketball tournaments only widen the gap between these borrowed identities and the stories, rituals, and sacred geography of his true inheritance. Even the name the parents give their brown-skinned, Indian-featured child seems strikingly inappropriate: John Smith, a name evoking the first historical encounter between English Europeans and Native Americans, opening a period of genocide. Marie Polatkin summarizes the young man's plight: "John Smith was screwed up . . . hurting. He didn't know up from down. He got screwed at birth. He had no chance. I don't care how nice his white parents were. John was dead from the start" (*Indian Killer*, 417).

After the first "owl feather" murder, two further crimes follow in quick succession: the murder of a young white man last seen at the Tulalip Indian Reservation Casino, and the abduction of a young white boy whose bloodied pajamas are sent with no further explanation to radio talk show host Truck Schultz. Schultz uses air time to deepen the chasm between Seattle's white and Native American communities, supplying his listeners with bogus history lessons. One such lesson describes the work of Marcus and Narcissa Whitman, a missionary couple responsible for removing Indian children from their eastern Washington State homes and erasing their Indian identities in religious boarding schools. Their mainstreamed children returned, the outraged parents murdered the Whitmans to revenge the crimes committed against their children. Schultz uses this real event as a call to arms in the current crisis: "We must defend ourselves, our families, our homes. We must arm ourselves and repel further attacks on our great country" (346).

The rage Schultz exploits is not far from the surface in both white and Indian communities. Lawrence Bird illustrates how destructive anger and disgust for the Indian community can be, in this case in training his own Indian son. He insists that his son use his Indian surname until he has earned the right to his white father's surname, a right gained only after passing a stream of tests:

"What was the name of the Indian who helped raise the flag on Iwo Jima during World War Two?"
"Ira Hayes."
"And what happened to him?"
"He was a hero."
"No, you idiot. What really happened to him?"
"He died of exposure in the winter of 1955. Passed out in the snow."
"Why did he do that?' "
"Because he was a dirty Indian." (93)

However, the plan backfires, and Reggie, filled with his own rage, drops out of college and out of his family as well. He is an urban Indian set adrift, his traditional roots severed, as his conversation with the truck driver who gives him a lift out of Seattle confirms: " 'So, where are you running to?' Reggie pointed up the highway, pointed north or south, east or west, pointed toward a new city, though he knew every city was a city of white men" (409). For Reggie, every choice is the same; none holds more promise than the others. There is no clear direction to move in and no homeland to receive him and to heal his wounds. This loss of heritage, direction, and homeland, for Alexie, outweighs any particular and immediate violence committed by his alienated characters.

JAMES WELCH (BLACKFEET, GROS VENTRE)

James Welch's *The Indian Lawyer* is more in the mainstream crime tradition than Sherman Alexie's works. Welch and the novel's main character, Sylvester Yellow Calf, are both Blackfeet; both attended reservation schools for their early education, eventually graduating from the University of Montana. The general setting of the novel is the mountains and plains of Montana; the particular setting is the state prison in Deer Lodge, an environment about which Welch has detailed knowledge, having served on

the Montana State Board of Pardons. Thus, Welch's own experiences inspired the milieu of his story, and he has a fine eye for the nuances of
reservation life as well as the often cut-throat culture of the prison population.

His hero, Sylvester Yellow Calf, is a young Indian man in his mid-30s
whose early childhood was marked by abandonment: his alcoholic father
left his wife and son, and his mother left him in his grandparents' care.
Where his grandfather is self-described as a rational man untouched by the
hocus-pocus of traditional medicine, his grandmother is a respected elder
matriarch in her reservation community; she gives her grandson the war
medicine pouch once owned by his great-great grandfather.

Nevertheless, Yellow Calf's connection to the traditional Blackfeet
world is tenuous at best. He accompanies his grandmother to giveaways,
naming ceremonies, and powwows, although for him these are primarily
social gatherings, any religious significance having slipped into the background. Yellow Calf fancies himself one of the "new Indian warriors"—
so described in the educational literature distributed by his high school
guidance counselor, a Crow woman named Lena Old Horn—the younger
generation of Native Americans that understands clearly that a professional education is the only way to "battle" the complex economic, legal,
and social structures of white society. Yellow Calf thinks he can rise above
the material poverty of reservation life as a "new warrior," with his continued success in high school basketball the single factor that anchors his
self-esteem.

Ray Lundsen, a sportswriter for the *Great Falls Tribune*, carefully follows Yellow Calf's high school career. He finds basketball serving the same
function for reservation youths as for inner-city African-American youths.
Intending homage to Yellow Calf, the acknowledged power player on the
Indian team, Lundsen writes a newspaper article that effectively disrupts
Yellow Calf's relationship to his tribal community, calling "him the heart
and soul of the greatest Indian basketball team this state has seen," dis-
missing his teammates as potential failures who "will have had their brief
moment in the sun and will fall by the wayside, perhaps to a life of drink
and degradation—so much a part of Indian experience," and challenging
him to "carry the torch" (*The Indian Lawyer*, 103). Lundsen proclaims
Yellow Calf a "winner both on the court and off, in the past, present, and
future, in life" (103). As his teammates read this vision of their own futures
on the reservation, they see themselves clearly as failed ex-jocks who sleep
in their clothes in cars and doorways, people already well known to them
as uncles, cousins, and even a father. The team and all who read the article
distance themselves from Yellow Calf as he inevitably reminds them of his
solitary success amidst their own limited futures. This perceptual shift
marks a critical turning point in Yellow Calf's personal history, for he
becomes as disconnected from the Blackfeet Reservation as John Smith, the

hero of Alexie's *Indian Killer*, was alienated from his authentic Indian heritage. Both Sylvester Yellow Calf and John Smith become urban Indians not at home in either the Indian world or the white world. The fateful newspaper article functions like an omen, as though Yellow Calf really were destined for continued acclaim. He moves easily from a basketball scholarship at the University of Montana to law school at Stanford, then to membership in a prestigious all-white law firm in Helena and finally to the Democratic candidacy for the congressional representative in Montana's western district. However, shortly after his acceptance of the offer to run for public office, his career takes an abrupt turn off the golden road to success.

Yellow Calf sits on a parole board for the Montana State prison system and spends a full day each month making parole determinations and gaining insights into the criminal mind. Despite his new understanding, he becomes the vulnerable target of a complex blackmail plot hatched by Jack Harwood, an accountant-turned-bank robber, who had served seven years of his sentence when turned down at his first parole hearing by Yellow Calf and his board colleagues. After a gang of Indian prisoners shaking him down for the unrecovered money on the bank job stab Harwood in the prison library, Harwood believes his survival depends on being paroled, but when that fails, he schemes to use his wife Patti Ann and two recently discharged convicts to make Yellow Calf his ticket to freedom.

Despite careful planning, the trap backfires, and each plotter in turn becomes the victim of the scheme. Thus, Sylvester Yellow Calf is both detective and victim, using all of his connections with the parole board as well as his knowledge of the criminal mind to resolve the threat facing him:

Sylvester had seen this kind of criminal before, they had sat across the hearings table from him, polite, repentant, earnest—and wicked with hate. They didn't know that you could see through their eyes to the blackness of their insides and you shuddered to think that such evil exists. They were the ones who cut the throats of families or hitchhikers because they just wanted to do it, to see how it felt drawing the blade of a knife across the windpipe, the jugular, the soft flesh below the ears. They wanted to know how it felt to smash a skull into pulp, to blow a hole through a face, to degrade and destroy a human body. He had seen them and he had shuddered. (303)

Yellow Calf admits his lack of experience in the front end of the criminal justice system, that is, investigation and apprehension. His critical strength lies in a mind trained by the legal process to observe and collect detailed information that can be marshaled into an effective defense. As a "new warrior," Yellow Calf will have to secure his victory through the power of words and strategic maneuvering. There is no tribal elder upon whom he can rely, nor are there spirit powers to aid him. Instead, he must trust reason, experience, and intuition. Like Philip Marlowe or the Continental Op, he moves through mean streets and must outwit and outreason those who would con, degrade, and destroy him.

LINDA HOGAN (CHICKASAW)

Oklahoman Linda Hogan's *Mean Spirit* describes the fortunes of the Osage people in the 1920s. In fact, three of our authors, Robert Conley for the Cherokees in 1873, Mardi Oakley Medawar for the Kiowa in 1867, and Linda Hogan for the Osage in 1922, vividly picture the 50-year period during which increasing economic, legal, and social pressures eroded the quality of life that the surviving Indian peoples had struggled to maintain. This period saw the rise of the Ghost Dance, a revivalist movement that started in Nevada and spread to the east, passing through Oklahoma on its way up to the Great Plains, the home of the Sioux and the Cheyenne. The Ghost Dance, a last spiritual call-to-arms, insisted that observing the proper rituals and purification would restore traditional ways of life. Despite the firm belief of practitioners, the bullet-ridden ceremonial ghost shirts now displayed in museums give silent testimony to the failure of this fragile hope. The end of the century witnessed the massacre at Wounded Knee, where 300 Lakota Sioux men, women, and children were cut down by the U.S. cavalry, left frozen in the snow, and then buried in a mass pit. Hogan describes both the Ghost Dance and the massacre, since they provide the broad context for the misfortunes of the Osage people, her primary focus.

This 50-year period of disaster, defeat, and death takes on personalized dimensions through the multigenerational story of two Osage families, the Blankets and the Grayclouds. Both families have become "town" Indians, living on farmland surrounding the city of Watona, a center that serves a mixed Indian and white population. However, this was not the original home of the Osage; instead, they bought this location from the federal government in 1861, moving there from the Neosho River in Kansas. Belle Graycloud, the matriarch of her family, was born in 1861 shortly after the move; thus, her life history mirrors the changes that impact the Osage in their new home.

After the initial move to Oklahoma, a split occurs among the people, some opting out of a town-centered life and retreating to the bluffs above Watona to better preserve their traditional ways. This group, the Hill Indians, ensures that the traditional roles of river prophets and sacred runners will continue. The other Osage who remain near the town develop a curious lifestyle, mixing traditional belief and practices with new ways. Many convert to the Oklahoma Indian Baptist Church, live in two-story frame houses, and adopt a European-American mode of dress. Belle Graycloud exemplifies this blend of conflicting lifestyles when she retreats to the root cellar to find solace in her "prayer cave," taking with her a Sacred Heart of Jesus candle, a bundle of cedar and sage, a vial of holy water from the sacred spring, and an eagle prayer feather.

The "town" Indians retain from their traditional heritage the knowledge that the health and stability of the Osage people are inextricably linked to the well-being of the earth. Oil discovered on Indian land effectively destroys this symbiotic state. The oil and the money from the drilling leases initiate a brief flash of material prosperity for the Indians, so most families can afford such luxury items as automobiles. Even Michael Horse, the traditional fire keeper, dreamer, and water diviner, purchases a gold convertible which he parks outside of his teepee. However, Belle Graycloud fears the quick riches, for "all along the smell of the blue-black oil that seeped out of the earth had smelled like death to her" (*Mean Spirit*, 29). An elaborate scheme is hatched to defraud the Indians of their land, its ultimate stage not a simple eviction of the Indians from their property but the murder of the Indian owners with all property rights reverting to white ownership. The murder rate is so high that Belle's husband, Moses, writes to President Harding, in what becomes a national scandal reported in the *Boston Globe* and the *Washington Post*. Moses' letter describes the attacks on the Indian community:

There's been some murders here in Indian Territory. It's even been in the Tulsa newspapers of late that a plot is underway against the Indians with oil money. One good young man is being held in connection with two of the killings, and we here know that he is innocent. There have been 3 recent murder deaths and 17 before that, just in this one year alone. We are asking if you will investigate these crimes for us. (*Mean Spirit*, 117)

Finally, a federal agency sends two officers to conduct an on-site investigation: a Lakota Sioux, State Red Hawk, and his colleague, who take up residence undercover in Watona. As Red Hawk becomes more deeply acquainted with the situation, he sees that the conspiracy against the Indian landholdings is both cleverly constructed and legally protected. He begins to despair of the successful outcome of his mission and to doubt that his advocacy and defense of Indian rights in Washington, D.C., have any real power to effect change. Slowly he becomes absorbed into the lifestyle of the more traditional Indians, spending more and more time with the resident "seer" Michael House and the Hill People, and also in silent, solitary communion with the earth and water spirits. Meanwhile, danger creeps ever closer to the Graycloud family. Their closest friends, the Blankets, have already experienced three mysterious deaths, including a presumed suicide in the town jail. Now Belle herself is shot on her own property. Her only safety lies in staging her funeral, then secretly seeking refuge with the Hill People. As the official investigations conclude, one man is convicted, another receives immunity for his testimony, and a third accomplice is killed by an "accident of nature."

However, this "resolution" does not return peace and safety to the Blankets and the Grayclouds. Belle and the "seer" Michael Horse had always feared dire consequences for their people once the earth had been violated by oil drilling. The land had been blackened by fire as it was hurriedly cleared by the oil interests. Torn apart and broken, the earth at times shows its rage by gas well blowouts that leave craters 50 feet deep and 500 feet across. Belle's grandson, Ben, voices the common sentiment when he asserts: "Some of us have broken all apart, like the earth just did. We have as much pain, it's on our faces and in our eyes. It's in the clothes we wear" (75). Michael Horse's prophetic vision addresses this joint brokenness of the land and the people:

[T]he people will go out of their land. They, like the land, are wounded and hurt. They will go into rocks and bluffs, the cities, and into the caves of the torn apart land. There will be fires. Some . . . will be restored to the earth. Others will journey to another land and merge with other people. Some will learn a new way to live, the good way of the red path. (362)

Thus, Hogan predicts troubled times ahead that only "the good way of the red path" can make endurable.

CONCLUSION

While each of our eight authors uses different geographical areas, tribal cultures, and historical settings for their dramas, nevertheless they highlight common themes. The most important is that quality of life for Native Americans is in direct proportion to the quality of their particular homeland, their source of identity. Owens and Hogan powerfully dramatize the theme of a wounded land and a wounded people. But even Alexie, Welch, and Walters, who do not spend a great deal of time describing the environment, affirm the same belief when they insist that the key to their characters' crises of spirit lies in their broken connections to their unique tribal space. There is no generic Indian Way, only particular tribes and Peoples. Medawar details the final years of freedom for the Kiowa before they will be confined to reservation lands. Her White Bear explains the essential connection between the people and the land:

I love the land and the buffalo and will not part with any of it. I have heard that you intend to settle us on a reservation near the mountains. I don't want to settle. I love to roam over the prairies. There I feel free and happy, but when we settle down we grow pale and die. (*Murder at Medicine Lodge*, 261–62)

A second theme important to the eight authors is the nature of spirit power: who claims it, and whether it is used positively or negatively. The following chart delineates the varying levels of power claimed by individuals, ranging from traditional elders to Navajo witches and Kiowa Owl Doctors. Finally, although seven of the authors write murder mysteries, only two use the standard detective fiction format. In most instances, the reader must become the detective, listening and watching for clues as the crime drama develops.

	Identity of People and Land	Role of Tribal Elder	Role of Specialist in Spirit Power	Classic Detective Fiction Format	Crime Fiction Format
Owens	x	x	x		x
Querry			x		x
Walters	x	x	x		x
Conley				x	x
Medawar	x	x	x	x	
Welch	x	x			x
Alexie	x				x
Hogan	x	x	x		x

The detective form does not come naturally to Native American storytellers, except when the crime and the questions of justice are tied to genuine historical events, as in the stories of Robert Conley and Linda Hogan, and to realistic depictions of modern crime both on and off the reservations, as in the stories of James Welch and Ron Querry. Sherman Alexie and Anna Lee Walters both use the genre to some degree for social criticism that depends on shock effect: to impact on a broad general audience and to present to mainstream readers issues that native peoples feel strongly about. The danger, of course, is for the message to dominate the story at the expense of the "mystery" and thus to lose the powerful awakening effect the authors intend. Louis Owens' approach, in contrast, is an interesting, surprisingly effective blend of historical questions of justice, social criticism, modern crime, and native spiritualism that invites mainstream readers into the world of Choctaw and Cherokee belief, yet uses magical realism to make the spiritual and historical events compatible with modern realism.

4

The Southwestern Detective Story:
A Reflection of the Land

We [Native Americans of the Southwest] are the land . . . the Earth is
. . . a part of our being, dynamic, significant, real . . . within [which]
we are given life, and in . . . acknowledgement we eat, . . . plant, . . .
harvest, . . . build and clean, . . . dance, hunt, run, heal, sing, chant and
write.

—Paula Gunn Allen, "We Are the Land" in
Lawana Trout's *Native American Literature*

And the exorbitantly redundant sun burned savagely in the powder
blue Western sky.

—Richard Parrish, *The Dividing Line* (104)

Understanding the unique nature of the Native American detective story
requires understanding the geography that it inhabits, the terrain over
which its detectives move and the daily realities its denizens encounter. The
world of the Native American detective is mainly a rural milieu, an open-
world setting of enormous distances, uninhabited regions, and isolated peoples. There is no better place to distinguish between urban detectives and

Native American detectives than in the Southwest, where so many fictional
native detectives find their homes.

Author	Detective	Tribal Affiliation
Rudolfo Anaya	Sonny Baca	Pueblo/Spanish/Anglo mix
Sinclair Browning	Trade Ellis	Apache
David Cole	Kauwanyauma (Laura Winslow)	Hopi
Cecil Dawkins	Ginevra Prettifield	Sioux (and French)
	Tina Martinez	Tsorgi Pueblo
Anne Marie Duquette	Jasentha Cliffwalker	Apache
Brian Garfield	Sam Watchman	Navajo
Kathleen and Michael Gear	Dr. Maureen Cole	Seneca
	Hail Walking Hawk	Hopi
	Stone Ghost	Katsina Anasazi
Micah Hackler	Sheriff Lansing	Tewa/Cherokee/white
	Gabe Hanna	Navajo
Tony Hillerman	Joe Leaphorn	Navajo
	Jim Chee	Navajo
M. E. Hirsh	Ben Naya/ Kwikwilyaqa	Half-Hopi
Rob MacGregor	Will Lansa (adolescent)	Hopi
Lauren Maddison	Laura Nez (FBI/sidekick)	Navajo
	Police Chief Albert Tsosie	Navajo
Kirk Mitchell	Emmett Quanah Parker	Comanche
	Anna Turnipseed	Modoc
Jake Page	Connie Barnes (assists)	Hopi
Richard Parrish	Jesús Chuy Leyva	Papago
Walter Satterthwait	Daniel Begay	Navajo
Martin Cruz Smith	Youngblood Duran	Hopi
Richard Martin Stern	Johnny Ortiz	Apache (part Spanish/ part Anglo)
Aimée Thurlo	the Blackhorse brothers (Gabriel, Joseph, Joshua)	Navajo
	Belara Fuller	Half-Navajo
	Justin Nakai (FBI)	Navajo
	Joseph Payestewa	Hopi
	Ashe Redhawk	Navajo

	Benjamin Two Eagle	Navajo timewalker
	Cisco Watchman	Navajo
Aimée and David Thurlo	Ellah Clah	Navajo
Robert Westbrook	Howard Moon Deer	A dislocated Sioux

GEOGRAPHICAL DETERMINISM

Southwestern Native American cultures encompass a region extending from southern Utah and southwestern Colorado through Arizona and New Mexico east to the west Texas desert, then south into Mexico as far east as Sonora and west into southern California and Baja.

The political boundaries imposed by the Spanish and later U.S. invaders and settlers distort the integrity of a region with common features north and south of the Rio Grande and across the state and provincial lines of the United States and Mexico. Although this larger Southwest was home to wildly divergent cultures, all faced similar shaping demands: a harsh environment that, for all its apparent diversity of field, forest, desert, and mountain range, was remarkably consistent in its lack of a resource crucial to the survival of all living things, water.

Today, much of this area is semi-arid or arid (under 20 inches of rain a year, an eight-inch average in some sections), although archaeological findings suggest past periods of greater rainfall and although the mountainous areas (peaks towering to 12,000 feet) may have verdant alpine forests and as much as 39 inches of annual rainfall. The distance from moisture sources has produced the desert regions, while a summer inflow of warm, moist air from the Gulf of Mexico brings more rain to the plains, producing what Richard Stern calls "climatic frivolity" (*Murder in the Walls*, 13). Rain comes in sudden cloudbursts—convectional thunderstorms. The overabundance of water in a short period is not absorbed easily into the soil, so dry gulches fill quickly and torrents of water plunge through deep sandstone canyons suddenly and violently. Winter snows covering the northern third of the region provide the water that helps flora and fauna survive the hotter months. The San Juan and Sangre de Cristo ranges of the Rocky Mountains extend into this region, as does the Colorado Plateau. There are plains and basins and rivers such as the Rio Grande, the Canadian River, and the Pecos. A flat strip of land, the Llano Estacado (Staked Plains), or High Plains, extends from Texas into New Mexico.

The general lack of water in the Southwest determines the life the region can sustain and the means of making a living that life has available. Even present-day irrigation schemes (grandiose versions of older methods) must confront limits set by climate and territory, limits reflected in the indigenous cultures of Native Americans. Native religions and worldviews reflect ways of coming to terms with the irreducible facts of life in a particular place and time, accepting boons with gratitude and making offerings in the hope that they will continue, and mitigating troubles with ritual and ceremony. Apart from some speculative influences from Mexico, the religious and spiritual ways of the Southwest reflect the flora, fauna, landscape, and climate of the Southwest, a region of dramatic contrasts and great diversity.

Stark contrasts between mountains and desert and dramatic scenery mark the entire region—rolling grasslands and wildflowers set against mesas, buttes, otherworldly towering red rock monuments, extensive valleys, colorful sandstone formations, and deep canyons whose appearances shift moment by moment with the changing light. David Cole's *Butterfly Lost* captures these contrasts as his characters fly up, down, and around isolated Arizona and Utah mesas, buttes, canyons, arches, and spires—often inaccessible even with four-wheel drive:

Two major rivers channeled gorges deep within a landscape of rock, the spires casting thousand-foot elongated shadows because of the early morning sun. . . . Everything was suffused with color, rock structures segregated into horizontal bands of color [by] . . . geological strata, looking . . . like holiday candles of many different-colored waxes, lighter colors on the top, blending down toward centuries-old dark bedrock. Blacks and browns formed the background for striking variations of ocher and umber, blending into tones of muted red, rust, yellow, and most of all, orange . . . shales, limestones, gypsum, jasper, siltstones, and mudstories. (251–52)

Tony Hillerman, in *Hunting Badger*, also spotlights rocks:

The tableland of multicolored stone, carved into a gigantic labyrinth by canyons, all draining eventually into the narrow green belt of the San Juan bottom. Multiple hundreds of miles of sculptured stone, cut off in the north by the blue-green of the mountains. The slanting afternoon sun outlining it into a pattern of gaudy red sandstone and deep shadows. (208)

The Southwest territory, home to a diversity of plants, boasts six of the world's seven life zones. The desert flatlands support cholla, creosote, prickly pear, and yucca, sage brush, rabbit brush, and black grama and bunch grass, as well as mesquite, cottonwood, and olive and cedar trees. Horny toads, lizards, snakes, jackrabbits, kangaroo rats, prairie dogs, and deer mice abound. Javelina, peccary, goats, pronghorn antelope, mule deer, bobcats, and even mountain lions also roam this territory, and buzzards fly above, constant reminders of the nearness of death. The malpais extends 40 miles south of Mount Taylor, filling the valley between Cebolleta Mesa and the Zuñi Mountains, with lava flow which Hillerman's Mary Landon describes as black ink suddenly frozen hard and which the Navajo call the blood of the Horned Monster. The Bisti badlands, once a sandstone plain, is now "a grotesquerie of shapes—tables, heads, layer cakes, twisted spires, exposed ribs, serrations, and weird forms" carved by wind and water exposing black coal deposits, crimson clay, and blue shale (Hillerman, *People of Darkness*, 160). The mix of colors—"solemn earth tones," gray-greens, rusty reds, soft browns, warm beiges, and "walls of living stone" glowing in the sunset—fascinates Lauren Maddison (*Deceptions*, 136), while Richard Parrish records the daily struggle for survival:

A red-tailed hawk circled slowly in the topaz sky. It screamed raucously, *kee-ahrr, kee-ahrr*. The sound dissipated quickly into the vast open space over the Sonora Desert. Again it screamed, harsh and piercing, and two more hawks darted upward to meet it . . . circling. One . . . swooped . . . suddenly and snatched a pocket gopher in its talons, swept off to a skeletal mesquite tree, . . . an outstretched dead limb. It held the gopher clenched in one clawed foot and tore at it with its hooked, razor-sharp beak. (*Versions of the Truth*, 9)

Survival of the fittest is not a metaphor here. Adaptation is paramount. Brian Garfield defines the extremes—up to 135 degrees in summer, deep snow drifts in winter.

Above 4,500 feet, cacti and desert grasses (blue grama grass, buffalo grass) still abound alongside juniper, oak, and piñon pine, wild onion, chamiza, and saltbush, as do coyotes, nighthawks, cougar, and black bear. Higher altitudes bring cooler temperatures, increased precipitation, and different flora and fauna. Ponderosa pines take over between 6,500 and 8,500 feet, and wildflowers (scarlet gilia, pentstemon, cream-white mariposa lily, wild geranium pink) peek through the undergrowth, but these give way higher up to Douglas fir, blue spruce, and aspen. There are elk, white-tailed deer, skunk, porcupine, bobcat, quail, duck, wild turkey, and migratory waterfowl, and an alpine ground cover of columbine, pennyroyal, and groundsel. Amid a ponderosa forest are the angry chatter of a gray squirrel, the song of a mountain chickadee, and the raucous cry of a Stellar's jay.

Above 9,500 feet, bristlecone pine, blue spruce, and subalpine firs dominate, as do bighorn sheep, mountain goats, marmots, and other high-altitude rodents. In winter, in the thin, dry air, the temperature could drop 30 degrees in late afternoon. Richard Stern describes an Arizona October at 7,000 feet as a sweaters-and-fireplace time, while atop the mountain slopes, to a timberline of 11,500 feet, where golden-leaved aspens glow, the first snow coats Lake Peak and Baldy (*Tangled Murders*, 11–12). His protagonist's mother freezes to death on the Jicarilla Apache Reservation during the winter of 1967–1968, and one murder victim lies buried in ski slope snow (*Death in the Snow*).

The mountains, deserts, buttes, and canyons of Navajo, Zuñi, and Hopi country provide an imposing natural backdrop for crime and malfeasance, a larger-than-human scale against which chaos and destruction struggle with balance and order. The distances reduce human scale; social squabbles seem ephemeral, petty. The largest Navajo reservation is 25,000 square miles—larger than New England—and sprawls across New Mexico, Arizona, and Utah, so tribal police work with New Mexico State Police, the Utah or Arizona Highway Patrol, the Bureau of Indian Affairs Law and Order Division, the Southern Ute Tribal Police, or even Hopi or Jicarilla Apache officers. Black Mesa rises over 7,000 feet above the Painted Desert, a plateau approximately the size and shape of Connecticut, according to Hillerman. On the Navajo Reservation, Shiprock (an eroded volcano core called "Rock with Wings" because by legend the first Navajos flew there from the north on its back) towers 1,700 feet above the surrounding desert and stretches miles southeastward across a prairie: a "great dark volcanic monolith . . . like the ruins of a Gothic cathedral built for giants" (Hillerman, *The Fallen Man*, 233). Rodney Barker, in *The Broken Circle*, celebrates the uniqueness of the Southwest's vast mesa-checkered high desert grassland and the views extending over 100 miles to where Colorado's mountains pile against the skyline: "Driving toward a horizon that seems to maintain its distance" confirms "the immense vastness" of "endless sky and pure space," and finally topping a rise and seeing the twinkling lights of a town "on the far side of what looks like open range forever" bring "the feeling of sighting land after a long sea journey" (11–12). The clear air and open spaces make the distant visible: Albuquerque shines brightly in the night from 100 miles away. Lauren Maddison's heroine, Connor Hawthorne, marvels at "the sheer breadth of the horizon" and realizes that she has never seen so much of the heavens at one time (*Deceptions*, 135).

Here, "down the road apiece" could mean a day's drive over uncomfortable back roads. Tribal police traverse four states—450 to 500 miles daily. Officer Chee thinks nothing of a 90-mile evening run across the Painted Desert or driving 200 miles to interview witnesses; such travel goes with his territory. In Hillerman's *People of Darkness*, Mary Landon feels they have traveled 1,000 miles that day, but Chee says it is only 250: "It just seems longer because a lot of it was dirt roads" (127). In fact, the roads the southwestern detectives travel range from "Divided Limited Access Highways, down through Gravel, Graded Dirt, and Ungraded Dirt to Doubtful Dirt" (148). Newcomers to the Southwest in Thurlo's novels face mystifying directions. "Turn at the rock with the petroglyphs," for example, might mean 40 minutes of wrong turns in an area where there are no telephone lines or houses or even clear-cut roads. "How could anyone stand being so isolated," the heroine of Thurlo's *Redhawk's Heart* muses (63). In *The Dark Canyon*, Micah Hackler describes the route to Chaco Canyon Monument: 21 miles down a dirt road with no sign of civilization and, during the "monsoon season," a washed-out road or a mud bog (14). This is partly why information takes time to reach the authorities. In Hillerman's *Listening Woman*, for example, a sheepherder in a remote corner of the

reservation tells a veterinarian about sighting a helicopter; the vet tells a
school bus driver, who passes the message on to the local trading post
owner, the natural distributor of messages and gossip, who finally tells a
tribal police officer—a process taking about nine months.

The rugged terrain, limited water supply, and isolation require expertise
to negotiate. "You could hide Kansas City out there," says Leaphorn (*Listening Woman*, 34). Hillerman's *Hunting Badger* draws on the real-life
1998 FBI backcountry manhunt for three heavily armed "survivalists" who
murdered a police officer, fled the Four Corners area in a stolen truck,
engaged pursuers in a shoot-out, and then vanished into the rugged Utah–
Arizona borderland wilderness; there they successfully evaded hundreds of
officers from more than 20 federal and state agencies, including Navajo
trackers. As Leaphorn notes, there are "enough canyons out there to swal-
low up ten thousand cops" (214).

Ironically, the distances and the geographical isolation often facilitate
tracing outsiders, setting up roadblocks, shutting off exits, and trapping
villains. Wheeled vehicles have only limited choices, and running without
a vehicle means certain death without a ready water supply. "Thirty miles
to a drink of water," says Navajo tribal policeman Tomas Charley in *Listening Woman*, "if you know where to find it" (24). In an urban environment malefactors can melt into the masses of people, but in the open
Southwest territory they stand out as intruders unless they already know
the terrain well. When the nearest movie show is 100 miles away, the
television reception is poor, and most people do not have electricity anyway, says the owner of a Hopi trading post, little things stand out, everybody pays attention to everyone else's business, and the bush telegraph
system of gossip and news flourishes (Hillerman, *The Dark Wind*, 34).

Furthermore, with only eleven waterholes in the Utah-Arizona border
area south of the Rainbow Plateau, half of them near habitations, there are
only six sites to check in a criminal pursuit because surface water in such
a dry region is a "magnet for life" (*Listening Woman*, 43). Finding a trailer
parked under a cottonwood tree might seem impossible in most places, but
Hillerman notes in *The Ghostway* that on the arid Colorado Plateau, cottonwoods grow only along streams, beside springs, or near snowmelt runoff; around Shiprock, they are only in the San Juan River bottom and along
the Salt Creek Wash and the Little Pajarito Arroyo. Furthermore, most
Navajo trailers would not have both electric and telephone lines, so Chee
can find the trailer in an afternoon's search.

Landscapes loom large in Native American religions. Black Mesa, for
instance, features prominently in both Navajo and Hopi beliefs. In *The
Dark Wind*, Hillerman delineates such ties:

Masaw, the bloody-faced custodian of the Fourth World of the Hopis, specifically
instructed various clans of the Peaceful People to return there when they completed

their epic migrations and to live on the three mesas which extend like great gnarled fingers from Black Mesa's southern ramparts. Its craggy cliffs are the eagle-collection grounds of the Hopi Flute, Side Corn, Drift Sand, Snake, and Water clans. It is dotted with shrines and holy places. For Chee's people it was an integral part of Dinetah, where Changing Woman taught the Dinee they must live in the beauty of the Way she and the holy People taught them. (99)

As a boy, Chee collected herbs and minerals for ceremonies and holy bundles at sacred places on the Eastern rim. Southwestern Native American detectives such as Chee find in this landscape the source of their power and commitment to community good. Before Chee pursues a dangerous criminal, he engages in the hunting and stalking ceremonies that tie the Navajos to their northern ancestors and follows Navajo directional orientation: "Everything has a right direction to it," he thinks, with the Navajo way being "sunwise," from the east, toward the south, to the west, and finally to the north, as the sun goes and as one turns upon entering a hogan (*The Dark Wind*, 154).

Weather extremes characterize the climate: the sudden storms and floods of spring, the parched red earth and cloudless skies of summer drought, the dark blue skies and autumn beauty that make the first blizzard "a dangerous surprise" (Hillerman, *The Fallen Man*, 163), and the bitter cold of air sliding southward from Canada, down the Rocky Mountains, bringing the snow, ice, and piercing winds of a "blue norther." Hillerman describes cold wet Canadian air pouring over the Chuska Mountain range, colliding with the dry, warmer air on the New Mexico side of the ridgeline and producing "a towering wall of white fog, which poured down the slopes like a silent, slow-motion Niagara" (*The Fallen Man*, 273). Chee and his companion look "into the vast San Juan River basin—dark with storm to the right, dappled with sunlight to the left" and see Shiprock "at the edge of the shadow line, a grotesque sunlit thumb thrust into the sky," and through some climactic quirk, the Hogback formation "already mostly dark with cloud shadow" (273).

Southwestern mysteries, to greater and lesser degrees, tie weather to the unique beauty of the landscape—the brilliantly blue sky, the rainbow sunsets, the play of light and dark across colored rocks, the long blue shadows undulating across a glowing twilight landscape. Chee, confronted with such beauty, experiences *hozro*, harmony with nature:

To the west the morning sun lit the pink and orange wilderness of erosion that gave the Red Rock community its name. Beyond that the blue-green mass of the Carrizo Mountains rose. Far to the north in Colorado, the Roman nose shape of Sleeping Ute Mountain dominated, and west of that was the always-changing pattern of lights and shadows that marked the edge of Utah's canyon country. But look eastward, and all of this was overpowered by the dark monolith of the Rock with Wings towering over the rolling grassland. Only five or six million years old, the geologists said, but in Chee's mythology it had been there since God created time. (*The Fallen Man*, 111)

In *Her Hero*, Aimée Thurlo describes "skies the color of burning coals" (7); Hillerman's sky in *The Dark Wind* is "a thousand gradations of gray from almost white to almost black, and—from the dying sun—shades of rose and pink and red" (136). In *Coyote Waits*, long streamers of ice crystals from the snowy white tops of great thunderheads glitter in the direct sun, while lower down, a fiery sunset ignites cirrus clouds (60–61). In *Skinwalkers*, "sunrays from below the curve of the planet" light "cloud banks on the western horizon," and convert "the yellow hue of the universe into a vague pink tint" (150). Such exquisite natural beauty is a fact of daily life, molding a worldview, expectations about life, and concepts of justice. Disruption of this natural harmony is self-evidently evil, and the investigator's role is to restore order.

FICTIONAL GEOGRAPHY

The unique, inescapable features of the Southwest landscape become more than local color in regional mysteries featuring Native Americans or would-be Indians. The landscape is often an additional player in the unfolding dramas. It reflects the character and values of its dwellers, hides their secrets, and threatens intruders. In crises, its distances make self-reliance not simply a virtue but a necessity. For many of the natives in modern detective stories, the land is sacred and unbowed, peopled by ancient gods and full of mysteries, yet familiar and comforting. An Easterner in M. E. Hirsh's *Dreaming Back* is shocked by "the sudden, incredible distance, weird Mars-red buttes and salmon cliffs carved by the wind and persistent thread of the river. . . . Undulating bluffs of rust and cream held barely in balance by the radiant sky. . . . An enclave dwarfed by the gigantic mesas and dark Pedernal ridge. The true face of the planet [is] . . . totally indifferent to the creatures moving across it or anything but the force of wind and water" (46–47).

This landscape, terrain, and climate shape detection in this region, with death from heat prostration or lack of water; drowning in sudden, unexpected spring floods; and rattlesnake bite or scorpion sting real possibilities. Tarantulas, centipedes, and desert reptiles crawl across the landscape; coyotes yip and howl; death lurks in shadows. In Janice Steinberg's *Death-Fires Dance*, the would-be shamanistic healer Dylan Lightwing, a New Age Indian "wannabe," born Lew Zeiglet, uses fast-spreading canyon fires to wipe out his San Diego competition—Native American and Mexican-American herbal healers. Stern's Johnny Ortiz burns tumbleweed to smoke out a sniper in *Murder in the Walls*, while a damp arroyo sandstone cave saves Aimeé Thurlo's protagonists from a desert fire in *Black Mesa*. Similarly, in Hillerman's *Listening Woman*, the updrafts from a canyon fire started by fleeing robbers to discourage pursuit nearly end Leaphorn's life, but a rainwater catch basin facilitates survival.

In most regional mysteries, knowledgeable Westerners use the land's hidden dangers to ward off malign intruders. Val Davis' *Track of the Scorpion* features one villain defeated by dehydration and energy-sapping desert heat and another incapacitated by scorpion stings. Hillerman's Jim Chee and Joe Leaphorn fear not carrying sufficient liquid on long patrols and getting stuck in wilderness areas with no canteen and no water holes nearby; their extra duties sometimes include hauling barrels of water to indigent desert dwellers. Brian Garfield describes the plight of reservation Apaches when white neighbors tap the reservation water supply to support cattle-heavy ranches, leaving a depleted water table, inadequate water for irrigation, and lucrative recreational enterprises reduced to mud. In *The Dividing Line*, Richard Parrish paints the misery of Papago Reservation Indians whose reservation water irrigates white lands upriver and who cannot afford to waste water on laundry or baths with so little available to drink.

Hillerman's *The Dark Wind*, however, features the other side of the coin: a dry wash turned torrent by a sudden cloudburst over Black Mesa. The Hopi have ceremonially beckoned the rains, and the storm which coincides with their sacred ceremony sends millions of tons of water draining down dozens of washes and arroyos and "ten thousand little drainage ways—all converging on Polacca, and Wepo, sending walls of water roaring southwestward to pour into the Little Colorado River" (208). Chee hears the rumbling and roar of boulders and brushwood propelled by the flood and exploits its expectedness to distract and thwart a corrupt DEA official/ killer. Thurlo's characters face winds like "a rampaging stampede," roads turned to mud, and turbulent irrigation ditches that can sweep the careless to their death (*Redhawk's Heart*, 59). Stern likewise describes furious flash floods that hurtle gigantic, weighty rocks and wipe out campers in a sheltered dry river bottom or, in a different season, snowdrifts higher than one can reach and snow blown horizontal as if "from a gun" (*Death in the Snow*, 113).

Snakes are ever-present in Southwestern lore. With a sleeping diamondback only six inches from her leg, the heroine of Sinclair Browning's *The Last Song Dogs* shoots it dead, only afterward recalling her Apache ancestors' refusal to kill rattlesnakes within their camp out of respect for the rattler's power and their ritual discourse to encourage their departure. Richard Stern's Apache hero Johnny Ortiz speaks rapidly in the old tongue until the angry buzzing ceases and the rattler moves on. Aimée Thurlo's archaeologists in *Spirit Warrior* proclaim a good stick the best way to handle the diamondback rattlers that inhabit their dig. Snakes figure prominently in Jake Page's *The Deadly Canyon* and Tony Hillerman's *Coyote Waits*. In *The Deadly Canyon*, they hiss and slither among the rocks; a deputy sheriff counts 60 rattlers from the safety of his vehicle, and a disgruntled herpetologist tosses a large rattlesnake into the arms of his intended victim. In *Coyote Waits*, their buzzing frightens urbanite Janet Pete, but young Taka Ji and Officer Chee follow the Navajo herpetological psychology: waiting for a snake to pass and then erasing its zigzag track in the sand, a sign of harmony with the desert around him. However, a villain whose greed caused three deaths is out of harmony, and he ends up with a large gray snake writhing from his neck, "its fangs hooked through the neck muscles" just below his left ear, its venom only inches from his brain (198). While backpacking in the Sangre de Cristos near Pueblo reservation land, Ginevre (Gin) Prettifield, the part-Sioux heroine of Cecil Dawkins' *Rare Earth*, encounters another natural threat absent from the urban detective story: an eight-foot cinnamon bear towering on its hind legs, "twisting its head slowly, heavily, one forepaw padding the air," and at its feet a sinking figure, "one bloody arm shielding a mask of gore that has recently been a face" (13). Though she bravely distracts the bear from its prey, it is too late to save the mangled victim, who gurgles up blood and dies in her arms. Later, the body's disappearance raises the question of death by bear or murder with other than natural causes and motives.

The region's mineral wealth, from turquoise to uranium and rare earth, is another natural feature vital to modern Native American detective stories; the possibility of such natural treasures makes credible the greed of outside exploiters and their attempts to bribe or terrorize tribal council leaders into advantageous deals. The land itself provides motive and rationale for criminal behavior. M. E. Hirsh's *Dreaming Back* and Dawkins' *Rare Earth*, set in the Sangre de Cristo Mountains, dramatize the inherent potential for villainy in rare mineral wealth essential to high-tech computer systems. In *Dreaming Back*, federal officials in Huey helicopters secretly conduct reconnaissance by night preparatory to removing a priceless superconducting mineral vital to computer defense systems, but private entrepreneurs willing to kill to win join the race as well. The mineral source is a large meteorite situated directly over a secret, sacred Hopi snake nesting ground; the Hopi believe that scattering the snakes would end their holy snake dance, the sacred cycle, and maybe not just their world but the world itself. Three Hopis strive to protect tribal secrets and the sacred snakes but have limited force against a cadre of wealthy, politically protected conspirators anxious to employ drills and backhoes to make a sandpit of the nesting ground. One Hopi asks, "Is the American public going to think our snakes . . . more important than having the fastest computer in the world?" (209). Clearly, the answer is no.

Not only is natural wealth taken and land destroyed in its taking, but environmental disasters remain. Hirsh describes the 3,000 open uranium mines abandoned around the Hopi Reservation, strip mining and slurries that suck the aquifers dry, people dying of cancer from the tailings, black lung disease from the coal mines, irreversible genetic mutations, and skies so polluted that villagers cannot use the old methods of sun rays through notched buttes to determine planting and ceremonial dates (*Dreaming Back*, 90).

The murder and potential murders in *Rare Earth* result from the high value of rare earths, the elements of the periodic table with atomic numbers 58 through 71. Such minerals are cheaper to work than gold; used in computers and television sets, they bring premium prices from Japanese electronics industrialists. Dawkins describes the rift valley near the high Taos Mountains as—"a place where the earth's mantle had split wide open and spread, letting all that magma bubble up to the surface in little volcanoes all over the place, bringing treasures from the deep. Not the deep cold sea but the deep hot earth"—and draws parallels to a similar valley in Africa, the center of the diamond trade (67). Dawkins, less cynical than Hirsh, ensures that her greedy would-be money makers are thwarted and the disputed 100 acres and their mineral rights returned to the Pueblo Indians, who choose to protect and preserve the land and its wildlife rather than benefit from the hidden wealth.

Likewise, the murders, attempted murders, and suicide in Hillerman's *The Fallen Man* link directly to the conflict between greedy landowners and mining developers drawn by molybdenum deposits "worth killing for" (101) and conservationist ranchers and Navajos committed to protecting the land from the effects of such strip mining: scenic mountains slashed and razed, crystal-clear creeks running gray with cyanide and mining effluent (291). Leaphorn reminisces about a beautiful trout stream winding through a narrow valley set between high mountains—the Red River canyon north of Taos—but learns that one mountain was reduced to a mile-long whitish heap of crushed rock and holding ponds full of effluent spillover, cyanide sludge that killed the trout and ruined the stream. In Hillerman's *People of Darkness*, highly radioactive uranium motivates the crime and serves as a murder weapon, while in his *Sacred Clowns*, the greedy and the ambitious scheme to dump toxic waste on reservation land. In *Spirit Warrior*, Aimée Thurlo discusses the ill-will and ill-health that the uranium mill at Shiprock caused by its failure to clean up the radioactive tailings the processing left behind after the mill closed down. In Richard Parrish's *The Dividing Line*, a powerful senator uses bribes and political manipulations to siphon off the wealth of minerals and metals (even gold) beneath Papago Reservation soil; while Papago die of disease, malnutrition, and hunger, the senator thrives, and his illegal stranglehold on reservation land has the force of law in a region characterized by political cronyism. Later Parrish novels expand on corruption in the granting of multimillion-dollar federal contracts and the cooked books of receiver companies. The deaths in Micah Hackler's *Coyote Returns* result from an obscure clause about mineral rights to Coyote Mountain in a multimillion-dollar timber deal that the Navajo leaders are anxious to close; if the deal goes through, the sacred mountain will be flattened.

Some crimes are peculiarly Southwestern. Trafficking in antiquities has become a mainstay of the Southwestern "Indian" detective story: petroglyphs hewn out of rockfaces, ancient objects stolen from ancient ruins, and sacred items dug up from burial grounds or stolen by irreverent youths driven by alcohol, drugs, or gambling debts. In part, the physical realities of the Southwest make such offenses possible—numerous archaeological sites, unexplored because of their isolated locations on reservation land. Along rural highways in Colorado, Utah, New Mexico, and Arizona, one can still see petroglyphs protected by cliff overhangs but unguarded and exposed to thieves. European collectors, particularly Germans, are featured frequently as either villains or the money source behind villains. In Anne Marie Duquette's *In the Arms of the Law*, set near Tombstone, Arizona, Athabaskan (Apache) Jasentha Cliffwalker, a bat specialist, finds her life threatened while rock climbing and her wits challenged by a brazen thief who cut from bat-cave walls three sets of ancient petroglyphs sacred to Cliffwalker's people and important to their sense of identity and continuity. In Page's *The Deadly Canyon*, blind Santa Fe sculptor and amateur detective T. Moore "Mo" Bowdrie pursues a ring of international thieves who steal kachina dolls, rifle Aztec artifacts from anthropological sites, and even chisel petroglyphs from their ancient rock settings. Page follows the tradition of such blind detectives as C. H. Stagg's Thornley Colton, Baynard Kendrick's Captain Duncan MacLain, and Roy Lewis' Eric Ward. Bowdrie's companion and sidekick Connie Barnes, a peaceful Hopi, bristles at the desecration of ancient desert ruins and longs to be as fierce as the Apache warrior women of her imagination in pursuing and punishing violators. Page's *The Stolen Gods* makes a heartfelt attack on the illegal trafficking in Native American religious objects: the theft of sacred objects means the loss of the "gyroscope" that guides Indian existence and without which they cannot pass on or practice the divine law of the tribe. His blind detective compares their loss to being "spiritually blinded" (188). With buyers offering a quarter million for carved Hopi gods, inevitably some non-traditional youth, hard up for cash, will be tempted. In this case, Connie Barnes' brother, Daniel Quanemptwea, of the Corn Clan, sells out his people and then tries to rectify his sacrilege in muddled ways that cost him his life. The items, originally hidden in a sacred shrine in the cliffs below Oraibi, are so sacred that Connie fears violating taboos and affecting their power by just looking at a photograph of them. References to other religious items on public display (a Zuñi kachina mask, a Northern Cheyenne umbilical fetish) suggest that the desecrations Page attacks are not all illegal. Furthermore, the problems the local museum has returning sacred items stolen a century before confirm the complexity of the situation: how to research ownership of over 300 sacred nineteenth-century Navajo medicine bundles.

In Walter Satterthwait's *Wall of Glass*, a Hopi illegally trades away his heritage (eagle-feather kachinas and burial-site artifacts, including an Anasazi mummy), while Hillerman's *A Thief of Time* tracks artifact trafficking (Anasazi pottery) and grave robbing (human bones for DNA studies). In Aimée Thurlo's *Breach of Faith*, compulsive gambling makes locals vulnerable to the high prices offered for illegally acquired native artifacts; a British anthropologist steals religious secrets, while a cancer-ridden billionaire covets genuine Hopi religious artifacts he thinks can save his life, paying well to replace originals with high-quality reproductions. Thurlo's *Shadow of the Wolf* likewise depicts outsider greed for Native American art, in this case, the recent creations of local Tewa artists dependent on a price-fixing dealer; and in *Spirit Warrior*, a Navajo lawyer and an Anglo archaeologist debate the competing claims of religion/heritage against science at a disputed dig. Micah Hackler's *Legend of the Dead* features a millionaire rancher's attempts to forcibly seize an ancient unexcavated Anasazi pueblo and its priceless artifacts. A reversal of this graverobbing theme occurs in *Talking God*, wherein the crazed Indian enthusiast Mr. Highhawk protests the Smithsonian Institute's collection of over 18,000 complete native skeletons by sending a museum official her grandparents' bones in a box. Similarly, Pawnee-Otoe Anna Lee Walters, in *Ghost Singer*, attacks the Smithsonian's grisly artifacts—human ears, scalps, skulls, and skeletons—through a Navajo's experience with silent ghosts who drive institute employees to suicide or insanity.

The proximity of Mexico, the open stretches of reservation land, and the possibility of quick money for impoverished residents make drug trafficking another Southwestern theme. In Louis Owens' *Nightland*, a narcotics dealer thrown from a passing plane is impaled on a towering ancient cedar; a coyote howls; lightning pierces the sky, flickering like "a snake's tongue," as the blood of the dead Pueblo drug dealer drips down the tree trunk (1). The Cherokee hunters who find the dealer's package of drug money then face a modern evil that takes ancient, mythic directions. In Hillerman's *The Dark Wind*, corrupt Drug Enforcement Administration (DEA) officials bring murder and a violent search for missing drugs to Hopi and Navajo territory.

The nature of the land inevitably determines the nature of the detective or police manhunt. Southwestern detectives depend on a patient, intuitive knowledge of the territory—the people, the customs, the land itself. It takes a Native American detective to recognize signs of witchcraft that others miss (such as flesh cut from palms and heels for corpse dust), to intuit the secret significance of prayer plumes at a streambed, or to understand that tribal incest taboos guarantee that the suspect Navajo could not have had sex with a local girl. Tracking skills are often vital to pursuit—reading the signs at a crime scene, as did traditional scouts. In *The Dark Wind*, the DEA "experts" misread the crash site tracks and accuse Chee of drug trafficking, while Chee, reading the signs correctly, discovers the DEA's involvement with the hoodlums, the location of the buried drugs, and even the probable identity of an eyewitness. Tracking figures prominently in Hillerman's *Hunting Badger*: FBI agents armed with high-tech equipment and expensive helicopters authoritatively but futilely search reservation wilderness areas, while Chee and Leaphorn combine their distinctive Navajo skills and instincts to track and actually catch murderers who have gone underground, as did their Ute fathers before them. They thus satisfactorily reverse the traditional nineteenth-century cooperation of Utes and the U.S. Army in tracking Navajos. Tracking is also central to Brian Garfield's *Relentless*, the basis of the 1977 CBS movie-of-the-week *Relentless* (screenplay by Sam Rolfe). In the film, Native American actor Will Sampson played Garfield's lead detective, Navajo tracker and Arizona highway patrolman Sam Watchman; Watchman pursues ex-commando bank robbers through Southwestern wilderness areas, drawing on the scouting and tracking skills of his heritage. This use of detectives as scouts returns to the origins of the Native American detective as scout in such nineteenth-century works as Judson R. Taylor's *Phil Scott, the Indian Detective: A Tale of Startling Mysteries* (1882) and T. C. Harbaugh's *Velvet Foot, the Indian Detective, or, The Taos Tiger* (1884). In fact, the largely unrecognized connection between Indian scouts/trackers and mainstream detectives, discussed in earlier chapters, dates back to the first encounters between Native Americans and Europeans, since the latter were often incapable of surviving in the New World wilderness on their own or of dealing with hostile acts without advice and help. Historically, Southwestern guides and trackers predated even the Huron and Algonquin, who led the French Jesuits in Canada.

SOUTHWESTERN HISTORY IN DETECTIVE FICTION

The Southwest has had a long human history, going back about 20,000 years to the first Native American cultures, the Folsom and Sandia cultures (named for the sites where artifacts were found). During 900–1000 A.D. the Anasazi built extensive cliff dwellings, roads, and irrigation dams, and the Mogollon Indians inhabited the southwest region of modern New Mexico. The Hopis and other Pueblo Indians trace their descent from the Anasazi and have maintained irrigated plots of maize, beans, and squash along the Rio Grande for close to 1,000 years. The Apache, Comanche, and Navajo had migrated into the region from as far north as Alaska by 1500 A.D. Novels such as Kathleen O'Neal Gear's and W. Michael Gear's *People of the Silence* imaginatively portray life among the Anasazi:

Straightpath Canyon's huge towns had been organized and built for defense. If one person screamed an alarm, within half a hand of time every town and village down the length of the canyon responded with an outpouring of warriors. *That* was their strength. They could push an enemy war party back against the canyon walls and literally shoot them to shreds.... Ten hands thick in places, [those impenetrable walls] could not be battered down or scaled—though she had watched very brave warriors throw up ladders in an attempt to do so. The Straight Path archers atop the walls had laughed as they picked them off. (535)

Other writers, such as James Hall Roberts in *The Burning Sky* and Louis L'Amour in *The Haunted Mesa*, imagine the Anasazi enduring until modern times in hidden canyons or in time warps. Some authors use this past to illustrate present problems. For example, in Stern's *Death in the Snow*, a modern archaeologist studying an Anasazi dig finds in the disastrous effects of drought on the ancient Mesa people's closely balanced ecology modern-day lessons about glitzy campaigns to develop new "communities" for wealthy Easterners in areas with no natural surface water for 60 miles (water usage will reduce the water table, producing ecological disaster). Though the details of Anasazi culture remain somewhat mysterious, encouraging literary speculations such as the above, the archaeological record provides indisputable evidence of rich, complex, and diverse cultures in the region for tens of thousands of years.

With the Spanish came over 400 years of written history, beginning with Alvan Nuñez Cabeza de Vaca in 1536, followed by Franciscan priest Marcos de Niza and his black slave Esteban in 1539, seeking the Seven Golden Cities of Cibola (possibly impoverished Zuñi villages, shining golden in the sunset). In 1540, Francisco Vasquez de Coronado also searched the area for the Seven Cities, as did Antonio de Espejo. Juan de Onate came up from New Spain (i.e., Mexico) through the Rio Grande Valley in 1598 and established the first European settlement in the region at San Juan Pueblo. Santa Fe was built in 1610, so the American Southwest was colonized by Spain 25 years before the Pilgrims landed at Plymouth Rock. The Spanish colonialists encouraged farming and sheepherding, built missions, enslaved the native peoples, replaced their names with Spanish ones, and undermined their traditional cultures. Aimée Thurlo's *Second Shadow* explores the resultant modern-day hatreds and suspicions endemic to Tewa-Spanish relationships when a Tewa architect takes on the restoration of a colonial home, a Taos landmark owned by the descendants of the original Spanish slavers.

By 1680, the Pueblo were ripe for revolt and, led by Tewa and Towa peoples, staged a fierce rebellion on August 10, driving the Spanish out of Santa Fe to as far as El Paso, Texas. The motivation for murder in Stern's *Murder in the Walls* is Spanish treasure (gold religious relics), hidden in the thick adobe walls of the 350-year-old Francisco Sanchez house (a fortified *torreon*, or tower/keep) 278 years earlier by a wealthy landowner fleeing this Pueblo Indian attack. Another history-based work, Page's *The*

Knotted Strings, turns on the reenactment of the same Pueblo rebellion against the Spanish conquerors. The novel's blind detective, Mo Bowdrie, muses about historical events that forced Tewa speakers to live among the Hopis or to intermarry with the Navajo, and that led Navajos to adopt some Tewa gods; he also observes the continuation of conflicts over tribal lands and their modern use. He notes that some Pueblos trace their origins back to 1200 A.D. and to the Anasazi, and that their residents proudly retain purely Pueblo sensibilities, despite Spanish names imposed during colonization. Page's *The Deadly Canyon* examines the ties between Hopi and Aztec: related languages, similar creation stories, even similar legends of contact with whites. Bowdrie's Anglo-Hopi girlfriend, Connie Barnes, provides ties to the Native American community and historical values and attitudes that endure: the links between seasons, crops, and spirits, snake dances, and the role of Hopi gods in human affairs. In *The Knotted Strings*, contemporary radical traditionalists called "Walk of the Warriors" wish to return modern Hopis to the lifestyle and ways of their pre-Columbian heritage by wiping out all European influence and rediscovering a utopian past. They argue that Native Americans are "the nation's landlords, and the rent is due" (165).

Thus, though mainstream readers might assume the detective is a purely modern figure dealing with contemporary issues and problems, many detective stories set in the Southwest hinge on the modern repercussions of past events. Shortly after the opening of the Santa Fe Trail in 1821, American General Stephen Kearny occupied Santa Fe and claimed New Mexico for the United States; by the 1860s, conflict with the native peoples was in full swing. Indian fighter Kit Carson, whose scorched-earth tactics of burning crops, salting fields, and killing livestock starved the Navajo into submission, is remembered for herding some 2,400 Navajos a grueling 300 miles to Fort Sumner (the "Long Walk"). Eventually, 8,000 Navajos were incarcerated and relocated. The army wanted to make them sedentary (controllable) farmers, not herdsmen and warriors. In 1868, the United States finally relinquished the experiment and allowed the Navajos to return to a small part of their original territory, in particular, the badlands, far from the land that white settlers wanted and too limited for grazing.

The heroine of Aimée Thurlo's *Spirit Warrior* recounts this history to prove her sympathies for the Navajos, whose sacred land she excavates. In *Cisco's Woman*, the history is central to the investigation, for an 1868 document, a treaty between the Navajo and the United States, has disappeared, as has the heroine's brother, who was hired to guard it. Detective Cisco Watchman says, "That treaty represents our tribe's suffering, our triumph and, most important of all, lessons learned in blood" (68). Micah Hackler, in *The Dark Canyon*, ties his modern mystery about the murder of a prominent anthropologist directly to two historical periods, the time when the Anasazi Chaco Canyon culture thrived and the period leading up to the "Long March." The eleventh- or twelfth-century Anasazi guardian of the dead, a demonic jaguar, wiped out nineteenth-century U.S. cavalry soldiers terrorizing locals while seeking Montezuma's treasure, and the terror lives on when modern greed for status and wealth again unleashes the jaguar. The diary of a law officer's ancestor links past and present and provides the key to the mystery.

Walter Satterthwait also provides a taste of this history in *At Ease with the Dead*. Therein, a respected geologist, anxious to encourage his daughter's budding taste for archaeology, stole the mummified body of a Navajo tribal leader from its secret burial place in 1925. The body had been interred in Cañon del Muerte in 1866 to hide it from Kit Carson, who had unsuccessfully pursued this particular native rebel. In Satterthwait's story, the dead man's modern descendants have terrible dreams about the repercussions in their community if this desecrated ancestor is not properly put to rest again. So fearful are they of the power of the dead and of the reality of their dreams that they send Navajo leader Daniel Begay to a private *belagana* (white) detective, Joshua Croft, for satisfaction. Begay, drawing on the resources of the Navajo community, works with Croft to discover who now has the missing body and why his search has precipitated recent unexplained murders. This unlikely team—the one looking to the past, protecting tribal secrets, and employing the oblique indirection of his heritage, the other straightforward, blunt, and grounded in the present— teaches the reader much about the differences between mainstream and Navajo attitudes toward physical distance, time, ancestors, history, dreams, politeness, hardship, violence, and social and personal obligation.

Hillerman's *Coyote Waits* postulates Navajo oral stories revealing the secret of where Butch Cassidy and the Sundance Kid died—not in Bolivia— but in the American Southwest. Cassidy's family claimed that he had returned to the United States in 1909, bought a farm under an assumed name, and lived life as an honest citizen until his death in 1932. However, various eyewitness reports suggest that Cassidy continued his life of crime with his old hole-in-the-wall gang. Hillerman has an impoverished shaman with a reputation for using crystals for finding things uncover Cassidy's missing body in a lava cave on Navajo land. The novel depicts the ambition and rivalry of university scholars trying to undercut the theories of their colleagues and the greed of underpaid graduate students anxious for lost treasure (in this case, nineteenth-century stamps from stolen postal bags). It also reveals a great deal about the dependence of scholars on translations in which interpreters may be lazy or wrong and on the memories of the elderly reporting what they were told in their youth.

Micah Hackler and Richard Parrish investigate more recent history, the period before and immediately following World War II, respectively. Hackler speaks of the arbitrary authoritarianism of the 1934 Indian Reorganization Act, which ignored "the tapestry that intertwined the family and clan groups with the community as a whole" and replaced it with a government-determined structure (Hackler, *The Dark Canyon*, 88). Parrish targets the Dawes Act and its policies meant to destroy Papago and other Indian cultures, end the reservation policy long term, and yet keep the Indians from the rights of citizenship; he also targets Catholic and Mormon missions as historic centers of abuse overlaid with the illusion of piety. His Catholic missions grow rich amid reservation poverty, and his nuns and priests are contemptuous of those to whom they teach humility and passive acceptance, echoing Native American indictments of Spanish missions in the Southwest centuries earlier. His Mormons are land grabbers and womanizers, using the Papago to serve strange fantasies about the Lamanites, a Lost Tribe of Israel. His courts are corrupt and blind to the injustices perpetrated on Native Americans—treatment as second-class citizens, without even the right to vote in a country that demands the sacrifice of their youth in its wars. If this were not enough, a reservation border with Mexico means rivers polluted not simply with human waste but with the dangerous chemical runoff of industry that would be illegal in this country. In *Versions of the Truth*, cholera in the reservation water from sewage in Mexico is killing off Papago, while in his other novels it is tuberculosis, dehydration, malnutrition, and the myriad of other diseases to which the impoverished are prey.

Thus, this region's rich history validates interesting studies of the modern ramifications of this past.

RANGE OF INDIGENOUS PEOPLES

The Southwestern Native Americans who have been treated in detective fiction range from the ancient Anasazi dwellers of Chaco Canyon, Aztec, Mesa Verde, and Canyon de Chelly to the Hopi, Zuñi, Tewa, and other Pueblo peoples, the Navajo, the Papago, the Pima, the Apache, the Yaqui, and the Southern Ute. The discoveries, theories, and speculation of archaeologists about the ancient peoples of this region have resulted in numerous mystery novels that hinge on the archaeology itself or the value of long-buried artifacts. For example, Val Davis' *Track of the Scorpion*, a Nicolette Scott mystery set in the New Mexico desert near Los Alamos, depends for its denouement on whether or not the archaeologists in the book have theorized correctly that the Anasazi comfortably endured a period of drought due to underground water sources beneath the *kiva*. If they are right, the aging archaeologist and his amateur detective daughter will have a water supply to sustain them until the desert sun does in their deadly pursuers. If they are wrong, they will die of dehydration long before the villains' bullets find them. Throughout the novel, however, the archaeologists educate both fellow characters and readers about the Anasazi, answering questions like "What kind of Indians would live in a godforsaken place like this?" (257), and "Why [did the Anasazi] leave, if there was water to be had?" (260).

The range of peoples in this region means a variety of customs and perspectives quite different from mainstream ones. Southwestern detective stories often aspire to the cultural sensitivity modeled best by Hillerman to call attention to characteristics of culture ranging from etiquette and manners to mores, folkways, and deeply grounded beliefs about time and physical space that derive from a different worldview. The Hopi tolerate contact with dead bodies, but the Navajos will not touch them nor enter a place where a person has died; nor will they speak the names of the dead. When a skeleton is found at the top of Ship Rock, Leaphorn asserts that no Navajo would kill on that sacred mountain, nor even be disrespectful enough to climb it; only a white man would dare such an outrage (Hillerman, *The Fallen Man*, 91). Most Southwestern Native Americans avoid direct eye contact out of politeness, but looking directly into the eyes is a traditional Navajo way of suggesting disbelief. The Hopi and other Pueblo peoples such as the Tewa prefer crowding together in family groups; their towns push buildings together and have a high population density. The Navajo prefer to scatter to separated, isolated spots and to place a hogan or ranch in harmony with nature: near water, grazing land, and a road, but also with a beautiful view that could be soul healing. For the Navajo wealth symbolizes selfishness. Thus, a successful rodeo champion stopped winning rodeo competitions for fear that his fame was unhealthy and would put him out of harmony (*The Fallen Man*, 193). Hillerman's *The Dark Wind* gets its title from a cultural distinction. The Navajo call any driving emotion leading to loss of control and judgment a "dark wind." The whites in the book, in contrast, believe that revenge is sweet, and a father and a sister both lust for revenge. This idea of vengeance is as alien to Chee and the Navajo way of life as is the idea that someone with money would steal. Hillerman makes clear the Navajo love of bawdy puns but also their strict incest taboos, their deep commitment to privacy, and the daily rules that guide their actions: don't step over people, don't walk where water has run, shuffle to erase a snake's trail so it won't follow you home, and don't watch a dog urinate or you will go crazy. Traditional Navajo culture, reports Hillerman, permits a harmless lie, but that lie can only be repeated three times, at which point the liar must tell the truth or, on the fourth telling, be locked into the deceit (*Skinwalkers*, 172).

Both Hillerman and the Thurlos build into their stories the Navajo tradition of waiting outside a house or hogan until invited in, of shunning physical contact with strangers, and of keeping personal names secret, instead using relationship descriptions, such as aunt or uncle. The Thurlos call attention to gestures: the Navajo way of thrusting out the lower lip to point or the unique body movements which enable a Navajo to recognize a non-Navajo in dim light. Such close observation of interesting cultural differences has brought freshness and new life to the detective genre.

INDIGENOUS BELIEF SYSTEMS

While the Navajo have no religion in the white world's meaning of that term and, as Hillerman notes, no word in their language for religion, they do have a geographically based creation story. According to their tradition, the Holy People emerged from the underworld to kill the monsters that roamed the land between the four sacred peaks of Navajoland (Mount Taylor, Blanca Peak, Mount Hesperus, and the San Francisco Peaks); that done, they created the *Dineh*, the "People." Thus, the land itself is the center of Navajo sacred belief. The Navajo have a complex system of maintaining balance, peace, order, and harmony and a set of stories to explain the nature of their universe, for example, Coyote grabbing the blanket where First Man had put the stars to hand place them in the sky and simply tossing the remaining ones out to form the Milky Way. The saying that one doesn't have to go looking for Coyote because Coyote is always out there somewhere waiting sums up the Navajo expectation of imbalance and chaos waiting to take control—through alcohol, greed, vengeance, and so on. Basic Navajo metaphysics teaches that everything has two forms, the outer and the inner, that order, law, and harmony are essential to survival, and that Coyote is a metaphor for chaos and disorder. Hillerman argues that when the Navajo migrated out of Mongolia, across the land bridge that then spanned the Bering Strait, and moved down the continent to the Four Corners area of the Southwest, they brought with them not only a community-centered Asian philosophy but also the mystical idea that thoughts and words could affect reality: "To speak of death is to invite it. To think of sorrow is to produce it" (*The Fallen Man*, 77). These same qualities impress Page's Mo Bowdrie: "Navajos, in particular, believe that speech—talking, singing—actually creates the world. Or recreates it. Makes it harmonious and whole when it's gone to hell. You think until you know how it should be, then you put that into speech, and that is what the world becomes." In *The Stolen Gods*, he calls this worldview "artistic," "almost romantic" (219). This notion, rather than any Western concept of religion, guides their ceremonial practices.

Hillerman's *The Dark Wind* sensitively contrasts Navajo/Hopi beliefs through Chee's friendship with a Hopi tribal officer nicknamed Cowboy and a Hopi sorcerer from the Frog Clan. This aged, respected holy man, who has repeatedly damaged a government well and windmill to prevent the water of a sacred shrine from being drained off, agrees with Chee that, "There are higher laws than the white man's law." He narrates the Hopi story of their emergence through the *sipapuni* to discover that Masaw was the guardian of this world, the Hopi choice of the short, hard corn ear that determined their lifestyle as opposed to the Navajo choice of the long, soft ear, the migrations that led to their present pueblos, lifestyles, and rituals. The point that Hillerman makes through Chee is that, despite major differences in attitudes toward space, community, and religion, the Navajo and Hopi share values that the white man cannot fully appreciate or even perceive, and that their respect for the land and tradition suggests that they have more in common than their long-standing conflicts and even warfare might suggest. In *Breach of Faith*, Aimée Thurlo likewise contrasts Navajo and Hopi attitudes toward the dead, burial practices, and the afterlife.

The Hopi and Zuñi have, say experts, preserved more of their ancestral heritage than have any other Indian tribes in the United States, as their enactment of the pageants of their traditional ceremonial system and retention of their indigenous social structure confirm. Their kachina cult seeks to maintain a harmonious balance in the universe and encourage weather conditions beneficial to agriculture. In *Dreaming Back*, Hirsh provides some background on the Hopi snake ceremony, its ties to the creation story of Spider Woman creating life and taking steps to keep the earth in balance and to the prophecies of Massau (variously spelled Masaw, Masau, Massau'u), the god of death. His half-Hopi Ben Naya, known as Redbird in Hollywood films but called Kwikwilyaqa by the old men (after the kachina who wore white men's shoes and imitated people, like an actor), recalls the feathered snake dancers entering the Tesuque Pueblo plaza in his youth:

Silently, they circled it, bodies painted black and white, with zigzags of snake-lightning on their kilts. Antelope priests called to the clouds and a rattle of shells asked mother water to bring rain to the fields. Two by two the dancers came, one holding a wriggling rattler in his mouth while the other charmed it with a feather. He could see its forked and darting tongue. And then a snake escaped from where they were kept, aiming straight for a row of women, and he still remembered their startled cries, the flash of white leg-wrappings as they scrambled up onto their chairs.

Gathering the snakes, the dancers ran down to the valley, setting them free to carry their messages. If it always was done this way, the spirits would understand the signs and rain would always come. The only magic he had ever believed in because that day it poured. . . . Spirits of dead people were supposed to come back as rain to say goodbye. (43–44)

Another Hopi, Randall, an educated person with a master's degree, confirms the depth of such belief: "Eight thousand Hopi, praying to their sacred pile of rocks, surrounded by two hundred thousand Navajo and two hundred and fifty million pahanas [whites]. All of whom needed Soyal [the sacred snake ceremony] to be done just right to bring the sun back" (108). Randall rejects attempts to force biblical parallels to Hopi religious tradition (endless space before genesis, a serpent, a world destroyed by flood, an evil fallen angel); for him, the snake dance shows the unity of life, a working of the web that makes up the universe.

Jake Page's introduction to *The Stolen Gods* details the traditional yearly visit of the kachinas ("beaked figures adorned with paint, evergreens, bells, and turtle shells"), their songs "in low, aeolian voices" and their dances "to the hypnotic rhythms of a drum" set against the Southwestern landscape: small clouds of dust stirred up by the wind in imitation of the larger white clouds against the browns and reds of the baked earth and the bright blue of the sky. The cornmeal offering (appropriate food for the spirits) helps them on their journey to the Hopi fields, where the rain spirits are enjoined to provide sustenance for crops. In addition to the rituals tourists might see, says Page, are the ceremonies, prayers, sacred objects, and rites that the Hopi keep secret from the outside world and that form the philosophical core of their worldview. Page also notes that propinquity to the Navajos has affected Hopi belief, leaving them fearful of "hostile shades, witches, wolfmen," and other phenomena which were not originally part of the Hopi demonology (*The Stolen Gods*, 81). Rob MacGregor covers much the same territory in his young adult novels *Prophecy Rock* and *Hawk Moon*. His amateur detective youth, Will Lansa, learns the spiritual ways of his tribe, faces a powerful witch, prepares to dance the kachina spirits to their home in the San Francisco Mountains, and receives guidance from *Masau*, who becomes his spiritual protector even when he returns home to Colorado. MacGregor depicts *Masau* as a figure of balance between light and dark.

Martin Cruz Smith's terrifying detective-horror novel *Nightwing* sets the Hopi spiritual system against mainstream rationalism, and his *Masau* is a much darker, more destructive figure than MacGregor's. Smith, who has a Pueblo family background, imagines an ancient Hopi shaman, Abner Tasupi, attempting to bring on the end of the world because of white corruption and exploitation of the environment. The shaman's medicine unleashes or coincides with (Smith leaves the two possibilities open) the movement of vampire bats into the multitudinous caves of the Arizona desert, a migration from Mexico that will make their eradication impossible and deny humans any sort of safe nighttime activity. Youngman Duran is an assimilated Hopi deputy sheriff, a friend and protector of Abner's who has sought cultural authenticity by returning to the reservation but who nevertheless considers Indian medicine no more than tomfoolery for tourists.

As the vampire bat threat becomes undeniably real, Duran is joined first by his Anglo girlfriend, Anne Dillon, a public health nurse on the reservation, and then by Hayden Paine, a professional immunologist obsessed with the vampires and convinced that their sudden, inexplicable movement north of the Mexican border promises an unstoppable plague, perhaps an end to human life as it has been lived in the region. The combined efforts of these characters end Abner's threat, but not before Duran, caught between his Hopi heritage and his white girlfriend, on the one hand, and the shaman and the scientist's interpretation of the bats, on the other, is forced to answer what Smith poses as "the Hopi questions": "When was I born? Where did I come from? Where am I going? What am I?" (*Nightwing*, 10).

SOUTHWESTERN "INDIAN" DETECTIVES

Not all Southwestern detective stories are truly related to the land, the climate, and the culture; not all are really "Indian" in any authentic sense. Given the many cultures of the region, the heroes and heroines of Southwestern detective stories usually vary in their degree of Native American blood, with most characters half, a third, or some undefined part Apache, Navajo, Hopi, Tewa, or even Sioux. As a consequence, some of their creators feel free to focus on the superficial qualities of Otherness rather than to directly confront a truly different culture. Such mixed-blood detectives wear their "Indianness" as they wear their other Western accouterments—the long black hair, cowboy hat (or bandanna) and Western boots (or beaded moccasins, if occasion demands), rugged jeans, tooled leather belt and, of course, the outward signs of native authenticity—Southwestern jewelry, which can sometimes be no more than costume. In Dawkins' Prettifield series, part-Sioux Santa Fe investigator Gin Prettifield sports a $1,000 silver-and-turquoise concho belt with her fashion jeans and peasant blouse and frequents a crowd enthusiastic about local art. For her, being "native" is a fashion statement and a cocktail party conversation piece, and the fellow "Indians" she might parley with tend to be wealthy or on the edge of wealth. Characters in Richard Stern's novels (both male and female) wear silver-and-turquoise buckles and flannel shirts, and combine education, a comfortable income, and ethnicity, as do those in Robert Westbrook's Howard Moon Deer series.

La Cienega investigator Trade Ellis, whose area of practice is 30 miles north of Tucson, is pleased with the compliments her cheekbones win her and confesses to ironing her curly black hair to look more authentically Apache but claims equal pride in her Scots grandfather and her full-blooded Apache grandmother (naturally, a powerful medicine woman). Ellis expresses gratitude for their having raised her to have a "deep regard" for her Apache ancestry, but adds, "Not a bad thing at all, especially now that it's become so damned trendy to be a Native American" (Browning, *The Last Song Dogs*, 11). Basically, in terms of plot, for Ellis (her Apache name is "Pretty Horse"), being Native American means owning an isolated pueblo-style ranch house, having grazing title to 16,200 acres of ranch land, and doing tasks usually associated with males: rounding up cattle, mucking out her own stables, and even branding. Being Native American also allows her the right to make glib remarks about Indian behavior and attitudes and to occasionally tip her hat to her ancestors' history. At a ceremonial sing on the San Carlos Reservation, where her grandmother resides, she remarks, "Gloria Steinem and that bunch would probably not be happy here—the men always do the public speaking and prayers" (*The Last Song Dogs*, 199). This Apache insistence on male dominance is one reason she gives for turning down her relatives' entreaties to live on the reservation.

In Stern's Johnny Ortiz series, being part Apache is an attitude and a look that creates expectations in others. Ortiz, the trilingual police lieutenant of Santo Cristo, New Mexico, is of mixed blood (Spanish, Anglo, and Apache): the Apache genes dominate his appearance, the Spanish blood affects his temperament and personal style, but the Anglo experience dominates his investigative method and lifestyle. The front blurb of *Tangled Murders* sets up reader expectations of the traditional scout role: "In New Mexico's landscape of vast wilderness and ancient lore, he'll track a suspect through hell and back." While it is precisely his ability to match footprints at the scene of the crime with those of the murderer, to put himself into the head of the man he tracks, and to anticipate his moves that marks his detection in *Missing Man*, visual footprint verification is not acceptable evidence in a court of law, so his final means of detection must be urban centered (despite bodies dumped in the desert) and his "lore" standard investigative procedure. Nonetheless, Stern retains the illusion of a practicing Indian scout by having Ortiz discover trails and signs that others miss, and fellow investigators comment about his tracking ability verging on the "supernatural": "that damned Indian would track a man through hell and out the other side, and then stake him out on an anthill" (*Tangled Murders*, 10). Friends allude to Ortiz's "scalping-knife look," Apache features and expressions that seem "carved in stone" and strike terror in suspects. His smile, says one acquaintance, makes one think of being staked out naked and honey covered atop ant hills, and Ortiz himself admits appreciating his ancestors' reasons for roasting a villain over a slow fire. His coworkers conjure up images of him squatting on his heels, wearing an Apache-style breechcloth and headband, "staring into the smoke of a tiny fire, seeing visions invisible to ordinary folks" (*Tangled Murders*, 57–58). His girlfriend thinks of him as "a great hunting cat on the trail" (*Murder in the Walls*, 139). Villains fear that he is measuring them for "an anthill or a skinning knife" (*Murder in the Walls*, 140). Ortiz himself makes comments like the following:

You find bear tracks. . . . You may never find the bear, but you can see that here he turned over a rock and there he found some wild honey and in a third place he ate some berries. . . . You may not be able to say what color he is, but you know his size, and how he moves. (Stern, *Death in the Snow*, 155)

Despite presumably admirable intentions, these ordinary tales of love triangles, drug smuggling, mobster control of resorts, computer theft, and high-tech surveillance include references to cosmetic Indianness that to a modern eye seem almost racist in effect. Ortiz may look exotic, but he is no Apache scout. Apart from superficial appearance, there are no good reasons to cast him as an alien Other. His final unraveling of events is straight out of Poirot or Columbo, with the clever detective gathering round him a set of suspects and enumerating the chain of evidence and reasoning that leads to villainy unveiled, or laying out his case point by point for the local district attorney. His approach is as linear and rationalistic as could be asked for by any forensics instructor in an FBI training program.

Unlike Stern's Ortiz, Robert Westbrook's Howard Moon Deer is not even from the Southwest. He is a highly assimilated Sioux working his way through college (a degree in psychology/sociology) by doing the legwork for a blind private detective in and around Taos, New Mexico. Though he occasionally muses on the cryptic lessons taught him by his great-uncle Two Arrows, he knows "more about Paris bistros and who won last year's Princeton-Harvard game" than about Native American customs (*Red Moon*, 108). In Westbrook's *Warrior Circle*, the crazies his investigation stumbles on are part of a men's encounter group, New Agers enacting what they think are Native American rites of manhood under the desert moon. Costumed as Silver Bear, Black Wolf, Coyote-That-Sings, Cosmic Turtle, and so forth, they act out what they learned about ancient ceremonies from the Internet website www.shaman/rules.com, not realizing that they harbor in their midst a psychotic killer. Westbrook's *Ghost Dancer* has Moon Deer untangling the affairs of a U.S. senator shot dead with an arrow, while the client in *Red Moon* believes that his stepfather, a dissolute artist, has stolen the client's mother blind and is involved in at least one murder. Except for his appearance and his racial classification, Moon Deer is an Anglicized "Howie" and performs like any other amateur detective, tracing down a stolen Georgia O'Keefe painting in *Red Moon* and dealing with a decapitation in *Ancient Enemy*.

In many novels, then, there is no question about the Native American detectives working in a shamanistic native tradition rather than the Western tradition of Holmesian logic, because these so-called native investigators are not truly native in any deep-seated way that affects their perceptions, points of view, and approaches to life. In an age-old American process of appropriating superficial Indian characteristics to express mainstream yearnings for freedom, exoticism, and authenticity, these writers ignore or diffuse core native values, instead retelling conventional detective plots. They avoid the challenge to the readership inherent in incorporating truly different ways and values, allowing the fiction to focus on comfortingly familiar turns of plot and minor quirks of character.

Nevertheless, the majority of the detective stories set in the Southwest treat indigenous cultures with respect and with a concern for authenticity. The natives of this region see their community, culture, and philosophical beliefs tied to the land, and their perceptions of reality are not mainstream. The authors who most credibly depict Native American detectives make those ties and perceptual differences integral to their stories. The detective stories of Cecil Dawkins, Sinclair Browning, Richard Stern, and Robert Westbrook fail at this task. The next chapter will discuss authors who are more accomplished at incorporating authentic cultural issues, and who, even when they fail, at least make a genuine effort to capture difference. These Southwestern detective stories make the question of shaman or Sherlock and of traditional native ways versus mainstream ways central to their authors' methods and concerns.

5

The Southwestern Detective:
Shaman or Sherlock?

One hundred fifty years was but a sigh in the memory of the people. History did not happen and then go away for the people of the Sangre de Cristo Mountains, it festered and grew into the bones, blood, and soul. It stayed to inhabit the memory, and so the people learned to accommodate the ghosts of the past. People here lived and breathed history. It was all around them. In the mountains, around the plaza, in the adobes of old haciendas, . . . the ghosts of the ancient past still walked, appeared, spoke, did mischievous things like the duendes [dwarf spirits] of the forest.
—Rudolfo Anaya, *Shaman Winter*, 168

Most readers turning to a Native American Southwest detective story expect the exotic. The dramatic Southwestern geography and history lend themselves to mysticism, to expectations of the inexplicable. The popularity of television's *The X-Files*, the notoriety of Roswell, New Mexico, and the UFO "movement," and numerous other challenges to the assumption that what we see is what we get show that many modern audiences are ready to at least entertain the possibility of perceptual complexity, of layers of reality not immediately apparent. The bedrock assumptions audiences have

about Southwest native religions heighten this expectation of the supernatural: here, the visible world is infused with deeper meaning, and natural
features become philosophically and spiritually complex. In the Southwest,
one may drive along a two-lane blacktop, a defining modern experience,
and see in the red rock formations a petroglyph figure seeming to wave
from the rock face—one's perception of reality can change quickly. So too
the strikingly unique ceremonies with kachina spirit dancers, snakes, and
mudheads visually prompt other ways of understanding the familiar world.

Barker's *The Broken Circle*, a fictionalized account of a local incident,
begins with fact—Farmington, New Mexico teenagers maliciously killing
and mutilating Navajo males—but ends with Navajo witchcraft succeeding
where American justice failed: a local tells the investigating journalist, "A
Navajo shaman put a curse on them [the killers] and they're all dead" (7).
Released after a minimal jail sentence as juvenile offenders, these killers of
Indians, says Barker, experienced justice one by one in unusual ways—
struck by a bolt of lightning (literally out of a blue sky), crushed to death
in a trash compactor (having fallen in during a drunken stupor), and severely injured when carjacks mysteriously dropped a car down and per-
manently damaged nerves. A Navajo has the final say about the
punishments reflecting the degree of each boy's evil, the universal order
restored, and the sufferers "restored in beauty" (320).

Barker quotes an anonymous turn-of-the-century poem about the threats
of the Southwest—the tarantulas and centipedes hidden under every stone,
the ever-present perils of "the dreaded cactus," "noxious weeds," and "a
million different breeds" of such threatening flora, and the paths that all
"lead straight to hell"—to argue that the Farmington Indian murders and
the Navajo view of how balance is restored are a product of the region, its
geography, its isolation, and its unique cultural perspectives. While Barker's
only detective is the liberal journalist who details events, his materials introduce the fictive questions raised in Southwestern mysteries: A good detective will certainly need to understand the culture, psychology, sociology,
and regional uniqueness of the people with whom she or he deals, but at
what point does knowledge give way to belief in the guiding force of the
supernatural? Can a detective practice ratiocination and logic and yet explain crime as a product of supernatural forces with supernatural counter-
forces? Can readers be asked to believe that spirit warriors truly haunt
museums and ancient pueblos, that curses kill, and that only sacred rituals
can truly defeat evil? Such questions are central to fictive works in which
the detectives are pure blood and, to some degree, tied to the ways of their
ancestors.

In Hillerman's *People of Darkness* (1980) Mary Landon protests to
Chee, "But you can't be both a Navajo medicine man and an FBI agent"
(75), and she is proved right. Chee tries hard to be both but finds community pressure limiting his duties as a shaman, except for serving a hand-

ful of sympathetic relatives. A major question raised in the detective fiction featuring Native Americans is whether two opposing worldviews can meet in a single person. Is such an amalgam credible or even likely? The question applies equally to the detective-fiction genre at large: Can detective fiction be ratiocinative and yet reflect the spiritualism of the native tradition?

SHAMAN

Most Southwestern detective stories to some degree detail Native American religious belief, but their handling of religion varies greatly. In some cases, religion is peripheral to the main story, misdirects, or merely titillates. In most cases, the writers take major liberties with native religious beliefs.

Like Westbrook's *Warrior Circle*, Janice Steinberg's *Death-Fires Dance* exploits the shamanistic to mock New Agers who participate in Indian rituals to discover life's elusive secrets. Steinberg's Dylan Lightwing leads Indian wanna-bes like himself in sweatbath and drum ceremonies, singing in his version of Navajo, using drum, chants, and herbal mixtures to satisfy their desire to participate in Indian wisdom. A total fraud, his Indianness as fake as his shamanism, he schemes to steal the power and the herbal secrets of his competitors in the New Age market niche while spouting inanities about secret native ceremonies. The shamanistic overlay serves a satiric function: the intentional sham confirms the villain's hypocrisy.

Cecil Dawkins' *Clay Dancers* provides another twist: shaman spiritualism to create terror in an otherwise conventional plot (a stolen diamond necklace, professional battles in the academic community, a nascent love story). Set on an Anasazi archaeological dig near Santa Fe, New Mexico, Dawkins' mystery draws on the New Age interest in crystal, tektites, meteors, and Indians that *The Santa Fe Rembrandt* exploited but adds to these feminist theories about hunter-gatherer gender equality that supposedly resulted in strong female shamans. The theory is that the venerable Pueblo men-only kivas were womb symbols once controlled by female religious leaders before matriarchal society yielded to patriarchy. Dawkins' detective is Tina Martinez, the niece of the Tsorigi head man (a Pueblo group almost decimated by smallpox). Her uncle has authorized her to observe the outsiders, since the site is on land to be turned over to the Pueblo shortly. Tina squeezes into the excavated kiva, discovers the mummified remains of a *kwiyo*, a female shaman, walled in with a meteor fragment and a dignitary's cloak of Mexican plumes, and experiences a frightening memory fusion with her shaman ancestor. Her kiva-inspired insights offer a model of historical detection carried out through otherworldly means—her discovery settles the question about ancient female power—but does little to further the modern-day investigation of the theft, the crime in question. The novel never pulls together the various plot strands and disparate characters, leaving the impression of a grab bag of interesting but unrelated Southwestern elements.

Also intriguing is Lauren Maddison's infusion of the supernatural into an adventure/detection story, *Deceptions*, which moves midstream from Washington, D.C., to Navajo territory. Its FBI heroine becomes the pursued, threatened victim, while her local Navajo sidekick, Laura Nez, a special agent on assignment from a secret government agency, dominates much of the book's second half. Though up to date on the latest surveillance systems, Nez is also a skilled tracker; her weapon of choice an Uzi, she settles for a heavy rock when necessity compels. Seemingly totally assimilated, she deeply respects her aged grandmother, her clan head, whose special powers she cannot dispute, and the hidden significance of dream time, "another dimension, a place out of this time and space" (242). She argues that, "The Navajo don't see their spirituality as separate from their lives"; that is, the traditional Navajo "lives" his or her religion from sunup to bedtime, employing "rituals and prayers for even the most simple activities—planting, building, slaughtering sheep, hunting" (244). When Nez is wounded, another Navajo, Police Chief Albert Tsosie, who has tracked her through the desert, helps get her to her grandmother's secret cave in time to save her life through extraordinary means: an ancient healing ceremony, glowing crystals, and a gateway into another dimension. In this case, the shamanistic does not solve crime, but greed for ancient native secrets motivates the string of murders that ultimately brings Nez back to her grandmother and her tribe. Likewise, in J. A. Jance's *Kiss of the Bees*, a Tohono O'otham teenager, the intended victim of a serial killer, discovers her spiritual powers and her tribal ties as she battles to survive. Such writers as Maddison and Jance may have gotten on the bandwagon of Native American detective fiction, but they do not make the differences in cultural perceptions, attitudes, and beliefs central to their mysteries.

In contrast, Kathleen and Michael Gear, Micah Hackler, Aimée and David Thurlo, and Rudolfo Anaya all toy with alternative visions of reality, with shamanistic powers at work paralleling ratiocinative detection. The Gears alternate between modern and ancient, with shamanism played against the intuitive "science" of archaeology. Hackler experiments with varied ways to introduce native spirituality into his stories; the Thurlos plunge their heroine deeper and deeper into the conflict between shamans and skinwalkers; and Anaya intermeshes the everyday and the supernatural world of dream visions and shaman powers to merge time, external realities, internal instincts, and dreams into an inseparable weave.

Kathleen Gear and Michael Gear

Kathleen Gear's and Michael Gear's Anasazi mystery series alternates between a modern archaeological team and the ancient peoples whose graves and homes they excavate to suggest that the actions of long-dead witches can reach across centuries to harm present-day people. In *The Visitant*, the discovery of a mass grave of women and children, some with heads smashed by large stones traditionally used against witches, sends archaeologists Dusty Steward and Dale Robertson seeking help from Chaco Canyon tribal representatives (Magpie Walking Hawk Taylor and her great aunt Hail Walking Hawk) and from an internationally famous Senecan physical anthropologist, Dr. Maureen Cole. The physical remains from which Cole derives scientific data speak in a different way to Hail Walking Hawk, a "ghost talker" who hears ancient voices and knows how to send restless spirits to the Land of the Dead. Cole too experiences supernatural contacts but refuses to admit their reality.

The modern archaeological investigation parallels the story of a thirteenth-century serial killer attacking the Katsina People, an offshoot of the Anasazi. War Chief Browser sends for his great uncle, Stone Ghost, to uncover the criminal who threatens his people's lives and their annual inter-pueblo religious ceremonies. The clubbing of a female religious leader and the first body, seemingly that of Browser's mutilated wife, awaken fears of witchcraft. The killer is someone among them who draws on Anasazi spirit powers to evil ends. The past and present investigations dovetail as the ancients discover in the Anasazi ruins a corpse being stripped of muscle tissue, and moderns uncover a bowl of corpse dust (ground muscle tissue); both ancients and moderns undergo purification rites to protect against spirit powers. Stone Ghost combines shamanistic powers, close observation, and logic to piece together disappearances from neighboring communities, while the archaeologists discover a pattern suggesting a methodical testing of the effects of head injuries on different motor skills.

The intersecting plots illustrate the long-term negative impact of child abuse. However, while Stone Ghost stops a killer with multiple personalities, Hail Walking Hawk is too weakened by cancer and by the loss of ancient rituals to combat the evil released by removing the protecting slab from the skull of the witch Two Hearts, whose evil deeds Stone Ghost exposed. Thus, despite discussions about the right of science to ignore superstition, the Gears' Anasazi mystery series makes shamanistic spiritualism a reality. Ancient evil unleashed provides an open-ended story ripe for sequels. *The Summoning God* repeats characters and patterns, this time with 33 charred children's bodies excavated in an ancient kiva and with Stone Ghost conducting a modern-style autopsy, while the modern archaeologists find clues of warring religious factions and vanishing resources that produce witchcraft and murder.

Micah S. Hackler

Balancing two ways of seeing the world gives many popular writers problems. Micah Hackler weighs the supernatural equally with the ratiocinative, while the supernatural elements dominate, equal, or replace the ratiocina-

tive in the works of Aimée Thurlo. Only Tony Hillerman consistently translates Native American spiritualism into forms mainstream readers can
respond to both emotionally and intellectually.

Hackler's Southwestern detectives fluctuate between ratiocinative and
otherworldly investigations. His part Tewa, part Cherokee Sheriff Clifford
Lansing traces his ancestry back locally 150 years but is totally assimilated
and, despite his affinity for the Pueblo peoples, wary of the intuitive and
mystical. An outsider, excluded from secret rites and blood-based clans,
Lansing pits logic against experiences that defy rational explanation. Hackler includes a shaman only in his first book, not as an investigator but as
an instigator/problem solver; however, his stories incorporate the religious
beliefs of a number of tribes, particularly the Mayan, Anasazi, Zuñi, and
Navajo. Possibly supernatural events frame *Legend of the Dead* and *Coyote
Returns*. In *Legend of the Dead*, an autopsy report of a .22 caliber bullet
undercuts the initial illusion of death by vengeful spirits, though a respected, elderly traditionalist, Joseph Windwalker, "The Father Who Walks
on the Wind," reasserts the spiritual as a viable parallel reality. A Zuñi
Kiahlo, the keeper of tribal memories and ways, he walks between the
spiritual world of the *a'doshle*, or guardian spirits, and the world in which
a distant U.S. government can decide the fate of his people's sacred land.
The ancient Anasazi ruins he protects figure in his people's creation story
(emergence from the *Shipap*) and their ancient ties to the Aztecs. To con-
vince a state senator that the site merits federal protection, Windwalker
summons thunder, wind, and spirits, "three figures, as tall as the kiva roof,
wearing ceremonial robes elaborately decorated in feathers and fur, wheeling . . . in strange, contorted dance" and behind them "dozens of other
figures, their hideous faces gauzed by the flying sand" (100).

Confronting white villains, the disarmed sheriff, senator, and others
stone their attackers from the cliff-dwelling ramparts, as did the Anasazi,
and the echo of voices combines with thunder to suggest an army of
thousands at work; in the haze of a sandstorm, the number of participants
seems visually to multiply as well—as if the shaman has summoned supernatural powers to punish sacrilege and satisfy ancient Anasazi spirits. Are
these real Anasazi warrior spirits or a shared hallucination? Do the *a'doshle*
the aged shaman claims to have summoned save Lansing from a bullet, or
is his survival a trick of the wind? Unless these spirits actually exist, the
defeat of the villains makes little rational sense—stones and sand cannot
defeat bullets; yet Hackler provides no final judgment, only Lansing "want-
ing to believe it was more than just his imagination getting the best of him"
(244). Clearly, however, the shaman anticipated conflict, secured the sacred
site, and quite possibly defeated the villains and saved the sheriff.

In *Coyote Returns*, Sheriff Lansing again sees events through the lens of
a rationalist, while his deputy, Gabe Hanna, in discovering his Navajo
identity, interprets the same events within the framework of Navajo oral

tradition. Where Lansing sees greed-inciting motives, Hanna sees the mystical maneuverings of the Coyote god, whose whimsical magic, partly recounted from Coyote's perspective, frames the ratiocinative tale. The novel begins with a traditional story about Coyote teaching deer to dance and with Coyote dragging a Navajo traditionalist to the roadside to ensure proper burial. Coyote, inciting mischief to exercise his power and remind native peoples of his significant role in their cosmology, punctuates the narrative. The final image is of him trotting north to cause instructive mischief among northern tribes. A compromising death in incriminating circumstances, threats to the dead man's daughter, and shots fired at Sheriff Lansing's girlfriend necessitate an official investigation that uncovers a grab for mineral rights. Parallel to the investigation is unusual wild coyote behavior and interference, always in time to save Lansing. Hanna's and Lansing's very different investigations dovetail, providing contrasting perceptions that end in the same reality—villainy exposed and a community rewarded. However, unlike Lansing, Hanna, an urban Navajo come home to tribal land, finds his dreams of coyote activity repeated in reality, though Lansing must contend with the mystery of a coyote taking shots meant for him yet leaving no tracks, no blood, and no body. Presumably, Coyote has interfered in human affairs, perhaps through animal mediaries, because the sacred Coyote Mountain is at stake.

In Hackler's *The Dark Canyon*, Lansing has a larger role than as a representative of the rational beleaguered by the supernatural. A diary from his great-great grandfather forces Lansing to remedy disorder in the spiritual world left by the long-vanished residents of Chaco Canyon, even as he denies belief in the supernatural. A horrific nocturnal predator killing sheep and humans in secluded areas of Lansing's county is a Jaguar God that even repeated point-blank gunfire cannot stop. Loosed 100 years earlier by renegade U.S. Army soldiers who stole from a Chaco Canyon burial ground a fist-size emerald jaguar totem, the jaguar is the spiritual tool of an ancient shaman whose spells programmed it to guard the canyon dead. Lansing's great-great grandfather, Virgil Lansing, buried the emerald under his house along with a diary explaining its significance. The sheriff resists this old tale but has no alternative rational explanation to account for the Jaguar's powers. Ironically, a trio of anthropologists, one helping Lansing reconstruct his ancestor's diary, the others excavating in Chaco Canyon, speaks most forcefully for the reality of the Jaguar Cult and the sacred nature of the tombs. The scientists are more open than is Lansing to nonmaterial explanations of events and ultimately agree to keep the ancient cemetery a secret (no burial site has been found at Chaco Canyon to date).

An ambitious book, *The Dark Canyon* boldly cuts between character and plot events to interlock more than half a dozen main characters in initially separate settings and situations (Anasazi believers, nineteenth-century skeptics turned believers, twentieth-century rationalists encountering living nightmares) into a coherent, interwoven plot, all connected by the supernatural rampages of the Anasazi Jaguar God. This effective strategy allows Hackler to depict the dusty, gritty realities of archaeological digs and related academic politics and betrayals without drifting too far from his signature character, Lansing, who is himself credibly drawn into the scientists' competitive jealousies and who ultimately must face the fact that his personal experiences defy rational and scientific explanation.

Turning on Apache tribal divisions going back centuries, Hackler's *The Shadow Catcher* celebrates the power of dreams and visions, even as its Apache characters debate the efficacy of modern medicine as opposed to shamanism. The terrible images of murder dreamt by the twelve-year-old great-grandson of a Jicarilla Apache shaman, once a very powerful medicine man, parallel the actions of a serial killer who Sheriff Lansing pursues. As the killer scalps his victims and leaves behind the feathers of an owl and his signature (*Se-ka-la Ka-am-ja*, "The one who never dies"), Sheriff Lansing once again moves into a bizarre world of Native American legend and magic where, in a moment's flicker, the stars disappear and the chill air left behind betrays territory where a spirit walks. The shaman, a self-proclaimed shadow catcher with visions of the future, predicted that an oil rig on tribal land would bring death and sorrow to the tribe, and that the great-grandson, unbeknownst to his more assimilated parents, has inherited his great-grandfather's mystical foresight. Lansing's nightmare visions become part of the investigation when the present killings are linked to the strangulation of three children years before (an act that has long haunted Lansing). The murderer, the former apprentice of a respected medicine man, has been gathering knowledge from tribal medicine men across the continent, learning to twist shamanistic powers to evil ends (assuming the body of an owl, he steps out of time and place, leaving behind a string of bodies). For believers, the parallels between the Apache creation story's incest taboos and the villain's family history explain the origins of this particular evil. Moreover, the shaman's medicine bundle, used as his great-grandson directs, enables Lansing to overcome the villain and to rescue his own kidnapped son. Yet Hackler does not fully credit the supernatural explanations that dominate the story, for the powerful evil shaman-villain wears a bullet-proof vest, a triumph of up-to-date technology and a sign of distrust in his medicine, and is aligned with a local businessman who wants Apache land ceded generations before. His final death by lightning bolt is either just punishment from offended tribal gods or a quirk of nature in territory renowned for peculiar weather.

Aimée Thurlo and David Thurlo

Like Hackler, Aimée Thurlo infuses her mysteries with native spiritualism and suggests inexplicable ancient forces at work, despite detectives who are wary of shamanistic phenomena and are more comfortable with Western investigative tools. Her later works explore native ways to knowledge employed when normal investigative methods fail.

In her Harlequin Intrigue mysteries, the shamanistic/spiritual serves multiple functions. At times, it provides misdirection. Thus, inspired by New Mexico's San Ildefonso Pueblo, *Black Mesa* emphasizes the alien features of Tewa religious ceremonies. It begins with a practice session for a sacred ceremony honoring the blue-headed masked god of the Summer People, with his corn husk ear pendants, striped horn, and sacred clown attendants. Then the heroine stumbles upon an even more secret desert ceremony and, pursued by eerie figures in mule deer masks seemingly seeking her death as atonement for sacrilege, flees along an arroyo as a ubiquitous blue pickup joins the chase. Navajo FBI Agent Justin Nakai suspects her of illegally photographing sacred rites until his investigation dovetails with the disappearance of a Tewa friend, and missing tribal funds that suggest criminal motives for murder and attempted murder. His belief in evil, but not in Tewa spiritualism, provides a rational counter to the white heroine's fears of witchcraft and supernatural intervention, and his explanation of hunting and tracking signs makes the mysterious seem logical. Ultimately, a dishonest art dealer with mob connections engaged in money laundering and fraud turns out to be the villain, not Tewa secret society members nor Tewa spirits.

In other books, spiritualism provides a cultural foundation contrasting with mainstream attitudes. In *Redhawk's Heart*, Navajo lawman Ashe Redhawk offers prayer sticks to Changing Woman at his ancestral shrine at Rock Ridge and sees in the stone formations of the Lukachukai Mountains a world of secrets where the Navajos sing sacred songs, perform holy rituals, and pray to the guardians of the Diné, ancient warriors trapped in mountain stones. "Attuned to the rhythms and cadences of the desert," he is "like the Diné of old . . . a warrior whose beliefs [give] . . . him strength" (9) and whose tracking skills and powers of observation make him a valuable crime scene investigator. Ashe sees no conflict between being a policeman and a traditionalist, but the witness protection officer who works closely with him does. She finds the land as stark and barren as Mars and its inhabitants' responses to her ignorance of customs, folkways, and territory at times as harsh and unforgiving as the land. Thurlo's novel turns on that officer's coming to terms with the geographic and cultural differences that define her case. Despite Thurlo's emphasis on Ashe embracing the secrets of his tribe and accepting the past and tradition as integral to his being, ultimately, it is his solid, trudging police work that breaks the case and proves that different is not necessarily right or wrong, just different. Where the outsider sees an isolated, impoverished old woman, Ashe sees a highly respected trembler, whose ability to diagnose illness places her at the heart of a tribal network interlocking the community and its shared knowledge. Cultural contrast and supernatural skill further this plot but do not drive it as the book's central theme.

In still other books, the shamanistic vaguely hints at supernatural forces at work beyond our understanding. Thus, Thurlo's characters trust the power of corn pollen, amulets, and family or tribal tokens or fetishes shaped like animal spirits (mountain lions, bears, or armadillos) to ward off evil and protect from spiritual danger. Cisco Watchman, the skeptical tribal detective in *Cisco's Woman*, has always understood Navajo belief intellectually (pollen creating peace and contentment, the wind bringing news, or thunder finding things), but he trusts his own skills more than any spiritual assistance. However, he reevaluates his attitude when his grandfather's carved stone armadillo fetish deflects a bullet shot at him point blank. In *Spirit Warrior*, set on an Anasazi archaeological dig, a Navajo lawyer turned amateur investigator says, "Being Navajo isn't easy in today's world" (47). Despite his modern education and cause-effect rhetoric, he finds harmony and spiritual protection in a medicine pouch containing corn pollen and rock crystal, but he is not happy about facing inexplicable lights or intangible evil, extrasensory experiences that "open a crack" in his thinking, "like being shown another time or place where sand talks and the sun rises in the west," a place where the ideas that he takes for granted and that make his world stable no longer apply, where "there are no sturdy pillars to lean against for support" (158). Whether the evil force is a dishonest archaeologist, amorphous *chindi* (evil spirits), one of the Navajo twin gods, Slayer, or an Anasazi spirit warrior with glowing eyes offended at archaeological sacrilege matters little; nor does logic. Why would an Anasazi spirit attack a white archaeologist when a Navajo, the traditional enemy of the Hopis (the descendants of the Anasazi) is available? Or is desecration the only inspiration for attack? Why, then, isn't the whole archaeological team wiped out, including the hero and heroine? Can the connivings of a greedy professor explain away all of the mysteries? More important than logic to this plot is the frightening effect of eerie wailing, "like the agonized cries of the damned" (245), the black amorphous sentient darkness of the cave, the stench of a slaughterhouse, and a dead villain with an Anasazi flint knife embedded in his neck.

In *Shadow of the Wolf*, a greedy Anglo art dealer manufactures the signs of the supernatural (a Tewa witch's bundle and voodoo doll), but *Second Shadow* mixes bogus witchcraft (witch signs coupled with construction accidents), Tewa protective rituals, and what the hero and heroine assert is genuine spiritualism: a medicine man's and a clairvoyant aunt's warning of danger, the family totem spirit—a mountain lion—stalking the site and (along with the quartz life stones that carry the souls of her ancestors) protecting the heroine from danger.

In Thurlo's *Four Winds* trilogy, the investigative yields to the supernatural, as the blessing/curse of a nineteenth-century medicine man tests three brothers, and the supernatural undercuts the ratiocinative. The three brothers warn against "the Anglo world blindness" to the magic and miracles of "*dineh's* history" (*Her Hero*, 155). Healers battling skinwalkers reflect the ongoing conflict of good and evil in the town of Four Winds. In *Her Destiny*, a skinwalker's spirit bowl precipitates a chain of events requiring the *hataalii* (healer) powers of Sheriff Gabriel Blackhorse. Though a Los Angeles police officer for five years, Blackhorse's reaction to crime is not that of the street-wise urban cop but of a Navajo shaman, using the flint hawk inside his medicine pouch to protect against the *chindi* that drive the villain to misdeeds and death. In *Her Hero*, an assimilated Navajo who dismisses Navajo spiritualism as "superstition" finds herself in need of a *hataalii* singer-healer and in love with a traditionalist, a shaman who follows the Navajo Blessed Way but who has been framed for patricide.

Thurlo pits the Navajo concept of finding strength through harmony and inner balance against the evil that skinwalkers unleash, and her shaman hero must use black flint, charcoal, corn pollen, and ritual spells for protection and cast spells, shift shape, and walk unseen to counter contamination by *chindi* and defeat his skinwalker enemy. By story's end, the heroine has reevaluated *hataalii* powers and traditional beliefs and found reassurance in her savior's deep-rooted ties to the Navajo community. In *Her Shadow*, the enchantment continues through a little raven carving made by a sick Navajo peddler; a cycle of mysterious illnesses tests friendships and exposes villains. Chains of events test character against chaos and violence to expose evil, restore harmony, and strengthen individuals, as the traditional detective story quickly yields to supernatural intervention (shape-shifting villains).

Breach of Faith explores the Hopi belief in religious curses and in the clan as a religio-political unit: individual wrongdoing rebounds on family and community. Gilbert Payestewa, blackmailed into stealing sacred healing items entrusted to his family and clan, not only dies but brings down a kachina curse on every female in his bloodline until his clan is wiped out or the sacred objects returned. He also endangers his tribal policeman brother, Joseph, who must recover the missing items to save family honor and lives. Ultimately, this single misdeed threatens the health of the entire pueblo, which has lost its spiritual protection. Thurlo's Hopi characters firmly believe that the Hopi kachina spirits destroy the thief because he perverted sacred rites, and Thurlo's FBI agent, Glenna Day, becomes a believer herself when her health and fertility are miraculously restored as thanks for her service to the Hopi community. In *Timewalker*, another FBI agent, Julia Stevens, on a stakeout for a bank robber using stolen money to purchase Navajo artifacts, finds unexpected assistance from Benjamin Two Eagle, a nineteenth-century Navajo warrior trapped in time by the force of twin amulets and locked in an ongoing struggle with one of her ancestors, a bloodthirsty officer under Kit Carson. Two Eagle's tracking, warrior, and *hataalii* skills enable him to outthink the FBI investigators, prevent past evil from infecting the present, and restore the balance of justice.

David Thurlo joins forces with Aimée Thurlo in the Ella Clah mystery series—*Blackening Song, Death Walker, Bad Medicine, Enemy Way,* and *Shooting Chant*—novels that purposely pit the ratiocinative against the supernatural to give credence to the otherworldly. The heroine of this series, Ella Clah, is a trained FBI agent, home for a family visit after her father's murder in *Blackening Song*. She has no official standing on the case but hopes her special expertise will help her see what locals have missed. Ella thinks of herself as "a no-nonsense, show-me-results agent" (48), but her new reservation experiences plunge her into the heart of a struggle between traditionalists and modernists, a struggle her Christian minister father waged for years before his ritual slaying by skinwalkers.

The Thurlos very clearly intend for Ella to represent the reader's perspective initially as she moves into the world of Navajo magic, a world that she no longer intuitively understands. Her instinct is to seek logical explanations of the bizarre and make evidence add up empirically. As events become more and more inexplicably tied to the supernatural, Ella's *hataalii* brother, the FBI's chief murder suspect, provides spiritual explanations. He sees the Clah family as historically benign guardians of their tribe's sacred ways, and he identifies as skinwalkers their enemies, the murderers and troublemakers who have brought on the evil that threatens to engulf the community. These skinwalkers call on psychological and supernatural forces of terror and mayhem through incantations, corpse dust, and bone slivers. In *Death Walker,* they stalk and kill elderly tribe members who carry in their memories the tribe's collective wisdom. In *Bad Medicine* and *Enemy Way,* they exploit the disarray created by racism and the generation gap. And in *Shooting Chant,* they set traditionalists and activists against those who would embrace white technologies to improve their crops, brood stock, and quality of life.

As the series progresses, Ella Clah acts less as the outside perspective and more as a convert, returning to her family and to tribal faith in supernatural realities. Where once she acknowledged, almost against her will, some of the benefits of traditional medicine, very quickly she becomes convinced that enemies of the Blessed Way are shifting shape and invoking spirit powers to undermine her family and that, if her family and tribe are to survive, she must join the extrasensory forces she rediscovers within herself with the longer cultivated powers of her brother and mother. Ironically, *Enemy Way* evokes supernatural evil while at the same time it realistically depicts the miseries of modern reservation life: alcoholism, drunken driving, racial tensions with local whites, criminal militancy, alienated youth gangs preying on their own community, and secret tribal discipline groups discouraging cooperation with all official authorities, tribal or otherwise. In *Shooting Chant*, Ella's peaceful brother has joined the activist Fierce Ones, a traditionalist group that vociferously opposes a personally profitable contract that tribal leaders made with a medical supply company, not simply because they believe more Navajos should be hired but because they fear it is in some dread way contaminating their community. The murder of a Navajo factory guard, the kidnapping of two tribal leaders, the slaughter of prize show animals, and the theft of health clinic records of pregnant reservation women foment conflicts between progressives and traditionalists, and Ella must walk a tightrope between the two, battling deep-rooted superstition and trusting her instincts and the tools of her profession to sort out misleading information and uproot a terrorist plot that threatens her unborn child, her family, and her tribe.

The Thurlos' odd mix of rational and supernatural usually ends with mystical shamanism defeating the dark forces of chaos and individualism, restoring balance, and returning the community to the Blessed Way. Yet, even amid peace and harmony a tension remains, the possibility of fear and superstition bringing future dangers against which the Clah family must unite.

Rudolfo Anaya

Rudolfo Anaya's Sonny Baca series blends magical realism with crime fiction, making the shamanistic integral to Baca's private investigation—a way of recognizing and confronting evil outside of the realm of logic and ordinary experience. The series begins in *Zia Summer* with an elusive villain (Raven) and his cult followers trying to blow up a truck carrying high-level nuclear waste. Committed to chaos and destruction, Raven employs black magic to further his ends. Baca's guardian animal spirits are coyotes, and like them, he is a survivor. The coyote is also an appropriate guardian because of his racial mix: he calls himself a "Nuevo Mexicano," a mestizo mix of Hispanic and Pueblo Indian. In their first confrontation, Baca as coyote and Raven as the dark bird of the forest (a familiar figure in Indian mythologies) battle in the Sandia Mountains north of Albuquerque, and an ancient Indian medallion Raven had used to create chaos deflects a bullet that would have killed Baca. In *Rio Grande Fall*, the conflict continues with a sinister trail of corpses, including a balloonist shot down while participating in the Hot Air Balloon Fiesta de Alburquerque. In *Shaman Winter*, Raven is again after plutonium but not merely as an ecoterrorist. Baca sees him as "a demented Sun King," determined to turn against mankind the gift of light and fire of the original Raven of native mythology (85). Raven has insinuated his operatives into a highly classified nuclear project at Los Alamos, his goal mass destruction.

Though a Southwestern racial blend, Baca returns in a series of dream visions to his Pueblo Indian genetic makeup, meeting himself in his ancestors in *Shaman Winter*. Baca initially believes that dreams are "incoherent, random images" that come "out of nowhere," symbols of subconscious activity for the conscious mind to interpret (4), not exterior realities to be dealt with and obeyed, as defined in Native American spiritualism. However, his confrontation with Raven, the powerful and mysterious villain who kidnapped his fiancée in *Zia Summer* and who put him in a wheelchair in *Rio Grande Fall*, changes Baca's understanding of himself and his reality. Baca's neighbor, Don Eliseo, a Pueblo Indian elder, guides him step by step in the process shamans undergo to master and direct their dreams and thereby to acquire power over reality. Baca realizes that the strange dreams of his ancestors tormenting his nights have been set in motion by Raven, the Bringer of Curses. Raven has entered Baca's dreams to destroy his history and capture his soul. This personification of the destructive forces of the universe is symbolically destroying, one by one, the four significant women in Baca's ancestry who formed his biological being (for Pueblo Indians, the genetic line is matrilineal).

Meanwhile, in the everyday world of Albuquerque, Raven is kidnapping young girls who symbolically represent Baca's female ancestors in the dream world. Baca is hired to find these vanished girls (one of them the mayor's daughter), with four black feathers the only clues left at each kidnapping scene. In this case, however, defeating the villain and rescuing his victims can only be accomplished in the dream world, and failure will mean that Baca will no longer exist, because his ancestors will have been annihilated and the whole history of the region will have been changed. Baca, as an educated man of reason, resists this idea at first, but when no other explanations make sense, he takes Don Eliseo's teachings to heart. Thus, *Shaman Winter* is a mystery like no other. Like a Navajo tapestry, whose mix of colors and shades forms a unified whole reflective of the land and the people who produced it, so Anaya's novel creates a New Mexican mix, a blend of cultures, races, and ways of living, perceiving, and interpreting the world that is, to a great degree, alien to mainstream America but that, within the novel's context, is nonetheless asserted as a viable, energized alternative worldview. Baca stares at the barren winter landscape of tawny rolling hills, the blue Sangre de Cristo Mountains, and the clouds gathering around the Jemez peaks and thinks of the "kachina spirits of rain and snow gathering on the mountains," the redemptive glow of the divine sun blessing sacred places, and the light that drew the original inhabitants and that continues to draw artists and holy people to New Mexico (58). He intuits the strength born of the state's unique amalgam (Indian, Spaniard, and Anglo) combined with the power of the land. Don Eliseo helps Baca understand the Pueblo vision of universal interconnectedness and the chaos inherent in creation, and thereby understand his enemy:

This was one of the remaining spiritual centers in the country. The Pueblo Indians knew that. Here where the covenant with the ancestral kachinas had been made lay a great power for the good of mankind. . . . In la Nueva México Raven had found the spiritual center he needed to destroy . . . the spiritual heart . . . to blast the dream apart. Go right to the heart of thousands of years of ceremonies that sustained life. (82)

Shaman Winter alternates between past and present, dream and waking, with the constant threat of the real world vanishing with the dream and of the dream annihilating the past and, thereby, the future.

Baca merges in his dreams with Andres Vaca (the "B" and "V" in Spanish are closer than in English), a Spaniard under the command of Juan Pérez de Oñate, the newly (1598) appointed governor of New Mexico. Vaca has fallen in love with a unique, spiritually gifted Indian woman, Owl Woman (Mujer de Tecolote), the daughter of an Aztlán shaman. She studied with Tenochtitlán Aztecs and brings to this joining of Spaniard and Indian a sacred obsidian bowl, a polished Calendar of Dreams from her people's ancestral holy place in Tula, Mexico, one she says holds their dreams and destiny. The local archives confirm Baca's dream characters' historical reality and his genealogical ties to them, and Owl Woman comes to Baca in visions of the Anasazi departure from the Four Corners region in A.D. 1500 and the migration into the Rio Grande Valley of the people who would become the Pueblo Indians. Her sacred bowl becomes a dream symbol of Baca's obligation to defeat Raven to preserve his ancestral reality and a symbol of the power of his Anasazi/Tula/Pueblo ancestors who support him in his dreams. Furthermore, Don Eliseo guides him through the Toltec creation story to delineate the glyphs spiraling the bowl, the Toltec concept of cyclical births and deaths of suns, and of destruction as necessary for creation.

The next round of historical dreams begins with the early seventeenth century, when missionary zeal, fired by the spirit of the Inquisition, led to the persecution and hanging of Pueblo medicine men who resisted conversion, the destruction of ceremonial kivas, and the burning of native masks, fetishes, and other religious paraphernalia, as well as a prohibition against snake dances. His dream moves then to 1680 when Popé led the Pueblos in the Taos Rebellion and drove the Spaniards out of New Mexico, south to El Paso and to another ancestral couple separated just before their wedding by the eruption of violence.

The third historical dream sequence occurs in the 1840s, with Colonel Stephen Watts Kearny imposing a U.S. government, a new language, and a new legal code and Kit Carson corralling protesters (particularly the Navajos). A friend recounts for Baca the "begets" and marriages that tie Hispanic and Pueblo families to his bloodline, generation after generation, and concludes that everyone is everyone else's cousin—that is, relatives of one sort or another. In his dream, Baca sees Raven as a U.S. Cavalry soldier stealing away another of his female ancestors.

Aptly, the non-dream locations for Baca's encounters with Raven are sacred places, such as Bandelier National Park, where the ancestors of present-day Pueblo Indians lived in caves carved into volcanic cliffs and farmed corn, beans, and squash on the canyon floor:

The entire plateau was a place of the ancestors, and the peak of the mountain a shrine to their spiritual ancestors. The kachinas [Anasazi], deities of rain, lived on the mountaintop. And because a sacred time in the cycle of the sun was drawing close, it was time to pray to them.

Or in Raven's case, to threaten them with the fire of the plutonium pit. . . . "He disrupts the sacred circle every chance he gets." (*Shaman Winter*, 89)

Raven is darkness struggling against light to disrupt the harmony of the universe. But Owl Woman brings Baca a vision of the kachinas blessing the pueblos and the land with water and growing seeds, "their rattles sounding like falling rain, their breath the breath of life, cold and invigorating"—the "Lords and Ladies of the Light" that Don Eliseo prayed to (98). This vision helps Baca battle his elusive enemy in his final dream.

There is a New Age quality to Anaya's vision—the concept of a world consciousness (a collective memory across time and space), of a philosopher coughing in China creating hurricanes in the tropics, and of memories and dreams curing spiritual sickness worldwide and affecting other dreams. Also, it is difficult to separate the truly Indian in Baca from the New Mexican, the shamanistic from New Age spiritualism. However, Anaya's vision transforms the detective story into a totally unexpected spiritual history of races and cultures in conflict, merging amid violence to produce a new mix most unlike the American heritage of Plymouth Rock but nonetheless an alternative history dating far back in prehistory. Baca does research, consults experts, and pursues a villain, but when his pursuit turns inward and his major confrontation occurs in the dream realm, he no longer functions in the mainstream detective tradition.

SHAMAN AND SHERLOCK

In *Coyote Waits*, Hillerman's Joe Leaphorn smiles at the oxymoron "A Tribal Policeman-Shaman," for, from his point of view, the two professions are "utterly incongruous"—just further confirmation of his colleague Chee's fatal flaws as a policeman, his individualism in following private rules, and his romantic illusions about heritage (18). His hair knotted at the back, Chee relies not only on his official weapon, a pistol, but also on his deerskin *jish* (his Four Mountain leather medicine bundle with flint arrow points, pouches of pollen, and "talking prayersticks") (19), healing

ceremonies dependent on geographical directions, ritual poetry, sandpaintings, and pollen to control natural powers and to restore beauty and balance. Leaphorn sees Chee as a loner, "marching to his private drummer,"
and characterizes his attempts to be simultaneously a *hataalii*-policeman as
"impractical," like "being an investment banker and a Catholic priest at
the same time. Or a rabbi and a clown" (144). For Leaphorn, shamanism
suggests "the dangerous mystical fringe of the supernatural," but for Chee
it means a life of harmony spent preserving traditional ways to improve
his people's lives through the reassuring past.

Unlike the shamans in the works of Dawkins, Thurlo, and Hackler, however, Chee is neither overpowered nor possessed by the supernatural. Instead, for him, being a shaman rationally affirms duty, community, and
heritage. Initially, Chee stands at the crossroads between two worlds. An
avid reader, he subscribes to *Esquire* and *Newsweek*. He graduated from
the University of New Mexico and the FBI Academy ("with distinction" in
anthropology and sociology); a Sergeant of the Navajo Tribal Police, he
daily ponders causal chains and deductive reasoning, but at some deep level
of his being he is "Long Thinker," his secret war name, a traditionalist
committed to Navajo ways. These opposing selves perpetually war within
him, as he struggles to decide whether his future will take him closer to or
farther from his heritage.

His personal love relationships—first with the blue-eyed blonde teacher
Mary Landon and later with assimilated Navajo defense lawyer Janet
Pete—force him to face the implications of assimilation and to deal with
the differences between Navajo and white perceptions. He and Mary, curious about each other's worlds, repeatedly contrast their ways of perceiving. Navajos see a dwelling in terms of location, setting, or environment
rather than physical condition. Thus, Chee, thinking of Mary's reaction to
his home, realizes his trailer looks "cramped, crowded, slightly dirty, and
altogether dismal" to white eyes, but he himself never normally notices its
state: "His trailer was simply where he lived" (*The Fallen Man*, 274).
Through Mary, Chee gains insights into the opposition between white and
Navajo realities. She complains that he tells her about his family, not about
himself personally, but as a Navajo he defines himself by his family, not
by his individual acts. In fact, normally, before he would consider inviting
a young single woman on a date, he would want to know both her mother's
and father's clans in order to avoid the incest taboos of a complex clan
system. Traditional Navajos do not say someone's name in their presence;
Chee sees names simply as reference words for when the person is not there.
That very idea disturbs Mary's sense of rightness. When Chee and Mary
visit a Navajo hogan, he sees as refreshing the complete silence of a Navajo
home when no one is speaking (no TV, no traffic noise, no sirens, no clock
ticking, no refrigerator humming), whereas she finds it eerie. The white
man's custom of demonstrating attention through periodic (and meaning-

less) interjections rather than the courteous, attentive silence of Navajo etiquette irritates Chee. He speaks when he has something to say; Mary speaks to fill uncomfortable silences and, sometimes, to hide her true thoughts. By his standards, she is too blunt, too direct; by her standards, he is too oblique, too indirect. Chee cannot understand why whites plant grass and flowers where they do not grow naturally and turn animals into dependent pets; Mary considers such control of nature normal human activity. These cultural differences, taken one by one, are interesting but encountered on a daily basis in an intimate personal relationship are divisive.

When Mary finally opts for college and life off of the reservation (she doesn't want her children attending impoverished Navajo schools nor adopting a Navajo worldview), Chee discovers that he cannot abandon his commitments to his people and culture. In *The Ghostway*, seeking a missing teenage witness in Los Angeles, he sees the devastating effects of rootlessness, of loss of culture, of Navajos trapped in urban poverty, degraded by alcohol, prostitution, and crime, without their language, elders, traditions, or healing ceremonies to restore balance. When he learns how few *hataalii* practice the sacred rituals and ceremonies of healing and blessing that make his people who they are, he cannot accept an anonymous position with the FBI among other disintegrating tribal groups—the dream job Mary had planned for him. With Janet Pete, Chee at first thinks Navajo blood will suffice to bring harmony to their relationship, but he discovers that her assimilation has separated them in a thousand ways that cannot be overcome. Material possessions, fame, and reputation are an inescapable part of her value system yet are totally at odds with the Navajo Blessed Way.

In giving up these potential loves, Chee confirms his traditionalism and commits to Navajo values. His later relationship with Bernadette Manuelito holds more promise for long-term stability because of the skill with which she blends traditional values and ways with her position as a tribal police officer. Chee studies as a *hataalii* and clearly believes in powers beyond logic and reason, as does Manuelito, but he is not overpowered by superstition or magic. He enjoys debunking illusions and magic (like that of the Hopi Trading Post owner West). Instead, his shamanism is defined by a knowledge of traditional ways to promote harmony, ward off evil, and restore balance to damaged lives and spirits. Consequently, his shamanism is more credible and more understandable than the purely supernatural experiences described by Dawkins, Thurlo, and Hackler. It is also more in accordance with what serious students of native religions agree is the goal of shamanistic practice, as distinct from the flashy, superficial trickery beloved of popular depictions of shamans.

In *People of Darkness*, Hillerman does gracefully what Micah Hackler struggles to do: he effectively and seamlessly parallels the worldview and acts of a shaman with those of a detective. On one level, as a law officer,

Chee realizes that a greedy engineer who discovered a rich uranium deposit under his oil well intentionally blew up the rig, supposedly dying on site, took a new identity, and years later purchased the mineral rights, making himself a multimillionaire. However, the villain has had to take furtive steps to get rid of the six Navajo roustabouts who survived the explosion and could link him to his discarded identity. Knowing of their membership in the Native American Church and their defiant use of peyote as a sacred drug, despite denunciation from the Navajo Council, he has given them a secret amulet symbol of their cult identity, a mole made of pitchblende, the hottest uranium ore. Worn close to their bodies, it guarantees leukemia/cancer and death. However, when the son of one of the dead six contracts the same disease from his father's secret amulet, the villain, fearful that modern medical scrutiny will reveal his treachery, hires an assassin to eliminate the son and the evidence. The assassin awakens the suspicions of Jim Chee, and the plot unravels. The story hinges on greed and murder, then more murders to cover foul play. It ends as thieves/killers fall out.

On the other hand, from the Navajo point of view, the mysterious deaths of seven Navajos, six members of the Native American Church and all related and belonging to a secret Mole society (the "People of Darkness" of the title), point to witchcraft—an act out of harmony. The mole plays only a trivial role in Navajo mythology, as a predator and a symbol of the dark underground, with access to unseen subsurface worlds. That underground connection associates the mole with the Dinee evolutionary rise to human status, but Chee finds no religious or ceremonial reason for a Navajo choosing the mole as an amulet symbol, except that oil wells drill toward the nadir in the mole's domain; therefore, the amulet itself points to outside origins. The leader of the six, the peyote chief, was a witch who had broken from the Blessed Way of balance and harmony and whose witchcraft tainted all that he touched. He claimed his peyote visions had saved the original six Navajos from the oil rig explosion, but all died later (as well as the son who inherited his father's medicine bundle). Their relatives attributed their deaths to corpse sickness, since one by one they became mysteriously ill with a white man's disease and wasted away. When the body of the seventh Navajo, the son, disappeared before the autopsy, officials and locals assumed relatives who did not want the corpse tampered with stole it. However, Chee understands that Navajo attitudes toward death would keep them far from a body, especially that of a bewitched relative whose *chindi* might injure them. On the other hand, a witch might snatch a body for corpse dust. When Chee discovers that the wealthy entrepreneur who hired him founded the Mole society, had its secret black mole amulets carved for each member, and benefited personally from sending men burrowing underground to remove riches (a reversal of the Navajo creation story of the first people emerging from a hole in the earth's crust), he acts against the entrepreneur as a healer would against a

Navajo wolf (one out of harmony). The man has violated the natural laws by destroying his past in fire and recreating himself with a new identity. Chee thinks of an owl stalking a rabbit and recites the Stalking Way before facing his would-be assassin. He sends the purveyors of witchcraft (in this case, a bank check and a hired assassin) back against the witch, just as traditionally he would invoke an Enemy Way, a traditional formula to reverse the witchcraft. The ceremony always requires using something that the witch used, perhaps a piece of human bone that carries the witch's power against others, or some personal item. Chee takes satisfaction from acting as Changing Woman taught his people. His strategy is effective; the villain/witch dies, as does the assassin. Peace and order return, and beauty and the spirit are renewed (a respected shaman conducts a ceremonial Enemy Way: eight days of songs, poetry, and sandpaintings among relatives and friends).

Chee's special knowledge enables him to deal effectively with reservation crime and to know which questions to seek answers to. In *The Ghostway*, the crime scene of a gunshot victim (a criminal) leaves Chee uncomfortable. He knows how a Navajo body should be laid out in death and is puzzled that the ritual way is only partially followed. The hair left unwashed and other signs suggest a limited knowledge of Navajo customs. Furthermore, the abandoned hogan disturbs his concept of harmony. Its west wall has been stoved in to let the *chindi* escape, and its smoke hole has been stopped up, both traditional acts, but Chee asks why a traditionalist would allow someone to die slowly in his hogan instead of carrying him into the pure open air ("as the Dinee had done for a hundred generations"). A death inside would require the home owner to abandon that valued home forever, and this beautifully situated hogan has been well cared for over a long period of time. Further investigation shows too that the owner failed to remove sacred items built into the structure in traditional ways. Such details are meaningless for outside investigators and non-traditionalists, but to Chee, they suggest that the surface appearance intentionally misleads. This knowledge guides Chee to the missing owner, who had been murdered and disposed of before the stage was set to mislead the police.

In order to get the knowledge he needs as a detective, Chee must overcome his personal fear of *chindi*. He reasons that the death occurred outside of the hogan, so *chindi* are absent, yet he feels contaminated: "From this talus slope in this dying light, in the dead stillness of this autumn evening, the rationality of the university [where he was educated] was canceled" (*The Ghostway*, 56). To Chee, stepping into the contaminated hogan is an unnatural act, out of harmony with his inner Navajo sense of rightness. As a *hataalii* advisor, he recommends that the murder victim's granddaughter undergo a healing ceremony, because she too has entered the possibly contaminated hogan; ultimately, he participates in a healing ceremony for himself—just in case. However, he decides that the real sickness comes from stepping out of being a Navajo into being a white man—a sickness that runs rampant in Los Angeles.

This internal conflict between reason and spirituality is inescapable, even in minor matters. The pride that Chee feels in Navajos successfully improving their irrigation and farming methods (instituting large swirl patterns for efficient water distribution) is balanced by his distress at uprooted desert plants and changed landscapes (*Sacred Clowns*), just as his understanding that Anglos dropping the cremated ashes of relatives from a Navajo sacred mountain are seeking harmony with nature does not stop him from horror and repugnance at the ghost sickness that such corpse dust spreads through the community (*The Fallen Man*). Chee hates skinwalkers, because they cynically use Navajo religion against believers, exploiting Navajo credence in supernatural explanations of illness, bad luck, and a host of other worries. In *Skinwalkers*, Chee must prove to a desperate mother that he doesn't meet the characteristics of a witch, while the man who has sent her against him does; if he fails, he will die.

Unlike Thurlo's characters, Chee doubts that witches can change shapes and fly; for him, witchcraft is not a supernatural force but a malicious choice of imbalance, conflict, and ugliness over the Navajo Way of peace, beauty, and community (*Skinwalkers*, 73). He sees it in the activities he combats as a tribal policeman: witches are those who sell whiskey to children, who waste family funds on personal pleasures instead of feeding hungry relatives, who get drunk and knife friends, and who beat wives and abandon children. Chee thus understands this traditional belief as a symbolic counter for social disarray. He also combines an educated man's belief in "penicillin," "insulin," and "heart bypass surgery" with a parallel Navajo belief "that something far beyond the understanding of modern medicine controlled life and death" (*Skinwalkers*, 139).

Consequently, through Chee, Hillerman makes the Navajo spiritual world accessible to modern readers, while stressing its perceptions, values, and rules for personal, social, and environmental interaction as meaningfully different from our own in sometimes unbridgeable ways. Hillerman so effectively captures a Navajo world vision that he has not only earned the Center for the American Indian's Ambassador Award and the Navajo Tribe's Special Friend Award, but he has also been paid the highest compliment: Navajo readers mistakenly assuming that he is Navajo.

SHERLOCKS

The two most credible ratiocinative Southwestern native detectives are Tony Hillerman's Joe Leaphorn and Brian Garfield's Sam Watchman, both Navajos. This tribal affiliation makes sense, because of all the Southwestern tribes, the Navajo are the least "spiritual" in the mainstream sense of the word. They traditionally have had no belief in a god or gods (though contact with Christianity has changed oral wisdom). Instead, Navajos live according to an ethic which values harmony above all else. Though a distinct, unassimilated group with their own living language and culture, the 200,000 or so Navajos have nevertheless demonstrated a creative ability to accommodate mainstream demands and ways without losing their own, just as Chee attempts to live in accord with the ways of harmony. Rooted in the land, they are renowned for reading nature and sign. During World War II, Navajo code talkers adapted Navajo ways to urgent American needs, using their language as a code uncrackable by the Japanese, and the Navajo trackers who have helped the FBI hunt fleeing felons are equally invaluable. Garfield's two novels and Hillerman's *Hunting Badger* demonstrate how these tracking skills reflect the logic, experience, and tenacity of the trackers. Their inferences and conclusions, like those of Sherlock Holmes', are grounded in a thorough understanding of their environment and human psychology, at times bridging the ratiocinative and the intuitive in their pursuit of criminals.

Unlike Leaphorn and Watchman, Richard Parrish's Chuy Leyva, a Papago, is not a central detective figure, but his importance increases with each volume in the series. He is a down-to-earth, practical, hardworking tribal police officer, whose legwork enables the Anglo BIA lawyer whom he assists to force the law to protect the rights of the tribe and its members. David Cole's series investigator Laura Winslow was once and becomes again Kauwanyauma, Butterfly Revealing Wings of Beauty, a disenchanted, disaffected Hopi beauty who has spent much of her life off of the reservation but who returns to Arizona Hopi country as a bounty hunter and general investigator specializing in extracting computer information. Her preferred methods are high-tech, but personal connections to the injured and deceased necessitate more direct investigative procedures.

Joe Leaphorn: Navajo Logician

In contrast to Chee, Leaphorn is a rationalist and a skeptic. A graduate of the University of Arizona, he is a lieutenant in the Navajo Tribal Police and moves up in rank with time. Chee calls him "our supercop" and describes him as "old as the hills," "knows everybody," "remembers everything," "forgets nothing," and "handles the tough investigations wherever they are" (*Coyote Waits*, 103). Leaphorn is a Navajo in his appreciation of the land and commitment to the reservation, but his professional training (including a master's degree in cultural anthropology), his strong powers of observation, and his skepticism about witchcraft, skinwalkers, and evil spirits distance him from the problems of reservation and tribal life and the difficulties that traditionalists face with assimilation. He dismisses Navajo witchcraft as a hangover from tribal captivity that keeps Navajos from dealing realistically with everyday problems, and he is uncomfortable even discussing witches, not because of characteristic Navajo silence on the subject but because of personal dislike of such beliefs (*Skinwalkers*, 72). He may be Navajo enough to be nervous around his dead wife's unmarried sister because of traditionalist expectations that he marry her, but he is sufficiently distanced to not take this obligation seriously. He is direct and to the point, as Navajos usually are not.

The title that two separate acquaintances bestow on him in *Coyote Waits*, "the Sherlock Holmes of the Navajo Tribal Police" (46, 162), accurately describes Leaphorn. He has the mind of a policeman: he does not believe in coincidences. To him, a good detective seeks patterns and motives that make meaningful the seemingly random. His disbelief in coincidence is a vital part of both his investigative power and his Navajo experience. Leaphorn expects random coincidences seen from a new perspective to fall into place, like the pieces of a puzzle or kaleidoscope: turned the right way, they suddenly make sense, revealing motive and modus operandi (like the meaningless rock painting that, seen from a certain young lady's distant home, clearly says "I love Jen") (161). Leaphorn excels at finding patterns, solving the mystery in *The Fallen Man* purely by ratiocination from his home at Window Rock. Initially irritated at Chee for allowing his trailer home to be shot up (with Chee inside), he gradually pulls together disparate threads—a skeleton on Shiprock Mountain, the sniper-murder of a canyon guide at Canyon de Chelly. As he fills in the details with information from a variety of sources, he uncovers a causal pattern that Chee's groundwork confirms. Leaphorn maps out his cases on his double-sized print of the Automobile Club of Southern California map of "Indian Country," using coded pins: red for incidents of witchcraft, yellow for problems "with no priority beyond their inherent oddity," and so on (*Coyote Waits*, 88). A yellow pin amid a cluster of red suggests relationships between cases that Leaphorn will explore. In *Skinwalkers*, an epiphany occurs when all of the pins on Leaphorn's map cluster together and confirm that four or more homicides are really a single crime with a single motive (260). Even in retirement, with a good map and an assistant to feed him details, however seemingly irrelevant, Leaphorn, like Sherlock Holmes, can see connections where others find none. Just as Holmes discovered meaning in a dog that did not bark, so in *Hunting Badger* Leaphorn sees a radio that wouldn't play as the linchpin in a developing theory that time proves true.

Leaphorn's view of crime is informed and practical. He distinguishes between the types of crimes that whites and Navajos would commit, calling in the FBI or state police if the m.o. suggests an outside rather than a homegrown criminal. As the policeman of a small, gossipy community, he has learned the value of information exchange, sharing gossip and details to encourage civilians to share private knowledge too. This Navajo way of gathering information unobtainable otherwise is also good local law enforcement. As a Navajo, he lives the slower pace of reservation life and can distance himself from the crime and the immediate demands of his job in a balanced, insightful way. Informed about the differences between Hopi, Navajo, Zuñi, and Apache modes of operating and thinking, he can evaluate them objectively while intuiting unspoken concerns. The time element figures importantly in Leaphorn's cases—who did what, when, and how. When need be, Leaphorn scouts the crime scene or tests a theory about criminal activities. He might spend several hours observing tracks to add one fact to an evidence chain that will blossom into a confident understanding of act and motive. In sum, Leaphorn is a highly competent, dedicated policeman, a cutting-edge investigator and professional skeptic, dependent on deductive reasoning and cause-effect explanations of behavior and events but acting within a slower-paced community than the urban mainstream.

Leaphorn, like Chee, is Hillerman's foil for cross-cultural analysis, but Leaphorn's difference is limited. He pays for a sandpainting ceremony to pacify relatives but does not expect healing results. Yet, as a Navajo, he appreciates power and meaning beyond surface realities. On the one hand, he values the technical ingenuity that produced a dancer's carved wood-and-leather mask and the dancer's art, clacking in perfect time to the drum to create the illusion of a great bird with snapping beak and hooting cries. On the other hand, for an instant he also envisions the Zuñi spirit behind the mask, Shalako, the courier between gods and men, bringing fertility to seeds and rain to the desert when the Pueblo people call on, feed, and bless him: "Now it danced, swooping down the earthen floor, its great horns glittering with reflected light, its fan of topknot feathers bristling, its voice the hooting call of the night birds" (*Dance Hall of the Dead*, 147). This dual outlook provides glimpses of Navajo (and Zuñi) visions of reality, while remaining true to the perspective of a modern professional: skeptical, aware, and closely observant of events and human nature. His new girlfriend, Professor Bourebonnette, remarks in *Hunting Badger*, "Nothing changes. A century later and you have the same problem in the same canyons" (145). Leaphorn agrees to some extent as he examines his people's past and their knowledge of the land to better understand modern crime. Despite modern weaponry and high-tech aids, a Vietnam-veteran Ute who robs a Navajo casino is simply acting out Ute-Navajo warrior conflicts from a century earlier. The Navajos who pursue him act in the pathfinder tradition of detective fiction, with tracking skills central to detection.

Highway Patrolman Sam Watchman

Brian Garfield's Navajo police officer, Sam Watchman (Tsosie Duggai), was a precursor of Leaphorn, with the first Watchman novel coming out shortly before Tony Hillerman's first Leaphorn novel. Garfield based his hero on a fellow University of Arizona pre-law student, who planned to repay his many family members for financing his schooling by police work.

His bright, attractive, real-life model "could keep a room full of grad students in stitches with his droll digs at anthropologists of the 'Lo, the Poor Indian school,' " says Garfield. By making Watchman a highly competent Navajo Arizona highway patrolman, Garfield hoped to provide his hero with "a larger—less restrictive—landscape than a single locality would have provided" and to explore long-standing Apache-Navajo intertribal sensitivities and mutual skepticism.

Watchman mistrusts coincidence and, like the early Leaphorn, is a pathfinder: his finely honed tracking skills and logic based on a knowledge of the land enable him to read volumes in details that FBI men cannot comprehend as evidence. Garfield is interested in Watchman as a competent professional on home territory, set against those with more authority but less expertise and an inadequate knowledge of the Southwestern desert and high country. At age 33, Watchman, whose features are as "bone-craggy as those of a Frederic Remington warrior," has been a cop one-third of his life, with three commendations, two citations for bravery, and five written reprimands (*Relentless*, 17, 41). Self-described as "easy going," he has a comfortable give-and-take with his Anglo rookie partner: though good humored about Indian stereotypes, he is competitive and hard-nosed when his skills are questioned and his ethnicity disdained. The following exchange with his partner is typical:

"You guys never had any writing at all, did you."
"Didn't need it. That old chief said words that are true sink deep in a man's heart and stay there."
"How's anybody know what this old chief said if nobody wrote it down?"
"There was some anthropologist. He had a tape recorder. You ever see an anthropologist without a tape recorder?" (*The Threepersons Hunt*, 42)

His is the only Arizona police car in 15,000 square miles, so he cooperates with Utah and Nevada police officers who share his respect for the realities of place and season.

In *Relentless*, Watchman is always one step ahead of the bumbling FBI agent supposedly in charge of pursuing five bank robbers after a million-dollar heist. Out of his depth and quick to leap to erroneous conclusions, he believes technology infallible, even when the Southwest defies such confidence. Watchman immediately recognizes the military nature of their suspects' operation (led by an ex-Green Beret officer and his right-hand man), discovers their means of flight, and anticipates not only the possibility of sudden storms but the escapees' response if their plane crashes in high mountain country (as it does). He already has insider information, since he and his partner stopped one robber for speeding before the crime occurred. Moreover, by acting on his territory and gratuitously killing a fellow Navajo policeman, the criminals, commando specialists in evasion and killing, have provided him a personal motive for pursuit; they meet their match in Watchman.

The FBI man expects to simply march into back country without the necessary supplies that Watchman enumerates: a jeep, food, heavy clothing, rifles with infrared snooperscopes, walkie-talkies, mud boots, and so on. But knowing how to prepare for high country pursuit is only one of Watchman's many advantages. Garfield notes, "From boyhood his eyes had been trained to read signs left in the earth's surface. You learned these things quickly when you grew up hunting strayed sheep across the broken badlands of the Window Rock country" (30). Where others see a jumble of intertwining ruts, Watchman reads the comings and goings of several vehicles. Computerized organization and modern technology might work well for sealing off superhighway networks in urban areas, but Watchman doubts their efficacy when a blizzard blows into the high country. This is his home ground and his jurisdiction, and when the FBI agent plays it safe, Watchman takes the chances necessary to do his job, setting or spotting ambushes equally well, and anticipating double and triple blinds. In a fast-paced, exciting mountainside chase sequence, Garfield demonstrates the ingrained survivalist skills that drive Watchman, skills quite different from the tourist sporting feats in which the FBI man takes pride. Simultaneously, he dramatizes with depth and insight culture clashes amid a hostile environment (a full-blown blizzard).

Equally exciting, *The Threepersons Hunt* is a gripping story of the tenacious pursuit of an escaped prisoner—Apache Joe Threepersons. Watchman, as a token Indian, must not only track down a Southwesterner with a knowledge of the land equal to his own, but he must also deal with the interference Apaches create to hinder a Navajo investigator, including the occasional sniper. He explains to his Anglo captain: ". . . [R]ight now we've got Hopis and Navajos murdering each other over the rights to a few useless acres of land, and the Apaches are laughing themselves silly every time somebody gets killed there. A Navajo going onto the Apache land, that's more of a foreigner than a white man" (30). It is flash flood time in the 2 million-acre territory to be searched (half of the Apache reservation), and the Apache policeman assigned to help Watchman sympathizes with the escapee and laughs as Watchman consults a topographical map of craggy mountains, badlands, and forests: "Man if you need a map of this country, you ain't never going to find him" (11).

Garfield captures the complexities of white-Indian relationships and Navajo-Apache animosities and the motives that would make an innocent man accept blame for murder. Watchman's great-grandfather had ridden with General Crook, tracking down Geronimo, because fighting shoulder to shoulder with white soldiers was the only way to battle a traditional enemy. Now Watchman deals with growing evidence that the Apache he pursues is no killer and that his job is not just to return a prisoner but to discover what really happened five years earlier. He sees through the witch talk about the escapee's sister and recognizes a supposed road accident as murder (hacksawed tie rods). Ultimately, it is as much his tracking and cross-country running and riding skills as his reasoning out who did what and why that close his case.

Chuy Leyva: No Stereotypical Tonto

Richard Parrish, like Hillerman, humanizes Native Americans and makes their collective and personal experience as victims, suspects, and detectives accessible to mainstream readers. However, unlike Hillerman, Parrish sets his novels in and near post–World War II Tucson, Arizona, in order to provide a fitting time frame for novels concerned with battles for human rights and constitutional justice. Furthermore, he makes his central detective a world-weary Bureau of Indian Affairs lawyer, Joshua Rabb, an outsider to his community, the Southwest, and the Papago reservation, because of his New York Jewish origins. Having experienced firsthand the horrors of the Nazi concentration camps and the racism of German fanatics, Rabb finds common cause with the residents of the San Xavier del Bac Papago Indian Reservation and, as the series progresses, echoes the famous speeches of Arizona defenders of democratic principles such as Justice Levi Udall (Udall's 1948 ruling brought the Papago voting rights and equal citizenship denied even after World War II service). The Rabb novels include legal procedure but are not legal procedure novels per se, because the people take precedence over the law and its implementation.

Hillerman made Native Americans equal actors on the fictional stage of the detective story, their friendships, setbacks, and successes a matter of personal interest for readers. Parrish follows Hillerman's footsteps: his Papago characters achieve a wholeness missing in most popular fiction, and their suffering teaches that no decent human being can allow the abuse of the defenseless (whether Jews, blacks, or Papago Indians) without being diminished and tainted.

Furthermore, Parrish paints vivid portraits of Papago tribal police, like Police Chief Jesus "Chuy" Leyva, whose father is on the Papago tribal council. Ex-Marine Leyva is a decorated war hero of unquestioned courage, his warrior skills proven on the battlefield—two silver stars won at Iwo Jima and Guadalcanal. He is tall and well built, with bulging biceps and forearms like a weightlifter, obsidian eyes, and shaggy black hair held back with a twisted red muslin headband. He wears cowboy boots and, low on his right hip, a brown leather "gunslinger" holster with a Colt Single Action Army .45. Leyva, who understands that his real role is to protect his people from the injustices of a white-dominated court system and society, interprets his police duties flexibly; increasingly as the series develops, he serves as a competent, practical, good-humored, earthy official investigator whose sharp observation of crime scenes and knowledge of local people and politics enable Rabb's legal battles.

Especially after villains use locoweed to kill Rabb's employer's son, Chuy willingly resorts to whatever works to protect the innocent from the outrages of the blindly racist and politically corrupt. When needed, he camps out in Rabb's home to protect his family from local thugs, and he disguises himself as an impoverished Indian to investigate across the border. As the series progresses, Chuy the sidekick becomes a more significant investigator in his own right, not only doing the legwork (serving warrants, transporting bodies, and doing surveillance) but also providing a sharp, reliable interpretation of people and actions. He knows all the gossip. He stands tough against bullies who would discredit his office, and he faces snipers, a jailhouse beating by rednecks with badges, and threats of death with courage. When ordered to help the FBI arrest a fellow Papago with two university degrees in anthropology and a prestigious museum job because he broke the nose of an abusive official who denied his right to vote, Chuy takes time to eat with the family and makes the FBI treat the prisoner with respect.

In *Nothing but the Truth*, he helps Rabb link mob murders of Hasidic Jews with the Papago man who Rabb defends; in *Wind and Lies*, he opposes Mormon extremists who prey on Papago women and confiscate reservation land, using free food, entertainment, and a philosophy that appeals to Papago males (polygamy/male supremacy). Chuy has a double task: to protect his fiancée, Magdalena, from rape and murder and to win Arizona Indians the right to vote, serving as Rabb's test case against Arizona's "guardianship" laws. Rabb cites the real-life case of Pima Indian and Arizonan Ira Hayes, a Marine who helped raise the American flag on Mount Surabaci, a symbol of all brave fighting men, yet who was denied voting rights; Rabb asks about the arrogance and injustice that denies Hayes his full citizenship while demanding from him "the possible sacrifice of his life so that *it* can continue to vote?" (288). Rabb's righteous and compelling rhetoric and Chuy's personal strength of character make this series a winner.

Parrish could have chosen to make so representative and worthy a Papago a man of spirit power respected for his "medicine," but instead Chuy is a man apart. He recognizes *I'itoi* as the sacred protector and the totem animals coyote and buzzard as equally important with man, because he sees the power of the old religion in "the rain and the wind and lightning . . . in this great desert that the Papagos had inhabited for countless generations"; however, neither Christianity nor Coyote spirit power control his life or mind (*Wind and Lies*, 75). Instead, it is the survival and betterment of his people—his social conscience—that is the driving force of his life. Parish rejects popular "shamanistic" alienation—attitudes and perceptions different from the mainstream's—for a common humanity. His Papago are too poor to afford a change of clothing; they depend on Bureau of Indian Affairs aid or charity, and they suffer from all the diseases that accompany poverty and malnutrition. Their regular diet is *nopalitos* (cactus fruit) and cornbread. Vigilantes and law enforcement officers find them easy scapegoats and even the best can be undermined by the complexities of the court system. In *The Divided Line*, vigilantes kill and mutilate a Papago male who is physically incapable of the rape of which he is accused, despite a court recognition of this incapacity in a verdict of innocence; the case is not mistaken identity but willful racism. In his job, on a regular basis, Chuy must look into the hearts of those around him and see darkness, violence, ignorance, and brutality. His love for Magdalena Antone, the granddaughter of the former chief and the Rabb family "acculturation girl" (a cross between a live-in maid and a participant in an acculturation program designed to teach natives their place in the white world), helps readers see him as a whole person. Together, Magdalena and Chuy help the Rabbs break through cultural stereotypes to see the Papago as fellow human beings, and the readers break through their mythology of what Indians "should be" as opposed to what they in fact are.

Computer Hacker Laura Winslow/Kauwanyauma

New Yorker David Cole, co-founder of NativeWeb, an Internet corporation for Native Americans and other indigenous peoples, has created a troubled amateur detective, neither a traditional detective nor a traditional Hopi; on the outlaw fringe of mainstream life (jailed seven times from Yakima to Sonora), she has been running away from herself and her mixed identity for much of her life. Taught traditional ways by her Hopi grandparents and relatives (the four worlds, the different clans, the kachinas, and the dances), Kauwanyauma (alias Laura Winslow) rejected her heritage in youthful rebellion against conservative relatives and an elusive father, a rodeo star who followed the circuit and was an unfaithful husband. She ran away with another rebel, Johnnie Begay, and traveled the trail of the American Indian Movement (AIM) and activist Native American protests, loading weapons at Pine Ridge while battling the FBI. This explosive violence tainted her relationship with Begay, but it was the ill will which erupted between the Navajos and Hopis when the federal government designated Navajo land for Hopi use that spilled over into her private life and finally destroyed her relationship with her lover. When he vanished with their daughter, her life became a series of aliases to avoid FBI detection, escape her Native American identity, and immerse herself in computer data, hoping someday to discover information to reunite her with a daughter whose teenage years she had missed. Along the way, she burned off the butterfly tattoo that had symbolically connected her to her heritage and her tribal name.

The name Laura Winslow is only one of numerous false identities she assumed and discarded, but she is at a personal crux, abusing the drug Ritalin to target her mind and moving from one self-destructive relationship to another. She has become an expert electronic tracker of people who want to stay lost. The bounty hunter for whom she gathers data has walked out on their partnership, pursued by a vicious horse mutilator. At that stage of her life, the action of *Butterfly Lost* begins, and a search for missing gods and missing girls becomes a search for personal identity after 20 years of running. Her new Navajo boyfriend and partner, Kimo Biakeddy, asks, "How do you sling off what you were?" (101), and when she dismisses her Hopi butterfly-girl self as another lifetime, he concludes, "There are no other lives. . . . Just this one" (159).

Hopi elder Patrick Valasnuyouoma has had a frightening recurring vision: a giant kachina guides him beyond the ancient stone villages on the three Hopi mesas to a high desert plain where Hopi butterfly maidens, their hair done up in the traditional butterfly whorls called squash blossoms, their faces powdered with sacred cornmeal, are violated and ridden like animals by sharp beaked creatures of darkness; he recognizes the maidens and sees Kauwanyauma also present in his vision, squeezing to death the two hearts of a witch. However, by the time a blind, elderly Hopi persuades Winslow to search for his missing granddaughter and to see the elder at Oraibi about his vision, both the visionary and his great-grandson have been cruelly murdered on their home territory, and Hopis are armed and fearful of witches, their sacred root gods missing. With the village shut to outsiders, Winslow sees in the young radicals who guard the entrances with rifles the angry self of her youth. She no longer believes in the ancient gods, witches, or dream visions, but she understands murder and violence, recognizes the need to find the missing Hopi girls (the granddaughter is one of many) and missing artifacts, and accepts the case. To her angry assertion that she doesn't believe in Hopi witches or Navajo skinwalkers, a Hopi police officer observes that his police training conditions him to disbelief too, "but people believe in them" and "there's no sense going against that belief" (107).

Ironically, investigating the lives of the missing teenagers is like reliving the hormonal surges, rebellion, and search for change and mainstream materialism that characterized her own teenage years:

Bahana [white] culture was constantly . . . bombarding young reservation women and eroding clan and tribal distinctions. MTV, movies, videos, dances, drugs, magazines like *Cosmopolitan* and *Glamour* passed from girl to girl, crinkled and dog-eared articles about Madonna, the dead Diana, Janet Jackson, a hundred other young women glowing with the tides of fashions, jewelry, sex, money. *You Too Can Have Multiple Orgasms!* All these influences urging them toward Flagstaff, Las Vegas, Phoenix, LA. Anywhere Outta the Rez.

I ran away when I was fifteen. (*Butterfly Lost*, 14)

It also means remembering the traditional manners she had long forsaken, such as avoiding direct questions and dealing with the incredibly circular conversations Hopis engage in with those outside families or clans, "responses withheld while they explore the entrails of the stranger's words for signs and possibilities" (12). A visit to a Hopi village reminds her of the timelessness of the pueblos, as she observes, for example, "the smooth spots worn on the latch side [of a low doorway], just at that place where for hundreds of years somebody's hand had reached for steadiness to open the door" (36) and as she talks to people who think the past is the present. The plea of the village elders touches her heart: "If we do not care for our children, no matter how wild and unbelieving they may be, if we do not care, our whole way of life will die out as surely as corn without water" (39). She is stunned that they consider her one of their own "wild and unbelieving" youths and can recite her family ties. "How could I forget?" says one elder: "You think that with another name you can deny who you are. But you can't run from your blood" (41). Thus, Cole makes her discovery of evidence and responsibility a journey of self-discovery as well.

Winslow warns the tribal leadership, "I can't guarantee anything. . . . I only look for information. I do not work like a detective in some TV show. I'm not licensed to do anything like that, nor do I want to. I will *try* to find information" (18–19). And initially this is true. Her investigation begins with computer searches related to buying and selling artifacts, but to find which girls are missing she must confront the silence of Hopi families united against outsiders and the pain of youngsters who have been injured and escaped alive, like Mary Nataanie, who was raped but who feels guilty for having fled when the rapists turned their attention to her friend, Judy Pavatea, the granddaughter of Winslow's client. Her investigation ties in with the rodeo circuit, raises old memories of her father and her lover, and connects a series of horse killings and mutilations to the missing Hopi girls, who begin showing up similarly gutted and mutilated. By then, Winslow knows that she is trailing a serial killer, a white bull rider with delusions of stealing Indian power.

Her investigation becomes less and less the passive acquisition of data off of the Net and more and more the active search of a driven avenger, in the mainstream tradition of the detective as the protector of the innocent and of the community at large. In pursuing answers, she antagonizes a Navajo tribal police officer, who is most unlike Hillerman's Leaphorn or Chee in his violence, racial hatred, and cruelty: he nails a live, angry rattlesnake to her doorstep and threatens her with obscene phone calls. She interviews witnesses, sets traps to catch traffickers in stolen artifacts, photographs rodeo suspects to enable Mary to identify her assailants, and employs confrontational methods to both recover the Hopi gods and identify and punish the rapists and the serial murderer. Only when she has used her computer as a weapon in a just cause and fulfilled her responsibility to all the dead and mutilated butterfly maidens can she find some peace. However, she finds this peace not in returning to the traditionalist Hopi mesas, nor in reentering the mainstream urban world, but in finding her own niche in an Arizona small town (Tuba City). There she rediscovers old friends, makes unexpected new friends, and does what she does best (computer investigations)—not under a string of aliases, but with the identity she has denied for too long, that of Kauwanyauma, Butterfly Revealing Wings of Beauty. The next books in the series follow her career as she grows to fit this identity and setting.

Kirk Mitchell's Emmett Quanah Parker and Anna Turnipseed

Drawing on his real-life Southern California police service as a SWAT sergeant and on his assignment to the joint patrol force of Paiute, Shoshone, and Comanche deputies serving the Indian reservations of Inyo County, Kirk Mitchell has created a convincing native law enforcement team consisting of Comanche Emmett Quanah Parker and three-quarters Modoc Anna Turnipseed. Parker is an experienced investigator with years in Oklahoma City P.D. Homicide and in his present position as a Bureau of Indian Affairs (BIA) Criminal Investigator. He has a history of defying authority when need be and of contempt for unwarranted or unnecessarily violent FBI interference in tribal and BIA matters. When undercover investigating members of a radical Sioux faction of AIM, who robbed banks to finance their terrorist activities, assassinated rivals for tribal office, and planned hits on state officials, Parker participated in a Sun Dance alongside some of those he was investigating and stopped the FBI from turning a religious sacrament into a blood bath, keeping them at bay until he could separate the men to be arrested from innocent dancers. Turnipseed, in contrast, is a neophyte G-man, an FBI rookie fresh out of Quantico, innocent, foolhardy, and eager to prove worthy of greater trust.

Both are outsiders in their chosen professions, forced to deal with teasing about their "savage" Indian natures and, even worse, with the easy belief that all Indians are motivated by "mindless superstition" (*Cry Dance*, 108) and share a "conspiratorial affection for one another, centuries of intertribal war notwithstanding" (38). Parker is a reformed alcoholic who still battles the strong tug of liquor; as a child, Turnipseed was sexually abused by her alcoholic father and has still not come to terms with nightmares of incest. Parker, having lost one partner to violence, feels protective of her, though she resents what she interprets as his distrust of her competence. She knows that she is the token Indian on any FBI team but feels ready and competent and asserts her claim to full equality with Parker, despite growing proof to the contrary. Like his illustrious namesake, Parker appreciates women, but unlike the Quanah Parker of legend, he keeps ending up in divorce court. However, from the very beginning, despite his constant irritation with her, he feels that Turnipseed could be the real love of his life. Yet organizational demands send him investigating in one direction and her in another, thrust into potentially life-threatening circumstances with only an hour or so crash course in undercover strategies.

Cry Dance is a fast-paced, exciting story of a psychotic serial killer who slices off the faces of his victims, as if to count coup and separate their souls from their identity. As Mitchell's investigative team examines the crime scene for clues, seeks motivations, and unravels the connections between Indian casinos, BIA land exchanges, and Rastafarian mobsters, Parker's apprehension mounts, and he struggles to fully explain his intuitive sense that they are being set up:

Long ago, a Lakota friend, a pilot—a brother, even, before the law separated them forever—had flown him over the rolling hills at Little Bighorn, telling how Crazy Horse had drawn Custer on with just forty warriors, lured him on with the promise of sudden opportunity until there was no going back. It seemed like that now. A setup based on a quick and easy solution to Stephanie Roper's murder. A Comanche of the last century would have called this inner buzz a vision. A veteran cop might justify it as a hunch. Emmett felt stranded in between. (47)

His instincts prove true. A trap has been laid, and the only questions are when it will be sprung, by whom, and to what ends. Yet, like the members of the elite Comanche warrior society of the nineteenth century, who staked themselves to the ground before giving battle, he feels that he has staked himself to this investigation and cannot turn his back on it without loss of honor.

Mitchell repeatedly captures the ways in which Parker's and Turnipseed's jobs leave them "stranded in between," as they are sent into ill-defined situations demanding innovation, courage, and quick wits and must mislead the Native Americans whose trust it is their job to win. Yet, they find ways to do what they feel they should do. For example, the old Chemehuevi woman exploited by gambling interests to justify a new casino is the last of her tribe and has no one to dance the sacred chants to see her soul across the chasm after death (by Chemehuevi belief, Parker can never cross over because he lacks the necessary pierced ears). Parker visits her often to learn the Chemehuevi chants and dances so he can see her soul into the far land in the traditional Chemehuevi way. Parker's and Turnipseed's unique perspective qualifies them to see among Native Americans what other BIA and FBI officials would miss: the social indicators of something out of place, unspoken, or covered up, the significance of family ties that demand unexpected loyalties, and the modern applications of the lessons of history. Where the Spanish explorers had dismissed the Kaibab as shy and cowardly, Parker sees them with a Comanche's vision: a people whose "marginal existence in a hard land, living on lizards and roots much of the year, had ingrained caution in them" (130). This knowledge makes him scruti-nize a Kaibab casino manager other agents would dismiss as unrelated to the case, especially when he learns the man is undergoing a Soul Loss cer-emony.

Scattered throughout Mitchell's novel is esoteric information about tribal beliefs, for example, the Modoc confidence in the immortality of snakes because they shed their skins yearly and the Southern Paiute vision of the world as a round ball suspended on a cord from another earth above it. Mitchell sets Parker's conviction that gambling simply turns reservations into "criminal enclaves" (82) against the view of a Lakota Sioux, who calls it a means to self-reliance—employment for the unemployed and funding for health clinics, tribal courts, and tribal officers. Parker sees Indian pros-perity repeatedly built on "a rug that could be pulled out from under the tribes at any time the courts decided sovereignty was just a romantic myth," as they did in 1890, when the Allotment Act stripped the Comanches of the rich grasslands they had leased profitably to Texas cattlemen and gave it instead to white settlers (81). For him, the great lesson for the Comanches was to avoid being a "one-industry people," since the last time they were they ended up "squatting on piles of buffalo bones, eating stale army ra-tions" (82).

Spirit Sickness, set on the Navajo reservation in New Mexico, is a page-turner, a Thomas Harris-style thriller in which Parker and Turnipseed must face Navajo teenage gangs, drug trafficking, intertribal and bureaucratic conflicts, and another serial killer. During the course of their investigation, Turnipseed has several near-death experiences, and Parker tracks a mad-man across rugged reservation terrain. The case begins with a burned-out police car containing the bodies of Navajo tribal policeman Hank Knoki and his wife, and it soon pits Parker and Turnipseed against a psychotic killer who believes he is the Gila Monster of Navajo myth. Turnipseed, still traumatized from the physical and psychic injuries she endured in *Cry Dance*, is even more disturbed when their rational investigatory techniques seem to fail them. Ratiocinative training confronts bedrock Native Amer-ican spirituality, mythology, and superstition. While interviewing suspects and weeding out lies and misdirection, in order to anticipate the killer's acts and prevent a final bloodbath, the two investigators must draw on the native heritages they thought they had left behind and must think like their ancestors, for whom dreams were reality and who employed ritual means of overcoming evil ones and their terrifying dream realities.

Cry Dance and *Spirit Sickness* extend the tradition of the native tracker/investigator, providing new perspectives on assimilation and tradition, the cultural foundations of insanity and crime, and the modern Native Amer-ican as a product of distant history and recent globalization.

CONCLUSION

For some writers, the Southwest is what it too often was in the old cowboy-and-Indian shoot-'em-ups, the adventure stories cranked out from the 1930s through the 1950s, only with Indian protagonists. The landscape provides a dramatic stage on which to play out perfectly conventional tales unrelated to the indigenous cultures. Linking the environment to the life-ways of the indigenous inhabitants and understanding its shaping forces on them over centuries and millennia requires a leap of the imagination. It has been far easier to show the sufferings and triumphs of European settlers traversing the alien desert and mountain passes on wagon trains and stage-coaches, bringing an alien European culture with them. Virtually no twentieth-century film set in the Southwest meets the criteria delineated above, that is, of showing how environmental realities dictated the lives of native peoples.

Popular fiction has been more successful than film at this portrayal, thanks mainly to the accomplishments of Tony Hillerman in virtually inventing a new genre, the modern Southwestern detective story. While works such as Oliver LaFarge's *Laughing Boy* had successfully linked the people, culture, and landscape of the Southwest, Hillerman's insight was to create native detectives who belonged in the social and physical setting and to show the world through their eyes. The detective/crime novel, more than any other popular genre, explores social problems and assumptions about the basic human issues of justice, fairness, and assimilation into mainstream culture. Only Garfield recognized this potential as early as Hillerman, but wrote only two Watchman novels, while Hillerman kept writing, developing the traditional, spiritual Chee to counter the skeptical, rational Leaphorn. With these two characters, Hillerman could probe the inner lives of Native American characters, the psychology, intuition, and logic that defines a way of seeing. Garfield contrasts his approach with Hillerman's: "Tony's steeped in the tribal folklore and history—he's firmly grounded, where I mostly tended to pick my way through fairly limited areas where I felt I had some understanding." This firm grounding in history and tribal folklore, culture, and way of life makes Hillerman's fiction truly reflect the close ties between the land and its inhabitants, so much so that, as noted above, he has been celebrated by Navajos and sometimes even mistaken as a tribe member.

The enormity of Hillerman's achievement can be appreciated in the struggles of his followers and imitators. Garfield, neither follower nor imitator, confesses he moved happily on to other projects, leaving the Native American detective to Hillerman's superior knowledge of the people and place. (He also notes the difficulty of sustaining a series without repetition, praising Hillerman's deep knowledge and imagination.) Parrish, though capturing his Papago subjects with sensitivity and precision, relies on an outsider's perspective. Hackler's interesting experiments remain just that, attempts to establish a way of representing two widely differing ways of thinking, one rational, materialistic, and modern, the other intuitive, spiritual, and traditional. Aimée Thurlo learned from Hillerman, and her most interesting observations about native culture seem to echo his. David Cole counters the Hillerman tradition with a heroine who rejects her heritage and tribal ways but investigates crimes that force her to relive the conflicts of her youth caught between the traditional way and total assimilation. Kirk Mitchell opens up the Hillerman tradition to a wider mix of tribes than normally appears in detective fiction and introduces to mainstream readers the varied directions assimilation takes.

Southwestern novels, then, employ many different approaches to the region. Some simply use it as a backdrop for stories that could be set elsewhere; others make the crime unique to the area, but the detective and detection remain conventional. Still others use the detective form to satirize New Agers and sham practitioners of so-called native shamanism. Some, like Garfield, stick totally to the practical, everyday world with the detective as scout and hunter weaving his or her way through conflicting cultural attitudes. A few plunge fully into the spiritual, losing the ties to Western logic and ratiocination at the heart of the detective story, their tales verging instead on horror and fantasy/magic. Hillerman began with the detective as scout and hunter but approached shamanism through Chee. However, he has kept a necessary distance—a Navajo looking at the unique properties of the Zuñi or the Hopi but as an outsider, a Navajo with a Western education seeking in his tribal tradition spiritual beliefs that could unify and bind the tribe as a healthy social unit, recognizing the ties between mental health and physical health, believing in the power of evil, but accepting Western logic and reason as necessary for the investigative path. Hillerman clarifies the obstacles and inherent contradictions that plague Chee's struggles to practice shamanism while simultaneously serving the community as a police detective—until in the most recent novels, his detective has been forced to recognize that the only Navajos who call on him as a shaman are either close friends and relatives or villains after his blood. By exploring the religious and cultural differences that infuse the region while retaining Western detective methodologies and approaches, Hillerman remains firmly in the genre, as does Cole, while the Thurlos and Hackler move into other areas, with the Thurlos combining romance and horror conventions and Hackler mixing folklore and horror. For all of these writers, however, the Southwest is an unmistakably unique setting and brings to the novels a potential for special crimes and murder weapons, and special investigative needs.

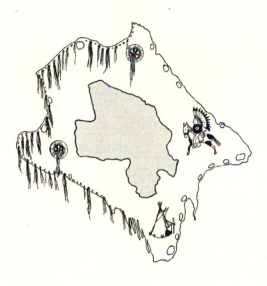

6

Shamans and Sherlocks:
Unravelling Crime in the Mountains
and on the Plains

The sun burrowed into her bare arms and the asphalt burned through
the soles of her pumps as she strode through the intersection, the din
of the city—horns and sirens, the growl of engines—rising around her.
She looked just like the throngs of lawyers and secretaries and bankers
. . . tailored linen dress, hair . . . clipped at the nape of her neck. But
she was not one of them. Not because her skin was brown—she passed
others with brown skin—but because she belonged to this place [Den-
ver, Colorado]. This was where the villages of the *Hinono eino* had
stood, where her people had traded with whites coming onto the land,
. . . [and] had died, their blood soaking the earth that lay buried under
asphalt and piles of brick.

—Margaret Coel, *The Story Teller*, 30

Despite high-tech farms and modern cities, extensive rural regions of the
Midwest remain much as they were when the Plains Indians roamed the
region. Today they still roam, in modern guises. Native American detectives
from the Plains and Rocky Mountain regions include:

Author	Detective	Tribal Affiliation
Peter Bowen	Gabriel Du Pré	Métis (Nez Percé, Ojibway, French, Chippewa/Anishinabe mix)
Margaret Coel	Vicky Holden	Arapaho
James Doss	Charlie Moon	Ute
	Daisy Perika	Ute
Katherine Eagle	Zane Lone Bull	Half-Lakota Sioux
	Jesse Brown Wolf	Sioux
Ed Gorman	Cindy (Morning Tree) Rhodes	La Costa (a fictitious tribe)
Fred Grove	Boone Terrell	Osage
Jean Hager	Mitch Bushyhead	Cherokee
	Molly Bearpaw	Cherokee
Mercedes Lackey	Jennifer Talldeer	Osage
Ronald Levitsky	Shaman (assists)	Lakota Sioux
Mardi Oakley Medawar	Tay Bodal	Kiowa
John Miles	Johnelle "Johnnie" Baker	One-sixteenth Choctaw
Sandra West Prowell	Kyle Old Wolf (assists)	Crow
J. F. Trainor	Angela Biwaban	Anishinabe (Chippewa)
Manly Wade Wellman	David Return	"Tsichah" (a fictitious tribe, possibly a mix of Cheyenne and Pawnee)

GEOGRAPHICAL DETERMINERS

This section explores two related regions, the Great Plains and the Rocky Mountains. The Rocky Mountain region extends from Colorado north to Wyoming, Montana, and southern Alberta, Canada, and includes "the broken buttes and arroyos, jammed against the foothills" leading to the Rockies (*The Dream Stalker*, 119). The Great Plains encompasses the heartland of North America, from northern Alberta in Canada, south into the Comanche Staked Plains and the grasslands of northern and central Texas. From north to south, this is a distance of some 2,000 miles. From east to west, it ranges from the Missouri-Mississippi valleys to the foothills of the Rockies, an area of approximately 1 million square miles. In addition to the mountainous Western states, this region encompasses what are today Oklahoma, Kansas, Nebraska, and the Dakotas.

Similar ecological imperatives govern Native American economies and cultures in this region, despite the territorial range from desert and semi-desert terrain in Utah, Nevada, and the Texas-Oklahoma panhandle to higher rainfall and sometimes even fairly wet environments in the Missouri and Mississippi valleys. These varying climatic Plains conditions produce vast savannah-like grasslands, wild grains, thistles, clumps of sagebrush and scrub brush, and shady cottonwoods bunched along river beds. Novelist John Miles describes lower-elevation southern Colorado plains:

[S]lightly rolling arid country, bare yellow dirt pocked by ugly little gullies torn open by the infrequent gully-washer deluges, studded by clumps of half-dead sage-brush and an occasional tumble-weed or chunk of dried-up cactus . . . in the distance . . . the indistinct blue lines of the mountains, . . . making everything closer seem so much more barren and lifeless. But here and there it wasn't lifeless . . . local Utes clung to a hardscrabble existence on the basis of a cow or two and a garden watered by the bucket on the days the old well sucked up enough brackish moisture to allow it. (*Tenoclock Scholar*, 48)

These extensive grasslands once made the plains home to vast herds of buffalo (some 60 million or more). Today, prong-horned antelope and wild horses populate the western Plains areas, and varieties of deer range widely, while mountain goats and herds of elk still abound in the mountains and their foothills. Meadowlarks trill, red-winged orioles chatter in grain fields, wild turkeys gobble, and crows call raucously. To the usual list of badgers, blacktail prairie dogs, gophers, marmots, raccoons, skunks, and porcu-pines, Angela Biwaban, in Trainor's *High Country Murder*, adds the numerous rodents (Western harvest mice, deer mice, pinyon mice, whitefoot mice) that protect plains and canyons from swarms of grasshoppers and cicadas, and the coyotes and red foxes that in turn control the rodent population (27). James Doss captures a predator in action in *The Shaman's Bones*:

The golden eagle circled, its hungry yellow-flecked eyes focused on the crest of the reddish mesa where the occasional small mammal darted among the junipers. The magnificent bird caught a thermal, soared upward, then folded its wings. *Kwana-ci* dived over the wide canyon to an altitude . . . just above the [mesa] crest, then spread its wings to glide toward the brownish-red cliff. . . . Focused on the center of the predator's retinas was a small gray form [a cottontail rabbit] that moved in the shadow of a long-dead ponderosa log. (220)

The weather varies enormously, with startling shifts of sun and shadow, hailstorms, sudden rains, and temperature extremes: "windblown and sun-scorched all summer, adrift in freezing snow all winter" (Coel, *The Eagle Catcher*, 17). Tornadoes are common, and when there is a drought, tem-peratures soar well above 100 degrees Fahrenheit, and prairie fires threaten rural homes. Rising water can be a major problem. A local in Peter Bowen's *Thunder Horse* warns a rider that it is three hours from rain to flood in the canyon he travels, and within the time limit a 20-foot-high muddy wall smashes into the gully, tumbling boulders and shattered trees. Even today, the Plains present demanding challenges to residents, with summer and winter temperatures nearing the limits for human habitation, unpredictable storms threatening economic and personal devastation, and an empty, lonely landscape offering few resources and scant social support. Throughout their recorded history, the unforgiving Plains shaped the character of its residents, creating free, independent spirits often larger than life and self-defining in their often eccentric reactions to their environment. Like their counterparts, the Cossacks, the mounted Plains people lived (and still live) heroically in the imagination, a folk distinct from all other Native Americans.

FICTIONAL GEOGRAPHY

Detective novels set in this region marvel at the space and distance, the flatness of the plains, the tall switchgrass, dry as kindling in summer, the drizzle, and the thick "tapioca" mud of springtime. In *Specimen Song*, Peter Bowen's detective, Gabriel Du Pré, memorably describes this mud: "six inches of gumbo . . . attached tenaciously to the sole of her boot. . . . mud the consistency of peanut butter" (150). Margaret Coel captures the stillness of the plains, the sapphire skies ("an enormous blue bowl inverted over the earth") (*The Dream Stalker*, 118), wisps of white clouds, and the clear luminescence as the first daylight glows in the east and spreads "fingers of pink and orange and magenta across the silver sky" (*The Ghost Walker*, 16). Her series detective, Father O'Malley, describes a Plains spring in which "the earth and the sky seemed to flow together, almost to exchange places, so . . . the mountains [seemingly] rose out of the clouds themselves"; the spring rains generate shimmering impressionistic landscapes, and "the slim, green stalks of goldenrod and sunflowers" spike the ditches (*The Dream Stalker*, 37, 63, 137). Surrounded by mountain peaks, Coel's high meadows are a "cool oasis" on burning days, their grass "the color of emeralds" (57). The wild country and the scarce population make it easy to get away with murder. Fort Washakie's police chief notes that a missing body could be located anywhere in 3,500 square miles of Wind River Reservation territory, with the chance of finding it a zillion to one if someone does not want it found (28).

Coel distinguishes a deep Wyoming winter, what the Arapaho call "the Moon When the Snow Blows Like Spirits in the Wind," from Eastern ones by killing power: deep, powdery snow, snow-crested roads like sheets of ice, blasts of frigid air driving snow and hard frozen ice slantwise and plummeting temperatures, a frozen landscape—weather so life threatening that no local would fail to stop for a stranded vehicle. In the opening blizzard scene from *The Ghost Walker*, O'Malley gulps in "icy air that punctured his lungs like a thousand sharp needles" as his body numbs— the "cold slipping over him like a sheet of ice"—and hypothermia sets in (4). James Doss describes Colorado's February snowflakes as "wet goose-feathers," falling incessantly for three days and producing drifts large enough to "lose a team of horses in" (*The Shaman Laughs*, 91). Bowen captures harsh Montana Decembers: howling winds, glittery pale gray sky, and snow so fine it freezes the lungs of cattle and horses that inhale it; one bad winter, as temperatures dropped to 60 degrees below zero, a blizzard filled coulees 100 feet deep with snow so that 90 percent of the range cattle died, and in spring "the tops of the cottonwood trees had dead cattle in the forks of the branches" (*Coyote Wind*, 66).

In Trainor, Forest Service mountain roads are rutted, unpaved, steep, and treacherous, even for a mountain goat, and the beauty of the 12,000-foot frigid peaks, with glistening, icy spires set against a cerulean sky, tons of snow, and thick forests of Engelmann spruce on the lower slopes, is offset by the very real threat of sudden avalanches four stories high roaring down mountainsides, flinging blocks of ice the size of dump trucks, breaking trees like matchsticks, and pummeling all in its path—particularly if there are chinook winds. This is pickup truck and four-wheel-drive territory. Trainor's heroine muses on the irony of distances in mountain territory: only 40 miles from her destination as the eagle flies, but the mountainous terrain extends her journey by 100 miles.

However, the region offers pleasures as dramatic as its drawbacks. Jean Hager captures the varied beauty of northeast Oklahoma's brief spring: the brilliant, cloudless sky, the sparkling spring green of the trees and new grass, the "blue mist" of wildflowers beside the fencerows, and the pink blossoms "like puffs of cotton candy" decorating the redbud trees (*Masked Dancers*, 27). For Hager, autumn is "like an indolent beauty who's all dressed up with no place to go," dawdling from September through November, and sometimes lagging on to the end of December: "Leaves . . . paint the countryside crimson . . . orange . . . yellow," flaunting themselves "in a grand, flamboyant display" (*The Redbird's Cry*, 1).

The Cherokees of Hager's novels live in one of 14 counties carved from the Cherokee Nation in 1907: the rolling hills and prairies west of the Grand River, the wooded areas of the Ozark plateau east of the river (with "hickory trees, native walnuts, elms, and blackjack oaks") (*Ravenmocker*, 1). Local Cherokees see in the "huddled" hills between Stillwell, Oklahoma, and Tahlequah "the backs of huge guardian beasts" offering "protection and security" (*Seven Black Stones*, 17). One aged medicine man living in a cabin deep in the woods near Going Snake Mountain takes pride in the thorny bushes and briars that discourage frequent visitors and in the mythic quality of the landscape: "Overhead, bare limbs created snaky patterns against the cold blue sky" (*Night Walker*, 171). This same medicine man, during a ritual to dispel evil from an ancient site, sits in the frigid dawn, seeing in his ceremonial fire writhing figures, a wolf's face, a severed hand, and other horrors. The stark, empty setting, inhospitable and cruel, invites its human residents to project their inner fears and insecurities outward into myth and legend.

Whatever the season or the particular locale, authors of detective stories featuring Native Americans connect history, tradition, and native religion with terrain wherever possible. Just as the urban, hard-boiled detective story of Chandler and his fellows featured American cities as active settings (sometimes almost as characters, as in Chandler's L.A.), so the Indian stories feature landscape as being as important as characters. In Doss' *The Shaman Laughs*, Deputy Sheriff Charlie Moon describes the legend behind the Three Sisters rock formation: three Pueblo sisters, hiding from raiding Apaches, were captured by a lone Apache brave, but their prayers to the spirit Sina-wa-vi brought bolts of lightning, transforming them to stone so they could always remain a part of their homeland and be remembered by their tribe and reducing the Apache to a smaller chunk to punish his deed (235). The Plains is a special place, with a colorful, exotic history and character of its own.

RANGE OF INDIGENOUS PEOPLES

This territory encompasses a wide range of indigenous peoples, from the Comanches in the south to the Cheyenne and Nez Percé in the north, with Ute, Pawnee, Kiowa, Arapaho, Shoshone, Sioux, Crow, Mandan, and many other tribes in between. The Oklahoma territory includes peoples removed from the south, such as the Cherokee, Choctaw, Chickasaw, Natchez, and Creek Indians.

SUBGENRES FEATURING NATIVE AMERICANS IN DETECTIVE FICTION

Most Western detective stories set in the nineteenth and early twentieth centuries dramatize the historical distrust of whites for Indians and the conflicts between cattlemen and Indians. Rarely do they provide a Native American perspective. Loren Estleman's Montana Indians in *The Stranglers* are typical: the Wild West Show Indian—a Ute pretending to be a blood-thirsty Blackfoot demonstrating warrior skills on a mangy buffalo to amuse his white audience—and the unpredictable and dangerous generic "bad" Indian, without tribal connections or loyalty, such as Virgil Blue Water, who betrays anyone if paid enough. A. B. Guthrie, Jr.'s *The Genuine Article* characterizes Indians as unpredictable and inscrutable, sometimes as wild savages, other times peaceful, but never law-abiding in white terms. The interpretation of events, whether Indians massacred a prominent but unpopular cattleman or whether a white murderer left signs that would shift the blame to Indians depends on Indians and whites having very different ideas about sexual behavior: an aging Indian husband pimping for his beautiful young wife, the white killer, desirous but unwilling to pay for the young wife's favors. Lewis B. Patten's *Death Stalks Yellowhorse* also reflects white distrust of local Indians, with the citizens of Yellowhorse automatically blaming a vengeful Indian for deadly nightly raids that white greed motivates. Though written recently, the plotlines reflect attitudes that seem dated, and the methods of detection are more haphazard than readers expect in a detective-centered crime story.

The historical Western detective story has little vitality as a subgenre and has few high-quality practitioners, but Ed Gorman's novels rise above stereotypes. His *Hawk Moon* mixes the Western and modern detection through a serial murderer whose modus operandi recurs in the same town in 1887 and in the present—the nose and one arm slashed off beautiful Indian women. Because this m.o. also matches Apache-style punishments for infidelity, both nineteenth-and twentieth-century investigators look for suspicious Indian males with motives. However, a reputable white father and son who consider themselves above the law have perpetrated these race-driven murders. Through his brave, educated native heroine, Cindy (Morning Tree) Rhodes, a La Costa (a fictitious tribe), Gorman provides insights into native perspectives and into the psychology of Indian-white relations.

A recent subgenre is detective stories featuring non-Native American detectives in Western settings and revolving around stolen Indian religious or burial artifacts and some form of New Age spiritualism. Typical is Lise McClendon's *The Bluejay Shaman*, set in Montana's Grand Tetons, which includes Native American activists, a New Age women's group engaged in moonlit "native" rituals, defaced religious objects on a reservation mission, a false "native" prophet (the bluejay shaman), fake petroglyphs, and Native American Church peyote rituals.

Sandra West Prowell's *The Killing of Monday Brown* more realistically captures Montanan Crow outrage at tribal graves desecrated by greedy grave robbers. Having Crow Indian police detective Kyle Old Wolf's cases intersect with those of private detective Phoebe Siegel enables Prowell to sensitize readers to a Native American perspective, as Kyle Old Wolf sensitizes Siegel. To help her understand how his people feel about such grave robbings, Kyle Old Wolf suggests that Siegel multiply by "about three hundred years and several thousand people" the feeling of loss and desecration she would experience if her policeman father's body were dug up, his bones tossed about, his torso ravaged by the elements, and everything of sentimental value buried with him (his rosary, police shields, rings) stolen; that way she might somewhat approach "what Indian people feel" (38). To solve this case, Siegel clashes with concepts of reality very different from her own. Suffering through the claustrophobia and drug-induced hallucinations of sweat lodge ceremonies, interviewing witnesses who claim to converse with powerful dwarves and have dream visions, and personally experiencing differences in attitudes toward private property, private space, body ornaments (finger-bones and scalp-locks), and aggression make Kyle Old Wolf's warning "Their ways are different" (63) seem much too mild. These ways are so alien to the mainstream that Siegel, despite her deep respect and affection for Kyle Old Wolf, cannot see past them.

Prowell contrasts Native American and mainstream behavior with a sensitivity missing in the westerns.

REGIONAL HISTORY IN DETECTIVE FICTION: TYING PAST TO PRESENT

Plains and mountain history appears in detective stories set in historical periods or with roots in the past. Cherokee Mardi Medawar, for example, sets her nineteenth-century Kiowa tales of detection on the Plains and makes their solutions depend on insider knowledge of tribal and family relationships, Kiowa customs, and competition between tribes.

Modern detective stories featuring Native American detectives tie past and present, old and new. Doss traces the ancient pageant of geological and cultural history that shaped the dramatic scenery and indigenous human societies. He describes a multicolored canyon between two pleated skirts of the Wind River Range, with layers from different periods marked by different colors (the blue clay of Eocene oil shale, the sulfurous orange and pale yellow bentonite from Cretacious volcanism, and, at the bottom, fiery red Jurassic sandstone, saturated with iron oxide), and he traces its inhabitants from hardy mammoth hunters and then Arapaho and Bannock shamans leaving red handprints on sandstone boulders as signs of secret vows, to fierce Crow warriors gathering ingredients for war paint, and finally to the Ute, who made Cradle of Rainbow Lizard canyon home long before whites came (*The Shaman's Bones*, 98–99). A modern Ute shaman important to his plot draws strength from this canyon's beauty and special powers. Doss also ties past and present through references to famous historical incidents that live in local memory, such as the battle in which Shoshone Chief Washaskie ripped out and ate the heart of Big Robber, the chief of the Crow nation, an action that gave Crowheart Butte its name and confirmed the Shoshone claim to the Wind River region.

In *Becoming Coyote*, Montana creative writing professor Wayne Ude ties past and present, imitating Native American oral tradition through a narrative mix of stories, legends, history, and customs. Mainstream readers might not fully appreciate this tour de force without learning about native belief systems, for the novel suspends, overlaps, or circles conventional time. The narrator, suffering from headaches that end in temporary blindness, has visions in which three shifting worlds are superimposed as he watches two men stalk an old buffalo:

I could see differences in the ways they moved, the ways they wore the museum clothing: Charley as though he had traveled entirely into the time perhaps a hundred years before when those clothes were new, and was now walking through that time toward the eternity within which buffalo had walked this continent; and Joe clumsily, as though he hadn't fully left his own time, hadn't moved completely into the world through which Charley pursued a still-older buffalo. Moving over the entire scene as we passed back and forth was the airplane's shadow.

Billy White Bull [a tribal elder] would have insisted that . . . part of Charley had always been in eternity, where the buffalo lived: that part from his Coyote heritage which was, if anything, older than the buffalo and its breed: existing before eternity, and surviving beyond it, Coyote, carrion-eater, hunter, thief, able to eat anything, whether alive, or dead, or rotten, or never alive, gathering everything to himself for no purpose, but to keep his own shaggy, flea-bitten, crack-brained life going and turning everything to that purpose, just as Charlie must be turning this buffalo hunt to some purpose of his own. (17–18)

Coyote and coyote stories punctuate this narrative, for the "breaks" territory Ude covers is Coyote land (reservation territory just 40 miles south of the Canadian border), and one of the lawbreakers being pursued, Charlie Many Rivers, bears the nickname "Coyote" because of his Métis blood and his Coyote Trickster ways. In fact, this adult Rivers is thought to be the famous Métis rebel Louis Riel himself, or his reincarnation.

Ude makes his amateur detective, Snook, a non-reservation Indian, cynical about the old ways. Snook describes how the old people speak of fasting in order to hear "voices just beyond hearing": "Their vision would blur and they would pierce through to another world, come back with knowledge. I come back with a hang-over" (1). Despite such cynicism, by the story's end, Snook acquires such insight, experiencing physical debilitation and blurred vision; while spending the night in a trance in an ancient cave, he has visions and hears voices from another world. He has seen the return of the buffalo and has found one of his tribe's long-missing, powerful medicine bundles hidden in a secret cave by an aged medicine man protecting it from theft by museums and anthropologists. Moreover, in broad daylight, he has been guided by Coyote and by an old-fashioned Métis cart that only he seems to have seen. He has told us that no one knew any more what the objects sticking out from the medicine bundle in the museum were except for a sense of their age, importance, and holiness, but he comes to believe personally in their power. Where once he would have scoffed when Billy White Bull said that new Coyote stories are evidence that Coyote is still around (no human would dare make up a Coyote story), now he takes Coyote's continued interference in human life as a given.

As the representative of the Tribal Museum and the tribal police, the first-person narrator sets out to investigate the theft of clothing and artifacts from the Tribal Museum and hunts down the culprits as a way to keep the FBI from interfering in the pursuit and blowing it out of proportion. Basically, the theft is a minor affair perpetrated by two spirited local youths (Charlie Many Rivers and Joe Thunder Boy), smitten with the dream of living out the old ways. One local has purchased a single buffalo hoping to someday produce a herd, and the young men are on a tear to hunt it down as their ancestors would have and to bring buffalo meat to their families to signal their warrior prowess. They steal, not for financial gain, but as a lark—to acquire buckskin clothing, bows and arrows, and cowponies so they can hunt buffalo in the old ways. Their trackers sympathize with the youths, as is evident from Snook's comment, "I hadn't ever tasted buffalo either, and I'd only seen a few, over in a park in Dakota once, and it did seem a god-damned shame that an Indian, even just a three-quarter Indian, should go through his entire life without once tasting that meat" (15). Thunder Boy, eventually done in by sunburn and heat prostration, surrenders, but Rivers endures until captured—before he can harm the buffalo. Upon returning the stolen regalia and weapons, a little sweaty but unharmed, the youngsters, in effect, get slapped on the wrist for their prank.

However, the story is much more than a hunt for two thieves. It is tied to the question of land, assimilation, and culture loss, to the Métis battle for freedom from Canada in the 1880s, and to modern regulations that limit herd size on reservation land. Snook sees the event as perhaps Rivers' first attempt at shape shifting (the tribe is convinced he got better at it) and ties it to more recent events involving Rivers doing the unexpected and skirting the law. The investigation is an excuse for Ude to contrast the complexities of contemporary reservation life with the witty parables of oral history, to show the present taking shape from the past, and the future from the present. As the title suggests, the shape-shifting Coyote Trickster dominates the action, weaving events into a continuous loop in which past and present merge, and metaphorical and magical realism dominate. The final result is a Native American concept of justice exemplified, a divided reservation community reunited, the offenders brought back into the community, and a non-believer so manipulated by Coyote's reweaving of reality that he recognizes the reality of the old ways. Rivers becomes a famous sculptor producing weighty images of buffalo.

Like Ude, but without traditional storytelling forms, Montanan Peter Bowen envisions the past fused to present and future through the Métis (half French, half Native American mix) ancestry of his characters. He describes traditional Metîs activities and patterns of behavior down through generations. As a musician, his series detective Gabriel Du Pré maintains the oral tradition of the voyageurs, the French fur traders who explored Canada and North America by canoe, preserving the songs that recorded their troubles, conflicts, loves, and lives. Du Pré might play a tune about the sounds the cart axles make as people hunted buffalo and pre-pared pemmican for the long, cold winter. As a local Montanan, he sees in the world around him reminders of the past, for example, a bad winter such as the one the Métis endured when chased south by the English in 1886–1887. Initials carved in a cave conjure up the Red River Rebellion, and the long skulls in an ancient burial site remind him of the blue-grey eyes and pale hair of the Mandans, an unusual Siouan tribe decimated by disease around the time of Lewis and Clark's Pacific expedition. Such knowledge enables him to set the record straight, as when movie makers rewrite the past, hiring Du Pré as a consultant at $200 a day,

while they made some piece of crap about a Sioux kept a pet grizzly—they thought grizzlies ate soybeans or something—and every time this Sioux killed a buffalo he held a wake for it. All the Sioux's relatives keening over this fine buffalo, good fellow, strong, brave, great singer and dancer, forgive us for making stew out of you our brother. The Sioux was extreme badasses, and before the whites give them horses and guns they was eating each other and any Cree that they could catch. As in, "We feeling peckish, so it is you, Least Muskrat, Apologies to you for we are eating you our brother." But never mind. (*Coyote Wind*, 30)

Bowen's detective hero may be politically incorrect, but he always has his-tory on his side.

In *The Story Teller*, Margaret Coel interlocks past and present with the history of a nineteenth-century ledger—a U.S. Cavalry accounting ledger appropriated and used in place of a buffalo hide to pictorially record im-portant historical events—an eyewitness account of Arapaho history. Oral tradition suggested that the Arapaho fought alongside the Cheyenne at Sand Creek, but the ledger in question proves beyond a doubt that the Arapaho were indeed massacred there on November 29, 1864, and therefore that the tribe qualifies for the compensation already awarded other tribes. In doing so, it refutes white history books that record no Arapaho presence and a Cheyenne historian who denies Arapaho partici-pation to keep the federal funds for his people. Coel captures Vicky Hol-den's outrage at artifact brokers who would break this valuable tribal record into single pages (their relation to the whole thereby forever lost) just to increase the price tag for the ledger from $1.3 million to triple or quadruple that sum. An elderly Arapaho had spotted the ledger book in a Denver museum in 1920, long before a federal requirement that museums return to Native American tribes artifacts sacred to tribal religion and tribal ways. When the artifact does not appear on the list of holdings given the

council, Holden is charged with recovering this Arapaho treasure and vital
historical record. Historian Coel's approach works neatly to show how past
and present interact, and how, despite all the influence of modernity, Arapaho traditional practices can have a place in the modern world. Oral history, ironically, proves more reliable than vaunted computer tracking of
artifacts and the scholarly record kept by academics.

These fictive linkings of time and place grow directly out of the beliefs
of Plains Indians.

INDIGENOUS BELIEFS

The religious-spiritual systems of the Plains Indians were somewhat distinct from those of other tribes. The Plains Indians believed in the multi-
faceted nature of divinity, a faith Margaret Coel gives voice to through her
Jesuit detective:

All around, the land dipped into arroyos and rose into bluffs. The breeze ruffled
the wild grasses; the sagebrush and cactus shivered as if the earth itself were moving.
The earth is alive, the elders had told him many times. A creature, like other creatures, growing and changing and becoming: ever showing the same face. On days
like today, he understood. (*The Dream Stalker*, 57)

Unlike the particularized forms of worship of the desert people, the Plains
nomads had many ways to worship the Great Mystery, the divine, whether
in the silence of nature or in varied religious practices as they petitioned
their God in the Sun Dance and in the Sweat Lodge. Their belief in the
universality of divinity enabled them to more readily accept the symbols
and trappings of Christianity as one of those many ways.

Coel convincingly delineates the amalgam of Christianity and Arapaho
traditional belief that infuses the St. Francis Mission Church with a special
spirit. Built by tribe members 100 years ago, the Arapaho mission church
of her fiction and of reality (the real mission, located between Lander and
Riverton, Wyoming, is much as described in her novels) brings together
native and Christian religious images, depicting the crucified Christ as a
warrior staked to the ground "so that enemies might vent their anger upon
. . . [him] while the people escaped," the Risen Christ as a triumphant warrior, the Virgin Mary as an Arapaho woman, God the Creator as a thunderbird, and the Holy Spirit as an eagle feather (*The Ghost Walker*, 17;
The Eagle Catcher, 86). The pulpit is a native drum, the arched ceiling
above the altar is Arapaho sky blue, and the panels above the entrance
depict the first encounters of the Jesuits and the Arapaho. The lines and
circles painted on the church walls symbolize the journey of life (*The Ghost
Walker*, 17). Chains of linked circles symbolize the connectedness of all
living things and remind worshipers of the roundness of the Earth, sun,

and moon (*The Eagle Catcher*, 86). The stained glass windows are collages of native religious symbols and color symbolism such as those found in a star quilt or a special necklace with red, white, and black beads and yellow porcupine quills—colors symbolizing "the four sacred movements at the center of life: the four winds, the four directions, the four seasons, the four periods of the day, the four quarters of the world" (*The Ghost Walker*, 27), as well as the four hills of life and the four quarters of creation. A yellow daffodil on the wall near the altar offers a reminder of springtime and resurrection, even in winter. The drums beat at Sunday Mass, the Our Father is signed in native sign language and whispered in Arapaho ("*Heesjeva hene Sunauneet: heneseet vedenau . . .*"), and the Christian message is proclaimed alongside Arapaho traditional belief (*The Ghost Walker*, 43–44; *The Dream Stalker*, 116). Since the latter is symbolic and abstract rather than located in particularized totems, sacred figures, or elaborate festivals and rituals, the two systems match fairly smoothly.

A funeral scene at the mission church likewise reflects the fusion of Christian and native beliefs. The Christian sermon delivered, the Arapaho ritual begins. An elder thanks Mother Earth for home, sun for light and warmth, and the animals and birds for sharing their lives with humans and then beseeches Shining Man Above in the Arapaho language to permit cedar smoke to mark the dead man's way to the spirit world. Then all the mourners share in the smoke as a smudgepot is carried among them (*The Eagle Catcher*, 135). A saddle, a symbol of the dead man's worldly goods, is buried atop his casket to accompany him in the other world, and a blessing with holy water is followed by the steady beat of drums; mourners take the fortuitous appearance of a circling eagle as a blessing, a promise of harmony (147). *The Eagle Catcher* ends with a "smoking," cedar smoke wafted through the air while an Arapaho prayer chanted drives out the evil that had defiled the community: "The sacred cedar smoke crawled over the ground like fog, then rose and drifted through the crowd, symbolizing respect for life, for all living things" (241). There is no conflict with Christian incense burned in European-style censers; the rituals complement each other rather than clash. In *The Dream Stalker*, another corpse is carefully adorned with sacred paint before drumbeats conduct his spirit to his ancestors (170). The elders entrusted with such ceremonies belong to the Big Lodge People, who care for and protect the Arapaho's sacred objects (such as the sacred pipe). The wake will seem familiar to adherents of Catholic and other Christian faiths that practice similar celebrations of the dead; the ceremonies differ mainly in their Arapaho content.

As its title suggests, *The Ghost Walker* also explores Arapaho attitudes toward the dead that contrast with orthodox Christian notions. Father O'Malley cannot persuade an Arapaho to drive him to the scene of a crime, because Arapahos fear the terrible repercussions of contact with an unblessed or improperly blessed corpse. A ghost not shown the path to the

Jesuit Mission on The Wind River Arapaho Reservation.

sky world will stumble about in terror, seeking its ancestors' land and causing mayhem in the process. When the body turns up missing, natives attribute local accidents—a burst radiator hose, a rolled truck, a slip in the bathtub, a fall through a barn floor—to the straying, rambunctious ghost. Such a view makes Christian talk of raising the dead seem like a threat rather than a hopeful promise.

Intertwined with formal religious beliefs are cultural practices, for most Native American spirituality is rooted in the everyday, in social behavior, in interaction with nature, in family routines. For the Arapaho, the cloud-topped Wind River Mountains, "their great blocks of granite, their ponderosas and lodgepole pines swept with white powder," are a "sacred space, the Middle Earth, a gift to the Arapaho... from Shining Man Above," a physical representation of universal harmonies (*The Ghost Walker*, 157). Powwows celebrate the harmony and peace that are the secret to a good life, with dancing, chanting, and wearing symbolically colored and decorated attire the traditional ways to move toward harmony:

The drums started beating, and the loud thuds rolled through the air like thunder. Then the singers began chanting in high-pitched voices as the dancers flowed into the arbor, ... a sea of colors. The women were in dresses, blues ... reds ... purples ... golds. Some wore buckskin dresses with long fringed sleeves and skirts. The men wore silk shirts and shorts topped with breastplates of polished bones and aprons covered with shimmering glass beads. All the dancers had on beaded moccasins and ankle-cuffs of white Angora. Some had wheels of red and orange feathers twirling on their arms and backs. Long yellow feathers, like stalks of prairie grass, sprouted from headdresses and bent in the wind. (*The Eagle Catcher*, 4)

Balance, order, and harmony result from the individual finding his or her proper place in nature, community, and family. Coel's Father O'Malley hears the ties to nature in the flatness of an Arapaho voice, "as if the man were speaking into the wind" (*The Dream Stalker*, 2). Arapaho children, taught that respecting elders is part of the natural order, gaze into the distance rather than disrespectfully look directly at an adult. Natural too, from a traditional perspective, are the gender divisions of warriors bringing home the food and women waiting on others. Though the day of the warrior belonged to "the Old Time," the warrior spirit seeks expression in modern means to power, prestige, and dignity (*The Dream Stalker*, 96). Promises are empty words until backed by action. The Arapaho way values politeness and provides no excuse for breaking the forms of courtesy. It also values sharing, which is why Coel's heroine Vicky Holden insists that gambling goes against the Arapaho way, a taking for personal gain rather than the proper giving.

Unlike many mainstream Christians, the Arapaho make no distinction between Sunday devotions and everyday life, seeing religion as a guide to even the most prosaic social interactions. The Arapaho way is a seamless whole, not a fragmented set of activities. Indian time is in harmony with a rural life, unhurried, like the seasons; when O'Malley tries to beg off from sharing a second pot of coffee, he realizes that the excuse of not having time makes no sense to the old woman he visits, for, from an Arapaho perspective, people have nothing but time.

Holden respectfully consults a "grandfather" about a dream that puzzles her; as the keeper of the sacred wheel and as one of the Four Old Men who represent the spirits guarding the four quarters of the world (the four directions) and controlling the directions of the wind that provides air to breathe, he has a power that awes the tribe he helps guide and awes the thoroughly modern Holden as well:

Only men with great composure and control ever became one of the Four Old Men. They had great self-discipline, even over their thoughts, since whatever they thought could become true. . . . think[ing] bad thoughts . . . could mean disaster for the People. (*The Dream Stalker*, 144–45)

The old man says he foresaw Holden's visit and when she relates her dream of a bear becoming a person and guiding her, he prays in Arapaho, asking the Great Mystery Above to accept an offering of food, tobacco, and fabric and to hear the supplications of the People. Chips of cedar heated over coals of cottonwood cleanse the room so he can touch the sacred wheel. A sacred bundle of buffalo hide protects the wheel, a cornerstone of the Sun Dance ceremony. Coel describes it as follows:

It was round, formed of a single branch, with ends shaped like the head and tail of a snake—a harmless water snake, meek and gentle, like the snakes that lived in the buffalo wallows. Blue beads were wrapped around the top, and eagle feathers hung from four points around the wheel. Carved into the wood were the symbols of the Thunderbird, which represented the spirit guardians of creation; *Nahax*, the morning star; *He thon natha*, the Lone-Star of the evening; and the chain of stars, the Milky Way. All of creation, all of its harmony, was contained in the sacred wheel—a reminder through time to her [Holden's] people that *Nih'a ca* [the Divine Mystery] was always with them. (*The Dream Stalker*, 146)

After a blessing to help Holden walk in balance and find the center of her life, the old man returns the sacred wheel to its protective bundle and explains the symbolic meaning of her dream: If her heart is pure, Bear will make her strong to protect the earth and help her people, but if she chooses pride over purity and service, the earth and its rivers will be poisoned (her fight against storing nuclear waste on the reservation makes the interpretation seem most apt). Holden, feeling as protected by this interpretation as by a power symbol on a warrior's battle shield, grows confident in her struggle against the nuclear storage plan, despite strong opposition.

Such beliefs and cultural practices inevitably result in a very different attitude toward crime and justice. Native Americans from this region value rehabilitation over punishment, and harmony (bringing the offender back into the fold) over isolating offenders. Even though many Plains groups are nominally or actually Christian, deeply rooted indigenous values can override more modern attitudes, replacing concerns with Old Testament-style justice with a craving for order and balance, the idea behind many rituals and ceremonies involving the concept of *medicine*.

SHAMAN

The shaman novels of this region vary from ones in which the shaman is the central detective and engages in totally otherworldly activities (as does Mercedes Lackey's Jennifer Talldeer) to those in which the shaman is an adjunct or a parallel investigator, assisting or advising the police or main investigator and actively engaging the forces of evil in a way quite different from the official investigation (as do Doss' Daisy Perika and Bowen's Benetsee).

Mercedes Lackey's Jennifer Talldeer, a.k.a. Kestrel-Hunts-Alone

Perhaps the most otherworldly shaman detective from this region is the Tulsa, Oklahoma, Osage-Cherokee heroine of Mercedes Lackey's *Sacred Ground*, Jennifer Talldeer. To the outside world, the petite (under five feet) Talldeer seems totally assimilated, an educated, modern private detective with a college degree in criminology, her mastery of English impeccable, her attire fashionably stylish, her knowledge of mainstream law impressive, and her care of her aged grandfather (Frank Talldeer) admirable. She helps battered wives enter the witness protection program and defy criminally abusive husbands; she investigates shoddy businesses, assists insurance investigators, and even disarms a bomb. A highly competent professional, she deals effectively with lawyers, judges, policemen, and ordinary citizens; she researches and deciphers government documents, treaties, and normally inaccessible historical data (diaries, private papers). She questions witnesses, gathers factual data/evidence, and seeks clues and patterns that expose relationships and explain events. She also does genealogical research and initiates suits against museums that have violated laws about confiscated tribal property. As the novel advances, she becomes involved in the case of Native American activists (including a former boyfriend) accused of sabotaging construction equipment at the site of a new shopping mall being built on an ancient burial ground.

Despite this professional facade, in her private life she is Good Eagle Woman, a community-centered Osage-Cherokee who attends powwows, joins in traditional Fancy-Dancer Contests, and helps identify and discipline peyote users who disrupt gatherings. Her major service is to recover sacred objects from private collections and museums that have acquired items illegally. A visit to a county museum awakens her to the existence of "souvenirs" taken from the local Indians (scalps, skulls, medicine bundles, sacred pipes, and even shaman bones), souvenirs that need a ritualistic burial or, in the case of sacred items, a return to the tribe from which they were taken. Her self-appointed task is to aggressively track down thousands of missing relics, to buy them or in some way remove them from profane white hands, and to return them to the tribe from which they came, whether it be Osage, Lakota Sioux, or some distant northwestern tribe. Like her grandfather, she adjusts old ways to new to make practicing tradition feasible: using an electric sauna for a sweatlodge, preparing sacred tobacco in a fruit dryer acquired at a yard sale, and purchasing cornmeal for ceremonies at a chain grocery, sweetgrass and cedar smoke in incense form from an esoteric bookshop in Tulsa, and crow beads and porcupine quills for traditional embroidery from a Tulsa specialty shop. She even adopts traditional practices from the Lakota Sioux when they fit her needs.

However, Lackey, as a renowned science fiction author, is not content with simple detection, nor even with questions of the dual nature of individuals torn between family or tribal heritage and assimilated self. Thus, she endows her heroine with supernatural qualities invisible to her neighbors and coworkers: extrasensory, shamanistic powers passed down in the family generation after generation. When Talldeer touches Lakota Sioux relics, she feels something akin to an electric shock that identifies one item as having great power; as it throbs and pulsates, she envisions its creation by nineteenth-century shamans and Fed-Exes the entire box to a Lakota elder with great relief. Talldeer's grandfather, whose secret name is Mooncrow, may look old and frail, but he is a powerful Osage Medicine Man, the descendant of one of the most famous shamans of their tribe, Watches-Over-the-Land, and through him Talldeer has learned to sense the power of sacred items, to shift shape as Kestrel-Hunts-Alone, to enter the spirit world, to evoke animal and bird spirits, and to shield herself and her associates from evil assaults. Watches-Over-the-Land, envisioning the destructive power of the white world, taught his descendants to camouflage traditional ways behind an assimilated facade, to attend white schools and learn white ways, but to secretly continue tribal medicine ways "under the 'porches' of the white ways" (*Sacred Ground*, 18). Mooncrow and Watches-Over-the-Land send their spirit selves to assist Talldeer in the spirit world.

In her secret third identity as a powerful shaman, Talldeer discovers truths behind the illusions of the visible world, placates the Osage Little People (vengeful spirits protecting burial mounds), and battles evil forces in full Osage regalia and warrior's roach. The construction of a suburban shopping mall has not only defiled a sacred Osage burial ground but has destroyed the grave of Watches-Over-the-Land, scattered his tools of power, and released an ancient evil he had once imprisoned in a willow tree. Kestrel spirit Talldeer foresees the barren spiritual and physical waste-land that will result if that evil fulfills its mission and kills the Osage eagle totem spirits. By novel's end, science fiction takes over as a Native-American-style Star Wars battle ensues, a clash of spiritual forces in which a deadly evil pursues Kestrel-Hunts-Alone, Mooncrow, and Watches-Over-the-Land through changing realities and shifts of shape. Crazed warrior spirits hurl electric bolts from television sets, zombies murder on command, and good and evil battle in multidimensional, alternate "other" worlds. In the spirit world, a kestrel wards off scrawny blackbirds with the aid of eagles (Mooncrow and Watches-Over-the-Land), while in everyday reality, hitmen in a black Lincoln try to drive Talldeer off the road but are them-selves forced over a cliff when an Eagles-line bus blocks their way.

Talldeer's sweatlodge ceremonies and rituals for placating angry spirits may reflect some native religious traditions, but *Sacred Ground* is a sci-fi fantasy hybrid far afield from detective fiction and Osage vision. Such is the hazard of extending the detective genre too far afield of its roots in Enlightenment reason, ratiocination, and scientific criminology.

James Doss' Daisy Perika

James D. Doss sets his novels in Southwestern Colorado, in and around Granite Creek, a small mountain town. Despite their titles, Doss' shaman novels do not go as far as Lackey's in asserting supernatural shaman pow-ers. In fact, Doss leans toward mainstream rationalism and resolution but remains tied to Native American mysticism. Doss' shaman is an aged Ute, Daisy Perika, a Native American version of the traditional British eccentric elderly sleuth. Like Agatha Christie's Miss Marple, Patricia Wentworth's Miss Maud Silver, Josephine Tey's Miss Lucy Pym, or even more aptly, Heron Carvich's Miss Emily Seaton, a.k.a. "The Battling Brolly," and other energetic senior sleuths, she is independent, resourceful, and zany, a par-tially comic character but nevertheless formidable in her idiosyncratic cre-ativity. Like Carvich's Miss Seaton, Perika stumbles upon crime in a serendipitous way, but with the additional flourish of mystical connections to a powerful Ute *pitukupf*, or magical dwarf. Perika's crime solving irri-tates officialdom, but her meddling produces results.

Perika lives in a flimsy aluminum trailer house in the narrow Cañon del Espiritu on the Southern Ute Reservation, and her nearest neighbors are shepherds with adobe homes on the rocky banks of the Rio de Los Animas Perditas, the River of Lost Souls. She supplements her diet with the wild potatoes, acorns, berries, and other canyon foods her ancestors lived on, and gathers *yerba del buey*, alum root, yarrow, woundwort, and other local herbs to cure bleeding, headaches, upset stomachs, aching joints, and so on. Her shamanistic activities are well known among her people, who respect her magic and medicinal remedies but joke about her coffee being strong enough to melt spoons and cure impotence. She teaches children traditional formulas for warding off evil, for instance, a chant to deflect the anger of spiders toward the Navajos (traditional Ute enemies) if a child kills one of their species.

The dreams and visions she reports to the authorities (in particular, Charlie Moon, the deputy sheriff and her nephew) ultimately make a weird symbolic sense, but her skeptical nephew is most unwilling to accept the parallels between his real-life investigations and her dream vision experiences. His nearly seven-foot height makes him feel the master of most situations, and his approach to his profession is highly orthodox police procedure. He is typical of the younger generation, educated at white schools, unable to speak the Ute language or to understand his people's traditional ways. For him, Ute traditionalism is *passé*, and his aunt's practice of the old ways is embarrassing and irrational: a dotty old woman, nearing senility, she is to be spoken to softly and respectfully, but not to be taken seriously. Where she sees an active spiritual world affecting daily realities, he sees only pedestrian facts, the raw data that becomes evidence and clues to criminal behavior. He is solicitous and amiable, but clearly a non-believer. From her perspective, he has lost touch with "the old ways that had sustained the People since time began" (*The Shaman Laughs*, 92). Consumers of British mysteries will identify Charlie Moon, like Daisy, as a native version of a stock figure, the orthodox policeman completely convinced of the efficacy of procedure.

Though Doss starts each novel with Daisy Perika's visions of reality, he seems unsure as a writer about how much credibility to allow her on a consistent basis. Her degree of involvement in the central plot varies from book to book, with some taking her role more seriously than others. Despite comic moments, she always sees into a realm to which others are blind. As Deputy Moon and Chief of Police Scott Parris investigate the murder of a physics graduate student in *The Shaman Sings* and link it to her discovery of "room temperature" fusion to make superconductors cheaper and more viable, Perika punctuates the narrative, worrying about visions she has had of Coyote, the servant of *pitukupf*, and of his warnings about a Dark One, and seeing in nature signs and portents:

First snow would come soon, with the Moon of Dead Leaves Falling. Tonight, the sky was as clear as the water in the Piedra. Her pulse quickened when she realized that the waning moon was not far away from the earth; he [the moon] was just there . . . sitting on Three Sisters mesa, resting for a moment on the stout shoulders of the stone women. The shaman could count all the round pockmarks on his silver face. Even *Akwach* seemed very near, as if Nighthawk might fly to him and perch on his handle. Her grandmother had told her, "*Akwach* is the dipper that pours out the stars. When the morning comes, all the stars have been spilled into the darkness."

"That is fine for the stars," Daisy muttered. "*Akwach* will gather them up again before the twilight comes. When I am poured out into darkness, Grandmother, who will gather up my soul?" (8–9)

Her neighbor reports balls of fire, a phenomenon usually associated with witches, and his discovery of raven eggs and owl feathers nearby—witches' tools to bring illness and death—confirms the association, especially when his sheep die in a big wind. Perika too has seen the fireballs and, remembering her grandmother's warnings about Chimney Rock being the gathering place of powerful witches, she finds herself threatened by witches she recognizes, including a university scholar who had attended the last Sun Dance. She still hears the monotonous rhythm of the drum which frees her spirit to travel to lowerworld, and though she feels too old for the arduous work of a shaman, what the dwarf reveals to her on her dream vision journey down the river of death heightens her sense of impending danger and drives her to warn the police authorities, for the sake of the community at large.

Daisy's seeming ramblings about the servant of the Dark One at work among whites and about a young woman swallowing four black stones make just enough sense to transform what seemed like a clear-cut case of murder over a romantic or domestic issue into something darker and more challenging. Later, Perika, warned by her dwarf, hides from the murderer the police pursue to her home, and Doss describes the dwarf and old woman together, though he reports, "A visitor would have seen no one in the shelter with the Ute woman, but the old shaman perceived much that was invisible" (232). This first Perika novel cautiously suggests otherworld activities at work alongside our own reality (the dwarf destroying the villain to keep Perika's gifts coming) but carefully leaves open the possibility that Perika herself may have set the death snare and that the witches and spirits are fantasy, not reality. The episodes seen from Perika's perspective can be explained away as the visions of an unreliable narrator, a hallucinating true believer. A rational explanation, however, is partially offset by Parrish, a trained mainstream investigator sharing Perika's dream visions due to his Celtic heritage. Parrish occupies a point of view midway between Perika's spiritualism and Charlie Moon's rationalism, an opportune perspective that Doss exploits to a greater and lesser degree in the novels which follow (Perika tells Parrish, "You see things . . . know things. But you don't believe what you know") (127).

In his later books, Doss merges Ute beliefs with Christianity, converting

Perika to a regular Roman Catholic churchgoer who makes the sign of the cross to force witches to flee, and whose first thought upon seeing her neighbor after his unusual disappearance is that angels, not Ute spirits, had taken and then returned him. He carries this Christian overlay further in *The Shaman's Game*, in which a local priest helps carry out a traditional Ute burial in a secret canyon site, and in *The Night Visitor*, in which the priest wins Perika's promise to no longer leave gifts for her dwarf spirit. Nonetheless, Perika's magic remains the product of Ute, not Christian, mysticism. Her grandmother had taught her about water spirits, Badger, Bear, and the demon *Kwasigeti*, who comes for people's souls, and, in the ancient petroglyphs on canyon walls, she sees reminders of past shamans and the elemental earth spirits they communed with, such as the dwarf who speaks to her. Her grandfather, a respected shaman and sage, taught Perika to see what others could not, to perform rituals with chants to the four quarters of the world, to offer tobacco to the dwarf spirit, and to heed the warnings when cold wind spirits beckon. She chants the songs her ancestors sang as they crossed from Asia to the Americas, the sacred songs of the Great Mysterious One, and when in sudden trouble, she prays to the Great Mystery for assistance. When she feels uneasy, she knows something bad is afoot in the spirit world, and a shamanistic journey to the subterranean Middle World where she might ride a giant buffalo with ember eyes through an eerie forest of lifeless creatures confirms her instincts. Thus, Daisy Perika as shaman-with-Christian-influences is a far cry from Margaret Coel's Arapaho, with their seamless blending of native and European in an elegant illustration of Christian synchretism, the renowned capability of the religion to absorb different cultural elements into a coherent whole. Perika remains mostly Ute, and her forays into Christian belief systems are not always convincing.

The Shaman Laughs carries readers deeper into the fantastic horrors of the spirit world, as prize livestock are slaughtered and mutilated as part of some secret rite in Cañon del Serpiente, and a site where Anasazi women once ground corn becomes the scene of human sacrifice. Daisy travels to the lowerworld and sees an owl with pitiless eyes ripping its prey, a portent, says the dwarf, of some barbarous, taboo act. Even the down-to-earth Moon, whose grandmother had extraordinary powers, dreams of a shaggy-headed beast with curved horns and shining black hooves, dismembering a struggling human victim, and discovers that he is still Ute enough to fear corpse sickness. Perika's symbolic narrative of spiritual events witnessed in the canyon might be her way of telling the police that she had seen an actual murder, a kind of indirect language with which to report an ordinary crime, but the Ute part of Moon thinks not (167), and the nightmare visions Parrish experiences on his own make him believe in a supernatural force at work as well.

Yet, the horror is actually workaday, local residents being frightened into relocating so radioactive waste from nuclear power plants can be stored in Perika's sacred canyon. In light of the eviction-storage scheme, the supernatural events seem hoaxes, purposefully concocted to drive credulous traditionalists from their canyon, but their perpetrator is a madman who has discovered in his dramatic role the pleasure of mutilation, murder, and cannibalism. Perika breaks character by taking physical action different from her normal interpretive role, burning down the Economic Development Building housing the federal storage project papers and taking purposeful (and comic) revenge on an FBI man who accused her of serving dog meat to a guest; such acts seem like healthy, non-shamanistic responses to federal interference in private Ute lives. After being served up as authentic supernatural events, the magical elements seem to fade away, either being explained as hoaxes or, again, as surreal visions in Daisy Perika's possibly unstable mind. Given the truly vivid and memorable depictions of the Colorado region and the sharply drawn characters, this uncertainty about the reality of events is somewhat disappointing. Is the final answer provided by a shaman or a Sherlock? Doss finesses the question.

In spite of lyrical descriptions of Colorado's mountains and canyons, of the varied people over history awed by that beauty, and of the mystical ties between the land and its inhabitants, *The Shaman's Bones* concerns drug running, tribal politics, cannibalism, crucifixion, and stolen shaman power. Daisy Perika's nightmare visions of a heavy rain of blood, a floating corpse, and a strange tapping warn that fellow Utes will die, a warning that Moon and Parrish ignore. Later, a dream of a child's untenanted grave suggests special danger. Doss introduces a second Ute shaman, an eccentric old man named Blue Cup, who sends his spirit and his deaf Shoshone apprentice, Noah Dancing Crow, to recover a powerful, stolen sacred object, a whistle from the bone of an eagle's wing. Perika is involved because the thief, Provo Frank, has left his five-year-old daughter Sarah with her. The police suspect that Provo ritually murdered his wife (nailed her upside down to a tree) near the City Limits Motel in Wyoming.

Between action scenes are shamanistic prayers/prophecies and Perika's unsettling visions of spiritual mayhem. Ironically, both Perika and Blue Cup, despite shared visions of a world beyond ordinary perceptions, are witty and irreverent, enjoying a good joke at the expense of the uninformed. As Blue Cup teaches his apprentice, readers learn too, for example, about the significance of the three circles associated with the sun and the five circles of the Tunnel Between Worlds, proper behavior in a sacred place, the contents of a medicine bundle, the meaning of some petroglyphs, the nature of the Middle World, and so on. At one point, Perika plunges into the dream world, where she youthfully pursues a great white owl through the fog between two worlds, meeting Navajo, Cheyenne, Shoshone, Apache, and Ute dead and playing the Navajo shoe game with a Ute in order to bring young Sarah back from the land of the dead; of course, when the shaman regains consciousness from her fall, Sarah is there beside her, and Doss once again lets readers decide whether she really brought Sarah back from the land of the dead or whether Sarah had simply come out of some hiding place on her own and Daisy's experience was what Moon calls a foolish dream. The apprentice's report of Blue Cup being struck by lightning also varies from what readers are told occurred: Blue Cup experiencing a vision, offering sacred deerskin and eagle feather ceremonial garments, and choosing to pass into another reality. However, what the apprentice does tell police is enough to make Moon fear he himself might end up dreaming the old dreams and singing the old songs, unable to distinguish between substance and shadow (307) and to make him follow the old ways to return a powerful artifact to the spirit world.

A series of Sun Dance rituals (Dancing Thirsty) around a beribboned, striped sacred tree (a cottonwood pole) within the enchanted circle unites the characters and events in *The Shaman's Game*. This grueling healing ritual in which Shoshone, Paiute, Sioux, Kiowa, Ute, and white worshipers dance for several days, accompanied by a bone whistle, unexpectedly results in healthy dancers dying—by natural causes, says the official report. However, Moon suspects foul play, while Perika actually sees an evil presence, a witch, at work, like a hawk swooping down on vulnerable sparrows. When tribal reporter Delly Sands is injured, supposedly while seeking the identity of the witch behind the recent deaths, Moon, enamoured of her youthful ways, suspects, rightly, that he might be fighting forces beyond his understanding. If Perika is correct, Sands used age-old shamanistic methods to steal healing power from a sacred ceremony, a stratagem Perika has the specialized knowledge to recognize and thwart. Doss, however, is not content to end with Ute spiritualism and turns instead to a biblical parallel with Samson and Delilah (Delly's full name) and the more prosaic explanation of poisoned darts.

Likewise, *The Night Visitor: A Shaman Mystery*, with its many characters and tangled plot, asserts preternatural causes, only to undercut them. Perika is haunted by an apparition, a silent, disheveled *matukach*, or white "magician," while sharing her trailer home with eight-year-old orphan Sarah Frank from *The Shaman's Bones* and *The Shaman's Game*. The apparition is linked to a voracious whirlwind that unearths a 31,000-year-old mammoth on a local dude ranch and thus draws world-famed paleontologists, archaeologists, and greedy collectors to the scene. The second find, a flint blade, results in an unexplained disappearance, a murder, and the additional discovery of the skeleton of a Stone Age Caucasian hunter, crushed beneath the beast. While Moon tracks down modern-day villainy, supernatural forces draw his aunt into a grim, related murder from the past as the long-dead cry out for justice. Moon understands that the ancient and the rare have traditionally inspired avarice, mendacity, and murder, and readily deduces sound investigative hypotheses to explain events. While Doss employs dark and dangerous dream visions to suggest that ancient evil threatens Perika and the two young girls in her care (one the daughter of the murder victim), he separates Perika's mystical visions of past events from prosaic modern explanations and eventually provides a human perpetrator. Readers are left wondering whether the spirit from the past is a fantasy that Perika and young Sarah Franks share or an alternate reality to which Moon and rationalists like him are blind.

Thus, Doss combines shamanistic revelation and practical police work, asserting through Perika, and sometimes even Moon, Parrish, or local Utes, the validity of a spiritual vision, then undercutting this assertion to suggest, as Hackler does in his New Mexico stories, that the visions are simply symbolic representations of reasonable events in a rational world. Doss also provides, as creatively as any writer in the Native American detective genre, a persuasive milieu, a Colorado setting so sharply drawn and convincing that the untraveled can appreciate the state's wonderfully odd cultural mix in cinematically stunning physical country. The exotic otherworldly beauty of such settings gives credence to supernatural possibility, lending geographic authenticity to plot, character, and event. Doss, however, backs away from a full acceptance of the intuitive, creating instead a mix of perspectives which lets readers decide where reality lies.

SHAMAN AND SHERLOCK: THE BENETSEE–DU PRÉ TEAM

Peter Bowen's Native American detective series, set in and around Toussaint, Montana, in the Wolf mountain range, combines the sacred knowledge and skills of an aged shaman, Benetsee, with the intuition (and occasional logic) of a droll, quirky Montana cattle-brand inspector, Gabriel Du Pré, who doubles as a deputy when the need arises. A Métis, whose Cree, Chippewa, Ojibway, and Nez Percé blood is mixed with French and Scots, Du Pré takes pride in his complex heritage, playing the songs of the French voyageurs on his fiddle and singing the laments composed when they trapped and traded for furs in the seventeenth century, far from home and loved ones. He is very much a mountain man, reflecting the values and prejudices of the local community—loyalty to friends and family, contempt for ignorant outsiders, enjoyment of hard liquor and a warm woman, and stoic respect for the harsh cruelties of nature (bear attacks, sudden avalanches, killing cold). When he plays his fiddle on an important occasion, he dresses in the same style as did his great-grandfather: Nez Percé–style beaded moccasins, quill-work vest with natural dyes, white deerskin gaiters. He drives an old boat of a police car or sometimes borrows a friend's pickup truck or sports utility vehicle, hunts game in season, despises environmentalists meddling with local concerns, and performs all the types of physical labor mountain dwellers have need of, from mucking out stables

and shoveling hay into feedracks to driving a backhoe. He has no tolerance
for flatlanders, officialdom, Texans, or stupidity. When an inexperienced
young cowboy flies into a rage and beats his horse for shying from a rattlesnake, Du Pré has no sympathy when the horse falls on the cowboy's
leg; he swings the bleating ill-tempered youth over the back of the abused
horse and proclaims, "I hope he dumps you and kicks you to death,"
adding, "he does, I buy him, feed him oats and carrots everyday, molasses.
. . . You're too stupid to live" (*Coyote Wind*, 9). When someone shoots at
him, he shoots back with deadly accuracy. Eccentrics dominate British fiction—from the characters of Charles Dickens to those of John Mortimer
and Jonathan Gash—but Du Pré is a true American eccentric, one whose
irascible but charming oddness arises directly out of the land he inhabits.

Du Pré accepts as simply nature's way the fact that bears waking from
hibernation have feasted on murdered environmentalists buried under the
snow in *Wolf, No Wolf*. He tames a blind owl in *Long Son* and is not
really disturbed when it eats the family cats; he is equally sanguine about
an innocent-seeming youth of Métis heritage using traditional Indian methods to eliminate drug dealers operating a cocaine/heroin factory on a local
ranch. When a mountain rescue is needed, Du Pré does what it takes, even
facing an avalanche to rescue a missing person in *Wolf, No Wolf*. He says
he is no detective, but the regional sheriff tells him his official status as
cattle inspector makes him the only identifiable official the police can call
their own, and his family's more-than-a-century residence locally means he
probably knows somebody who knows something that will help solve the
case. Law enforcement officers cannot investigate without local help, so he
takes on the job. Relatives assert his blood duty to help. Bowen makes
Du Pré seem a completely normal part of his rough and quirky Montana
environment.

Du Pré goes to earth in Toussaint, a village emblematic of rural Montana, with the Toussaint Saloon his staging area for confronting the outside
world. The saloon, like an British pub, is far more than an eating and
drinking establishment for, apart from the school, it is the only meeting
place for the locals, a somewhat shabby, run-down building but a repository of trust in personal relationships and a forum for open communication
between the diverse folk of the area, impoverished Métis, struggling ranchers, Du Pré's multimillionaire friend Bart, occasional tourists, migrant la-
borers following the wheat combines, and even FBI agents consulting Du
Pré. The Toussaint Saloon is as much of a throwback as Du Pré himself,
a whiskey and tobacco-smoke environment where people run tabs and
serve themselves behind the bar when the proprietors are busy. A resolutely
politically incorrect Montana spirit reigns, not simply in social attitudes
but in Du Pré's detection as well: when the FBI cannot deal with serial
killers in *Notches* (the title alludes to notches as counters of people dis-
patched, as well as to means of displaying corpses), Du Pré and a trucker

friend, Rolly Challis, become a two-man posse hunting down and punishing the guilty in the best traditions of the Old West. Whereas in *Coyote Wind* and *Specimen Song* Du Pré's dealing out of frontier justice is staged as *High Noon*-type shootouts, in which the kill-or-be-killed situations reduce the affront to current sensibilities, in *Notches* the villains are sent to their rewards by pure execution. Du Pré suffers guilt and the condemnation of Harvey, the FBI special agent, but the novel stays firmly unapologetic about the need for vigilante action when the established authorities cannot act. This unfashionable refusal to give way to the modern world gives Du Pré much of his charm. His detective-story progenitors are Dashiell Hammett's The Continental Op and Mickey Spillane's Mike Hammer, both lone wolves who sorted out criminals and dispensed hard justice as they saw fit; Du Pré's Métis heritage and his Montana environment, however, provide cover for detective values long considered extinct in popular fiction and here make sense of the typical hard-boiled attitude that a detective must do what he must do.

Du Pré has no mystical powers, but unlike James Doss' skeptical detective, Moon, he relies unquestioningly on his shamanistic source, heeding Benetsee's cryptic warnings and advice about how to conduct his laid back, informal, offbeat investigations. Benetsee, in turn, relies on Du Pré as a regular source of whiskey, beer, tobacco, and amusement and as an apprentice of sorts (or maybe an eager birddog) who can go where Benetsee cannot. In *Specimen Song*, for example, Benetsee sends Du Pré off on a Métis canoe expedition that will trace the path of the voyageurs down a Canadian river, but his motive in doing so is to bring Du Pré into contact with the serial killer responsible for the death of a young Cree woman at a Smithsonian Institution country music celebration. To prepare him for this journey and for the encounter with a psychopathic Indian hater who batters Métis women to death with primitive weapons, Benetsee performs a special ceremony. He whirls a bull roarer on sacred land, recounts for Du Pré the weeping murdered women he has envisioned on their way to the Star Trail, and arms him not only spiritually with a protective obsidian knife amulet but also physically with six magically marked black stones to be hurled from a slingshot as soon as Du Pré identifies the murderer. Du Pré must figure out the who and the why and set the trap to confirm his suspicions, but he takes to heart Benetsee's warning that identification of the murderer will require immediate retaliation or Du Pré will himself be killed; thus, when the moment comes, Du Pré walks away from the dead villain and does not look back. When he faces a pair of sadistic torturers and serial killers in *Notches* and fears his lover's daughter might be their victim, he needs the elusive Benetsee's help, not simply to get inside the heads of the killers but to keep what he learns from becoming a part of his own psyche.

However, Benetsee is no New Age shaman. At times, he seems like just a very old and smelly drunk:

"The hunter dream the deer and the deer come," said Benetsee.
"Shape you in, I don't want to see what you dream come at all," said Du Pré. The car smelled like the drunk tank. Benetsee belched, adding a little more to the stench. (*Coyote Wind*, 89)

At other times, he seems like a con artist, creating "ancient" pipes from red stone (admittedly quarried 5,000 years earlier), fitting them with a modern willow stem and decorative chicken feathers, and selling them to ingenuous tourists. Still other times, he is a very clever thief, stealing items from seemingly inaccessible places. In addition, he can be very contrary, disappearing when Du Pré seeks his advice, persuading Du Pré to plunge into icy water and roaring with laughter at the spectacle, wearing vermilion and carbon face paint and Stone Age attire and dancing and chanting and waving a white bone *atlatl* at an archaeological site to drive reporters into a frenzy, and never telling everything he knows about a given situation. Du Pré, however, understands that his antics and silences can be equally informative if one has the patience and wit to figure out what they mean.

There are always coyotes around Benetsee, who calls these tricksters "God's dogs," because they can tell people things if one can figure out what Coyote is saying and how much he is toying with humans. Du Pré argues that the ancient prophets must have been a lot like Benetsee—"No damn wonder folks killed them. Irritating sonsofbitches" (*Coyote Wind*, 67)—but he also admits Benetsee knows things there is no way he should know—riddles, weather, really old songs and chants, and details about Stone Age peoples, how they navigated, how they hunted, and even how they wove their snowshoes or lashed flint spearheads to the spear shaft. The 95-pound Benetsee plays the willow flute the Métis way, speaks modern and ancient dialects of numerous tribal languages equally well, and even chants in a high, keening ululation the eerie, atonal burial lament of the Horned Star People—Caucasian travelers from the north 12,000 years earlier. Benetsee looks at a dinosaur tooth Du Pré is asking about, and says, "Oh, him, . . . I know him where he is" (*Thunder Horse*, 71). Sometimes Benetsee just gives Du Pré special tobacco to smoke: "Pretty soon you smoke that," said Benetsee. "You know when and where and for which man. Smoke it, watch the smoke rise, go to his tired soul on the Star Trail" (*Coyote Wind*, 132). Du Pré smokes and suddenly knows who, what, when, and where and acts immediately on that knowledge. Whether this is magic or simply the result of released tensions is left up to the reader. Other times Benetsee's singing along evokes in Du Pré visions of the past; a long canoe paddled across black water as a man in a beaked mask and feathered costume in its bow imitates an eagle.

In *Wolf, No Wolf* controversial legislation to introduce grey wolves into ranch territory sends tempers rising, but when urban ecoprotestors, disguised as hunters, cut the fences of local ranchers, drive their cattle off leased public land, and release wolves, someone takes offense and kills the wolves and their releasers. These acts provoke bumbling federal agents into confrontations with cowboys and Indians, including old Benetsee, whose eccentric ways meet their guidelines for dangerous activist Indians. Du Pré helps get his rich outsider friend Bart appointed acting sheriff to protect locals from just such stereotyping, while Benetsee uses his extraordinary powers to teach federal agents just how unwelcome they are and how dangerous and unforgiving mountain country can be. Coyote tricksters associated with Du Pré and Benetsee keep appearing at propitious times, and Benetsee warns day-tripping urban protesters that they come with bad hearts, will kill a lot of people with their foolish talk, and will be eaten up by the place if they stay (and some of them are).

Both *Coyote Wind* and *Thunder Horse* pull Du Pré into the past, through the discovery of a plane missing for 35 years and of a skull with a bullet hole in it in the first and of a *Tyrannosaurus rex* tooth and an ancient burial site that offers clues to the origins of his Métis ancestors in the second. In the first, Du Pré discovers that his father is the killer—but with good reason. In the second, he learns that a Métis hero, Gabriel Dumont, once hid out in a cave so sacred to the Crow that they are still willing to kill to protect its secrets, and that that cave was sacred to ancient peoples going back many thousands of years. Both stories confirm Bowen's argument that the past is inescapable and that it is inextricably bound in unpredictable ways to the present; as a result, a good Western detective must weigh the present against the past in order to decide the future.

In contrast, *The Stick Game* concentrates on present criminality—not that of a crazed individual but of an unethical company that is out of control. When Du Pré's lover, Madelaine Placquemines, persuades him to investigate the disappearance of the teenage son of a distant cousin and the misfortunes of many more youngsters on the Fort Belknap Reservation, Du Pré connects a high incidence of birth defects and mental and physical problems (blindness, deafness, mental retardation) to a gold mining operation adjacent to reservation land. Later, when the missing youth turns up dead in a well, Du Pré discovers a water supply poisoned by heavy-metal waste products leached into the water supply. Aided by an archaeologist, a retired mining executive, and a local doctor, Du Pré proves the mining company's responsibility and cover-up. During this investigative process, Bowen provides interesting facts about native dialects, customs, rituals, and the harsh Montana environment. As in *Long Son*, Du Pré approves of a youthful Native American youth seeking personal and tribal justice on his own, in this case by forcing the mining company to admit criminal liability.

Notches is a definitive Du Pré novel, with the action firmly grounded in Toussaint but with Du Pré ranging out from the tiny settlement to protect his beloved Madelaine's "babies," her two teenage daughters and the other young and vulnerable women of the area from serial killers. Madelaine explicitly connects her man's defensive forays to those of their Métis ancestors, warriors who would roam up to 20 miles away from the campground to ward off threats. Du Pré repeatedly visits Benetsee's cabin to enlist supernatural help in the needle-in-the-haystack task of identifying mobile serial killers, and along the way we learn of the impossibility of ever finding murderers who strike randomly at defenseless girls and women and then move on. The ratiocinative detective's primary assumption is that all crimes occur for some reason, and that these reasons or causes can be teased out through exploration of who had means, motive, and opportunity. Serial killings, however, as the real-life Ted Bundy and Green River cases referenced in *Notches* make clear, are essentially irrational and motiveless; the aberrant sexuality involved has motivations unclear even to the perpetrators, who seem to be obeying demons invisible to normal people and perhaps experts as well. In the open reaches of Montana and the West, means and opportunity, the two categories of exclusion developed to narrow down suspects in crowded urban areas, become, ironically, unhelpful: many people out West are armed and capable, and the excellent highway system provides easy and unobtrusive access to hundreds of square miles of lonely killing fields. Since dedicated serial killers are aware of how paper trails are left in the modern world, they act to make tracking almost impossible. (Here a killer working stretches of highway installs huge gas tanks in his van to eliminate gas purchases and the resultant traceable records.) FBI man Harvey Wallace (whose Blackfeet name is Weasel Fat) and his colleague agent Pidgeon (herself "Redbone . . . Black, Cherokee, white, Mexican, French") (46) admit that even the FBI has called in psychics to find such killers, an admission of how useless modern ratiocinative methods are against figures of pure evil, "animals," as the characters repeatedly call them.

The frustrated FBI agents hope Du Pré might find their serial killers (although Harvey worries about having to arrest his Métis friend for murdering them), and Benetsee's intuitive help is suggested as a possible method of locating their whereabouts. Benetsee, however, has disappeared on one of his trips to Canada, leaving a young acolyte who is no help to the detective; the shaman's message is that the case will be solved before the next snow, a typically pointless prediction given that Montana sees snow in July on occasion. Du Pré is thus forced back on his own resources, returning to the ways of his ancestors when they needed to protect their tribe. Unlike similar situations in other Indian detective stories in which the investigator indulges a full ritual of authentic or supposed shamanistic activities to evoke intuitive insight, Du Pré simply behaves as a Métis warrior would, tracking long hours with minimum sleep and food and staying on the alert with maximum concentration. Bowen describes Du Pré's tracking methods:

Du Pré stopped and he breathed deeply and he set his mind to lock out sounds and the wind and all that was not in his first sight, to bring the ground up to his eyes, see what was on it that shouldn't be there.

At the place he had begun, when he returned to it after a time spent walking slowly, he glanced toward the center of the loop and he saw something circular. (95–96)

What Du Pré finds is a socket lost from a socket wrench set. Later, at a crime scene, he again takes his time tracking, noting that some man walked through the area the day before in the afternoon: "Du Pré got down on his haunches and he looked at the faint print of a bootsole, a hiking boot with five stars up the center of the sole" (160). He counts ant tracks across the trail, into the faint depression, and "on toward whatever it was that the ants were working on," and he notes the anthill standing 20 feet away; he observes that a bombardier beetle had scuttled across and, on the basis of these signs from nature, concludes, "Maybe twenty-four hours. Less, I think. Yesterday afternoon, late. No dew, no rain" (160).

But Bowen is unsentimental about presuming the worth of older ways when newer ones are more efficient; Du Pré washes his jerky down with whiskey, drives in his old police cruiser up to the foot of the overlook where he will camp, uses an electronic tracking device and cell phone to set his trap, and in general recognizes that he is not operating in the eighteenth or nineteenth centuries. As does Doss, Bowen locates shamanistic and Sherlock approaches in different characters, but unlike the Colorado writer, the Montanan, no doubt aided by the earthy, atavistic setting in the northern Rockies, credibly links his detective with a rich and coherent Native American heritage. The Métis culture, with its ancient links back to a variety of Indian tribes and to Canada and its French and Celtic influences, offers a range of possibilities absent with tribes more ethnically "pure." For example, the Métis voyageurs ranged from eastern Canada west to the Red River and over to Du Pré's Montana and down the Mississippi to Missouri and New Orleans. While they hunted buffalo like their Plains compatriots, they also traded up and down their watery byways, communicating with a wide variety of cultures and people. Du Pré's easy relationship with the FBI and other practitioners of modern ways, despite his personal disdain for the newfangled, his accommodation to modern technology when absolutely necessary, and his ability to range far afield from his headquarters in Toussaint are easily explained given his Métis heritage. Adaptability to landscape, climate, and culture was powerful Métis medicine, and Du Pré still knows how to practice this virtue. The past is an integral part of the present; Benetsee's intuitive shamanism is not, like Perika's, an isolated throwback to a much earlier time but rather a part, though an odd part, of the Montana Métis culture.

SHAMAN OR SHERLOCK: KATHLEEN EAGLE'S CONTRASTING APPROACHES

Although Kathleen Eagle is primarily a romance writer, two of her romances, *Sunrise Song* and *The Night Remembers*, partake of the conventions of detective fiction and thus are worthy of mention here. Technically romances because the love relationships in both novels take precedence over all else, they nonetheless illustrate the dichotomy between a ratiocinative and a shamanistic approach to crime. The first, the ratiocinative, is a disturbingly realistic story of past wrongs perpetuated into the present: the lifetime commitments of Sioux Indians to the Hiawatha Insane Asylum for Indians, in Canton, South Dakota, with Bureau of Indian Affairs' approval; such commitments are mainly a way to steal Indian land but also to punish the Sioux for practicing their religion, speaking their language, or asking too many questions about the nefarious money-making schemes of whites. The second, the shamanistic, is a surreal mix of urban crime story and coyote myth: a tribal police officer who suffers a nervous breakdown when one of his children kills the other with his police weapon, who fights street crime as a shamanistic superhero, and who is finally restored to harmony by personal and shamanistic powers.

Sunrise Song, like Ed Gorman's *Hawk Moon*, juxtaposes two time periods, the late 1920s to 1930s and 1973, and two sets of cross-cultural characters in order to show how a crime can be covered up over generations and how ill-gained wealth can taint its inheritors. The key 1920s' figures are Rachael Trainor, the sister of the Bureau of Indian Affairs representative, and Adam Lone Bull, a decorated war hero whose younger brother has been falsely committed to the asylum and sexually abused by its director. Lone Bull's investigation of the asylum's committal practices is short lived, for his discovery of the financial ties between the BIA representative and the asylum director leads to his being committed to the asylum himself, drugged, and then murdered; ultimately, Rachel too is silenced. Fifty years later, the modern amateur investigators are unknowingly tied to the past by their genetics. Michelle Benedict is the niece of the former asylum director, and Zane Lone Bull, a mixed-blood Lakota Sioux who thinks he was abandoned by his parents, is the son of Rachael Trainor and Adam Lone Bull. Zane Lone Bull, like his father, is a war hero, having served with honor in the Vietnam War, and he brings his warrior skills to the fray that soon overtake him. Michelle initiates the modern investigation, for when the asylum closes, she feels a commitment to return the bodies of the Sioux buried on the institution's grounds to any relatives who may wish to rebury them on native soil. The discovery of an Adam Lone Bull brings

Zane into the investigation, and the pursuit of explanations that delve into the heart of his identity results in threats to the lives of the amateur investigators. The uncle whom Zane has dismissed as insane turns out to be the missing link in the investigation, the sodomized younger brother whose unwarranted commitment to the asylum cost Adam Lone Bull his life. With time, the uncle's memories help Michelle and Zane unlock the past. The ugly secret is the BIA and the asylum director stealing Indian land and maintaining secrecy by institutionalizing anyone who could testify against them. It is the representatives of authority and order who have abused their positions and have murdered to maintain silence, and the Sioux as a people have been so intimidated that they have had no way to voice their fears about what has happened. How can anyone, let alone the disenfranchised, stand against medical declarations of insanity, especially with friends and relatives fettered and drugged by the authorities who control the legal decision making? The investigative couple run up against the ill will and violence of those who still benefit from ill-gained profits, but social justice finally prevails, and the law steps in to help some Sioux recoup what had been stolen at great human cost. The ending exposes the secrets of the past, offers a comeuppance for the modern-day perpetrators, and offers some sense of wrong vindicated. The detectives' approach is very much in the Holmes' school of investigation: the uncovering of secrets through logic and persistence.

The Night Remembers turns from the rural to the urban, from detection to mysticism. Although not a murder mystery, this novel features crime elements: a raw, threatening, urban milieu, the stalking of Angela Prescott by a rich, powerful sadist, urban warfare resulting from drug territory competition, and the potential for sudden violence and possible murder. As in other urban crime stories, it sets prostitutes, drug dealers, teenage gang members, and other such down-and-outs of the metropolitan ghetto against the representatives of the law, in this case, Jesse Brown Wolf, a Sioux tribal policeman who attended the FBI Academy to train as a career law officer. However, personal trauma (one of his children killing the other with his police gun) has left him solitary, out of balance, and distanced from his tribal community and family roots. Like other city dwellers, he has undergone a shift of psyche, but for him this shift has put him in tune with his mystical, mythical connections to nature and the Sioux spirit world. He has become a shape-shifter, an amber-eyed coyote man with an underground den and a coyote pelt donned when he sets out to right wrongs. He enacts his policing role in unconventional ways that reflect the Sioux trickster tradition, communicating with animals and clowning about, yet also righting wrongs—stopping thugs from injuring the weak, chasing criminals and drug dealers out of the neighborhood he has made his own, and helping the needy find inner strength. As in the oral tradition wherein Coyote puts the broken pieces of himself back together, Jesse, in befriending and assisting others, regains his lost balance, reassembles the fragmented pieces of his psyche, finds a new family among those he has rescued from injury and possible death, and returns to his community with a new vision of himself and his role.

Thus, Kathleen Eagle, though writing in a romance tradition, exploits the division that characterizes the Native American detective novel, the split between Western logic and native spirituality.

SHERLOCK

One of the earliest Plains Sherlocks was Manly Wade Wellman's David Return. Wellman, who was part Plains Indian himself, made Return a member of the "Tsichah" (a fictitious tribe) and his father, Tough Feather, a tribal police officer. In his short story "A Star for a Warrior" (1946), Tough Feather tells his son, who has just gotten home from police college, that their goal as tribal police officers is to "make things better for all Indians" (8). Return pins on his shiny badge of authority and accepts his first assignment—seemingly an easy one—to persuade a pretty anthropologist to come back to town with him. Gathering materials for a book on native music, she has been trying to wheedle the secret songs of the tribe out of the young men whose duty it has been to memorize them, play them at ceremonies, and pass them on to their sons. However, Return arrives too late. He finds the girl dead, shot in the throat, the wound slashed with a knife. The three keepers of the sacred songs are camped nearby, and Return must use close observation and logic to fix blame. Because of their shared sacred mission, the three purposely try to thwart his ends, belittling his experience and providing misdirection, but his knowledge of sweatlodge rituals and tribal purification rules enables him to identify a compact war club as the real murder weapon and its owner as the killer.

The straightforward presentation of Return as an educated man of reason, exacting in his observation and cerebral in his methodology despite his youth, yet with special insights into tribal ways to perceive what white authorities would miss, sets the pattern for today's native Sherlocks. Wellman succinctly provides readers with background on tribal relationships, customs, and values as a natural part of his narrative, but it is the intellectual puzzle that dominates the story and confirms Return's right to wear the tribal star he has just donned.

Oklahomans John Miles, Fred Groves, and Jean Hager, Rhode Islander J. F. Trainor, and Coloradan Margaret Coel follow in Wellman's footsteps. They too rely on Native American detectives who figure out how crimes unfold, who respond in conventional European-rationalist ways, and who use logic plus the intuitive flash of insight that comes from experience, knowledge, and cause-effect processes of reasoning. These writers may occasionally work in the idea of another way of viewing reality, but the vision of investigation that drives their detectives is mainstream—interviewing witnesses and suspects, collecting evidence, piecing together clues, examining motive, means, and opportunity, and drawing conclusions through a combination of inductive and deductive logic and informed intuition. The degree of importance placed on the intuitive by each of the writers, however, reflects different positions on the role of traditional ratiocinative problem-solving methods in present-day crime detection involving Native Americans.

John Miles' sheriff, Johnnie Baker, may be one-sixteenth Choctaw, with her name on the Oklahoma rolls of officially recognized tribe members, but she is an assimilated blonde with Hollywood movie experience, who has gotten her job in Tenoclock, Colorado, as a form of local publicity because of her "stardom" and her cuteness. Consequently, except for what she calls a personal affinity for things native, she is totally assimilated and reflects mainstream attitudes, values, and methods. In Miles' *Tenoclock Scholar*, when a body is discovered with an arrow through its neck and a knife with Anasazi-style carvings on it shows up in the rubble of the burnt-down courthouse, racist white locals blame the Utes, the Utes cry "frame," hotheads on both sides escalate the troubles, and Baker is caught in the middle, trying to keep the peace while figuring out who is committing the crimes and why. When a local medicine man, Abner Wakinokiman, spouts ancient prophesies about an Anasazi curse, Baker deputizes her most vocal Ute critic in spite of city council disapproval. Caught by surprise at being involved as aids, not suspects, in the investigative process, the Ute prove instrumental in tracking down and saving a missing man. Nonetheless, the nativeness of Miles' novel is skin-deep, and with an African lion on main street and a man in a rubber skindiving suit stopping local thugs with an underwater stun gun, exploring deeper questions of difference is clearly not the author's concern. The novel ends with Wakinokiman performing a purification/protection ceremony with tobacco, sage, and corn before the opening of an Anasazi mound, and Baker feels "a sharp tingling of something, some archaic stab of emotion, half fear and half recognition" (245), but that is as Indian as it gets.

All the other writers in this group contrast native perspectives with mainstream ones.

Fred Grove's amateur detective, Boone Terrell, is a three-quarters Osage who is fearful of succumbing to the powerful draw of alcohol, who has played warrior by driving racecars in dangerous speedway events, and who, from a childhood spent playing Indian, knows the Oklahoma land where his friend has died while Boone was away on the racing circuit. He has been gone from home long enough to see the Osage Reservation with new eyes. He perceives fear in the faces of townspeople, hears of Osage bodies dumped heedlessly in ditches, and knows something is deeply wrong concerning the drowning of an old friend noted for his swimming skills. Boone is wary of everyone, for most of his high school buddies are long dead and the handful of survivors are drunks and failures. Furthermore, he has been away long enough to understand the con artists behind the smiles, handshakes, and seeming generosity of respected white community members. His murdered friend's features, seen in the sad face of the friend's small, full-blooded daughter, steel him to his purpose—to uncover the truth despite personal danger. However, he has no clear method of attack except to question official reports, view the terrain, and act on instinct. His investigation moves in intuitive flashes, whereby his understanding catches up with what his mind has already observed but has not made sense of.

In contrast to Grove's realistically conceived Osage, Trainor's amateur detective, Angela Biwaban, an Anishinabe "princess" from Duluth, Michigan, is clearly a fanciful, fictive invention. Though she rejects the label "Chippewa" as an ethnic slur, her Indianness, in the main, translates into a healthy distrust of institutions and governments and an affinity with hardworking, independent farmers and ranchers and with those on the fringes of society. Like Thomas Perry's Senecan heroine Jane Whitefield, she is a computer hacker skilled at extracting supposedly protected information and generating convincing fake identifications in order to inform her search for who did what and why. Verging on white-collar crime and creating red herrings to misdirect her parole officer and her dupes, her battle is class warfare, and her stands are against big brother justice (the prison system, parole officers, biased judges, racist police) and big business (banks, land and mine developers, insurance companies, construction companies)—all actively employed in corrupt and often illegal secret deals at the expense of decent, ordinary folk who do not know how to fight back. Thus the role she envisions for herself is an odd cross between an Indian Lone Ranger and a native Robin Hood, roaming the West battling establishment forces and rescuing the down-and-out or soon to be down-and-out and finding unconventional ways to transfer wealth from the greedy rich to the deserving poor. In sum, Trainor's premise is that his heroine's cultural heritage of being abused and downtrodden by broken treaties and a corrupt Bureau of Indian Affairs has awakened her sympathies for the downtrodden of white as well as non-white America, and she combines rural skills with sophisticated urban know-how to repeatedly defeat the powerful and would-be powerful. Anishinabe she may be, but basically this heritage translates into occasional dances at powwows (when relatives insist), traditional gifts to relatives (Mackinaw shirts), and a secret language to use with her grandfather.

Likewise, Hager's detectives are only loosely tied to the Cherokee community and are distanced from traditional ways of seeing, partly because the Cherokee have worked hard at assimilation into the mainstream for so long (many Oklahoma Cherokees are Baptists, their families Christian believers before their removal from the South, though they may see no conflict in praying to Thunder to cure disease). One Hager series detective, Mitch Bushyhead, calls Cherokee beliefs pure superstition, bugaboo legends to scare children into behaving (Stone Coat will eat your liver if you do not come straight home). Molly Bearpaw is slightly more sympathetic to the elderly, who practice traditional native ways of battling evil but basically views their practices as harmless or as the fuzzy-headedness of incipient senility rather than as a viable counter-cultural alternative. She is embarrassed by her childhood trust in what she as an adult has come to view as mere superstition. The elderly bemoan the loss of seasonal celebration rituals like the Green Corn dance and of taboos about intermarrying within a clan, and they fear a future without the old ways, but most of Hager's characters don't even realize that such rituals and taboos once existed, and many who do purposely don't teach them to their children, to free the next generation from what the present generation sees as a nightmare burden from the past.

Coel's native detective, in contrast, seeks deeper ties with the Arapaho community and supports traditional values for very modern reasons; her progression as a character is from the assimilation necessary to become a competent lawyer to a slow movement back into a tribal role accepted by and beneficial to her people. This progression allows Coel to provide deeper insights into Arapaho perspectives than Hager can into Cherokee culture. Both authors authoritatively report fragments from tribal histories, but the crimes Hager's detectives explore could occur in any small town in America, whereas the malfeasance Coel's detective investigates is tied to the land and the people and reflects real-world conflicts within the tribe and between the tribe and the outside world.

Fred Grove's Boone Terrell

Fred Grove's territory in his insightful detective novel *Warrior Road* is the same as that of Linda Hogan's *Mean Spirit*—the Osage reservation in post–World War I Oklahoma, a period of oil booms and methodical theft of Osage land and mineral rights. By focusing on two murders and one near murder, Grove particularizes a statewide pattern of victimization that characterized the era. He depicts the Osage as a peaceful people who never engaged in war against whites and whose code of politeness emphasizes indirection and avoidance of confrontation. Yet their sudden wealth due to the sharing of oil profits makes them easy targets because of their vulnerability to the glad handshake and to protestations of friendship backed by cheap gifts. Grove's hero bemoans his and his tribe's ineptitude and naivete, as Osage girls fall for the deceptive romantic patter of white gigolos seeking the wealth that becoming squaw men will bring, as ambitious white families adopt Osage children to control their oil titles and as Osage youths succumb to alcoholism and drugs and sign away their lives on insurance policies made out to loan sharks looking to cash in big on the accident-prone young men.

Boone Terrell may not know much of the Osage language, and he may have escaped reservation life for a large part of his adult life, but he is no mainstream detective. Like his fellow Osage, his instinct is to walk away from problems, so he has to force himself to speak directly, to confront officials aggressively, and to stay and fight even when the odds are very much against him. However, he takes offense when white males call him "boy," when a so-called Indian benefactor publicly humiliates natives seeking loans, and when the local sheriff throws him in jail on a trumped-up charge and then locks two thugs in the cell with him to rough him up. The more he is attacked and the more he is advised to get out of town while he can, the more he is convinced that his friend's death was no accident and that his friend's daughter's life is in danger. The local tribal authorities seem helpless in the face of white political power, and the aging white ranch hand who has worked alongside Terrell and his father for years is beaten and then strangled for standing by him. Against common sense, he decides that his life is meaningless unless he stands up for his friends and his people when it counts—even when they cannot or will not stand up for themselves. In doing so, he comes close to death several times. However, his persistence pays off eventually, and some of those who for too long participated in the deaths of Osage youths, the humiliation of Osage elders, and the theft of allotment checks, land, and mineral rights receive their comeuppance.

Grove's skill lies in the narrative voice, for Terrell shares in the vices and the virtues of his people, and as readers come to respect and grieve for Terrell, they come to respect and grieve for the Osage. As Terrell sees his hometown through mature eyes, he flashes back to memories of high school achievements and childhood games, of longed-for warrior visions and lovely girls and a sense of belonging that time has destroyed for him. When he talks to the mortician who signed his friend's death certificate, he defends tribal burial practices, painting the face so the dead man will be recognized by his dead friends, burying a cedar pole at the foot of the casket to symbolize eternity, blowing cedar smoke at the site to purify it, and leaving food at the grave for the dead man's journey. As he flees a vigilante posse led by the squaw man who married his dead friend's sister, he thinks of himself as Coyote, outwitting his pursuers, and he resorts to the trick of backtracking on his trail and other stratagems developed in his youth. Grove offers no long-term answers for a troubled and shameful period in this nation's history, but he does provide a hero for one town and insights that should supply readers with a more balanced perspective than history books. Clearly, many present-day Native American attitudes are grounded in the past, including the recent past treated by Grove.

J. F. Trainor's Angela Biwaban

Trainor's Angela Biwaban follows the modern tradition of the tough, resourceful, no-nonsense, female detective, who quite happily locks horns with large, aggressive males with superiority complexes. Aggressive about her Indian-ness and proud of her Black Bear Clan, she calls attendance at an Honor the Earth powwow "an antidote to Columbus" (*Whiskey Jack*, 16). Like Sara Paretsky's Chicago heroine V. I. Warshawski, what the petite Biwaban lacks in size she makes up for in spunk and gymnastic fighting skills, wading headlong into the fray, feet kicking and fists swinging—even when opponents are bulky "hick" police. From a crouch, she might launch herself like a human torpedo to strike opponents in the lower abdomen with her hard head, or lambaste a deranged man with a heavy kitchen implement. However, unlike Warshawski, Biwaban is basically a country girl, despite her easy acquisition of an urban facade. Her investigations depend on her familiarity with the terrain, history, and characteristics of rural regions and their citizens, her highly honed tracking skills, her tough physical endurance, and the survival skills her grandfather instilled in her. She scrutinizes the ground and recreates in her mind the scenario played out there. She carries with her a compass and a stainless steel survival knife with a mini-survival kit in its hollow handle ("a snare wire, nylon fishing line, sinkers, needles, tinder, lifeboat matches, a birthday candle, and a gauze pad") (*High Country Murder*, 299). In a pinch, she can make her own snowshoes, camouflage her tracks and location, find edible roots, and generate enough heat to survive a night on a snow-bound mountaintop; she can also find just the right herbs to aid a hangover or to stop bleeding.

She also has good instincts, a precognitive intuition that kicks in during times of extreme danger. This sixth sense usually occurs as a sudden awareness of hostile intent, an icy tremor at the nape of her neck and a spurt of adrenaline that either launches her into an attack or sends her running from the danger source. She attributes such responses to having experienced "random, senseless acts of violence" daily in the Springfield prison (*Corona Blue*, 10). Yet, she is basically good-hearted, empathizing with youngsters at odds with their families, single mothers having difficulty communicating with loved ones, and old folks whose stability and well-being are threatened.

When what her prison "mom" called her "fussbudget face" takes over, she is committed to investigation, no matter what the personal cost. Urban camouflage and duplicity are her specialties, the protective coloration of appropriate attire, diction, and accent, manufactured credentials, and a con artist's bag of tricks, as she dons the Corporate Angie look, the tough prison moll look, the innocent schoolgirl look, or whatever fits the need and occasion. Like Jonathan Gash's rascalish Lovejoy, Biwaban invites readers to share in her clever stratagems for faking documents, creating portfolios and cover stories, providing window dressing for a role, and applying age-old con games in inventive new ways to bait modern traps. (She claims that her master's in accounting from Montana State University is handy in unexpected ways.) Her duplicitous tricks derive more directly from confidence games than from detective strategies and, like confidence games, they are predicated on the foibles of the villain "victim."

Other key Biwaban detective strategies include theorizing as her grandfather (Charlie Blackbear) acts as devil's advocate and playing suspects off against each other. Having acquainted herself with the territory, players, and gossip in an investigation, she examines potential suspects for motive, means, and opportunity, sometimes discovering several compelling motives for a single crime or querying her own assumptions, as when she rejects her premise that a suspect is "a rational human being": "Wouldn't want to bet the rent money on that!" (*Whiskey Jack*, 228). Sometimes distracted by other villainy not directly a part of her particular case, she publicly confounds the evildoers before returning to her central investigation.

Though on parole from prison (having "borrowed" from a tax assessor's office to pay her dying mother's medical expenses and crunched numbers to cover up the "loan"), a warrant for her arrest under one of her numerous aliases keeps her undercover throughout the West—particularly South Dakota, Wyoming, and Colorado. The FBI has given her the code name "Pocahontas" but remains unsure of her real identity. As she travels, she joins conflicts between working locals and large conglomerate interests actively undermining their livelihood. In *Whiskey Jack*, the competing interests of loggers, spotted owl enthusiasts, drug dealers, survivalists, and Nazi skinheads in Washington State catch Biwaban in a deadly crossfire that necessitates a trap to catch a killer. In *Dynamite Pass*, the suspicious death of a forest ranger cousin leads Biwaban to uncover graft and corruption in the lumber business. In *Target for Murder*, a big-time Michigan land developer proves responsible for the death of Biwaban's oldest friend's husband and the theft of family property. *Corona Blue* begins with Biwaban driving a combine through a South Dakota cornfield, being suddenly sprayed with rifle fire, and spotting a dead body as she flees; it ends with Biwaban racing through rows of corn pursued by a child molester/murderer in a combine trying to cut her down. In between she angers local cops (stereotyped redneck racists with fixed images of drunken, no-good Indians) and thwarts a hydroelectric company which has ignored safety codes and a loan shark who has profited from lending farmers large sums only to call in the loans early.

Her strategy for undermining the greedy is to let their greed destroy them, to, in the disguise of an official or a hard-nosed businesswoman, offer them a chance for easy money (e.g., through a money laundering scheme); when they take the bait, she then uses the funds to pay back the loans of farmers or ranchers about to lose their land. She carries out stings to help widows recover stolen property, children their inheritance, and the indigent a place in their community. Such Robin-Hood-style activities keep her fleeing the law but also win her the gratitude of those she protects. A common Trainor pattern is for local farmers or ranchers to turn out at the end of a novel to help a neighbor bring in the crops or round up the cattle.

One of Trainor's most effective Biwaban mysteries, *High Country Murder*, combines a lost treasure from the glory days of Butch Cassidy and the Sundance Kid, a modern treasure from a successful heist, a proud daughter repeating her mother's pattern of fleeing responsibility, and a pleasing comeuppance for an unscrupulous lawyer/land dealer/loan shark. The novel's success rests partly on its location in territory that Trainor knows well, so the mystery reflects the region, and partly on the more sympathetic perspective of Biwaban's grandfather, who investigates as much as Biwaban and whose down-to-earth outlook undercuts Biwaban's occasionally romantic self-image and sometimes grating first-person narrative:

"So what do you have in mind?"

"*Nandobani*," I replied. An old word among our Anishinabe people, fraught with spiritual meaning. Going *nandobani* means giving up your normal life. You become a hunter of men. You melt into the forest, trailing your hidden foe, and then you take him out with a single well-aimed arrow.

Chief sighed. "Got another quarter on you?"

"*Eyan, Nimishoo.*" [Yes, grandfather.]

"Then why don't you drop it on the Colorado State patrol?" he suggested. "I'm sure they can do a much better job of protecting Sarah Sutton." (49)

Biwaban accompanies her supervisor from her South Dakota work-release program to northwestern Colorado when her supervisor's mother's vehicle goes off an icy road on Monarch Pass. There Biwaban finds a family in disarray, their ranch forfeited because of a mortgage called in early, the superior's daughter distraught at the loss of her beloved grandmother and her mother's distance, and the whole family squabbling over who to blame and what to do. Biwaban's grandfather has the mechanical expertise to figure out how the dead woman's brakes were rigged, to recognize the villain's weapon simply by sound, and to identify the tracks of a vehicle by wheelbase. In addition, he provides a credible audience on whom Biwaban can test her theories and to whom she can explain her stratagems ("That grandfather of mine! Every time I come up with a great theory, he runs it through the shredder") (196).

The Native American overlay of this series is exactly that, an overlay. Biwaban uses untranslated *Anishinabe* words and even Lakota, calls her parole officer "Kemo Sabe," describes Caucasians as "the new people," and occasionally tosses out tidbits of Anishinabe history. At the end of *Corona Blue*, when an electric shock nearly kills her, she dreams that her long-dead grandmother removes her from her cradleboard and cuddles her beside a campfire, where her parents stir boiling maple sap and a relative in traditional Anishinabe dress, roached and feathered hair, and red-and-white-striped face paint speaks to her gently. However, such tribal connections occur rarely, and what dominates instead is a socialist take on capitalistic corruption and a celebration of the "little people" that seems to conflict oddly with Biwaban's insistence on her title of "princess."

Jean Hager

One-eighth Cherokee Jean Hager depicts the practice of Western logic and intuition by highly assimilated Cherokee investigators who reject traditional tribal magic. Mitch Bushyhead follows routine police investigative methods; Molly Bearpaw faces mysteries as problems in logic, following her assumptions to their end in order to see facts in a new light; if one assumption does not provide a logical solution, she explores a new assumption and therefore another perspective on puzzling events. This approach of testing a hypothesis against evidentiary data and then supplanting it with one with more explanatory power is a staple of British detective fiction and its "cerebral" American imitators (as opposed to hardboiled U.S. crime stories). The crimes the two detect spring from jealousy, hatred, and greed. Their topical concerns are modern: wife beating (*Seven Black Stones, Night Walker, The Fire Carrier*); suspected pedophilia and bank robbery (*Ghostland*); construction fraud (*Seven Black Stones*); mental illness and theft (*The Redbird's Cry*); the illegal dumping of toxic wastes (*Ravenmocker*); drug smuggling (*The Grandfather Medicine, The Fire Carrier*); the AIDS virus (*The Fire Carrier*); blackmail and insurance scams (*Night Walker*); rural anti-government protesters (*Masked Dancers*); and a car theft ring and chop shop (*The Spirit Caller*). Adulterous affairs, lesbianism, and even incest cast false suspicion on some characters, and small town gossip provides false clues to mislead investigators. Even when there is the theft of an ancient relic and the murder of a Cherokee activist and storyteller during a Cherokee festival (*The Redbird's Cry*), or the illegal slaughter of bald eagles for ceremonial feathers (*Masked Dancers*), the unraveling of whodunit remains firmly grounded in mainstream logic and motives.

Bushyhead is a professional, the chief of police of the small community of Buckskin, Oklahoma; Bearpaw is an amateur who begins as an advocacy investigator for the Native American Advocacy League, her brief to protect Cherokee rights. However, her regular entanglement in local crime eventually brings her a new position funded by Chief Wilma Mankiller: Major Crimes Investigator for the Cherokee Nation Marshal Service in Tahlequah, Oklahoma. Bushyhead is half-Cherokee, but his origins have little effect on his daily reality. On the home front, his problems are those of a single father (his wife died of cancer) worried about how to protect his lively teenage daughter from the world's evil and from growing up too fast. At the same time, he struggles to maintain viable new love relationships, first with a local high school teacher with ambitions to higher education and later with a highly competent, attractive doctor from the Cherokee clinic. On the job, he must find ways to prevent local politicians and overzealous lawyers from undermining his investigations and methods to deal with marijuana as the second biggest cash crop in Oklahoma, and all that that implies. Occasionally, the private and the public meet, as when the murderer in *Night Walker* threatens Bushyhead's rebellious daughter, who has witnessed incriminating behavior.

Bearpaw, in turn, balances her friendship with her elderly neighbor, her commitment to a stray dog, and her growing love for a local cop with her advocacy and investigative duties. Her job involves her more in local Cherokee concerns than does Bushyhead's, but she, like him, is a product of the modern age, with male chauvinism more troublesome for her than any cultural or ethnic conflicts. In fact, her knowledge of Cherokee culture is secondhand, learned from a beloved aunt and based on her own purposeful attempts to learn such dying skills as finger weaving. As a woman, she feels more compelled to become a repository of her community's way of life than does Bushyhead, but she is nonetheless skeptical of the spirituality once inherent in tribal ways. Her neighbor, a former university history professor working on an oral history project for the Tribal Studies Institute, interviews the elderly about Cherokee customs and legends so that these will not die with their generation. Neither of these Cherokee detectives speaks the Cherokee language, though Bearpaw is learning some phrases. However, as the novels progress, both detectives gradually accept that, though they do not know exactly how, some tribal elders have a power to perceive what they cannot, as when Bearpaw's aunt dreams of her in danger in a sea of blood and Bearpaw finds herself fighting for her life on a crimson carpet.

Despite names such as Whitekiller, Fourkiller, Tenkiller, Fishinghawk, Flycatcher, and Kingfisher, except for the extremely old, most native locals are indistinguishable from the white population except in very minor, superficial ways (like eating fry bread and attending stomp dances). Education has turned young people away from tradition, as they learn the nineteenth-century origins of many secret Cherokee traditions and the twentieth-century origins of fashionable practices such as the Cherokee powwow; a recurring phrase among young adults is, "You can't turn back the clock." Only a very few, like 70-year-old medicine man Crying Wolf and 87-year-old Zebediah Smoke, who practices Grandfather Medicine with specially cured tobacco, live traditional lives and adhere to the old ways; they see an unspannable chasm separating them from their children and grandchildren. *The Spirit Caller* explores the fraudulent claims of New Age would-be Indians whose meditation groups and vision quests mix Cherokee medicine with the practices of otherworldly religions; one New Ager chants to contact a Cherokee ghost at the local Native American Research Library but finds death instead. In *Masked Dancers*, a high school principal revives traditional dances to span the generation gap, only to arouse angry protests from locals who find the loud drumming disturbing.

Hager's two investigators must deal regularly with oldsters who are convinced of the validity of their dreams and visions and who attribute any mischief or evil in the community to Cherokee gods and spirits—the punishing powers of the Apportioner or sun god; the evil spirit, Fire Carrier, who is associated with strange lights; the Immortals (*Nunne'hi*), who live under the mountains and under the waters; Stone Coat, who cannibalizes children; the Eternal Little People (*Aniqunehiyat'*), who look like miniature Cherokees; Thunder, who gave power to the birds and who can drive away *Uk'ten*, the fire-breathing dragon/serpent with seven spots; *Ahw'ust'*, the spirit deer; Slanting Eyes; the Red Man; the owl as harbinger of death; and so on. Crying Wolf, for example, engages in secret ceremonies to restore harmony and sacred chants for exorcising evil spirits awakened by intruders on an ancient Indian burial ground (*Night Walker*); likewise, Zeb Smoke employs ancient tobacco (specially grown in North Carolina to enhance its power) and charm songs to protect his dilapidated shack from intrusion; he also uses a seven-black-stones curse to turn evil back on evildoers (*Seven Black Stones*). These old men, secure in their knowledge, continue their protective chants and curing ceremonies after the crimes have had conventional solutions.

Hager's detectives must also deal with the fearful and superstitious who are more ready to credit witchcraft and black magic than mischief and crime. A member of the Cherokee secret organization of Nighthawk Keetoowahs, police assistant Virgil Rabbit passes on to Bushyhead insider knowledge about local gossip and local fears. Bearpaw attends an autopsy to confirm for fearful relatives that a dead man's brain has not been stolen by a ravenmocker (a witch) and to quiet locals' fears of a witch sucking the life force from the sick and elderly. Shrieking ravens, a fire in the sky, or the sound of someone stomping on the roof at night are all accepted signs of Cherokee witches at work. However, these Cherokee religious elements remain peripheral, providing only local color or misdirection, not explanations of methods or motivations. In fact, details about Cherokee history and belief contribute little to the psychology of the crime or the social interactions of the family units.

Hager always begins with the fearful gossip of a few Cherokees who blame things going wrong in their community on a witch or black magic or ancient gods terrorizing them for not practicing tradition:

It was the Apportioner who, in the dim long-ago had brought death to the people. Walking stick wondered if Mercer was right about the ancient Cherokee gods being mad at them. Maybe the Apportioner was thinking up more ways to punish them, even now. He squinted up at the blank blue sky, forgetting for an instant that the Apportioner became very angry when a man didn't look straight at her, but screwed up his face. That was why she had brought death to the people in the first place. (*Ravenmocker*, 9)

This "old way" perspective established in the first chapter or two, Hager then turns to a modern-style investigation that reveals a culpable human being engaged in illegal activities that lead to murder. In *Ghostland*, the setting is a tribal boarding school with students practicing gourd dances for the Cherokee Heritage Festival; the murder victim is a small child whose spirit, according to the oldsters, wanders in ghostland until blood revenge frees her to travel to the dark land in the west. Translated into modern terms, the old Cherokee way of hunting down a killer, says Hager, means a lynch mob punishing the most visible suspect. In contrast, the main thrust of her plot is the complicated nature of a Western professional investigation—the "misdirection" of so many suspects with secrets that could be misunderstood by outsiders—and the fact that the real solution is unexpected and totally unrelated to the original speculations. Only rarely does Hager suggest that Cherokee, Osage, or Choctaw ways of seeing might reach the same truth as logical detection, as when Crying Wolf's dreams provide symbolic clues that help Bushyhead unravel complexities. However, even these dream clues have rational explanations based on modern psychology. Usually Hager's context confirms that the community would be better off to completely reject superstitions. There is no attempt to explore how native ways might have served the past or how they might find modern expression in contemporary America; the primacy and universality of Western rationalism is a given.

Only *The Redbird's Cry*, set at the Cherokee Heritage Center and museum during an important festival, ties the crime to the community and tribal conflicts and focuses on Cherokee heritage beyond the initial chapters, though, as usual, this overlay serves only as misdirection. Associated with the center is an eighteenth-century village with modern Cherokees portraying the way their ancestors lived and dressed (on the model of Williamsburg, Virginia). The first crime seems to grow out of either a domestic dispute or a conflict between two political factions vying in court for recognition as the voice of the whole Cherokee Nation. Moreover, the means seems traditional—death by a Cherokee blowgun during a creation story narration—though later the overt means of death also proves to be misdirection. The second crime is the theft of ancient wampum belts given to the tribe in North Carolina, carried on the Trail of Tears and then loaned to the museum exhibition by the Nighthawk Keetoowahs. The context allows Hager to bring in interesting details on Cherokee basketry and other such topics, to expose the ignorance and prejudices of white visitors to the museum (mainly in vignettes depicting stereotypes), and to characterize the fears of the older Cherokees that these wampum belts have the power to disrupt the present and produce disaster (they blame the wampum for the sudden death). Most significantly, the context enables Hager—through the museum storytellers—to punctuate her story with Cherokee creation and trickster stories that seem related to ongoing events, but that ultimately prove misleading. Thus, in this novel Hager effectively employs Cherokee trappings to create the multiple plot threads and distracters that mystery readers expect before the final unveiling of who did what and why. However, as in her other novels, there is no supernatural Native American force at work, only the pathos of a sister driven to extreme and deadly measures to provide adequate psychiatric care for a schizophrenic brother. For the killer, the past has no value except to finance the present.

As a half-blood, Bushyhead is considered an outsider by the full-blooded Cherokee and is distrusted because "he hadn't been raised in the Cherokee way and therefore couldn't be expected to understand anything having to do with their Indianness" (*The Grandfather Medicine*, 78). Initially contemptuous of full-bloods as lazy and prone to violence against their own, especially when drunk, as dependent on welfare, and, in general, as a backward, superstitious lot, he reminds himself that their forebears (like some of his own) "had been painted savages brandishing war clubs, with scalps dangling from their lances," and he speculates that only "the flimsiest veneer" separated some from their ancestors (100). Though disturbed by their contempt for the police and their uncooperativeness, he is surprised that they manage to feed a family with only a few acres of "anemic farmland" and hunting skills; with time, he develops a camaraderie with the old medicine man Crying Wolf, who accepts him as one of the People despite his white mother. As the series progresses, however, readers have trouble distinguishing Indian from white unless a character within a novel calls attention to that distinction with the appellation "Indian," as in "that Indian woman." Hager notes that Cherokees had probably "intermarried with whites more extensively than any other North American Indian tribe," and yet pockets of conservatives continued to pass on knowledge of the old ways from generation to generation (201). This discussion perhaps gives too much weight to Hager's use of the past, however, for, in the main, the distinction between white and Indian plays little part in the nature of the crimes, nor in their solutions. Hager's characters eat cheeseburgers and apple pie, worry about being overweight, work in ordinary jobs, and engage in the activities of small-town folk typical in any American town. Moreover, Hager is at her best when dealing with strained family relationships, like those of Molly Bearpaw, whose parents drank heavily, whose mother committed suicide, and whose father, at the behest of her aunt, stayed out of her life until he turned up as a murder suspect in one of her cases—a proud but impoverished man Molly has hated all her life for reasons that prove completely false.

Hager is not really interested in finding compromises between past and present, between Cherokee and mainstream. Her insights into the Cherokee Way are compromised by her deep-seated belief that assimilation is inevitable and good, that artificial Indian trappings do not detract from that assimilation, but that stubbornly hanging on to the past is injurious. Her stories assert that: (1) given the Cherokee history of assimilation, many of the so-called "old" ways of the Cherokees were invented by whites; (2) the myths created by moderns seeking their roots are shams; (3) the true "old" ways were not necessarily good ways (scary stories to frighten children and to haunt them as adults; violent revenge for the deaths of blood relatives, i.e., lynch mobs; spousal abuse; superstitions that produce fear, panic, hysteria, and violence); (4) the contempt that conservative full-bloods feel for part-bloods is unfair and mutually destructive; and (5) assimilated Cherokees are no different from any other Americans, except in very minor ways, such as regional cuisine. Thus, though technically Native American, her detectives are no more than mainstream investigators in (somewhat) Indian costume, with their approaches to detection basically Western.

Margaret Coel

A resident of Boulder, a historian by trade, and a sojourner on the Wind River Arapaho Reservation, Margaret Coel is the best-selling, award-winning author of a detective series that features a detective duo, one Boston Irish, the other Arapaho. Her detective stories are repeatedly praised for their vivid Western landscapes, accurate and intriguing history, likable, compelling characters, quick, tight writing and fascinating mix of the modern and the traditional. On the back cover blurbs introducing her books, Tony Hillerman calls Coel a "master" of "new trends in mystery writing and of contemporary Indian culture," and she is indeed just that.

Her first three detective stories focus on her Jesuit detective Father John O'Malley, who was originally sent to Wind River Reservation as penance for his drinking problems but who has come to identify with and love the Arapaho and who is committed to bettering their lives both spiritually and materially. However, each succeeding novel gives greater and greater emphasis to a second investigator, a Lander, Wyoming, lawyer, Arapaho Vicky Holden (nee Singing Bird, sometimes called Woman Alone). In *The Eagle Catcher*, which features the murder of tribal chairman Harvey Castle in his teepee at a powwow, Holden does the plodding legal background work necessary for O'Malley to determine why Castle was murdered (stolen goods, annuities, and reservation land linked to a gubernatorial candidate). In *The Ghost Walker*, a subplot fleshes out Holden's past, her troubled marriage and divorce, and her daughter's difficulties, first as a young, assimilated Native American in Los Angeles and then as a cover for drug dealers setting up business on the reservation, and Holden's parallel investigation provides pieces of information that help O'Malley ferret out a murderer. In *The Dream Stalker*, Holden's role is more central to the plot, as she works actively against a tribal plan to lease land for storing nuclear waste and struggles to educate her family, friends, and fellow tribe members about the long-term potential dangers to their health and to their land, dangers that should outweigh any short-term financial benefits. Ironically, her stance on this issue places her in the ranks of two seemingly opposite groups—white environmentalists and traditional Arapaho grandmothers. (The younger Arapaho want the promised jobs.) The reservation conflict and threats on Holden's life alert O'Malley to the motives behind seemingly unrelated murder cases, but the real resolution of *The Dream Stalker* is thematic, hinging on the outcome of Holden's tribal issues (jobs versus the environment; personal greed and power versus community obligations); O'Malley's detection solves plot issues, not Arapaho concerns. In other words, this book marked a turning point for Coel, and in the books that follow, Holden comes into her own as the central detective, with O'Malley's side investigations dovetailing with her central investigation as hers once did with his.

Coel sets up interesting parallels between the two. Just as O'Malley moves from the mainstream toward growing sympathy for and identification with the Arapaho, so Holden moved away from the reservation community in order to become a skilled legal professional. Her end goal had always been to help her community and her people, but, short term, preparing to do so meant becoming an outsider, assimilating to the white culture as she acquired the expertise she needed and becoming a stranger to family and former friends. In the early mysteries, she spends the majority of her time off reservation and no longer participates in the tribal women's organizations. As she walks through a crowded room, avoiding the eyes on her, she fears a killer she pursues may be among those watching, and as she hurries past the Arapahos hovering in the driveway, no one speaks to her: "She was the outsider here" (*The Dream Stalker*, 143). Thus, initially Coel uses Holden to demonstrate the loneliness and vulnerability of the assimilated. However, with time, Holden's fortitude and courage return her to the tribe as a defender who can do outside the tribe what those within cannot. Her argument with O'Malley in *The Dream Stalker* about Arapaho knowledge versus Western science marks a pivotal point in self-understanding as she thinks of the narrow, profit-centered, short-term vision of scientists advocating storing radioactive materials on reservation land and the long-term, land-centered Arapaho vision: "Nothing is worth the risk of destroying a sacred place" (98). By the roundabout means of leaving in order to return, she achieves her original goal: finding her role within her tribe while working outside the tribe but closely with tribe members in ways useful to them. In this role of protector, she comes into her own as an investigator in *The Story Teller* and *The Lost Bird*.

The Story Teller explicitly sets two ways of knowing against each other in two different arenas. The first is Coel's forte, Western history, with the oral history of the Arapaho storyteller of the title set against the official history of the academic and museum establishments. Ironically, it is a document, a ledger-book used to pictorially record Plains Indian oral history, that finally turns the issue in Holden's favor, but the trail to the ledger-book is itself an oral one, the memories of a tribal elder passed on to a respectful listener. The second arena is in a new setting for Coel's fiction, Denver, but with the familiar struggle between Holden's intuitive grasp of the truth and the fact-based, methodical investigation of the authorities. O'Malley's own Jesuit blend of reason and spiritual understanding here plays more of a helping role, with the spotlight firmly on Holden, whose deep certainties about guilt and innocence prove correct.

The faith that the modern world places in written records approaches the absolute: history is what has been written down. Descriptions, lists, catalogs, recorded testimony, and published analyses—the whole panoply of written documents—establish what is "true" and "authentic." Other ways of recording particular events and the past in general, even though certified by long use, tend to be dismissed: oral histories are unstable, mutable personal narratives that are degraded by being passed down from individual to individual. However, Coel dramatically defends the validity of oral history. The novel shows through Holden's receptivity to the wisdom of her elders that cultures establish ways of correcting and controlling the tendency of particular individual narratives to wander off into eccentric paths: the storyteller has a distinct role and is unlikely to have made mistakes. He follows protocols, just as modern academic print histories do, and though the protocols are oral, they nevertheless ground the narrative in established patterns. Communal sharing of this history is a further control on the possibly biased or quirky perspective of a given oral historian or storyteller; the elders and the "audiences" of the story all provide checks and balances on the accretions and variations provided by an individual teller.

Oral transmission of history is, of course, not unique to Native Americans; all the abstract values of Indo-European culture were transmitted orally across thousands of miles and thousands of years in Europe, most of the time without benefit of texts; yet, while the discovery of Sanskrit allowed Europeans to recognize the root of the word "divine" in a Hindu priest's chant "diva," no such credit is given to Native American oral tradition. Holden is hired to represent the Arapaho tribe in its attempt to recover a ledger book recording tribal history from the Denver Museum of the West through NAGPRA, the Native American Graves Protection and

Repatriation Act, a federal law allowing tribes to claim back materials taken from them. The problem is that the museum claims no such book now exists and perhaps never existed, since computerized records make no mention of it. The museum authorities take the absence of a record as self-evident proof of nonexistence, even though, as the record keepers of a valuable artifact claimed to be missing by its Arapaho owners, they might well be considered self-interested. However, an Arapaho tribal elder, a descendant of No-Ta-Nee, the book's creator, confidently repeats to Holden his recollection of seeing the book at the museum in 1920.

After an initial doubtful reaction to the old man's memory—almost 80 years have passed, and he and the other elders are certainly self-interested parties, if only because of their wish to regain the ledger—Holden realizes her dubious response is informed by her status as a ten-year absentee from the reservation, making her a white woman in Arapaho eyes and to some degree her own, as well as by her lawyerly skepticism and rationality. However, she manages to shift into a less mainstream point of view when she realizes the degree of trust being put in her ability to accept Arapaho tribal memories as fact and to battle for them in the white world. She confronts the museum curator, who mocks her evidence as an old man's dreamy recollection, and later clashes with academic experts and a rare book dealer, her trust in the elder's story becoming all the more firm as she learns of the ledger-book's $1.3 million value and the sometimes evasive responses of the academic experts who all seem to have financial or other interests in the ledger-book remaining missing.

A parallel plot initially seems to have little to do with the ledger-book, for a young Arapaho woman asks Holden to check on the whereabouts of her missing fiancé Todd Harris, a graduate student in Denver. When told by a Denver detective friend that Todd has been murdered in a drug deal gone bad, Holden again must choose between her deep sense of Arapaho reality and Western forensic evidence (drug tests/police investigation). Holden's intuitive assurance that Todd could never be involved with drugs must counter the experts' insistance on evidence. The balance of the plot follows her attempts to prove the existence of the ledger-book in terms acceptable to the mainstream world, and almost incidentally at first, to prove Todd innocent of the posthumous charges against him. *The Story Teller* is Holden's story; John O'Malley is in Denver attempting to gain diocese support for an Arapaho museum at Wind River, and he is drawn into the story as Holden's helper rather than as the main detective.

The Story Teller is thus a truly cross-cultural story, as Holden struggles to balance her two roles of Western legal rationalist and Arapaho tribal communalist. The novel is unusual in the general run of detective stories for its literary emphasis on serious intellectual themes over plot and on character over a whodunit puzzle. Coel returns again and again to the paradox of being caught between cultures:

"Hey, wait a minute!" the secretary shouted as Holden stepped into a room twice the size of the outer office. She had surprised herself. How had she come to be so rude? Her grandmother would be ashamed; this was not the Arapaho Way. Was this what she had learned in the white world? (90–91)

Holden is painfully aware of such differences in style and manners, differences that define a culture's idea of its place in the social and natural universe. O'Malley, normally the rationalist in their detective team, defers to Holden when she wishes to follow the trail her ancestors took 100 years earlier to the Sand Creek battlefield, a defeat that figures importantly, since an Arapaho presence established by the ledger-book will affect present-day reparations. At Sand Creek, Holden almost hallucinates, seeming to recover a memory of herself and O'Malley together at the battle site 100 years earlier, but Coel wisely pulls back, the riders of Holden's vision seguing into some very real cowboys on the range and the scene avoiding a New Age staple, the heroine transported into the past. Holden's hunch pays off, and the necessary proof is obtained. O'Malley says toward the end, "Stories are very powerful" (195), a sentiment that speaks to the title of Coel's novel, the ledger-book, oral history, the communal cohesion brought about by shared visions, and, in fact, Coel's own detective genre itself. *The Story Teller* may rank as her best novel to date, a coherent, powerful statement about the force of the "fictions" we share.

The Lost Bird continues the emphasis on Vicky Holden, with a new distance between Holden and O'Malley enforced by their mutual recognition of their forbidden romantic attraction to each other. Holden's response is to draw closer to the Arapaho community, mainly through reconciliation with her ex-husband, while O'Malley suffers his own painful return to the past when his niece confronts him with her suspicion that he might be her natural father, since O'Malley's brother had married O'Malley's girlfriend on the rebound when O'Malley had joined the priesthood. As with *The Story Teller*, the Holden-O'Malley plots begin as separate strands which are then woven together. The theme of rational versus intuitive is less explicit in this work, though the two value systems involved in the two ways of seeing the world underlie the behavior of the crucial characters.

Two disparate happenings set the plot events in motion. A well-known Hollywood actress, Sharon David, asks Holden to find her birth parents on the Wind River Reservation, a place the movie star has decided must be her birthplace on the basis of some suggestive evidence and the process of elimination. Holden counters that the Arapaho never give up their children, particularly not in the period when the actress would have been born, a time of high infant mortality and of an almost desperate gratitude for living babies. She agrees to take the case, however. Meanwhile, 72-year-old Father Joseph Keenan, who served at the St. Francis Mission 35 years earlier and has returned sick and on the verge of retirement, is shot and killed while on a visit to a parishioner in O'Malley's Toyota pickup. O'Malley's attempts to narrow down possible perpetrators and to protect himself from a possible assassin are compromised by the arrival of his niece, Megan O'Malley, with her fears that her uncle-priest is her literal father. Holden acknowledges her forbidden and repressed feelings for O'Malley when she hears of the shooting associated with his Toyota and naturally concludes that he is dead. In this miasma of guilt and tangled emotions, Holden and O'Malley discover through separate investigations that a famous baby doctor who began his practice in Lander, a short drive from the Wind River Reservation, had managed a highly profitable secret adoption service before moving on to Doctor Spock-like fame and fortune in California. The pollution of water supplies that had indeed led to high infant mortality also provided a cover for claiming that healthy babies had been born dead in the Lander clinic. The phenomenally cruel theft of babies from their parents and of true identities from the grown children is the main theme of the novel, with the guilty secret shared by nurses and administrators festering over the decades and ultimately resulting in the death of the old priest.

Though not as explicitly dealt with as in *The Story Teller*, the encounter between two ways of seeing the world is also at the heart of the novel. Holden uses fairly conventional methods of detection to uncover the adoption scam—interviews, questioning of knowledgeable observers, examination of records—but it is her empathy for identity loss that gives her the insight to understand the larger picture. Native Americans, of course, suffered just this loss of their children to Indian schools located in distant states with the explicit goal of eradicating parental culture and influence on their young charges. (Chapter 2 discusses the effects of such schooling in the case of Slim Girl, in *Laughing Boy*.) If these secret adoptions are metaphorical of larger thefts of Native American identity, Holden's reaction is just as understandable, for she has given up pieces of herself "for her own good," just the rationalization given by the baby stealers for their crime: the children had far better lives with their adoptive parents, both materially and in their freedom from such pathologies as alcoholism and violence that afflict the reservation.

Questions of identity can never be parsed rationally, for identity itself defies rational analysis and measurement. O'Malley, his Jesuit reasoning notwithstanding, is committed to the essential mysteries at the heart of his faith, and both his contempt and Coel's scorn for bureaucratic Jesuits (recurring minor-league offenders or semicomic figures in her works) are measures of the profundities and complexities of the authentic Jesuit identity. O'Malley's compass remains true, in spite of the wild swings caused by the appearance of Megan. Holden's lodestone is leading her more and more toward her Arapaho identity, and it is this authentic self, a complex providing emotional comfort and familiarity that makes Holden such a valuable detective/investigator for her people. To be sure, she is helped by O'Malley's methodical analysis and his skeptic's reserve, as well as by his acceptance of the depths and validity of Arapaho Ways. But in *The Story Teller* and *The Lost Bird*, Holden comes of age as a true Native American detective, an investigator free of all the clumsy theatrical trappings of Indianness—from an exterior view, Holden is a thoroughly modern woman with her Arapaho features the only sign of heritage, yet thoroughly attuned to the concerns of her people, whose legal problems arise from cultural difference, not simply from human frailty.

CONCLUSION

The writers in this chapter on the Plains and Rocky Mountain Indian detectives illustrate the very different directions in which Native American detective fiction can travel. Lackey, Doss, and Bowen show the different degrees of credibility that shamanistic insights can be accorded. By crediting a whole system of belief alien to mainstream culture, Lackey is, in effect, working in the realm of science fiction, her preferred genre. Doss wavers between the shamanistic and the logical, at times crediting Perika with intuitive and spiritual insights that help her cut to the heart of a crime in a way that mainstream-style investigators cannot, while suggesting that much of what she experiences occurs in her mind, not in reality. Bowen provides the most credible shaman of the three, an elderly eccentric with an offbeat sense of humor, whose cryptic comments force Du Pré to apply his knowledge of people and place, distant history and near history to make sense of what Benetsee has expressed in native symbols. Eagle likewise experiments with the shamanistic and with ratiocinative investigation of past crimes, but in separate books, the one surreal, the other realistic.

Grove does not include the shamanistic at all; his is a realistic depiction of abuses perpetrated on the Osage people in a key period of their modern history. However, he captures the Otherness of the Osage people in his depiction of cultural attitudes and lifestyles that doom them to be dupes of scheming, unscrupulous whites and slaves of their own obsessions with alcohol, drugs, and gambling, and that incapacitate them for survival in the mainstream world. His hero rediscovers his ties to the land and to community, and in doing so he saves himself from self-destruction and the lonely anonymity of white individualism.

In contrast to these five, Trainor and Hager accept the essential rightness of the mainstream and modern viewpoints about crime and its solution. Indianness for both consists of cultural elements fairly near the surface: names, sometimes food and clothing, old stories, some traditions, and the like. Such a view is by no means contemptible—it is the conventional definition most Americans hold of culture, an assortment of indicators of heritage that points to a distant, unrecoverable past, a period to be viewed with nostalgia, perhaps, but very definitely as less than useful in the modern world. Time moves on, with past Ways self-evidently inferior because they are . . . past! If we consider how many Americans who claim an ethnic identity regard the places and ways of their origins, we see just how firmly Trainor and Hager occupy a mainstream view.

Coel, in contrast, entertains the possibility that the practices and outlooks of the past, in this case of the Arapaho, may well have a validity and even a virtue not always present in modernist mainstream culture. Appropriately enough for a historian, she sees strengths and admirable traits even among a people defeated militarily in the past and economically in the present. Her Jesuit detective, himself alienated and self-exiled out of the mainstream, is a bridge character who allows the reader to identify and give names to familiar, if now often unfashionable, strengths among the Arapaho: modesty, patience, self-discipline, tolerance of others, and fortitude. Coel is in a sense more anthropologist than historian, asking us to suspend the American obsession with newness and change in order to consider how the Arapaho fit into the traditional virtues of European-American society summed up in the Christian figure of O'Malley.

Coel provides no cheerleading for Indian values in romantic triumph over mainstream beliefs. Unlike escapist or tendentious writers who paint Native American culture in the golden hues of utopianism (a rude, demeaning way to regard a real, living people), Coel uses no rhetorical club with which to advance a mainstream agenda by gratuitously bashing one side or the other. Pathologies on the reservation are an important part of Vicky Holden's legal practice: spousal abuse, alcoholism, occasional violence, and despair. Yet the positive side of Arapaho culture is also presented in a balanced, evenhanded way. As with Tony Hillerman in the Southwest, Margaret Coel has the skill to present the complexities of cultural difference without taking sides, an ability far less common than is generally recognized. In Coel's works, we are also asked to suspend our faith in the Victorian idea of progress, the notion that the modern is, by definition, an improved version of the past, and that all change is for the best. This notion runs deep in U.S. thought, and Coel's Arapaho provide an elegant counter.

7

The Northwest: Shamanistic Horror amid Eerie Rain Forests

He stood on a steep basaltic headland, while the raging North Pacific thundered and crashed, sending up its fogs to embrace him. . . .

The beat of the sea ran deep in his being. The sea was his mother, his father, the breath in his body, the blood in his veins. Sometimes he thought that in the time before time he had been an *ekoale*, a whale. Or a *tgunat*, a salmon.

Behind and above him endless conifer forests, black in the blowing sea mists, sighed and whispered, singing their ancient songs. Far below, a whale rubbed off its barnacles on an upjutting sea stack.

His name was Musqueen and he was here in this special place at this special time to talk to the Earth. "*Tca-xel-qlix*, it is winter, the sacred season, when the Listening Ones visit mankind!" he shouted.

—Naomi Stokes, *The Tree People*, 1

The Northwest's physical setting of fog, sea, misty islands, dense old growth forests, high mountains, snowy peaks, and abundant water makes credible a spiritual setting of ancient gods and spirits still quietly asserting their presence in the raucous cough of a raven, the leap of a salmon heading upstream, or the sounding of a beluga whale. Like the Southwest, the

Northwest has very distinctive ancient native cultures manifest in occasional woodland petroglyphs, in ceremonial totems that rise above city
streets, and in ubiquitous carved cedar masks depicting terrifying spirits
that must be placated. The region's mix of eerie bogs, isolated islands, and
untraveled scenic stretches makes great detective story settings. The Native
American detectives from this region are all shamans, though the natives
assisting white detectives are not:

Author	Detective	Tribal Affiliation
Muriel Gray	Sam Hunting Wolf	Kinchuinick
Frank Herbert	Hobuhet as Katsuk, revenger and killer	Coastal Salish
Richard Hoyt	Willie Prettybird (assists)	Cowlitz
Father Brad Reynolds	Jesuit detective with Swinomish assistants	Swinomish
Naomi Stokes	Jordan Tidewater	Salish (Quinault)
	Old Man Ahcleet	Salish (Quinault)

GEOGRAPHICAL DETERMINERS

Although Colin Taylor in *North American Indians* places the Northwest
Coast native culture in a region extending "from the Copper River delta
on the Gulf of Alaska, south to the Winchuk River close to the Oregon-
California border," for the practical purpose of examining the Native
American detectives of the region, the Northwest consists of the states of
Washington and Oregon in the United States and the province of British
Columbia in Canada. It is bounded on the west by the Pacific Ocean and
extends inland into the Cascades Mountain range and down into the foothills of the Rockies in British Columbia. Because the Japanese current
warms the sea along this coast and because ranges of high mountains running north-south serve as demarcations of the coastal region, blocking de-
scending Arctic cold from moving to the west, the temperatures in this
region are less extreme than in the Plains and Rocky Mountains, or even
than in the same province or states a short distance east over the mountains.
Winters are wet and comparatively mild, while summers are pleasantly
cool. Water, whether in huge Pacific rollers on the coast, in bays, sounds,
inlets, and other inland extensions of the Pacific, in rivers and streams, and
in often constant precipitation—mist and fog—is a defining element. The
Olympic Peninsula has one of the highest rainfall rates in North America,
sometimes exceeding 200 inches a year.

The wind-swept coastline is spectacular, with sweeping curves, wide vistas, steep cliffs, and heavy forests sloping down to wide, sandy beaches in
Oregon and Washington or narrow, boulder-strewn strands in British Co-

lumbia. Lush green seaweed and barnacles coat rocks, while pieces of drift-wood, some the trunks of large Pacific Northwest trees, dot the shore. Currents may be swift and strong, with fierce undertows that pull swim-mers out to sea without warning, while large waves on some beaches can snatch away waders and even beach strollers in seconds, as if they had never existed. While pleasantly lush and verdant due to the rainfall, the coast gives a sense of the grandeur and power of nature absent elsewhere, reminding humans of their pettiness and impotence before ancient forces.

The sea is constantly at work. The pounding surf cuts many caves into the shore. In the tidal pools and protected inlets along the shore are sea birds of many types, middens, clams, brightly colored starfish, octopi, crabs, and sea anemones. Some tides come in quickly, violently, and thus dangerously; some create quicksand in the tidal pools or stir up whirlpools that could suck the unwary beneath the sea. Numerous rocky islands, inlets, and fiords remind one of the coast of Norway. Ferries are the main form of transportation across straits and between islands: the Washington ferries in the United States, the B.C. Ferries in British Columbia. In spite of modern technology, the rugged geography still determines the patterns of human movement, with direct routes over land often difficult or impossible. For the indigenous inhabitants, travel by sea was preferable to difficult treks over mountainous terrain and through very dense forests of Douglas firs, spruce, and cedar. Even today British Columbia's major highways are coastal, for narrow mountain roads with hairpin curves and sometimes little paving are perilous and nearly impassable in winter. Forests explode with impenetrable varieties of regional trees such as alder, cottonwood, arbutus, and scrub birch, and the canopy of boughs in forest glades protects a rich variety of life: vine maples and fragile maidenhair ferns, lichens, chubmoss, fungi, toadstools, mushrooms, devil's club, and bracken. In fact, over 12,000 plant species grow among the 1,000-year-old conifers of the Olympic Peninsula (*Wildcrafters*, 77).

The fact that the Quinault and other tribes traditionally buried their dead on the small islands dotting the coast, considered certain islands sacred, and warned of evil Salishan spirits left behind to guard sacred places height-ens the mystery inherent in the coastal areas. In fact, the misty Pacific Northwest landscape, with its dark forests, fog-shrouded islands, and glacier-capped mountains and jagged peaks, is ideal for evoking spiritual visions, for such psychic experiences often begin with literal ones. If the mind forms its way of knowing from its experience with seeing, with proc-essing visual information and interpreting it, then the Pacific Northwest landscape, with its shades of subtlety and many nuances, is a perfect phys-ical platform for a sophisticated, intricate mind-set. Long vistas are softened and modulated by mist, fog, and clouds, smoky views that promise—and often make the promise good—more complex visions just beyond the next stand of trees or just around the adjoining summit. Frank Herbert captures the mix of light and dark:

All around him lay a forest of mossy limbs—every limb draped with moss like green wool hung out to dry. The light, now bright and now dull as clouds, concealed the sun, alternately flattened the colors, and then filled the world with green jeweled glowing. At one passage of muted green, the sun suddenly emerged and sent a rope of light plunging through the trees to the forest floor. (*Soul Catcher*, 73)

The coastal mountain ranges suggest infinite regressions, lands beyond human vision perpetually shrouded in cloud and fog. The forests offer infinite perspectives, but in this case, up close and personal, with angles of vision changing constantly; as one ascends or descends ten feet along, everything looks different. There is also a fluid atmosphere of multiple liquids—ocean, straits, bays, rivers, creeks, streams, tidal pools, waterfalls, marshes, swamps, cranberry bogs, heavy dew, mist, drizzle, wind-whipped horizontal rain—water everywhere, and everything alive because of it.

As a result, the environment supports incredible varieties of wildlife, from frogs and insects to endangered butterflies; it is a bird-watcher's paradise with over 300 bird species (including ravens, eagles, hawks, spotted owls, woodpeckers, red thrush, brown pelicans, blue herons, white egrets, cranes, Canadian geese, swans, grouse, and ptarmigan). Whales and dolphins are visible offshore, with sea lions and seals on the coast. Along the water's edge and inland, plentiful aquatic life thrives, from enormous banana slugs (the unofficial mascot of Seattle) to bizarre geoducks, clamlike bivalves with protruding necks as long as good-sized trout. There are otters, beavers, woodchucks, and porcupines as well as 70 other mammal species. Elk and moose are commonplace in wilderness areas, and less prevalent but still present are black bears, wolves, coyotes, bobcats, and cougars. Although no grizzly bears are left on the Olympic Peninsula, they inhabit the north, British Columbia. Plentiful wild berries (blackberries, huckleberries, cranberries) are the bears' favorite treats. High atop mountain ledges are bighorn sheep. According to Naomi Stokes, the 900,000-acre Olympic National Park, a bioreserve, contains "the largest and best example of virgin temperate rain forest in the western hemisphere, the largest stand of coniferous forest in the contiguous forty-eight states, and the largest wild herd of Roosevelt elk"; it also boasts ten major rivers, 200 smaller streams, and nine plant types and seven animal types found nowhere else in the world (*The Tree People*, Author's Notes). Life and life-sustaining ecosystems abound in the Pacific Northwest.

FICTIONAL GEOGRAPHY AND WEATHER

Skye Kathleen Moody in *Rain Dance* describes typical Northwestern weather: a "dense gray drizzly morning," "a thick fog" shrouding Puget

Sound, "misty rain . . . falling nonstop for three days," and the possibility of a " 'sun break,' a rent in the pall through which sunlight leaks briefly, revealing wondrous natural beauty, including that sublime scoop of ice cream called Mount Rainier, the snowcapped Olympics and Cascades, Puget Sound's sparkling saltwater inlets, emerald islands, and amidst it all, Seattle's soaring urban skyline" (8). Richard Hoyt's *Fish Story*, whose grisly slash-and-hack murders result from Cowlitz Indians and local salmon fishermen competing for fishing rights, provides spooky images of labyrinthian underground Seattle as the fog rolls in, swirling around the tall ancient totem pole at the city's heart and muting the laughter and music from funky local bars.

In contrast to this urban scene, in *Wildcrafters*, Moody captures the isolation of the Northwestern woodlands, as searchers spread out seeking a missing Native American child, seemingly spirited away by a large elk:

Of course, they'd never find Paris Nighteagle, not in a million years. Anyone who knew this forest . . . knew how easy it was to conceal a secret, no matter how many searchers flooded the woods. Bogachiel preserve's deep hollows, overgrown with giant ferns and underbrush, produced ideal conditions for hiding. You could even build a camp, live beneath the forest's voluminous vegetation, and never be discovered. There were caves and hollowed-out stumps where you could hide something. Or bury something, for instance, a human body. There was Elk Pond, where, if you weighted down a human body, you could submerge it in three hundred feet of still black glacier water. There was the moss-draped, labyrinthian rain forest, where arcane secrets of evolution had escaped humankind's grasp for thousands of years. They [the searchers] were wasting their time. (65)

Frank Herbert's main character in *Soul Catcher* wanders through the mountains west of Seattle, in ground "so sodden" that it "oozed up at each step." Heavy overhead branches shut out the sun, and the undergrowth is so thick that "he could see only a few body lengths in any direction" (11). The result of his immersion in this wilderness is a startling sense of communion with the dead:

Somewhere, he had come through a tangled salmonberry thicket to a stream flowing in a canyon, deep and silent. He had followed that stream upward to vaporous heights . . . upward . . . upward. The stream had become a creek, this creek below him. . . . Abruptly, he sensed all of his dead ancestors lusting after this living experience. (11)

When a friend in need takes Angela Biwaban to the Olympic Peninsula and Vancouver Island, until she becomes attuned to the secrets of this forest, her movements, even in moosehide moccasin boots, are so much noisier than usual that she spooks a Roosevelt elk: "Big as a horse, dark neck and tawny torso, with a full rack of antlers. . . . He bounded over a fallen spruce log, vanishing into the shadows like a buff-colored ghost" (Trainor's *Whiskey Jack*, 168–69). Amid the dark greenery of the red cedar forest, her senses energize as she identifies the "sweet smell of deerfoot vanilla leaf," the "pungent odor of wild onions," and the "dull tang of spirea and Sitka columbine" and spots a dark area for setting a trap (169).

Muriel Gray, whose terrain in *The Trickster* is western Alberta, shifts descriptions from view to view to capture the infinitely varying nature of the landscape, its mystery and its immensity. Thick stands of almost impenetrable lodgepole pine forests on rocky cliffs—"a dark labyrinth of trunks" (86)—give way to the apparent openness of a ski slope, while the stone-hard solidity of a mountain tunnel suddenly shifts into a magically fluid liquid, and the huge flakes of the constantly falling snow cover all trace of human habitation. Her hikers are awed by the "strange . . . silence in among the trees," as if "life became muffled," "softer around the edges," in this primeval "sanctuary" of green and brown, with "twittering birds, scuffling animals, and that thick, syrupy silence" (125–26). In *The Trickster*, mountain blizzards approach "nightmare force," hurl "stinging bullets of snow" (43), freeze human beings into ice gargoyles (60), and leave them with hands like pig trotters from frostbite (80). Gray's winter snow is almost sentient, eddying around the dead, exploring them and their silenced vehicles (44). Flakes the size of golf balls clog yards and mouths, cut the town of Silver off from the outside world, and "pillow" every trace of topographical detail in thick white.

RANGE OF INDIGENOUS PEOPLES

In the northern part of the Northwest region live the Tlingit, Haida, Tahltan, and Tsimshian. To the south are the Nootka, Cowhichan, Chinook, Tillamook, and Kusa, and in between are the Bella Bella, Bella Coola, Kwakiutl, Nisqually, Quillayute, Clallam, Lummi, Cowlitz, Tillamook, and Quinault, many of them Coastal Salish peoples noted for traditional head flattening. Most coastal tribes occupied red cedar plank houses, structures large enough for an extended family and placed just above a river bank, so coast-hopping cedar ships and whaling canoes lined up below them. Their dwellings traditionally have high-pitched roofs and symbolically decorated fronts with abstract images of sacred creatures (Raven, Thunderbird, Whale, or Salmon) (Taylor, *North American Indians*, 59). Their main food has always been shellfish, fish (salmon, halibut), and other sea creatures (whales, seals, walrus, sea urchins), with smoking a traditional way to cure and preserve.

Inland, in the mountains and high plateaus of Washington, Oregon, and northwestern Idaho, are the interior Salish (the Okanogan and Columbian groups, the Shuswap, Coeur d'Alene, and Thompson), the Walla Walla, Cayuse, and Nez Percé, while on the plains of British Columbia and Western Alberta are the Kootenay, Lillooet, Assibinboin, and Kinchuinick, whose life ways are more like those of the Plains Indians, with teepees for homes and buffalo as the main food source.

INDIGENOUS CUSTOMS AND BELIEFS

The Northwest peoples firmly believed in guardian spirit helpers, in the healing power of shamans and the sacred power of ever-present cedar: cedar smoke, cedar chips, carved sacred cedar boards (Squa-de-lich), and carved sacred cedar staffs (Tus-tud). Cedar could heal, bring salmon, ensure a good hunt, and give power. A hunter needed a spirit helper to succeed in his tasks, and trees, natural formations, bees, and all sorts of creatures were thought to have spirit ties. Even jellyfish (called By-the-Wind-Sailors) carried the sacred messages of *Tyee Sahalee*, the Quinault Great Chief Up Above. When the blue medusa jellyfish died, it became sacred food (like the Christian communion host) through which the deity entered human souls.

The low level of human vitality in winter has always required guardian spirit ceremonies among the Coast Salish; spirit powers arrive and depart with the cold season. However, unlike the natives of the Southwest, the Northwest coastal peoples do not rely on hallucinogenics to achieve an altered state of consciousness. Instead, techniques for attaining dissociation are sleep deprivation, fasting (which produces hypoglycemia from lack of food and dehydration from lack of liquids), purging, sweating, exposure to temperature extremes, and hypoventilation of the sort one gets from prolonged diving (*The Tree People*, Author's Notes). Wolfgang G. Jilek, in *Indian Healing: Shamanic Ceremonialism in the Pacific Northwest Today*, demonstrates how Salish guardian spirit ceremonies, once banned but now revived and revitalized, help troubled and alienated tribe members overcome depression and various ills and reidentify with the group.

The potlatch, an occasion of feasting and gift giving once banned by mainstream law, has been revived as a Northwestern native tradition. The potlatch traditionally represented not simply giving for its own sake but giving to maintain social standing and to receive reciprocal favors. The coastal tribes had an elaborate social structure entailing tattoos, slaves, and other outward signs of wealth to indicate status. Anthropologists, according to Taylor, view potlatching as "a substitute for physical conflict" or "fighting with property" (62). Because it is celebrated by special songs and dances, much speech making, and even dramatic performances in ornate, highly elaborate symbolic costumes, the potlatch was and is important in transmitting tribal customs from generation to generation. Father Brad Reynolds, in *A Ritual Death*, describes a typical modern Swinomish smokehouse, a community building large enough to look nearly empty with 200 or 300 people in it. Welcoming totems topped by eagles with outstretched wings sit on either side of the heavy wooden, hand-carved doors, and inside

three [cedar] fires, crackling loudly, burned on the dirt floor in the center of the long hall. The room was hot and smokey, filled with the scent of burning wood. Staggered tiers of seating ran along both sides of the smoke house, separated by the fires burning in the middle. Four huge wooden support columns on either side supported the beams of the high ceiling. Each column was carved with a figure wrapped around the top half. (73)

As part of the local ceremonies celebrating a birth, a cloaked dancer, whose head is shrouded by a thick hood of braided rope, holds "a long pole, decorated with dark colored scarves" and shakes it slightly with both hands to produce the small rattling sound of deer hooves that will protect the group, especially the infant, from bad spirits. Other participants have painted their faces, mainly black, but some red. The young mother, her face painted black, her hair tightly bound and covered by a red scarf, cries out and begins pounding a steady beat on a drum, keening and then singing as others join in, and the ceremony of the Seeowyn ensues.

A Kinchuinick shaman in Muriel Gray's *The Trickster* voices a type of Indian pantheism that she attributes to this region:

"We have kept what the white man could not take from us. We know how the earth lives. They tell us with science what the raindrop is made of. We know in the hearts of our shamans what the raindrop knows, where it has been and where its spirit lies when it twinkles in the sun and harbors its rainbow.

"To forget our knowledge, to lose that great love of all that is alive, is when we become nothing. . . . What does the raindrop know?" . . .

[Sam replies], "That it falls from a sky it is part of, onto a flower that it is part of, into the ground it is part of, to feed the fruit it is part of, that feeds the man it was part of long ago before it fell. . . . It knows it will be a raindrop again as a man knows he will be a man again." (453)

Northwest tribes attribute healing properties to many rain forest plants. *Wildcrafters*, which features Native American victims but a non-native Park Service detective, enumerates the uses to which local tribes put an indigenous plant, the devil's club, whose bark serves healing and cosmetic functions:

Puget Sound shamans used devil's club in their magic ceremonies, and some Coastal tribes made fishing lures from the plant's thorns. The Lummi burnt the bark, mixed it with bear grease to make black face paint. Like a prick from its spines, the plant's berries were toxic. Native tribes stripped off the thorns and spines and applied the plant's bark to various ailments, from common colds to breast-feeding maladies to unpleasant odors. In recent times, some herbologists had claimed devil's club was nature's most reliable cure all. (Moody, 51)

When healing herbs fail, practitioners turn to secret rituals with cedarwood masks and elaborate costumes, sacred designs, carved cedar spirit boards, and cedar smoke. Evil shamans were traditionally executed in such a way that their departing spirits could be trapped in a living cedar tree, and bodies of the dead were sometimes hung high in cedar branches.

J. F. Trainor describes the seeming permanence of Klallam rituals suddenly defeated by industrial pollution laying waste to harvests of the sea:

For thousands of years, Klallam *tyhee* [shaman] had stood on the Gemini's banks, arms upraised, intoning the sacred prayer song, "*Nika kwisha lolo salmon kopa-chuck!*" And the silver-finned multitude had come, leaping and splashing. Year after year. Century after century. (*Whiskey Jack*, 193)

Thus customs and beliefs derive directly from the region's geography and climate, its flora, fauna, and unique Northwest properties.

SHAMAN

In mainstream fiction, stories which evoke shamanistic powers have traditionally been horror stories, bound by the convention that associates alien (i.e., non-mainstream) religious beliefs with the nightmare possibilities of the pagan and forbidden. Only recently have these powers been moved from the sci-fi and horror genres into detective fiction, where their religious aspects have assumed a validity and even partial acceptance on their own terms, particularly in stories set in the Southwest. In the novels of the Northwest, however, shamanism is still, to a great degree, associated with horror.

Frank Herbert's *Soul Catcher*

Typical of novels which exploit those horror elements implicit in the shaman story is *Soul Catcher* by science fiction novelist Frank Herbert. Herbert saw in the Northwestern natives' concept of the spirit world the opportunity to depict ancient terrors and powerful natural forces within the context of a modern-day murder story set in the state of Washington. In his novel, the shamanistic powers lie in the hands of a local youth, Hobuhet, whose sister's violent rape and resultant suicide commit him to vengeance in a traditional native way: by using the medicine powers and rituals passed on in his family to transform himself into an incarnation of the spirit of his ancestors, Katsuk, and to seek out and destroy the "deformity of spirit" brought on by the white world (78).

Hobuhet, a doctoral candidate in anthropology, reverts to his ancestral ways: "The spirit of the wilderness had seeped into him" (64). He waits for the full moon, fasting and purging himself by drinking seawater. Then he cuts out the tongue of a land otter and carries it in a deer scrotum around his neck until he can bury it beneath a rotten log in a place he can never find again; doing so makes it become his spirit tongue. He scrubs his skin raw with hemlock twigs, ties back his hair with a red cedar bark headband, and fasts, eating only the roots of devil's club. He calls on the names of the ancient dead and performs various secret ceremonies.

Herbert depicts young Hobuhet in ways that make his odd behavior understandable in Christian terms: he is possessed. That is, the process he undergoes to evoke visions and to disassociate himself from his assimilated graduate student self has enabled a soul catcher to seize his souls (in keeping with native tradition, he has two souls) and possess his body. In this possessed state, he acquires the power of totem spirits, a panther's strength, and a raven's sight. "Ka-" is the prefix for everything human and "-tsuk" the term for a mythological bird, and the name, says Herbert, evokes a number of meanings ("bone, the color blue, a serving dish, smoke . . . brother and soul") that all come together in this representation of a native deity, a human bird (9). As the soul catcher Katsuk, Hobuhet acts under an ancient native tradition of justice that seems much like the Old Testament injunction of an eye for an eye, kidnapping and ritually sacrificing the son of the U.S. undersecretary of state as retribution for white people driving his sister to suicide:

I have done all the things correctly. I used string, twigs, and bits of bone to cast the oracle. I tied the red cedar band around my head. I prayed to Kwahoutze, the god in the water, and to Alkuntam. I carried the consecrated down of a sea duck to scatter upon the sacrificial victim. It was all done in the proper way. (28)

Within the native context, he has been the equivalent of the mainstream detective, judge, and executioner, for he has identified the crime, attributed responsibility, and inflicted punishment. His act is blessed by the omens of falling stars, and it restores the balance of sky and earth, and when the mission he was called for is complete, Katsuk leaves Hobuhet's body. However, read as a crime story, Hobuhet, not Katsuk, is the deranged killer of an innocent child. He may use native myth to disassociate himself from his act, but he must suffer its consequences within the mainstream justice system. Herbert leaves both readings possible, depending on the context that the reader finds congenial.

Muriel Gray's *The Trickster*

Muriel Gray's *The Trickster*, which has a Kinchuinick central character, is set in an imaginary Alberta skiing town named Silver, in the Wolf Mountains. However, we will discuss it as a Pacific Northwest novel because, in mood and theme, it is far closer to the Northwestern shamanistic spirit than to the Plains spirit, as our discussion will make clear. *The Trickster* initially seems like a classic detective story, with a Native American suspect and a Royal Canadian Mounted Police hero, Staff Sergeant Craig McGee, but it then moves into a surreal world of shaman powers controlling horrific ancient evil released by an explosion and a resultant avalanche. The usual police methods of seeking causal links and examining motive and means simply emphasize the impossibility of a human perpetrator for a series of bestial murders and mutilations; instead, the mass murderer may well come from the spirit world. When the regular police are impotent and admit that demonic spirits may well be at work, the initial suspect, Kinchuinick Sam Hunt, must resort to ancient remedies to battle the evil that threatens to envelop his family, town, and world. But first he must undergo a change of heart, for he has battled his entire adult life to be more than "a superstitious, spirit-fearing Indian" (337). As his father warns him, shamans can choose only one of two paths—to practice good medicine or bad, with nothing in between—for if the dark enters them, they are lost (247). Sam Hunt's response is to reject both shamanistic paths and to choose assimilation instead.

In keeping with the Native American belief in the intertwining of past and present, the plot moves between events in 1907 that set in motion happenings in the present, suggesting links between Scots engineers, construction workers, and natives in their first meetings early in the century and their descendants almost 100 years later. Early in the twentieth century, the construction of a corkscrew railroad tunnel through the rock of Wolf Mountain releases an ancient, evil Kinchuinick spirit, an ice and stone Trickster that preys on both whites and Indians but most particularly tortures Chief Hunting Wolf, the tribal shaman. In the 1907 plot, a Scots clergyman joined Hunting Wolf to battle this destructive evil—without final success. In the present, Calvin Bitterhand, who was trained by Eden James Hunting Wolf, Chief Hunting Wolf's son, and who is the only medicine man on Redhorn, the 25 square miles of Kinchuinick reserve, understands the darkness that threatens whites and Indians alike but feels helpless in the face of white indifference.

He knows that to them he is "a useless drunken, old gray-haired Indian, stinking of his own dried urine," in threadbare clothes like skin, not fabric, and with "a face lined by abuse and tragedy" (182). Sam Hunt, the modern suspect turned hero, is the great-grandson of Hunting Wolf, but in his youth an unwanted homosexual experience with Bitterhand turned him against his mystical, shamanistic heritage and led him to methodically embrace the modern world. He has married a white woman, drives a pickup truck, watches televised hockey games, and loathes the culture of his abusive, alcoholic father. He no longer thinks of himself as Indian, and he calls Siouan, the language of his tribe, "the language of losers" (31). Yet, within the context of plot events, he can only be whole if he returns to the power of the old ways. He finds himself waking from blackouts, muttering in Siouan, and fearing the deeds that might have sprung from his unconscious mind.

Ironically, Hunt eventually acts as both a shaman hero within the native tradition and a Christ figure within the mainstream tradition, and the supernatural entity that he battles is both a Satanic figure and a distorted version of the Native American Coyote Trickster, Creator, and Destroyer, bringer of heat and death. However, where traditionally the Coyote Trickster, who can take animal or human form, promotes harmony through humorous exaggeration and negative examples of pride, obscene sexuality, and human excesses of all sorts, Gray's Trickster tests the outer limits of human capability in deadly, terrifying ways, using cold rather than heat, destruction rather than beneficence, and a questioning of all realities rather than self-understanding. Normally, one can laugh at one's own human frailty when laughing at the mischievous Coyote's mishaps, but one cannot laugh at Gray's Trickster, with its "huge, taloned limbs," "savagely curled [ice] claws" that "sheen like black blood through rotting veins" (162). This Trickster is an obscene "farce" of primal evil, a rotting excrescence of ice and stone that is nevertheless sentient and can draw power from the weaknesses and fears of humans. Hunt's Kinchuinick tradition provides him with the secret names of the monster he challenges (Sitconski, Inktomi, Inktumni). However, in rejecting his heritage he has forgotten the ways in which his people historically overcame this Trickster. As a result, the demonic creature has become stronger, merging with a malevolent, inchoate mountain being, roused from the depths of a living rock by miners and railroad men in 1907.

This modern Trickster has power over both the physical and the psychological. It forces deer, foxes, and other creatures to tear themselves apart, and it controls human hallucinations that bring to life its victim's worst nightmares: paranoid projections of lust, mutilated bodies, beating hearts ripped from the bodies of friends, and other distortions of fears and hopes, emotions that have become literal visions. It is a cannibalistic winter demon of ice, mud, and rock, a reflection of its mountain environment— older than Christianity. Furthermore, it mocks the Kinchuinick for rejecting the old ways and "hiding" among the whites, laughing sarcastically: "Oh, but I've enjoyed the search. So much misery. Such lost and useless lives. What has become of you, my fine noble people?" (314). To defeat it, Hunt must accept his Native American Kinchuinick identity as Sam Hunting Wolf, an inheritor of the shaman role who must make great personal sacrifices to imprison the Trickster and keep him bound. He must go into the wilderness alone and purify both his flesh and his spirit in traditional ways; like Christ, he must withstand the temptations of the Trickster; he must make a conscious decision to take upon himself the burdens of his people, to accept the old ways, to reject the materialistic trappings of his assimilation, to face his fears and, secure in the secrets of his ancestors, to defeat the historic spirit enemy of his tribe. He must become a Kinchuinick shape-shifter and take on the power to transport his physical body over great distances. Furthermore, he must accept that the battle will never truly end, and his sons must learn the Kinchuinick secrets and battle the Trickster as he has done. Thus Sam Hunting Wolf becomes the reluctant champion of an unknowing, uncaring humanity. As such, he and his wife return to the reservation, commit to teaching their children and grandchildren the old language, and presumably reject assimilation and modernism.

Ultimately, Gray asserts that the land itself—the caves, forests, mountains, and canyons—can produce a dark malignancy that endangers humans who infringe on its territory, possesses their minds and souls, and disrupts nature's balance. To counter such evil is beyond the capability of any detective dependent on reason and logic; for example, the supernatural events that Royal Canadian Mountie McGee witnesses (including nightmare visions of his dead wife's cancerous womb as a spirit version of her attempts to embrace him, innards exposed) call into question the Western understanding of reality, and ultimately he cannot cope. Instead, it takes the sacrifice of a Native American tied to the spirits of the land to defeat what the Western mind cannot admit exists.

Although McGee's investigation is ongoing, Gray confirms that justice and truth will elude conventional means of detection, that the truth might be hard for rational beings to accept, and that mainstream justice is irrelevant for the malevolent powers of the universe. Evil can be thwarted for the moment but always threatens to burst forth in new destructive forms that reflect past manifestations. Evil is not a social problem, as the mainstream would have it, but a condition of man and nature.

Naomi Stokes' *The Tree People* and *The Listening Ones*

Naomi Stokes' *The Tree People*, set in an ancient forest area on the Pacific Northwest's Olympic Peninsula, combines Salish witchcraft with detection in a story about environmental struggles over the cutting of old-growth timber. The novel pits white magic against black magic and a good Quinault shaman, Old Man Ahcleet, a direct descendant of a great pre-Columbian shaman, Musqueem, against a bad shaman, Xulk, and a red-headed Quinault witch, Aminte, with a Raven familiar. Ahcleet's ancestor had imprisoned the redheaded demon shaman Xulk (Aminte's ancestor) within a sacred cedar centuries before, but Aminte moves the local tree company's yellow tape markers so the workmen cut the old-growth tree, freeing Xulk to infect the land with ancient evil. Ahcleet uses herbal medicine to heal while Aminte spreads disease and casts spells. She weaves spells to enhance her physicality and to attract men to her forest home, where she then separates their souls from their bodies with a soul catcher. He, in contrast, struggles to reunite soul and body and to end the evil threatening his great-granddaughter (Jordan Tidewater) and her son.

Tidewater is a pragmatic, well-educated policewoman, a Quinault tribal sheriff who has purposely chosen a modern path, studying forensic logic and methodologies, employing modern technologies, and even planning to undergo state-of-the-art training at the FBI Academy in Quantico, Virginia. When confronted with victims who have had their throats slashed, been battered to death, or been killed by runaway machinery, her instinct is to apply the logic of motive and means on which she has come to depend. However, when the virulent infection that Aminte and Xulk have released threatens her son's life, instead of calling a medical specialist she turns to traditional ways of combating evil. Ahcleet had asserted her destiny as tribal shaman, and now necessity compels her to reject the investigative methods which had served her well as a law officer and open her mind to the ancient rituals and mystical experiences that shamans undergo to gain spiritual power.

As she did at the police academy, she must accept a rigid regime of physical and mental activities, though these differ markedly from her police experiences: purifying through fasting and sweat baths followed by a plunge into ice-cold water and a run through the forest, naked, greeting the four cardinal directions and calling on her spirit helpers to reveal themselves. The beaver and the snake Teb'ak!wab answer her call, and sacred body paint and physical torture at the hands of senior ritualists help her discover her sacred song and merge with an ancient shaman, La'quwamax, who had brought the Quinault the lesson of successful whaling directly from Thunderbird. Armed with a shaman's spirit helper, a sacred cedar-and-otter-skin shaman cape and apron, and a soul catcher, she first dominates Aminte's raven and wolf familiars and an ancient Quinault ghost board. Next, she overcomes nightmare threats to recover Xulk's bones and restore them to a cedar tree prison. Then she launches a spirit canoe on a psychic journey, during which she battles Aminte and Xulk. While Ahcleet guards her physical body and drives her canoe with his spirit powers, she travels through a land of dreams inhabited by bats, bears, cougars, and the dead spirits of her ancestors; she battles turbulent rivers and disorienting swamps in order to bring her son's spirit back from the Land of the Dead. This transforming experience returns Tidewater to her Quinault heritage and enables her to accept her community role as shaman, her people's spiritual link between past and present. The novel ends with her commitment to the ancient ways and to teaching her son to respect them.

The Listening Ones again begins with a seemingly straightforward investigation, with Tidewater specially deputized as a U.S. marshal to increase her authority to investigate the illegal killing of eagles and bears for body parts prized in Asia. However, she soon heads an investigation of two youngsters her son's age who were dismembered and left in eagles' nests on sacred land. The details of these murders suggest ritual sacrifices and intentional desecration. Because of her transformation in the first novel, Tidewater quickly gives up on Western investigative procedures and draws instead on her shamanistic powers, the collective wisdom of her ancestry, and the spirit voices of the listening ones of the title—her guardian totem spirits. Ahcleet and masked tribal dancers who engage in personal blood-letting battle both natural forces (waterspouts, tornadoes, earthquakes, fierce lightning, and a terrifying eclipse of the moon) and spirit forces (the dead seeking vengeance for past wrongs). Their combined efforts enable Tidewater to shape-shift into a cougar and later an eagle, but it takes a vision of Klokwalle, an ancient being revered by the Quinault, to help her finally defeat a South American shaman whose magic threatens the tribe.

CONCLUSION

Thus unlike in the Southwest and the Plains regions, where detective fiction straddles the fence between shaman and Sherlock, the powerful indigenous beliefs and the uniqueness of the Northwestern coastal and mountain terrain from which those beliefs sprang have strongly influenced the writers of detective fiction from this region. The congruences in the plots of Gray and Stokes show how very different novels about the region converge on similar notions about evil, the past, and the landscape. Instead of Western logic, these Northwestern stories offer mysticism and spiritualism, guardian spirits and shamanistic journeys through misty territory where strange creatures threaten and where humans mask as animals, animals take on human qualities, and trees are sentient beings. Evil springs from earth and trees and must be returned to them by those who know the ancient ways and can resourcefully apply the knowledge passed down orally from ancestor to ancestor to combat what has often been opposed and what must again be fought at some future time. Old growth cedar has power beyond its practical resilience and beauty; it interfaces with eternity.

The historical Duwamish Chief Seattle, in a speech responding to Governor Isaac Stevens' offer to purchase 2 million acres of Duwamp territory, spoke for his people, warning:

[W]hen the last Red Man shall have perished, and the memory of my tribe should have become a myth among the White Men, these shores will swarm with the invisible dead of my tribe, and when your children's children think themselves alone in the field, the store, the shop, upon the highway, or in the silence of the pathless woods, they will not be alone. . . . At night when the streets of your cities and villages are silent and you think them deserted, they will throng with the returning hosts that once filled and still love this beautiful land. The White Man will never be alone . . . the dead are not powerless. Dead, did I say? There is no death, only a change of worlds. ("Address," 55)

In modern Northwestern detective fiction, the ghosts of the native dead still walk, and their ancient spirits still affect the land and its inhabitants, white and native alike. Writers such as Herbert, Stokes, and Gray find the mountains, forests, rivers, and coasts indeed haunted by the spirits of the past. Their characters may seem superficially assimilated, but deep in their souls they are at one with their ancestors and, in times of trouble, it is the ancestral ways of knowing that rule the day, not Western logic or the Sherlocks who practice it.

8

Alaska and the Canadian Northwest Territories: Wilderness Challenges and Human Limitations

A distant rumble. Water rushing north. Boots thudding against wet tundra. Rhythmic panting. A moaning gust of wind. Willows trembling and bowing. A raven cawing sleepily from its perch atop a leaning, stunted pine. . . . Glancing over his shoulder he sees . . . squat alders, the snaking, thorny vines of berry bushes, a sea of autumn leaves, limestone peaks, cirrus clouds floating like brush strokes across a deep blue sky. No movement. No evidence of hostility or danger. But . . . the enemy is coming. . . . The wilderness is pristine, innocent, without guile. Unbridled, untouched by man.

Then he hears. . . . a shout. . . . He splashes across a shallow eddy and sprints uphill, . . . into a vast, merciless wilderness that stretches for more than thirty-five million acres.

He has no idea where he is going, only that he is running. . . . away from death.

—Christopher Lane, *Season of Death*, 2

As Lane's introductory quote suggests, the emptiness and isolation of the pristine wilderness is a perfect setting for murder and other forms of human villainy—far from those who might hear the cries of a victim or stumble across a decaying corpse—and nature herself makes disposal of the corpse a cinch—if not the ravens and the crows, then wolves, bears, and any number of scavengers. The Native American detectives from Alaska and Canada's Northwest Territories must learn to cope with the wildness of the land and the eccentricities and cultural differences of that region's sociological mix. These detectives include the following:

Author	Detective	Tribal Affiliation
Christopher Lane	Ray Attla (assisted by Sheriff Glen Redfern and Keera)	Inupiat Korean-Yup'ik Athabascan
	Shaman Maniilaq	Inupiat
Marcia Simpson	Lisa Romero	Half-Lummi
	Paul Howard	Tlingit
Dana Stabenow	Kate Shugak	Aleut
Garth Stein	Jenna Rosen	Half-Tlingit
	Shaman David Talmost	Tlingit
Scott Young	Matteesie Kitologitak	Inuk

GEOGRAPHICAL DETERMINERS

Alaska and the Canadian Northwest Territories are both arctic and subarctic, a region of snow and ice, walrus, and polar bears, as well as tundra (low, flat, treeless plains with bogs, lakes, and streams) grazed by musk-ox and caribou, though to the south are coniferous forests of pine, cedar, spruce, and larch, much like those of British Columbia and the U.S. Pacific Northwest. Technically, there are four different climates, with the subarctic divided into maritime, continental, and transitional and the transitional subdivided into Anchorage and the western coast from Bristol Bay to Point Hope (nearly 1,000 miles, says Father Brad Reynolds in *The Story Knife*, 60). Megan Mallory Rust describes a pilot's view of the 50,000-square-mile Yukon-Kuskokwim Delta, with the tall spires of the Alaska Range on its eastern border "jutting" through the clouds "like stalagmites piercing the surface of a subterranean lake," "the flat tundra plain" to the west stretching for "miles and miles of dismal monotony," and only three routes through mountains whose "magnificence" hides "menace" and whose blue-and-white glaciers brook no mistakes (*Red Line*, 1, 174).

North of the Arctic Circle the subsoil remains frozen year round, as January temperatures drop below minus-22 degrees Fahrenheit, and summer daytime temperatures average only in the 50s. Christopher Lane, in *Elements of a Kill*, describes winter weather:

horizontal snow and vengeful blasts of wind . . . create an impressive whiteout: nearly zero visibility. The weather . . . mak[es] the darkness even more complete, as if it were alive, intent upon crushing all hopes of spring, light and life. . . . like walking into an abyss. (79)

the howling wind, the near total darkness. . . . was like looking into a void, a black hole in space, where only cold and evil existed. (285)

Canadian Scott Young confirms the Northwestern Territories winter practice of leaving a vehicle's engine running because, with an outside temperature of −38 considered comparatively warm, any vehicle not left running would be not only too cold to start but also too cold to get into, and their summer tradition of anticipating and preparing the graves needed in winter when the ground is too frozen for digging. His hero gazes into "the impenetrable Arctic night," where all is blackness except thick particles of snow and ice caught in the runway lights (*Murder in a Cold Climate*, 26).

Though usually depicted as harsh and hostile, the region has several distinct ecological zones, with temperatures in the subarctic regions comparatively milder than those of the arctic region (from the 40s to 60s Fahrenheit along the coast in summer). Where Fairbanks gets piles of snow and icy wind, Sitka gets the patter of raindrops and shimmering fog—100 inches of rain annually. However, in winter, the 1,000 square miles of ice covering the Bering and the Chukchi seas create storms whose effects can be felt far inland:

Hurricane-force winds ripping through the region can drive pellets of ice and snow a hundred miles with the sting of a 12-gauge shotgun. The combination of tides and wind can stack islands of ice, some miles across and a hundred feet thick, . . . creating vast ridges and cliffs in the cold, white frozen seas. (Reynolds, *The Story Knife*, 60)

Thus in the main, Alaska's native peoples and those of the Northwest Territories have been and are at the mercy of the climate as few people are. By necessity, they have traditionally been resilient, resourceful fishers, hunters, and sometimes trappers, with the dictates of the seasons and of the migration patterns of game regulating their cycles of activities. Seal, walrus, and caribou were traditional food staples. The intensely cold, long, dark winter months, particularly January and February, are bleak and inhospitable, making outside activities difficult, if not impossible. Consequently, this period has traditionally been a time for community and family storytelling and for constructing the tools and weapons needed when the weather improves. It also suggests why the Inuit consider their homes microcosms of the outside world (Taylor, *North American Indians*, 81).

The famous Iditarod sled-dog race across 1,500 miles of wild territory is a modern reminder of how much this region remains a lonely, isolated, wild frontier, a territory where cars and trucks have limited access, and where boats, small planes, and helicopters are the most reliable forms of transportation. Marcia Simpson, in *Crow in Stolen Colors*, describes the typical road as "a washboard, a zigzag track punched along the side of the mountain, the rising curves precisely the arc required for the log carriers to get around," with precarious boulders above, and small rocks cascading down (125). Reynolds calls airplanes Alaska's "taxis" and argues that "there is no facet of life in an Alaskan bush village that has not, at some time, involved an airplane" (*The Story Knife*, 77), while J. F. Trainor's Angela Biwaban jokes that the distances and terrain necessitating air travel make the Cessna 180 "the Alaska state bird" (*Whiskey Jack*, 230). Susan Froetschel, in *Alaska Gray*, observes that Sitka, though Alaska's sixth largest city, is, like most towns in Southeast Alaska, "accessible only by air or water transportation," because all city roads stop abruptly "at water, forest, or mountains" (36). Thus, the standard arctic flight gear includes "a two-layer tent, primus stove, axe, snow knife for making an igloo, one Arctic-grade sleeping bag per passenger and pilot, watertight match container, candles, dried food, extra parkas if passengers didn't have their own, a rifle" (Young, *Murder in a Cold Climate*, 49).

Alaska has high mountain ranges (Mt. Denali, formerly Mt. McKinley, America's tallest promontory, rises 20,320 feet and on a clear day is visible from 200 miles away). Of its numerous volcanoes, some are unexpectedly active, like Mt. Redoubt, which sent suffocatingly gritty, corrosive ash down on south-central Alaska, or Mt. Spurr, which hurled ash and stones 60,000 feet into the atmosphere, and, says Megan Rust, rained volcanic fallout on Anchorage, 80 miles away (*Red Line*, 187). Rust, in *Dead Stick*, an Alaskan aviation mystery, describes the surprising agricultural richness of the floodplains:

[T]he Butte, a tall, rounded knoll . . . seemed to guard the fertile soil of the Matanuska Valley. The floodplain of the Mat Valley, the hotbed of farming in Alaska, was famous for the enormous crops grown there. Every year at the State Fair those gigantic vegetables stood in state—ninety-seven pound cabbages, zucchini squashes the length and breadth of a human arm, pumpkins so heavy they had to be moved by wheelbarrows. The greens owed their mammoth size to . . . the silty runoff of the Matanuska River, and the nearly twenty-four hours of sunlight dappling the Alaska summer days.

She could still taste the sweetness of the juice . . . from the immense Mat Valley carrots—two of the giants could produce enough flavorful nectar to fill a beer mug to its brim. (141)

The southern region shares the same variety of terrain, plant life, and animal life as the Pacific Northwest. Dall sheep inhabit the glacier areas;

caribou wander across tundra from Alaska to Canada. Black and brown bears frequent Chugach State Park, which boasts a grizzly about every ten square miles. Moose browse on aquatic greenery in the shallow lakes and streams and graze on birch bark, ferns, and leaves in the dense forests. Other wildlife includes the gray wolf, wolverine, coyote, red fox, lynx, marmot, beaver, otter, muskrat, mink, snowshoe hare, and the plentiful ground squirrel. In the spring and summer, giant mosquitoes attack everywhere, and salmon swell the rivers and streams. A Stabenow character measures the desirability of the land by its wildlife:

He saw a grizzly with two yearling cubs swiping salmon out of the river, startled a pair of eagles out of a dead cottonwood, surprised a black bear with three cubs into stampeding for . . . the nearest spruce, stopped counting moose after he got to ten and caught sight of a black streak that might have been a wolf. (Stabenow, *Hunter's Moon*, 5)

With a runway on such property, he thinks, anything is possible. Froetschel sees land as Alaska's "biggest resource," some of it pristine ("never stepped on by any human being"), some "shamelessly abused—clear-cut by logging companies, stripped by miners, and oversupplied with shoddy and downright ugly construction," and much privately owned by the indigenous peoples (*Alaska Gray*, 15). While landscape determines culture in all the regions discussed in this book, because of its dramatic impact on everyday human life, the geography (including flora and fauna) of Alaska and the Northwest Territories looms large in the detective fiction set in this frontier, sometimes becoming almost a character which moves the plot and shapes the theme.

FICTIONAL GEOGRAPHY

The park where Dana Stabenow's Kate Shugak lives is 20 million acres, bordered by the Quilak Mountains running north and east (on average, 16,000 feet high with 3,000 foot thick, 30-mile long glaciers in every pass), the Gulf of Alaska to the south, and the TransAlaskan Pipeline to the west in gently sloping, open land drained by the 250-mile-long Kanuyaq River, which is frozen over in winter and swollen with glacial runoff in the summer. A rain forest of "Sitka spruce, hemlock, alder, and devil's club" chokes the passage from seacoast to mountain but, as the land rises, the tree line thins to a region of "kinnikinnick, rock and ice" (*A Cold Day for Murder*, 20). In detective fiction, such geography means infinite murder possibilities and difficulty finding corpses.

One killer, from Anchorage, shares his strategy:

"I'm going to . . . bury the body somewhere in the woods. That's wilderness over there, thousands and thousands of acres of virgin forest. No one will find anything

for years, if ever, and by that time there'll be nothing left to identify anyway." He
grinned. (Rust, *Dead Stick*, 181)

Kate Shugak, having seen most of her hunting party killed on one ill-fated
expedition, thinks of the consequences if only the two murderers survive:

[I]f they were the only two survivors, who could disprove their story? The Alaskan
Bush was often loath to give up its secrets. Look at Baker Bob, the serial killer
from Anchorage who had kidnapped strippers and hookers and turned them loose
on the Mat-Su River delta . . . [to] hunt them down again. It was years before he'd
been caught, and the bodies hadn't been found until he led the authorities to them
himself. (Stabenow, *Hunter's Moon*, 202)

In Alaskan and Canadian detective stories, a walk in the forest might mean
sudden injury or death, if not from nature then from stumbling upon an
antisocial hermit's hideaway, a drug cooperative's marijuana crop, or a
survivalist group's secret compound. Natural predators decimate a body in
a short time, and an arranged plane crash leaves no questions asked.

RANGE OF INDIGENOUS PEOPLES

   This region is populated by Athabascans and Eskimos, though Eskimo
is the derogatory Algonquian word for "raw meat eaters" and is therefore
not a term the Alaskan Aleut and Yup'ik, or the Inuit-Inupiaq or Inuk
peoples like or use for themselves. Inuit (meaning the People/Humans) has
become the preferred generic term for all peoples formerly designated Eskimos. In fact, despite their extensive geographical range and tribal divisions, these native peoples have a fairly homogeneous language, religion,
social order, and economic system, though kinship patterns differ. The
Tlingit live in southern Alaska, and the Inuk, Athabascans, and Métis in
Canada's Northwest Territories.
   The northern native peoples adapted to their environment by developing
a typically short, stocky body that minimizes loss of body heat (Dana Stabenow's detective Kate Shugak is five feet tall and 110 to 120 pounds,
while Scott Young's Mountie Matteesie Kitologitak is a stocky five feet ten
inches). Their lives are spartan and communal, with survival of the group
traditionally more important than survival of the individual. The Inuit language's lack of pronouns for "I" or "me," "my," or "mine" reflects this
value. Kitologitak notes the absence of swear words in Inuktitut and the
difficulty of readjusting to eating nothing but flesh again when among his
people.
   The ice block igloo is the characteristic Central Arctic dwelling, but elsewhere the Inuit prefer an earth-covered mound dwelling, partly dug into

the ground, a bit like the soddy of the American West, framed with drift-wood and whale ribs, covered with turf, and aired through a rooftop smoke hole. In the warmer months, instead of a fixed mound dwelling, they might prefer a caribou or seal skin tent, which allows for a nomadic lifestyle over wide-ranging territory, trapping muskrat, snaring migratory waterfowl, or collecting bird eggs, berries, and plants to supplement their diet. The har-poon and the stone or ivory blade were the traditional hunting tools, but modernization has introduced more high-tech weaponry along with pre-fab housing, all in standard sizes and colors. Huskies and dog sleds are an inevitable part of Alaskan life, as are the *umiak* (a large, open boat) and kayak, and nowadays snowmobiles and the amphibious plane.

Novelist Megan Rust's heroine, who uncovers a nasty scheme to trade alcohol illegally to remote Yup'ik villages for valuable native artifacts, some stolen from grave sites, calls the Yup'ik themselves amazing because "thrown into the unfamiliar and hostile world of the white man," they retained their "serenity" and eked out a life "on the inhospitable terrain of Western Alaska," a land "virtually treeless, offering no protection from the howling winds," with no large animals to hunt and very little nourish-ing protein on the few small ones—the tiny marmots and pikas (*Red Line*, 28). In *The Story Knife*, Jesuit mystery writer Father Brad Reynolds admires the Yup'iks' survivalist skills and their ability to use every part of their catch, melting seal blubber into oil, cutting the meat into long, thick strips to dry, saving the whiskers to decorate a carved mask, and preparing the skin for *mulkuks* (shoes) or other warm clothing (3). In this novel, Reyn-olds makes an intricately carved, ivory-handled Yup'ik story knife (a chil-dren's toy for drawing stories in the snow) the murder weapon to misdirect the investigation away from attempts to gain legal control of oil rights. His story turns on the intimacy of village life where no secrets can be kept and where everyone—individuals and families—has an interdependent assigned role, whether leader, hunter, mother, or moocher.

ALASKAN HISTORY IN DETECTIVE FICTION

Alaskan history in detective fiction recalls the encounters between the native inhabitants and the early Russian explorers of the 1700s, the gold rush miners, the religious boom missionaries, and the disruptive 1971 Alaska Native Claims Settlement Act (ANCSA). This legislation ostensibly gave the six Alaskan tribal groups $1 billion and more than 90 percent of Alaska's private land in compensation for lost ancestral lands, but in reality it was an exchange for dropping over 200 tribal claims to Alaskan oil fields and to the proposed TransAlaskan Pipeline route (straight across the heart of aboriginal hunting grounds). *The Story Knife* humorously describes the Russian exploration of the Alaska coastline in 1830, the coming of Moravian missionaries 50 years later to build a Russian Orthodox church directly across from a Yup'ik village, and the local shaman's curses on this intrusive structure (in fact, flood waters carried it away) (38). Less humorously, Marcia Simpson describes the missionaries burning native art (masks, totems, cedar carvings) because of their spiritual associations and drowning out "the throaty, oboe music of their Tlingit names" with substitutes such as "Dan Jim, Violet Gamble, Simon Jack" (*Crow in Stolen Colors*, 57). Kate Shugak's relatives are all Russian Orthodox, with Aleut traditions just beneath their surface faith.

Less humorously, too, Reynolds makes the negative effects of the ANCSA central to his murder mystery. The settlement made villagers shareholders in one of twelve corporations in charge of distributing the cash and the 40 million acres of land, but it forbade selling any stock until 1992, when a sale of stock could mean loss of village land and rights. One villager explains:

This new threat was not wind that you felt stinging your skin, or water that you could see slapping against your boat. This new threat was much more dangerous. It had no smell, no taste, no feel to it. All you ever saw were its tracks—small rows of numbers running down columns of a page. And the voice of a *gussuk* [white man], telling you that the place where you, your ancestors, and your future children consider home might be taken away. . . . The trust of the entire village rested on a white man [a lawyer] who lived two thousand miles away from Soognyak. (*The Story Knife*, 134)

The ANCSA is also vital background to Froetschel's mystery. Locals needed legal proof of at least one-quarter native blood, but some natives who technically qualified could not prove their ancestry, while others simply paid the tribe in question to identify them as members. In Froetschel's story, the administrators of a local Sitka college dependent on government grants to natives to support its student population exploit the situation by filling the student body with youngsters who qualify for federal monies but not for university admission. Moreover, some of its staff and faculty have innovatively expanded the college's art department by having retarded native youths with artistic skills duplicate valuable indigenous artifacts in the school's native arts museum; these high-quality fakes replace the originals, which are sold abroad. Such trafficking in rare native items, a mainstay of detective stories featuring Native Americans, opens the door to discussions of, for example, Tlingit carving skills, the role of Raven in native culture, potlatches as an expression of wealth and artistry, and so on.

INDIGENOUS BELIEF AND CUSTOM

Eskimo religious belief has no central or omnipotent god, only a complex taboo system which reduces unpredictability and stress by appeasing numerous fickle and uncaring animistic powers related to sustenance and season. According to Taylor, such taboos required strict observance before a hunt, with rituals or chants to avoid offending animal spirits, and dietary rules about not mixing marine and land products under threat of illness or death. A dead seal might be offered a drink of water as a ritual indication of hospitality, thanks for providing the family with its meat and skin, with the hope that other seals will make the same sacrifice. A Yup'ik in Reynolds' *The Story Knife* pours a cup of fresh water into the mouth of a harpooned seal and says:

Quyana, nayiq. Thank you for choosing me. Thank you for coming to my boat and giving yourself to me. Drink, because you will be thirsty before your trip is over. And when you next see your brothers, tell them of the respect this hunter gives to you. (4)

Animals, features of the landscape, and even the weather, are thought to have spirits or souls, and human beings have several souls. There is the spirit of the fish, the spirit of the whale, the hunt, the sky, the caribou, the walrus, the ice, the snow, and so on. Stabenow's Kate Shugak captures the pantheism of this attitude:

There had been those moments [of spiritual communion with nature] next to the stream in the forest, the kiss of the wind on her skin, the strong and joyous pulse of the earth beating up through the soles of her feet. And she would never forget the animate, vindictive menace of the sea on board the *Avilda* during the ice storm. Or the enchanted dance with the aurorae on top of Angqaq. "I've felt what I thought was a presence from time to time," she said cautiously. "It was real to me." (*Play with Fire*, 184)

Saying the right ritualistic prayer to the right deities at the right times might win pity or aid and prevent starvation, freezing, or other negative possibilities. Or it might not, since these spirits are untouched by human anguish. Amulets and bone or tusk charms hung on one's body or in one's home might ward off malign spirits.

Spirit forces permeated the northern native's world. Family and friends, fearful of injurious spirits released by death, left the sick to die alone; not even a shaman tended the dying because of the power and danger of the spirits of the dead. Traditionally, the dead have been left in the wilderness to return to the land, consumed by ravens, wolves, bears, and foxes. For the Inupiat, death is a transition period, during which the lazy wait in a humiliating netherworld, while good hunters go to a place of plenty as all await reincarnation, perhaps as a caribou, fox, or whale, or as a human. A child named after a brave hunter now dead, or an ancestor, is thought to receive the dead one's soul along with the name.

The shaman played a major role in daily life, discovering why hunting had been poor and how to propitiate the spirits, treat illness, drive out madness, change the weather, and deal with crises. Dream visions carry dark meanings, and the old stories are parables for daily life. Lane's Ray Attla repeatedly dreams traditional myths which apply to his own life, such as the story of how a brave young man captured the sun and brought daylight to his people. Or the story of the wicked mother who blinds her son, uses his skills to kill an attacking polar bear, then half starves the boy while gluttonously dining on the bear herself, until he regains his sight, understands her treachery, harpoons a white whale, and lashes her to its back before setting it free. Shugak explains that the Aleut believed in the connectedness and interdependency of life, with salmon, for example, knowing that they serve as food for the People and accepting their self-sacrifice so the People could live (Stabenow, *Play with Fire*, 183). Thus, hunters dressed in new clothes and decorated their harpoons and kayaks with walrus whiskers, ivory charms, and beads to respect the salmon's sacrifice. Yearly ceremonies honor the animals that feed and clothe the People.

Stabenow, in a Liam Campbell mystery *So Sure of Death*, featuring a story knife as a murder weapon, salmon, artifacts, military secrets as motivators, and native islanders and salmon fishers as suspects, sums up the native cultural attitude about time and speed and the importance of being in harmony with natural cycles:

It never helped to rush anything in the Bay [of Kulukak], and it was offensive to the Natives besides, who had made a pretty good living for thousands of years by waiting: waiting for the fish to come up the river, waiting for the caribou to come down out of the mountains, waiting for the bears to wake up in the spring, waiting for the berries to ripen in the fall. Patience wasn't just a virtue for the people of the Bay, it was a way of life. (27)

This sense of nature's time, permanence, and repeated cycles permeates native culture. In *A Fatal Thaw*, Stabenow captures the spirit of the potlatch to reaffirm community togetherness and to celebrate significant events of passage, calling it "a paean to life and to those who lived it, a remembrance of the dead, an act of homage" (141).

In Simpson's *Crow in Stolen Colors*, a Tlingit Raven Elder finds death when he investigates a set of boulders that are in too straight a line to be naturally located. They bear petroglyphs carved by his ancestors 8,000 years before and placed by streams and rivers; displaying the round eye and sharp beak of Raven, they once called the salmon back to the waters that saw their birth. Now they are dislocated from their rightful places and in transit to foreign buyers:

His finger followed the outline of Raven's eye and beak. First People. Raven had tricked First People out of the Sun and Moon; had created a new people from Leaf. But Raven hadn't changed since someone spent years—years—carving his picture into this rock with a stone tool. Raven was Always.

His ancestors had carved rocks and totem poles so they would remember how Raven stole the Box of Daylight, how Grizzly Bear saved the people from the glacier floods, how Eagle was avenged against the great hunter. In case they would forget, they made masks and rattles and bowls to tell those stories with songs and feasts . . . [these are the same stories he now teaches his nephew].

"These rocks lived somewhere," he told the boy [his nephew]. "Each rock lived at one special stream or beach or ledge. Now they can't ever go home." (4–5)

First missionary zealots burned the totems, masks, and rattles, the old man thinks, and now the greedy steal the ancient artifacts that protect the land and ensure hunt and harvest, while the cities beckon the young away from their heritage. Modern detective mysteries depict the end result of centuries of white-native contact—the indigenous beliefs practiced dutifully by the elderly and scoffed at by the young, and crimes of desecration and theft of sacred artifacts in economically depressed areas where natives and whites alike scramble for survival. Simpson's Tlingit police officer, Paul Howard, voices native feelings about stolen artifacts:

"You lose this [several boxes of stolen artifacts], you lose a lot of the heritage of the Tlingit nation" . . . to Paul they were as dear as his own childhood, objects lovingly created, designed for a purpose, treasured for their usefulness. A whole culture of wood, of spruce root and cedar bark, replaced by Tupperware and stainless steel utensils. Even his grandmother had come to plastic and pottery, but each spruce root basket and wooden bowl on her shelves had a designer and a story, and he knew every story was true.

"This is Gonakadet, the sea serpent," she'd say of a carved wooden bowl. "Listen how Gonakadet tricked Killer Whale." (Simpson, *Crow in Stolen Colors*, 141–42)

SHAMAN

A mixed-genre shaman thriller, Garth Stein's *Raven Stole the Moon* combines elements of detection and horror with Tlingit oral tradition and belief. Set in a small, remote Alaskan town, it draws on native lore for its mystery: who or what is responsible for disappearances in and around a new, seemingly financially sound investment, the Thunder Bay Resort? Locals were told the resort would attract investment dollars and tourists and provide employment for workers dependent on seasonal fishing, trapping, guiding, and so on. Stein's amateur detective is a grieving half-Tlingit mother (Jenna Rosen) who has given up on her marriage, on the promises of corporate America, and on conventional answers, the official explanations for her son's disappearance. The story begins as a missing persons investigation, with Jenna convinced that her son Bobby did not drown, as the authorities and her husband assert (her husband, an official for the Thunder Bay Resort, seems to be participating in a cover-up, at least, so Jenna suspects). She seeks answers and is open to unexplored possibilities. Her journey to find answers becomes a form of personal empowerment, though her conventional husband believes she is suffering a nervous breakdown and possibly hallucinations.

That her son's body never surfaced gives her hope, and her Tlingit heritage leads to native explanations for his disappearance. The fact that resort officials hired a local shaman, David Talmost, to drive restless spirits from Thunder Bay spurs her to seek that shaman's unconventional means of searching. One frightening possibility is that the *kushtaka*, or Otter People, have stolen her son. Stylized on fetishes and totems with the body of a fish and two faces, "one upside down and one right side up, interlocked in some kind of battle" (162), these otter-like Tlingit water gods are shape-shifters who can appear as dogs or even as familiar humans to win the trust of those they stalk. However, an elderly Tlingit tells Jenna that, despite their power to fool, their unchanging eyes and teeth betray them. The Tlingit believe that these predatory gods live in a watery underworld, a transitional stage between life and death, and that they steal the souls of drowning victims. An elder tells Jenna that Raven gave the kushtake the power

[T]o watch over the woods and the seas and to rescue lost souls who are weak and on the verge of death and convert them into kushtaka. . . . When a person dies, the Tlingits burn his body so he can pass safely to the Land of Dead Souls. From there, his soul will return to his family. If he is saved from drowning by the kushtaka, his soul will be trapped with them forever. (163)

Furthermore, the kushtaka take the shape of family members to weaken the resistance of prospective Otter people; they cast spells to sap their victims' strength. Stein makes these otter gods more than simply receivers of dead souls, for they actively take captives to defend their territory. The closed resort is located precisely over their watery spiritual home; on those resort grounds, Talmost has already fought with them for his life and soul and nearly lost. The shaman knows what happened to the boy and how to rescue him but is unsure of his powers. Only a strong shaman can free a soul the kushtaka hold, yet they had already tormented Talmost, turning him into an animal with hair and claws, stealing the fetus from his pregnant wife, and finally freeing him with dire warnings. Now he fears the consequences of taking them on again.

At this point in the narrative, all conventional detection has disappeared. The shaman and Jenna agree on a supernatural explanation of events and question whether or not her son has already been transformed into an otter being, how to rescue him if he has not, and how to free his soul if he has. Such a rescue, like that of Jordan Tidewater bringing her son back from the spirit world in a spirit canoe in Stokes' *Tree People*, will involve a spirit journey to the center of kushtaka power; it also carries the possibility of failure—shaman and mother forever trapped in a watery spirit world, transformed into otters themselves. Talmost calls on his strongest medicine powers; Jenna steels her will to her task. Talmost gives her a mini-course in kushtaka behavior, their fear of dogs, because dogs see through their illusions, their inability to endure contact with processed ore or cooked food, the fact that human blood breaks their spells, and the native belief that they are neither evil nor bad, just powerful proselytizers. Fasting and purification renew his commitment to the shaman's way. However, before he can act, the kushtaka take Jenna to their watery world.

As in most novels featuring shaman powers, Talmost arms himself with medicine power for the journey and for the spiritual battle against powerful forces. He recruits Jenna's abandoned husband and her new lover to perform the rituals necessary to help him win the battle while his spirit is out of his body, traveling through the world of the otter people. What follows is a paranormal underwater journey to the spiritual nest of the kushtaka, a search through a network of passageways, caves, and lodges, and terrifying psychological battles with creatures who shift shapes to look like the shaman, Jenna, and her son. The shaman brings a sensual, furry Jenna back from the kushtaka spell by contact with the metal of his knife and blood from a gash he cuts in his hand. Then the two of them actively seek her son through the tunnels and chambers of the nest.

The absence of empirical confirmation of events or psychological explanations is deeply unsettling. In terms of the investigative plot, a mother has rejected the official theory of her son's drowning and searched for him, aided by an insightful member of the community; together they assert their discovery of his whereabouts: held prisoner against his will by mythic creatures. They claim to rescue him from the kushtaka so his soul can join his grandmother's in the Land of the Dead. But what does this all mean? Has the main character indeed had a total psychological breakdown, with her description of events a wishful projection? Does the shaman actually stand up to the real otter gods and, with the force of a mother's love to strengthen his own medicine and determination, overpower or fool them? Has the boy's soul been freed? No reliable narrator answers these questions, and no firm evidence guides reader response. Jenna has faced her grief through this process; the shaman's confidence is restored; the husband is chastened. However, such resolutions involve psychological shifts in perspectives rather than the "hard evidence" of changed physical events in the plot— the son's body recovered, for example—described by a reliable narrator.

SHERLOCK WITH SHAMANISTIC INFLUENCES

The harshness of Alaskan terrain and life necessitates a realistic, survivalist view, and this view dominates the detective stories of this region. Fears among the indigenous people of animal spirits and spirits of the land accord easily with the region's commonplace deaths by natural circumstances, given causes such as plane crashes, accidents at sea, icy waters, blizzards, bear attacks, or simply a lack of wilderness survival skills.

Christopher Lane's Ray Attla

Christopher Lane's Inupiat Eskimo mysteries directly counter Western rationalism with native spiritualism. A ratiocinative Inupiat adult is set against older traditional natives and native youngsters, both with special powers to see truths in dream visions or to intuit truths in some preternatural way. Lane's representative of deduction and reason is series police officer Ray Attla, a very prosaic, good-humored investigator with little tolerance for spiritual nonsense. Lane's representatives of shamanistic powers, however, differ from novel to novel; they serve as surrogate detectives, not always directly active in the plot but with knowledge vital to its final resolution. In *Elements of a Kill*, Attla's aged grandfather Charles warns Attla of his dreams of danger, and though the detective denies their significance except as reflections of his fears of marriage, his own dreams are fraught with threats. In *Season of Death*, the shamanistic voice is that of a young Athabascan girl with the gift of special sight through fragmented visions, while in *A Shroud of Midnight Sun*, Attla's own four-year-old daughter Keera has seen details of his case in ways that are unclear to him but that obviously derive from her family and tribal heritage. Moreover, Attla's grandfather and his elderly shaman friend Maniilaq call Attla the "crooked boy" because he is unchanging and traditional but also new and adaptable; they believe he has been favored since childhood by the *Great of Tuungak* (spirit forces) and thus has powers of which he is not cognizant or simply denies. Lane draws on traditional Inupiat, Inuit, and Yup'ik stories and religious beliefs about the spirit world and animal guardians to infuse his detective novels with a native vision of reality quite at odds with the vision Attla has acquired with his academic degrees. Lane also captures the close ties between the Eskimo view of reality and the unique terrain the Eskimos inhabit, showing how murder investigations in this northern wilderness, out of necessity, differ markedly from mainstream urban investigations.

Orphaned at age three, Attla had been raised by his grandparents in traditional Inupiat ways, learning to "harpoon bowhead, stalk game, seine for sheefish, hunt for seals," use the drum artfully, dance ritual dances, and participate knowledgeably in seasonal celebrations (*Season of Death*, 20–21). As an athletic youth, he had won several ribbons in the Eskimo Olympics, making his grandparents proud. His grandfather, a skilled whaler, regarded the changes brought by whites over the last 100 years as not simply unsettling and threatening but as a series of curses—disease, alcoholism, a loss of livelihood, oil spills, microwaves, televisions, and high-tech means to harvest the land and the sea. Attla's early lessons were about the Inupiat connection to the Land and their adaptation to its whims and desires; his grandfather taught him "to honor and accept the Arctic rhythms, to appease the fickle gods, to accept and endure the love-hate relationship that forever bound them to the territory that now bore the label Alaska" (128).

However, once Attla had attended high school in Barrow and the University of Alaska in Anchorage and then obtained a degree in criminal justice, exposure to new people, books, ideas, and philosophies gave him a perspective quite different from that of his grandfather and a worldview that challenged his grandfather's ideas as old-fashioned, superstitious, and no longer viable in a world determined by change. Where the family story is that his height (six foot one or two, several inches taller than the tallest Inupiat) is a gift from the gods to make up for the loss of his mother at such an early age, Attla understands the genetics that suggest one of his ancestors was probably a Quaker missionary. At age 28, he is in good shape, with quick reflexes, thanks to a regimen of physical training. He finds his people's vague system of supernatural causes and effects a disturbing "sick delusion" (*Elements of a Kill*, 151). He has studied forensics enough to do his job well for the North Slope Borough of the Barrow Police Department but usually has self-evident cases such as firearms accidents or drunks or hunters freezing to death.

Despite few murders in Barrow, Attla has adequate experience to "read" a crime scene, ask pertinent questions, and conduct an investigation effectively. Yet, deep down, he knows that he has returned to Barrow because, despite his sophistication, technological expertise, and impatience with "backward," "injurious" Inupiat ways, he is still an Inupiat, tied to home and tribe in inexplicable ways. Lane contrasts Attla's arctic survival skills with the naivete and inexperience of Deputy Billy Bob Cleaver, a newcomer ignorant of proper attire to survive local conditions, and he provides situations outside of Barrow (usually while Attla is on vacation) that call on Attla's detective skills and deductive reasoning.

While a vacationing Attla visits his grandfather, a frozen body discovered in an oil pipe requires Attla's official presence. His grandfather senses a powerful evil, chants a blessing to give Attla strength and protection, and sends him off with a pithy warning to seek the light and avoid the dark, especially since adverse weather conditions, according to Inupiat elders, beckon hostile spirits to visit death and sickness on the living. Attla is patient and respectful but very much a non-believer: "Spirits, ghosts, shamans. It was all very spooky, especially at this hour with the wind howling outside, but he was no longer a kid and he had work to do" (*Elements of a Kill*, 16). Later his grandfather radios warnings from the local shaman about angry spirits, multiple killings, and personal danger for Attla, just as Attla receives news locally of a second murder. Attla's hurried visit to his grandfather results in an Inupiat funeral dirge, chants about an evil hunter, warnings about the dangers of dark *anjatkuts* (evil shamans) and of an influential Inupiat, and much more that leaves Attla convinced that the old shaman is actually a sham (the shaman gives him a crucifix as a protective amulet!). Nonetheless, as the story line progresses, Attla's dream of animal spirit protectors corresponds to his sidekick's vision of where to find Attla's half-frozen body, events in the case make an odd sense of the shaman's cryptic comments, and the crucifix provides unexpected protection as a weapon.

Gunshot, not hypothermia, killed the first unidentified man in *Elements of a Kill*. Furthermore, attempts to sever the head with a curved blade and missing muscle/cartilage from the underside of the tongue (sliced out with a curved blade) suggest to Attla mimicry of the traditional Inupiat way of killing and displaying a bear so its spirit will be reincarnated instead of haunting the hunter. Everyone else assumes that the ritual slashes confirm an Eskimo roustabout as killer, but Attla is unconvinced. Instead he seeks motive and opportunity and asks questions that lead to cocaine abuse, drug smuggling, and other criminal activities that may or may not be related to the murder. He asks who the victim was and why his body had been desecrated and hidden. A series of near-fatal "accidents" captures the vulnerability of human beings in the face of an Alaskan storm or simply Alaskan winter weather and suggests that Attla is close to the killer. A malfunctioning battery is not simply an inconvenience; it is a matter of life or death. When his snowmobile breaks down, Attla feels the cold "stalking him, watching him, bending low, draping itself over him like a garment," making his fingertips tingle and his nose and toes go numb, slowly turning him into "an ice sculpture" or what local jokesters call "a popcycle" or "an Eskimo pie" (90). Doggedly persisting in his investigation, despite several near-death experiences, he eventually connects the shaman's words to the players involved and their secret roles. The denouement provides a somewhat rational explanation for the murders and places them within an understandable attempt to punish those who had violated Inupiat trespass taboos, though it also seems to confirm the shaman's more metaphorical attribution of responsibility.

In *Season of Death*, Attla takes fellow officer Billie Bob Cleaver to see the passing of the caribou herds on their annual migration, but the occasion turns into a shakedown kayak trip to awaken his Inupiat police buddy Lewis to what could go wrong were he to set up adventure trips for outsiders as he hopes to do; on this trip the inexperienced Cleaver, the guinea pig outsider, barely survives Lewis' erroneous assumptions about his knowledge and capabilities. The trip starts badly when fly fishing leads to Attla's discovery of a human skull and his more appalling discovery that Lewis has failed to bring along any means of contacting the outside world. Everything that could go wrong on the trip does. The travelers lose vital survival supplies to icy waters when their kayaks roll over, and they nearly drown because Cleaver's frantic struggles keep Attla from righting their craft immediately. They encounter life-threatening rapids that leave Lewis, who forgot to check with park reports on river conditions, well battered, a shoulder dislocated. Attla and Cleaver portage the rough section, but doing so brings even greater danger—a marijuana/hashish farmer with sophisticated greenhouses hidden in the forest and the will to kill all intruders. Lane captures the effects that Alaskan nature has on human attitudes in Attla's nightmares:

[H]e found himself staring . . . directly into the bulging eyes of a caribou bull. Thick muzzle to the ground, antlers just a foot away, it continued nibbling at the tundra. The barrel-chested animal studied him, seemingly unafraid, for a full minute before backing away . . . and moseying out of sight. As he departed, others came into view: scraggly white-and-brown coats milling about in a low dense mist. . . . hundreds, thousands, tens of thousands of animals. A living sea drifting slowly south. Heads bobbed and nodded at the ground, antlers jerking skyward, then disappearing into the layers of clinging fog. . . .

The sense of loneliness was overwhelming. . . . Framed by this freak phenomenon of nature, he had the impression that his life was without purpose: small, insignificant, impermanent, that it would have no lasting effect whatsoever on the world, . . . would in no way impact the march of history. (143–44)

Event after event in the bush confirms this sense of human impermanence and inadequacy in the face of inexorable nature. Human crime and bad behavior take on different dimensions in this kind of territory.

When Attla and his fellow officers finally reach an archaeological dig where they can get help, they discover that the skull they have found may well be that of a missing archaeologist and that all is not well in the camp. There are armed Asian guards, conflicts with a nearby mining operation, and nasty secrets. Attla's attempts to get outside investigative help take him to Kanayut, the northernmost Alaskan Athabascan settlement just in time for the Festival of the Nomads and a potlatch, to celebrate the coming of the caribou. The participants, adorned in caribou-hide clothing with sparkling beadwork, their faces painted bright red, insist that Attla participate or else he will ruin the spirit of the dance and anger the village leaders, one of whom brandishes a spear. Threats turn into good-humored fun-poking that ends with much laughter, at Attla's expense.

At the festival, a local youthful visionary confirms the identity of the skull, warns about a crazed murderer, talks about the daughter Attla does not even know has been conceived yet, and calls Attla a Lightwalker who has the power to outwit and overcome Nahani, a dark figure of evil. She later explains that Attla appears surrounded by light in her visions. As in Lane's other books, despite Attla's cynicism about journeys to the spirit world, his detective work eventually confirms the mystical experiences he undergoes. In this case, the Athabascan girl insists that a Lightwalker cannot succeed without a seer as a guide; besides, she can show him where the skull's body lies, and she does. Her inner voice tells her how to disarm plastique explosive on board the dead man's plane, and Attla's dreams of traditional stories such as those about Raven stealing the light suggest that he and this Trickster god share qualities: "You an' Raven, a-like," says his dream uncle (*Season of Death*, 296). Whereas the mysticism can perhaps be dismissed in Lane's first novel, in this second it has unquestionable validity that leaves even Attla without means of firm denial.

In the third book in the series, *A Shroud of Midnight Sun*, Attla is again on vacation, this time at a resort outside of Anchorage. Attla hopes to spend quality time bicycling Mt. Alyeska while his wife attends a conference. Instead, a spill into a berry thicket lands him near a body and a report to the authorities brings in the FBI. The novel also introduces a bumbling local Korean-Yup'ik lawman, Sheriff Glen Redfern, who doubles as a church pastor. Redfern, with only two weeks of law enforcement training at a special school in Anchorage, really needs Attla's expertise to help him unravel what proves to be an arsenic murder. Lane mixes Japanese industrial espionage, mobsters, false identifications, and adultery into the investigative brew, playing these recognizable murder mystery situations off against the odd precognitive ramblings of Attla's daughter Keera, childish jabber which parallels the murder and subsequent events: Raven pursuing a man to his death from a ski lift. Keera recognizes the dead man's car and later uses a story knife to recount events for Redfern's daughter, who is her age. The Redferns think she has the prophetic gift that the *angulcaq*, the old shamans, called "seeing into the night," but Attla rejects as nonsensical both their explanation and the view that a mythical bird committed a crime (59–60). For him, an investigation must be conducted strictly by the book, with "meticulous, painstaking inquiries, interviews, research, forms, procedures . . . not wild guessing games" (62); the Redferns' casual acceptance of otherworldly powers interfering with daily life deeply disturbs his rational worldview. Cut brake hoses, interdepartmental rivalries, a valuable stolen computer chip, and the telling signs of lying witnesses are more his cup of tea. Nevertheless, in his dreams, characters from Inupiat mythology bring clues that fit his case and shift-shape to suggest realities hidden behind everyday masks. Though he dismisses these dreams as the subconscious working overtime to make sense of details he has not yet consciously registered, their warnings come true as the loose ends of his case come together and reveal motive, means, and opportunity.

Throughout this series, Lane's method is to have Attla debunk native spiritualism yet be surrounded by believers whose visions and warnings dovetail with his police work. The effect is often comic, with Attla struggling for insights and connections that his grandfather or children intuit. In effect, Lane uses a rationalist hero to, oddly enough, give credence to the irrational or extra-rational. A slightly comic edge adds to the overall debunking, as in the following exchange between Attla and his police captain:

"They [the FBI] act like we're a bunch of aborigines."

"We are aborigines," Ray said, "Technically speaking." (138)

But the two indigenous police professionals have the sophistication to use Inupiat as a code for communications that the FBI cannot decipher, to deduce the motivations that produced murder, and to place responsibility where the FBI cannot. In an Author's Note to *Season of Death*, Lane says he hopes that his mystery series will "foster a sense of respect for the Native people of Alaska and the fascinating, beautiful, sometimes unforgiving land they inhabit."

SHERLOCK

Marcia Simpson and Dana Stabenow both choose native heroines who cannot speak their tribe's language and have been, to a greater or lesser degree, separated from the native groups of their ancestry. Simpson's heroine is self-described as "half Indian, with an all-white mind," who knows nothing about Native American ways except the stories everyone knows: "My [white] dad didn't want my mother to 'turn me Native' " (165). Stabenow's heroine has closer ties to family, but her parents feared she would be handicapped by Aleut in an English-speaking world, so growling curses are all she knows, and though her grandmother has tried to bind her to tradition, she has sought her separate way. Yet, she always carries an ivory Yup'ik-carved otter, "part talisman, part amulet, and part good luck charm," a link to her ancestors since Aleut souls might be reborn in otters (*Hunter's Moon*, 92–93). Scott Young's Inuk detective likewise has followed his ambition, in his case, away from the small, isolated villages where he grew up to Ottawa and the seats of political power (he represents his government in negotiations with the Russians where an understanding of Siberian Eskimos is required); he has married a beautiful blonde who has contempt for his family and tribal ways; yet when the need arises, he returns to his roots to investigate in ways closed to outsiders.

Marcia Simpson's Lisa Romero and Paul Howard: Tough but Caring

Marcia Simpson's heroine, Lisa Romero, is a totally assimilated half Lummi who has come to Alaska to settle down, far from the tragic memories of her Mexican-American husband, a police officer shot in the line of duty. Her father was an attorney, and through father and husband, she has acquired the habits of observation and reasoning that make her, when necessity compels, an effective amateur detective. Her husband taught her keen marksmanship, and, on her own, she has mastered the skills necessary to keep her small craft, *The Salmon Eye*, an old wooden halibut schooner, afloat and operative; she has learned through trial and error that Alaska's "rock-strewn waters" are "no place to make a mistake" (*Crow in Stolen Colors*, 8). Romero has settled into the rustic town of Wrangell as the proprietor of a freight service and traveling boat-bookmobile, carrying library books (and chickens or whatever else needs transporting) to isolated islanders and losing herself in this hauntingly beautiful but also treacherous landscape. However, her loss has made her a reticent loner, emotionally frozen, still grieving, and though she has a new lover, she remains oddly disengaged in the relationship. A friend lists what he considers her stupid behavior: going to the rescue of capsized kayakers during a northeaster, hiking a notorious wilderness area above McHenry without a bear gun, and pushing her vessel through rough seas on fumes when she lacks the fuel needed for the trip (69).

In *Crow in Stolen Colors*, her half-lab Sam directs her attention to an oddity on the rocks, a seven-year-old boy, alone, half-frozen, amid a fast-rising tide. His undaunted courage, reticence, and unwillingness to burden his grandmother with the dangers which have brought him so close to death win her heart. The discovery of a murdered adult in a nearby inlet lends credence to his account, and the rest of the novel describes her efforts to protect young James Kitai from thieves and murderers who want the tribal secrets he carries as nephew and heir of his village's chief (now dead), particularly the location of petroglyphs on the "listening" stone and the ancient treasures reportedly buried beneath it.

Romero's motherly concern is played off against the fatherly obsessions of Tlingit police officer, Lieutenant Paul Howard, whom Romero sees as a dark, brooding spirit, "like Hi-ya-shon-a-gu on the Raven totem, charged with holding up the whole world" (166). Howard, who deals with everything from bears wandering into town and fish-and-game violations to disorderly drunks and stolen totems, has lost his son in a court battle with his white ex-wife, so he crusades to keep Tlingit youngsters out of the hands of outsiders. His efforts to separate young James from Romero plunge him into the conspiracy that swirls around her and almost costs him his life from a hurtling boulder. However, their antagonism hides a deep attraction that, with time, could help them heal their injured souls.

In the meantime, however, Romero and young James keep on the move to throw off their pursuers and stay out of the range of the bullets that fly their way and the arranged accidents that plague them (a hole in a vital hose, a cut anchor line). When James goes missing, Romero, with brambles tearing at her jeans and bog mud pulling at her feet, hurtles through dense moss seeking some trace of him. Simpson brings to life everyday fears intensified by the nature of the region—the bear who wanders in and becomes intoxicated from the whiskey he consumes, the shock of a black shape suddenly hurtling past in the twilight gloom, so close that Romero ducks and flings up her arms protectively, only to recognize the hoarse screech of a heron.

The plot hinges on a failing local economy and on the negative effects of urban attractions that lure away the native villages' most ambitious young people, destroy their tribal connections, turn them into drunks and thieves, and lead them to betray the secrets of their heritage to greedy outsiders. James' Uncle Crow, the town drunk, is such a man; he has told village secrets that have incited theft but, at the novel's close, guilt and family responsibility make him save James' life, keep his people's secrets, and rescue stolen artifacts: "Like Katlian, the Tlingit warrior, swarming over the rail of the Russian warship two centuries ago, defending his nation with a hammer in his hand. Except Crow had no hammer. No weapon at all, except his pride. That he wore well" (262). Simpson lovingly describes the quality and tribal-religious value of such stolen items as spruce baskets, bentwood boxes, amulets, Chilkat blankets, shaman masks, crest headdresses, box drums, carved salmon trap stakes, sea wolf hooks, nose rings, pendants, family totem poles, shame totems, and petroglyphs.

Dana Stabenow's Kate Shugak: Alaskan Confidence and Toughness

Like Romero, Dana Stabenow's part-Russian, mainly Aleut detective Kate Shugak is clearly in the Holmes tradition of ratiocination—observing the crime scene and suspects, interviewing witnesses, and gathering data— but is also very much in the hard-boiled American tradition of the detective as society's avenger. Despite her distinctive Aleut physical features—bronze skin, high, flat cheekbones, and straight black hair—she does not have visions or call on spirit helpers, or even have a sidekick who does. Instead, she is a hardy, self-confident, hard-boiled professional, with all the no-nonsense hunter-gatherer survival skills her people have developed over the ages for coping with arctic life. As the raised knife scar that crosses her throat suggests, she is a survivor who can endure tough times, hard luck, and vicious opponents.

Shugak is at home with the frontier roughness of the state, has grown up hunting, fishing, and fighting, knows about the local feuds, the eccentrics, the drunks, and womanizers, has in her memory the words to every high sea chantey ever written down, drives an Arctic Cat top-of-the-line snowmobile, and can predict the behavior of bears awakening from hibernation and moose or elk in rut. She knows how to make tea from fireweed and wormwood, to use sourdock paste to relieve itching, or to use horsetail as a diuretic or an abortifacient (*Hunter's Moon*, 159). She is, as her lover and friend Jack Morgan proclaims, a "Renaissance woman" who can do anything: be a deckhand in the summer, guide climbers up challenging peaks in the spring, "skin a Cat[erpillar machine], mine for gold, butcher a moose, fix an engine, . . . make jam, . . . guide a big-game hunt," or "get anyone to talk" (2, 110). Her close ties to the land—she feels at one with "the graceful arcs of tree limbs bowed beneath glittering frost, the ponderous dignity of a cow moose in snow up to her shoulders, munching on an alder" (*A Cold Day for Murder*, 170)—provide her with an enduring inner strength.

Moreover, she is not afraid to work undercover doing back-breaking physical labor to put suspects at ease. Unlike the urban detectives for whom going undercover means simply a change of fashion, mannerisms, or speech, going undercover for Shugak means hard labor as a deckhand on a salmon fishing vessel in *Killing Grounds*, as a roustabout doing wellhead cleanup and a host of other unpleasant tasks on a rig above the Arctic Circle in *A Cold-blooded Business*, and as a crewman sledgehammering ice off the deck and wrestling gigantic crab pots (two feet wider and taller than she is) in stormy sea conditions in *Dead in the Water*. She uncomplainingly tackles tasks that many men would find daunting. When furthering her investigation necessitates taking chances, she does so without fearing the consequences, for example, going overboard into icy waters in freezing rain to spy on drug smugglers onshore, then, wet and cold and in danger of hypothermia, struggling back to her ship to avoid detection in *Dead in the Water*. She has been to the edge so often that her senses are finely tuned to just how far she can push herself, but then somehow she always finds the reserve strength to go just a little farther, as in *A Cold Day for Murder*. Therein, her investigation takes her down a cargo platform inside an old mine shaft, a threatening enough proposition given the darkness, the dankness, and the prospect of collapsing tunnels. When the rotten platform gives way, she must pull herself back up the shaft inch by inch in the dark, hand over hand, enduring strained muscles and rope burns to survive. In *Midnight Come Again*, she works eighteen-hour shifts with an air shipping company, hauling huge containers on and off various vehicles to bury her grief for the murdered Jack Morgan. Hard-nosed, like "a double-bladed axe," with a growl "like a dull saw ripping through old cement" and movements like a cat (*A Cold Day for Murder*, 6, 9), she is wild and aggressive like Mutt, her powerful, intelligent male malamute-wolf hybrid, with something barely leashed shining in her eyes. When that inner demon is released, everyone around her should beware; an airplane crashed in her living room, a gunfight at her favorite bar, a bear attack, a body exposed by melting snow, and a womanizer who covers treachery with a smile and gets away with it all send Shugak over the edge in *Breakup*, and she ends up driving a bulldozer into and over the homes of the local feuders whose bullets have interrupted her peace. In *Hunter's Moon*, German arrogance and disdain for life (both human and animal) drive her to a murderous fury, and she uses all of her native and wildlife lore to turn grizzly bears, bogs, and even trees into dangerous allies.

However, her activities are cerebral as well as physical, as her penchant for opera, philosophy, and good books suggests. In *Breakup*, she reads the signs in the spring mud and applies her knowledge of human and bear psychology to recognize that what seems like a terrible accident is really murder by bear—a clever husband finding a seemingly foolproof way to dispose of his wife. In *A Fatal Thaw*, when a local confesses to killing eight neighbors, yet the spring thaw defrosts nine bodies, she asks why and deduces the answer: she lists suspects, examines alibis, and then, like Poirot, puts her "little grey cells" to work. In *A Cold Day for Murder*, her quiet moments of analytical thinking enable her to pull all of the pieces of the puzzle together, to decide who is dead and where the bodies are and why. In *Midnight Come Again*, despite FBI suspicions of her involvement in murder, drug smuggling, money laundering, and collusion with Russian criminals, she identifies the American villains long before the FBI does, solves a friend's murder, and helps thwart the Russian villains too.

Kate Shugak reflects the virtues of the Aleut people, though she has, to some degree, separated herself from them, reminding her grandmother that their blood is also that of Russian Cossacks, Jewish cobblers, and Norwegian fishermen, not just Aleut nomads. In the early books she is still rebelling against this stubborn, hard-headed, highly political grandmother, Ekaterina Moonin Shugak, whose position of power among her people makes her a leader in the movement to reject assimilation and modernization (prefab housing and government funding but not the electricity and running water Prudhoe Bay oil money brings). Ekaterina's goal is to preserve the communal ties of the past, to protect the young people from the materialism that assaults them on every side and tempts them into Alaska's urban areas, and to combat the waste of animal and human life she sees corrupting her world. Kate argues that Ekaterina cannot turn the village into a prison compound to keep young people at home and will have to drag herself into the twentieth century:

You want to keep the family at home, . . . the tribe together and . . . the old values what they were. . . . It's not going to happen. We have too much now, too many snow machines, too many prefabs, too many satellite dishes bringing in too many television channels, showing the kids what they don't have. There's no going back. We've got to go forward, bringing what we can of the past with us, yes, but we've got to go forward. It's the only way we're going to survive. (*A Cold Day for Murder*, 47)

Yet, every argument makes Kate think "fifty generations of Aleuts" are lined up supporting her grandmother's view (195). To escape Ekaterina's reach, Kate Shugak resides in Anchorage, spending five years working sex crimes as the acknowledged star of the district attorney's investigative staff, with the highest conviction rate in state history for her position.

However, when the heartbreaking experiences of dealing daily with abused, battered women and children, with no end to the pain, over-whelmed her, she returned to familiar family territory around Niniltna (population 800) in northern Alaska, got a cabin on national park land, and established herself as a private investigator. As the series begins, the FBI, so impressed by her record that it tried on several occasions to recruit her, seeks her help in bush investigations. Mainly missing persons, murder, smuggling, and theft, her cases usually necessitate cooperating with or working for state troopers or rangers such as Jack Morgan, her occasional lover and almost husband.

As the series progresses, she also comes to understand her grandmother's position, though it disturbs her to admit it. The Aleut are assaulted on every side by outsiders, mainly con artists and power grabbers manipulat-ing locals in order to take over fishing, mineral, and oil rights and monop-olies of art and artifacts. When a teenage relative talks about doing exactly what Kate did—escaping the boredom of village life by moving to fast-paced Anchorage—Kate argues the dangers and difficulties of big-city life. When tribal representatives to the Alaska Federation of Natives Convention die under mysterious circumstances, in *Blood Will Tell*, Kate's main client becomes her grandmother, who needs protection from those who would eliminate her crucial vote on contested lands; this "protection" means ex-posing those who interfere in tribal politics for personal profit. Throughout her lifetime, Ekaterina worked to persuade Kate to take over the clan's governing powers, and to Kate's personal amazement, she finds herself do-ing exactly that just before Ekaterina dies at the end of *Blood Will Tell*: Kate argues forcefully for her grandmother's stand at the Federation of Natives Convention, and in doing so becomes inextricably committed to protecting the Aleut and preserving Aleut culture as best she can. When she commits to helping an orphaned child get an education and realize her dream to be a bush pilot, she realizes that she has become the mentor that her grandmother was for her and that she can use her own understanding of why she rebelled to help this young girl cope with the future.

Thus, Shugak comes full circle from the rebellious, assimilated youth to the more experienced, knowledgeable adult who recognizes the truth of her grandmother's warnings: assimilation comes with a price, and the Aleut must resist total assimilation or risk annihilation as a people. With the death of the tribal matriarch, Shugak inherits the traditional role and bears the burden of Aleut need in the face of alcoholism, family violence, a sub-sistence economy, the temptations of materialistic goods, and the persuasive rhetoric of big business and advertising. In *Killing Grounds*, Shugak's case of a drowned fisherman, who has also been beaten, stabbed, strangled, and mutilated, intersects with a dispute over fishing rights. Only late in the game does she discover that her Aunt Edna's statement, "As long as the water runs and the grass is green, we been here" (76), really means not just that her four elderly aunties are discontented with federal treaties infringing on fishing rights but that they are, to some degree, personally involved in the murder and lying to her about their role in it. Ironically, she has been gradually forced into the role of tribal protector, even though it sometimes goes against her own good sense. In *Play with Fire*, she stands up for potlatches, totems, and beaded shirts against the strictures of obsessed religious fundamentalist missionaries. At the end of *Breakup*, with all of its spring disasters and its technical, social, and familial breakdowns, she worries about being trapped in a tribal role of authority and responsibility:

[T]here was the acute personal frustration of being thrust into a position of responsibility for the tribe, of shouldering duties and assuming obligations she had never sought and had certainly never wanted. It wasn't just the tribe, either, it was the whole goddam Park, Native and white, cheechako and sourdough, ranger and miner and homesteader, fisher folk and fish hawk. Predicaments R Us, You Bring 'Em, We Fix 'Em. K. Shugak, Proprietor. Meetings Mediated, Marriages Counseled, Murders Solved. She didn't even have to advertise, they came, bringing their baggage with them, whether she wanted them to or not. . . .
   "Emaa," Kate said into the gathering night, "They lean on me. All of them, they lean on me: How do I stand against it? How did you [Ekaterina], all those years?" (*Breakup*, 240–41)

And the answer is the howl of a distant wolf and the drip of melting snow.

Scott Young's Matteesie Kitologitak

Scott Young's Inuk (Inuvialuit) Matteesie Kitologitak, a Royal Canadian Mounted Police (RCMP) inspector, is a rationalist who must deal regularly with Inuit spiritualism. Yet, he does not reject the old beliefs of his people. His ties of respect to his mother and to tribal elders remain intact, though he sees them through a perspective transformed by the inquiring skepticism of the Western investigative mind and the methodical application of the tools of his trade. A graduate of the RCMP's courses on forensics, he knows about rigor mortis time spans, weaponry, fingerprints, footprints, materials under the fingernails, telltale threads or hairs, and so on. Sometimes, however, when the hunt is on and he approaches a solution, he gets a special feeling "like a sudden shiver" along his spine that warns him of danger ahead (*The Shaman's Knife*, 88).
   Kitologitak has risen in the ranks the hard way and is one of the few Inuit officers in the Mounties. Early in his career, he was chosen to head a

new unit that specialized in native crime, and now he has a reputation for effectiveness throughout Canada. Most notably, he stopped a native protest that would have been launched during the Queen of England's tour of the provinces by signing the protest document himself as the senior native officer in charge of security. This politic act won him acclaim from both sides. Over the years, he has learned to deal effectively with being talked down to or with mocking attempts to "snow" him, and he appreciates fellow officers responding to him as a competent equal. He knows his territory, has lived with hunger, isolation, and exhaustion, and understands better than most native motivations for murder ("to effect a change of home address for some female who was alluring to both killer and killee," to provide the sick or the elderly who have decided to end the burden they place on others an easier death by bullet than starvation or freezing to death on the open tundra or ice) (*Murder in a Cold Climate*, 11). He has also experienced firsthand in his marriage to a white woman some of the disadvantages of white custom.

Occasionally fellow officers or politicians will joke about him being a shaman who reads mashed ice worms or a polar bear hambone like tea leaves (11), but he resents such attitudes. He is no shaman. He is hardworking, observant, and methodical. He has a record of successes, because he is a competent investigator. He examines the evidence, the crime scene, and the players, and he reasons from them what seems out of place. His work requires him to fly in and out of isolated areas and to explore the local terrain by dogsled or snowmobile, so he must be able to size up a situation quickly, identify whom he can trust and to what degree, and proceed from there.

In *Murder in a Cold Climate*, Kitologitak is onboard a flight to the scene of one investigation when a gunman suddenly enters the off-loading plane and kills the gravely ill leading spokesman for native rights in the north. Eventually, three seemingly separate cases—a missing aircraft, a drug smuggling ring, and the terrorist-style murder Kitologitak himself witnessed—come together as he unravels the cause-effect chain that links them. Native pilot Thomasee Nuniviak and later a former military pilot fly him over the search area and read the sign of animals and humans from the air. Since his experience has confirmed the ease with which aircraft of executive size or smaller can purposely disappear, he postulates that the missing plane has gone off the radar screen to pick up cargo or passengers unseen by prying officials. He also enlists two more assistants, a local teacher (an experienced dogsledder with team) and a competent trapper who lost his legs to frostbite but knows the region and the locals well. With this unlikely pair, he finds all he needs to recover the missing man and missing plane and to solve the murder case. In direct confrontations with suspects with weapons, he takes no chances. One villain suffers three shotgun hits from about 20 feet away, and though Kitologitak mildly regrets not being able to take his testimony, he notes: "Leaving him alive would almost certainly have left me dead, an option I always tried to avoid" (192).

In *The Shaman's Knife*, Kitologitak's investigation of a bloody and brutal double knifing in the tiny Arctic village of Sanirarsipaaq, northeast of Cambridge Bay on Victoria Island, necessitates the assistance of the village shaman, who practices the "old ways" to knowledge and who is privy to the secrets of many local families. Kitologitak feels personally involved when a young man and his grandmother are killed, because their killer has critically injured his 90-year-old mother (she had investigated the strange sounds next door). Despite anonymous notes implicating noted carver/shaman Jonassie Oquatoq, and naming the shaman's handcrafted knife as the murder weapon, Kitologitak and local corporal Alphonse Bouvier soon have an assortment of suspects, one with a history of violence and a local reputation for unpredictable, unpleasant behavior that frightens even his parents and sister. Kitologitak has never heard of a shamanistic-related murder; he respects the village shamans as "the chief instruments of the fairly complicated set of tribal beliefs and legends that all our people once lived by" before the Christian presence overwhelmed them, and asserts, "You can't wipe out ten or twenty or thirty centuries of beliefs, including shamanism, just by teaching a lot of people to sing 'The Old Rugged Cross' " (21). The shaman of this story has had disconcerting visions that he thinks will aid Kitologitak's search—as they do.

Oddly enough, despite its setting, this mystery fits the Agatha Christie English village mode, with whispered secrets, scandals, and rivalries, and with witnesses all lying for various reasons. The difference, of course, is that in an Inuk village, the cultural traditions for handling wayward youths, generational conflicts, and authority differ greatly from those in British cozy mysteries. Young provides intriguing local details, including an interesting byplay between twin brothers, a shaman artist and an Anglican priest. Again, the negative effects of drugs on native young people, conflicting attitudes toward sex and sexual relationships, and village secrets loom large. Kitologitak's visits to his mother's bedside occasion oral storytelling and reminiscences about the harsh but fulfilling life of the Inuk some 60 to 70 years earlier, stories of migrating with the seasons, hunting polar bears with knives and spears, harpooning whales, and following the caribou.

Kitologitak's girlfriend Maxine, who is part Scots, part Slavey Indian, plays a significant role in the two novels, for unlike Kitologitak's wife, she understands native ways and can make his mother feel comfortable; she uncomplainingly eats raw *muktuk*, the edible part of the beluga whale, the meaty section between the outer skin and the blubber, and companionably braids the old woman's hair. Her positive behind-the-scenes activities contrast with Kitologitak's wife's indifference to his tribal attachments, to his affection for his aged, tattooed mother (who in her youth had harpooned whale from her kayak) and with his commitment to justice for his people. Kitologitak cannot divorce his white wife for political and professional reasons and laments the odd difficulty of ending a union in white society, since as an Inuk he could simply walk out of her life.

Over the course of his investigation, Kitologitak provides telling facts about his territory. For example, outsiders think something hidden in the snow will disappear, but natives know that "discards don't go away in the Arctic" and that "odds and ends left by weary and starving men a century or two ago are useful now as firm evidence that [early explorers] Sir John Franklin, for instance, spent much of a winter in one place, or Samuel Hearne in another" (*Murder in a Cold Climate*, 107). He explains the Inuit system of picking their own surnames, a practice which baffles whites, since naming is based on individual choice, not patronymics or matronymics, so three siblings might have entirely different surnames. He also describes the negative effects of Christianity, reporting on the infamous Belcher murders of 1941, in which some new converts, convinced that they were Jesus and the Holy Spirit, led their followers to methodically shoot or beat to death anyone who clung to the old beliefs. More significantly, however, he contrasts Inuk justice with white justice, a contrast that Kitologitak must deal with daily. For example, he describes the tradition of the Inumerit, a committee of mature, respected community members, who would decide if someone had broken the rules or taboos of a settlement, would summon the offender, and would make very clear the consequences of not abiding by their counsel. Furthermore, by Inuk custom, the elders of a community judged offenders, and the most extreme punishment they could inflict on a wrongdoer was banishment from the community. In the past, such a banishment would have meant certain death from starvation or freezing; it also carried deep psychological weight among a people for whom belonging to the group was the most important thing in their lives besides survival. Today, says Kitologitak, Canadian law has incorporated some native customs, recognizing the cultural significance of a punishment such as banishing. Thus, the solution to *The Shaman's Knife* turns on the question of banishment and on a lawbreaker ignoring his sentence, depicting the survival of an ancient tradition in modern law enforcement.

CONCLUSION

The Alaskan and Northwestern Territories detective novels are bound to the land from which they spring. Their heroes are rough-edged, strong, and capable. They have to be. The land, the weather, and even the wildlife require it. Most Alaskan and Northwest Territories Native American detectives are rationalists; they have long winters to think through the ramifications of word and deed; they appreciate silences, and behavior that is out of sync with regular patterns looms large on their horizons. Most value permanence, the past perpetuated into the present and retrievable in the future. They are surrounded by fellow natives who see that permanence involving the spirits of the land, the animals, and the people, and while none of the Alaskan or Northwest Territories native detectives are true believers in any faith, new or ancient, they respect the old ways while they themselves represent the new.

9

The East Coast and Great Lakes Nations: Modern Reincarnations of Past Glory

I . . . believe, like my Micmac and Penobscot ancestors, that we live more than the sum of the present moments in this visible world; we exist within layers of reincarnated, reinvented memories that shape-change and prod us across invisible boundaries into the many worlds of the mind. Until we gather unto us the Power to navigate there with confidence, we are lost and alone, savages in a dark forest.
—Mark Sullivan, *The Purification Ceremony*, 292

When the "present moments" of the above quote take place in highly ur-banized areas, such as in the Great Lakes and East Coast regions, then the native investigators must exist as "reinvented memories" of a lost past, or as displaced persons, far from their roots, or as assimilated modern rein-carnations, locked into the modern world but with invisible ties to the past. The following list of Native American detectives associated with this region confirms these possibilities:

Author	Detective	Tribal Affiliation
Michael Delving	Bob Eddison (Ahuludegi)	Dislocated Cherokee from Connecticut
Kathleen and Michael Gear	Old Panther	Algonquin
Abigail Padgett	Eva Blindhawk Broussard (assists)	Iroquois
Thomas Perry	Jane Whitefield	Seneca
Mark Sullivan	Diana (Little Crow) Jackman	Micmac/Penobscot
	The ghost of Sarah Many Horses (assists)	Dislocated Sioux from Vermont
Margaret Truman	Christine Saksis	Half-Passamaquoddy
C. Q. Yarbro	Charlie Spotted Moon	Ojibway

GEOGRAPHICAL DETERMINERS

The Eastern cultural region extends from the Atlantic Ocean to the far side of the Great Lakes and south from the dense forests of western Ontario to the North Carolina-Virginia coast. It is a highly diverse region of rivers and lakes, mountains and foothills, and tidewaters and coastal plains. In *People of the Mist*, Kathleen and Michael Gear describe the prehistoric Chesapeake Bay area in particular as a natural paradise:

The rich estuary's environment and temperate climate provided everything . . . needed for survival. Yearly migrations of waterfowl and anadromous fish provided a wealth of seasonal food resources. The forest provided nut harvests, and a habitat for turkey, deer, bear, raccoons, and other animals. From the marshes, the people collected cordgrass, wild rice, muskrats, arrow arum root for tuckahoe bread, and other foods. On shallow mudflats, they caught crabs, dug clams, and harvested oysters. Deposits of silty loam soil grew corn, beans, squash, tobacco, and sunflowers, among other agricultural staples. In such a land of plenty, only . . . applied English obstinacy and ethnocentrism could have led to starvation in the Jamestown colony in 1608. (i)

The Gears go on to remark on the wealth of resources and the natural beauty of the modern Chesapeake area, with its oysters, crabs, successful agriculture, and migratory waterfowl.

Because the Northeast coast of North America was one of the earliest settled areas of the nation, the tribes from that region, by and large, either were decimated by war, disease, removal, or migration or were assimilated into mainstream culture. The result is that only in the relatively remote Great Lakes region is there still a viable enough native culture to attract mainstream writers seeking to popularize an "authentic" native detective voice.

FICTIONAL EMPHASES NECESSITATED BY SETTING

The heavy population centers of the East Coast region make it very difficult to construct credible stories of rural tribal life. Consequently, to have convincing Native American detectives, writers must turn back in time, as do Kathleen O'Neil Gear and Michael Gear in *People of the Mist*, a murder mystery set in the Chesapeake Bay region 600 years ago (the Late Woodland II period, around 1300 A.D.). Or they must place modern East Coast natives in settings comparable to those of their ancestors, as does Mark Sullivan in *The Purification Ceremony*. Sullivan moves his Micmac/Penobscot heroine from her present home in Boston and from her childhood home in Maine to an isolated area of British Columbia, where the terrain, forests, and winter experience parallel those of her East Coast ancestors, and yet the isolation is more credible than it would be in modern Maine or Massachusetts. C. Q. Yarbro moves her Ojibway detective, Charlie Spotted Moon, to San Francisco, though this move fails to reinforce Spotted Moon's ties to the land.

Another option, one most common in this region, is to eliminate the native detective and instead tie the crime to native lore, history, mystical powers, New Agers, or casinos. For example, Judith Kelman opts for historical connections in *Where Shadows Fall*—a "Shmohawk" curse associated with a desecrated Indian burial ground to provide misdirection for a modern college murder. Likewise, the native American elements in Stefanie Matteson's *Murder on High*—murder by long bow, historical background on the indigenous ancestors of the Penobscots, conflicts over modern "native" casinos and New Age retreats, and a jokester's impersonation of an eagle-masked native deity with moose antlers—simply provide misdirection. Abigail Padgett, in turn, has her Southern Californian Anglo detective, child abuse investigator Bo Bradley, draw on the spiritual vision of her Iroquois friend and occasional psychiatrist, Eva Blindhawk Broussard. Broussard illustrates native influence reaching across regions: Broussard helps Bradley better deal with the Native American victims she assists, as in *Strawgirl*, where the rapist-killer of a three-year-old threatens another child but is thwarted in part by Iroquois mysticism. Steve Hamilton's *Winter of the Wolf Moon*, set mainly on the Ojibway Reservation in Michigan's Upper Peninsula and featuring retired Detroit police officer Alex McKnight, depicts the drug pushers who prey on the native community, selling "wild cat," a methamphetamine derivative, and the natives who pay with their lives for the measures they take to escape the reservation.

Still another choice is to focus on a fully assimilated central character of mixed blood, whose native identity expresses itself only in a general concern for all fellow natives. This is what Margaret Truman does in *Murder at the FBI*. Her heroine, Special Agent Christine Saksis, whose father was a full-blooded Passamaquoddy, is one of the 40-some agents of Native American descent in the FBI, and one of half a dozen agents assigned to investigate crimes on federal Indian reservations. From her father she has inherited blue-black hair, prominent cheekbones, and a copper hue, but she knows only a few words of Passamaquoddy and, despite derogatory comments about her being a "squaw" or an "Indian goddess," she is not Passamaquoddy in her point of view, culture, religion, or anything else. Her previous assignments have brought her into contact with representatives of other tribes (Apache, Zuñi, and Sioux in particular) who are standing up for their people in confrontations with the federal government, but her present assignment to the murder of an FBI agent at the Bureau's firing range is, in the main, unconnected to any "native" story. However, Truman uses Saksis' friendship with an Apache journalist (Bill Tse-ay) to connect a Washington, D.C., murder to the Arizona murder of a reservation Zuñi teenager and to prompt limited dialogue about ethnic tokenism in the FBI (Saksis' total assimilation into mainstream culture makes her the perfect token American Indian, from the Bureau's view) and about "the worsening plight of the American Indian under the Reagan administration" (121). Except in these ways, ethnicity is irrelevant to the mystery and to the means of detection: the collection and evaluation of evidence and testimony and then reevaluation from new perspectives or with new information.

The final alternative is to choose the Great Lakes area, where there is still a living native culture that moves between the United States and Canada, one that must retain tribal identity, deal with hard questions of assimilation, and make an ancient heritage viable in the modern world. This is the option Thomas Perry chooses for his Jane Whitefield mysteries. Perry creates a modern woman with a tribal life who has found a traditional role to enact through combining ancient ways and modern technology.

RANGE OF INDIGENOUS PEOPLES

This is the region of the Iroquois Confederacy (made up of the Iroquois, Mohawk, Oneida, Onondaga, Cayuga, Seneca, and later Tuscarora tribes), the Micmac from the Canadian coast, the Hurons from the Quebec region, the Mohicans (or Mahicans) of northern Vermont, the Pequot of Connecticut, the Winnebago and other Siouan speakers of the Michigan area, and the Powhatan Confederacy of Virginia. The Algonquian tribes (the Ojibway, Ottawa, Sauk and Fox, Miami, and Shawnee) ranged the Great Lakes area.

SHAMANISTIC SHERLOCKS

As indicated above, the Northeast region has been so heavily populated, industrialized, and urbanized that the landscape gives far less sense of its pristine past than does the geography of the other North American regions. Perhaps as a result, the Native American detectives from this region who practice the spiritual or the occult have limited credibility, since the setting undercuts a vision of humans linked spiritually to unspoiled nature. A historical perspective or a rural setting in the region adds credibility, where an urban setting does not.

Kathleen and Michael Gear's Old Panther

Prize-winning archaeologists with a dozen or so volumes in their First North American Series, Kathleen O'Neal Gear and her husband Michael Gear, like Ellis Peters, Peter Lovesey, Elizabeth Peter, and Anne Perry, write historical mysteries. They set their story of murder and intrigue, *People of the Mist*, amid the political and tribal complexities of pre-European Algonquian and Susquehannock peoples. An important young woman from the Flat Pearl village, Red Knot, the granddaughter of Hunting Hawk, Chief of the Greenstone clan, has been betrothed to Copper Thunder, the Great Tayac of the Pipestone Clan, whose tribe controls the inland trade routes. However, Red Knot is murdered with a war club on her wedding day, and consequently, a relationship intended to seal a tribal alliance now threatens to produce war, especially when warriors from the Water Snake tribe arrive near the time of the murder. A rival in love, Sun Conch, is high on the list of suspects, as is the man she loves, High Fox, who had hoped to run away with Red Knot before her arranged marriage. An elderly recluse, Old Panther (formerly known as Raven) investigates this potentially explosive situation. Once an insider high in the tribal hierarchy, he is now an outsider, a hermit who lives on an island in the middle of the bay and who uses people's fears of his witch powers to foster his reputation and protect his privacy. This feared but respected elder is the equivalent of the modern detective and, in the main, relies on reason and knowledge of human behavior to investigate.

However, because of the superstitious nature of the people with whom he deals, he also employs what others take for witchcraft in order to accomplish his ends. Unlike Copper Thunder, who carries a protective amulet engraved with "a creature part bird, part man, and part snake" that rumor says makes him invincible (53), Old Panther attributes his power to a concept of balance summed up in two matched figures: Ohona (a man-sized statue of wood, clay, and hide, painted in white clay, with faded red sunbursts on its cheeks, a thick black band around its chest, wavering lines down the arms, blue legs crisscrossed by irregular lines, bearhide hair, oyster-shell eyes, white dots, and a sad expression) and his opposite, Okeus (black with a white chest band, black dots, and a gleeful expression). These figures represent a philosophical concept similar to the Asian idea of yin and yang, with Okeus associated with chaos and Ohona with the order that comes through compromise. Remembering when the seemingly fierce

Great Tuyac was a fearful youth named Grass Mat, Panther brings him back down to size. He also takes the role of teacher-trainer to help Sun Conch better understand her world and to transform her from a fearful adherent of her clan to an independent warrior woman who sees the world with new cynical realism. His advice is to take life in fleeting instants, "unconnected to anything else, with no promise of another instant to come" (242).

As in any modern mystery, motive, means, and opportunity are central to Old Panther's investigation. The evidence forces the conclusion that motive alone cannot determine guilt, because so many people had good reasons to wish for Red Knot's death; it also suggests that the killer was someone the victim both knew and trusted. Furthermore, the suspicious behavior of the obviously innocent, who are not forthcoming about their movements, suggests multiple explanations of events. Also, some tribe members have tampered with evidence to implicate others for spite and for revenge for past grievances. This misdirection keeps the final results of Panther's investigation a surprise until the very end. Despite anachronistic diction (characters talk about assumptions!!!) and the awkwardness of individuals explaining tribal customs to fellow tribe members (e.g., how their own matrilineal system works), the details about daily life are based on archaeological and anthropological evidence and informed scholarly speculation. Dreams and interludes from a storyteller fearful of shadows suggest the intrusion of a spirit world, one Old Panther uses to practical advantage: to find a murderer in order to save a number of interlocked clans and villages from a destructive war.

C. Q. Yarbro's Charlie Spotted Moon

C. Q. Yarbro's Charlie Spotted Moon suggests a lawyer-sleuth in the American tradition first popularized by Erie Stanley Gardner's Perry Mason and later developed by Scott Turow, Steve Martini, and John Grisham—but with a twist. Moon does indeed check out witnesses and clues, develop theories of a crime, and delve into events to seek confirmation. However, his main methods are spiritual and mystical, not ratiocinative, for his Ojibway heritage, not his legal training, ultimately guides his path. Consequently, what initially seems a legal procedure series turns out to be otherworldly.

Though now a Californian, Moon looks to the Iron River Reservation, where his blind grandfather lives, deep in the wilderness of Saskatchewan, Canada, for his tribal roots; in fact, however, the Ojibway moved over 1,000 miles northwest of their original territory in the colonial east over a 100-year period. Moon is theoretically a Sherlock, a defense attorney caught up in urban crime—at an opera house, for example—and age-old motives (jealousy, greed, rivalry) with a rainbow coalition cast of suspects.

Yet Yarbro exploits the shamanistic possibilities by endowing her hero with inexplicable power to intuit behavior in ways impossible for his colleagues. Hillerman's Leaphorn rejects coincidence for sound rational reasons; Moon does not believe in coincidence either, but because of his mystical spiritualism, where others have hunches, he has native power. "In that place within him that was wholly Ojibway, he knew that Cadao [a private investigator] was in trouble," writes Yarbro, and in the very next scene, Cadao is found brutally murdered and mutilated (*Poison Fruit*, 166). In fact, Moon has extensive psychic powers.

Moon touches a bed, a cot, a carseat, or wherever someone was murdered, and the murder scene not only replays in his mind but so do other murder scenes enacted in the same spot: "The voices of the dead had taken hold of him" (*Poison Fruit*, 202). Only his grandfather's stern warnings about the need to keep warm when taking a spirit walk and listening to the cold voices of the dead, to ignore their commands, and to not let the dead take his hand keep him from being psychically submerged in those voices. In *Ogilvie, Tallant & Moon*, a bloody handkerchief speaks to him of violence and guides him to a body; later, a car ride reveals the means and manner of death. Some colleagues reject his " 'heap big medicine' crap" as "demeaning to Indians," and even his girlfriend is uncomfortable with talk about recharging the spirit power of a carved wooden amulet, warnings not to let the magic out of a spirit bag (a leather pouch), and trance-like states: "She never quite knew what to make of these times with him, when he was a shaman instead of an attorney" (*Poison Fruit*, 40, 214). "This special talent of his still made her skittish; she had seen too often the demands it made on him, demands that frightened her" (*Cat's Claw*, 150). When she voices her fears about such powers, he replies that everything worth valuing is somehow frightening.

Taught by his grandfather, Moon sometimes enhances these powers with sacred objects (carved symbols of power or a protective amulet) or with incantations and traditional rituals involving purification through herbs, oils, and sauna sweat baths. Appropriately enough for his San Francisco setting, a sauna helps him open the psychic doors of perception to trace the troubled psychological imprints of a murderer in *Cat's Claw* and discover the patterns that make his capture inevitable. In *Music When Sweet Voices Die*, Moon employs an Ojibway instrument for protection and guidance:

It was a flattish wooden oval that snuggled neatly in the palm of his hand. A leather braid went through a hole at one end so that the wood might be worn around the neck. On the wood were the carefully carved and painted symbols of his name, Spotted Moon. He held the wood in his hands for a moment, warming it, then slipped the leather braid over his head and tucked the wood into the rolled collar of his sweater, so that it could lie against his chest. Although Lieutenant Jacobs or

Lydia Wong would find the wood a curiosity, Charlie's anthropologist cousin or his grandfather or any member of the Iron River tribe of Ojibway would instantly have recognized the wood for what it was—a medicine finger . . . he felt his sensitivity increased as his senses became keener. . . . This honing of his perception intensified his focus. (151)

Thus prepared, Moon is ready to face danger in his own special way.

Occasionally, Spotted Moon reaffirms his ties to the earth and to his heritage before returning to the mainstream world of his vocation. Yet, throughout the series, there is an edge of mockery to the narrative voice. When he suffers from the common cold, instead of taking two aspirins and a glass of orange juice, Moon smears himself with a "vile-smelling ointment" and chants each symptom with orders for it to depart (*Ogilvie*, 94). When irritated by whites who reasonably misunderstand his power and confuse him with a Chinese or a Sioux, Moon angrily asserts that he is an Indian witch doctor (79). Later, he uses Ojibway "magic" (a special series of taps) to get the attention of a negligent waiter, to the amazement of his guests.

Perhaps such magic would have greater credibility on home terrain, amid the eerie forests and foggy lakes and bogs north of Lake Michigan. However, it seems out of place amid the banal realities of a cosmopolitan area, with an amateur detective who prides himself on his taste for fine wine, classical music, and gourmet cooking. Though Moon is offended by his associates' suggestion that his way to knowledge is akin to the nineteenth-century seance, it partakes of the hocus-pocus and fraud associated in most detective fiction with seances (despite Agatha Christie's trust in them). His way to knowledge may be like the paranormal flashes of insight popularized by the clairvoyants or psychics who sometimes guide police searches when all other recourses are closed. However, traditionally, such spiritualistic characters themselves are not detectives, and this is where the problem of credibility occurs. How can Moon be both a rational modern attorney, using established legal means of investigation, and a paranormal visionary, a soothsayer who reads spiritual impressions from material objects? Within the conventions of the genre, such behavior strains credibility.

Mark Sullivan's Little Crow and Sarah Many Horses

Mark T. Sullivan explores the junction between clashing cultures in *The Purification Ceremony* and *Ghost Dance*. In *The Purification Ceremony*, the worldview of the white trophy hunter, one obsessed with world-class records for antler spread, clashes with Micmac/Penobscot hunter-gatherer sensibilities (hunting for food, respecting the hunted, abhorring waste). In *Ghost Dance*, the Native American belief in spirit world power clashes with

Western skepticism and the use of spiritualism to con the gullible out of their wealth.

The Purification Ceremony is intentionally set in an isolated, frigid region of mountains and forests, populated by deer, elk, porcupine, ermine, and wolves. Like the British mysteries in which the manor house guests are cut off from the outside world by a blizzard, flood, or other natural disaster, the characters of this novel have flown into a remote area, seeking a wilderness experience, and they are sequestered from civilization by snow and ice. However, whereas the British gatherings—like that of Agatha Christie's ten little Indians—are all white, Sullivan places one real Indian among his victims/suspects and, as a result, the solution is not cerebral. Instead, it depends on a direct confrontation between two ways to power: that of a Micmac/Penobscot hunter and that of a Mexican-Huichol-trained *Mara'akame* (drug-driven sorcerer). Little Crow uses the tracking skills of the scout—close observation of nature—rather than the ratiocinative skills of a Sherlock Holmes. The opening emphasis on natural signs indicating an approaching harsh winter (broad, complicated brown spider webs, geese passing south before Labor Day, ermines becoming inordinately aggressive) and the wildlife activities before an approaching storm (cawing scrub jays, moose crashing through a clear-cut area, a whitetail doe feeding hurriedly on a flat) move the novel out of the British tradition and into a New World native vision of the natural world shaping human events. So too does a wilderness dweller's belief that nature presages the future with signs, that a hare killed viciously by an ermine foretells his own demise, especially when his fears come true. An old guide calls this isolated country "spirit country" (21), and his appellation proves apt.

As in the British tradition, the prospective victims are not nice people. They carry a lot of negative baggage and are uncomfortable with women in anything but traditional roles (sex object, mother, cook, and housekeeper). They are particularly suspicious of Diana "Little Crow" Jackman, because she is a competent, no-nonsense Native American hunter with an MIT degree in computer engineering, who feels herself their equal or better and who is unimpressed by their posing. As the hunt progresses and the killings begin, the whites initially blame her, because their dead associates have not only been shot down with arrows and strung up to freeze but also scalped and gutted as if they were deer or elk, with a tail feather from a hawk placed between their upper front teeth. Jackman is seemingly the only Indian around, and in their minds a hunting bow, feathers, and scalping equal Indian killer. Eventually, however, they realize that their survival depends on her woodcraft, hunter's lore, and hunter's instincts. She is the amateur detective who will unravel motive and method and who will confront and overcome the antisocial aberration that threatens this artificial community.

Despite their growing dependence on her for survival, she is no role model. Her mother, once a U.S. Congresswoman, suffered from Alzheimer's disease and drowned in a stream in which the family had often fished. Diana blamed her father's carelessness or intent for her mother's death, and she rejected both him and the native heritage he tried to instill in her. She is an environmental software writer in her mid-30s, and though she trains hard in a gym, she has not immersed herself in a truly wilderness experience since she went hunting with her father eighteen years earlier. Yet she is not comfortable being totally in the white world and, as a consequence, is undergoing a crisis in her marriage to an urban white and in her personal sense of identity. She has a problem with commitment and assimilation that has sent her scurrying into the forests of Maine, reliving her childhood lessons about traditional native ways of interacting with nature and, against her husband's wishes, training her thoroughly urbanized children in the survival skills of their ancestors. She has kept her fears about her mother's death to herself, and her husband is embittered at not being entrusted with family secrets (she had told him her living father was dead, but her father's suicide reveals her lies about family and past). Once they had shared his humorous teasing about her being "a wild Maine savage" he had tamed and civilized, but the joke became too much of a reality for laughter (*The Purification Ceremony*, 135). Her mother, father, and great-uncle were all tracking deer hunters and, at this time of personal crisis, she has hired out to track deer for trophy hunters. In doing so, she becomes caught up in a nightmare situation that requires calm and rational control, that calls on all of her training as a tracker-hunter guide, and that ultimately requires her to throw off her white facade and become the spirit-guided woods-dweller of her tribal heritage.

Sullivan's story hinges on the extremes to which a person will go to exact revenge outside of the law courts. A woman shot dead at her clothesline during deer season has been declared "accidentally" shot, and the responsible party has walked away from his deed with a reprimand. A member of Jackman's hunting party is the one responsible, but all are in the line of fire because all, except Jackman, share the same indifference to nature and to fellow human beings, and all are obsessed with possessing a trophy head, at any price. The murderer has studied Mexican Huichol methods of acquiring power through peyote-and-jimson-weed-induced hallucinations; he has cached adequate supplies for a month, killed the nearby logging company's winter guard, and destroyed all available radio equipment for contacting the outside world. His observation of Jackman's hunting methods makes him treat her with more respect than the others he hunts (feeding her to the wolves instead of hanging her up like a deer carcass), but his grief and his means of retaliation have carried him so far beyond the human pale that there is no going back. Here Sullivan is in the tradition of pursuit narratives, such as Richard Connell's "The Most Dangerous Game" and Geoffrey Houshold's *Rogue Male*, in both of which the hunter challenges the hunted to extreme acts of courage or foolhardiness and in which, as in this case, roles may be reversed and the hunter become the hunted. To end the hunter's killing spree, he must be tracked down and killed. Jackman's gradual realization of this truth results in a profound psychological change, whereby she must develop the extrasensory, paranormal Micmac/Penobscot powers her relatives have taught her but that she has never before drawn on or fully believed in. She has always followed tradition in small ways, such as thanking a killed animal for providing its meat as her food or leaving a lock of her hair in the woods when she takes a part of the woods away with her. She has dreamed for a month of a ten-point buck and in native tradition should follow that animal where it leads (hence the hunting trip). The night before the hunting party departed she dreamed of water turning to blood and soaking the white clothes she wore, a blood dream that in native tradition foretells violent death. To survive the reality her dream presages, she must become Little Crow, follow the *Puoin* or shamanistic hunting rituals, and merge with the spirits of the forest. Her greatuncle, a shaman, summed up the worldview in which she now operates, teaching her about the six levels of existence (Earth World, Ghost World, and the worlds beneath the Earth and the Water and above the Earth and the Sky) and about the life force or "Power" which lay under and permeated these worlds. Her great-uncle said that "everything he could see," "touch," "taste," "smell and hold" manifested this power, including humans, trees, stars, moss, and wind. Consequently, he called birches, fish, deer, and even mountains "living things like us" (*The Purification Ceremony*, 95). Her father had been both a skilled surgeon and a Micmac medicine man, and she also remembers his teaching about being "at the whim of the six worlds and the invisible Power that flows through it," about the "endless cycle of Power," which "our ancestors believed was everywhere around us," and about handling that Power amid chaos (57–59). Now she must gain the acceptance of the woods and become like a mirror, reflecting all around her, in order to "sense worlds that are invisible to most people these days" (111), and she must use dreams and the hunt as windows into other worlds (113). In the old stories of her tribe, the *Kinapaq* used Power for personal ends, "to run fast as the wind, to dive deep into water, to carry trees on their backs, but her family follows the tradition of the *Puoins*, "who used Power to cure" (155). Within the genre conventions of the detective story, her behavior from this point on would mark her as the evil entity working entirely outside of the mainstream social system as a rogue or an outlaw, but within a New World native tradition she becomes society's protector and avenger.

In order to right the imbalance created in nature by the disrespect of the hunting party and by the insanities of the murderer, Jackman forces herself to bring her life back into balance, to confirm her native identity as Little Crow, to open up her doors of perception to the spirit world and spirit powers of her ancestral heritage, and to restore balance to the forest in which she hunts. By this point, Sullivan seems to have left the traditional murder mystery conventions far behind and to have entered the world of the horror story and of the supernatural sci-fi tale. This is Mercedes Lackey territory, and Little Crow follows native ways much like those followed by Lackey's Osage heroine in *Sacred Ground*. Little Crow dresses for power, placing a Micmac quillwork and leather medicine pouch and a sprig of spruce close to her skin for protection and endurance. She calls upon the powers of the Micmac shaman from the ancient forests of Nova Scotia, for example, the power of her namesake, the crow spirit. To the Micmac, the crow is a seer that sees and feels from the sky what others do not, and it is crow power that gives her her name and enables her to shift shape and fly above hunter and hunted to anticipate traps. This is the universe of native spiritualism that depends on ancient chants and ancient ways of attaining spiritual harmony to battle the unpredictable forces of an unforgiving, brutal universe. As the snow billows around her, she discovers her place in the fractured terrain through which she runs, accepts the visible world as an illusion, and prepares herself mentally to counter unpredictability with unpredictability, "to change mind and intent at a moment's notice" (254). She merges with the spirits of animal, rock, and sky to "strip away the veils" that separate her from deeper self-knowledge (308). This knowledge and these skills enable her to escape a wolf pack, survive the winter's cold with only a wolf skin covering, and ascertain motive, method, and means of retaliation.

Ironically, however, even amid spirit battles, Sullivan ties the methodology back to her old world and to the mystery pattern of planning and predicting behavior. As she hunts a killer and tries to anticipate his actions and reactions, recalling the topography of the territory covered and past patterns of movement, she draws parallels between "executing a hunt" and "writing a good piece of computer software." She muses, "The trick to writing a good piece of computer software is to anticipate the pitfalls and snafus that might thwart a user, leaving her frozen at the keyboard, wondering where she went wrong in the electronic wilderness." In like manner, she "draft[s] scenarios as to how the killer might act as he approached the beaver pond" (187–88). As Mexican sorcery meets Northeastern shamanism (just as South American sorcery meets Northwestern shamanism in Naomi Stokes' *The Listening Ones*), the out-of-balance must yield to natural balance. As heroine and killer clash, both draw on the powers of invisible worlds and electric currents of surging power. He has taken the wolf as his animal ally, and datura gives him visions as paths to the spirit world. He prays to Tatewari, the God of the Sierra Madre, and his murderous acts are part of the purification ceremony of the title, a ceremony of vengeance for inflicted wrongs. To hunt him correctly, Little Crow must understand his pain, and ultimately she must breathe in his spirit, just as her ancestors breathed in the spirit of the animal they had killed. In this act, the evil that enveloped him is dissipated; his body can return to the earth, and his spirit can be reincarnated in the natural cycle of power transfer.

Sullivan's *Ghost Dance* is based on a similar premise: the natural order being disturbed and a need for special native ceremonies and encounters to restore balance. In this case, according to a set of letters included in the narrative, Sarah Many Horses, the niece of Sitting Bull and a practitioner of his mystical teachings about Ghost Dance power, came East with a traveling road show that provided her protection after the massacre at Wounded Knee. The confidence artist who heads the show and his brothers Joshua and Caleb Danby, take her home with them to Lawton, Vermont, where they set up a scam with seances and fake spirits. However, when Many Horses refuses to teach the secrets of the Ghost Dance (genuine contacts with the spirit world), he and his bevy of local power seekers, including the mayor and a priest, kill her and eat her flesh. As the novel begins in modern times, the small town of Lawton is shocked by a series of gruesome murders tied directly to that nineteenth-century incident. Someone is killing off the descendants of those townspeople who sought revenge for Sarah Many Horses's death and who divided up among themselves as reminders of this ghastly blight on the town's history her journal, a set of gold crosses, and the Sioux items associated with the Ghost Dance. Secrets long hidden will out, and the evil perpetuated by modern descendants of past murderers will overtake them. Like *The Purification Ceremony*, *Ghost Dance* challenges the boundaries of detective fiction and crosses over into horror; retribution crosses generations and comes in unlikely forms. Gothic elements include eerie spirits of the dead haunting a man already haunted by his own past, an abandoned, decaying, nineteenth-century structure, where a madman tortures victims as the smoke of various drugs curl up and befog both room and minds, and an ancient cave where flickering firelight casts shadows, and horrid scenes of cannibalism were once played out. There is some precedent for combining the detective story with ghost stories and other elements of gothic horror, for both ghosts and the gothic have appeared in detective fiction since the time of Charles Dickens, Sheridan LaFanu, and Wilkie Collins, though often as a hoax or fraud to be unveiled by the skeptical rationalism of the investigator and only occasionally as a genuine occult event. The two recur in the comic detective movies of the 1930s and 1940s, particularly in New England gothic detective tales of mysteries mixed with hauntings.

Neither of the two detectives in *Ghost Dance*—one a professional police officer trying to live down a bout with alcoholism (Andie Nightingale), the other an outdoorsman and a documentary filmmaker whose self-pity is destroying a promising career (Patrick Gallagher)—is a Native American. However, Gallagher has psychically dislocating dreams and visions that connect him to the dead Many Horses and make him her psychic repre-

sentative. Furthermore, clearly no amount of forensic evidence will satisfactorily explain these serial killings, for the only answers lie in the past.
As the murder investigation moves toward its climax, a voyage of discovery
into psychotic behavior of the past and present, the spirit of Many Horses
acts as a surrogate detective as she guides Gallagher's investigation, shares
with him the secrets of the Ghost Dance, and uses him to find her body
and return it to the Lakotas for a traditional burial that will set her soul
at rest. Thanks to this restless ghost, a modern killer—a descendant of the
two brothers who took Many Horses under their protection and then killed
her in such a ghastly way—can be stopped. Moreover, as his characters
open the door to the past, Sullivan places them more and more amid rural
settings such as those in which the nineteenth-century crime occurred, as
they claw their way up "a series of benches where shagbark hickory grew
in meadows of still, pale grass" to emerge from a pine break "into a
meadow choked by low junipers" as "scraggly dead leaves beat themselves
against beech whips," and the rained-on soil and woods give off "the scent
of moldering decay" (*Ghost Dance*, 117). As they go higher up the mountain, past trunks of mountain ash, cherry, and spruce, they hear an owl
hoot, a grouse drum, and a turkey gobble. They stand on a rock shelf that
juts from a cliff, push through a maze of wild raspberry, and discover a
wide, oval cave mouth, once a bear's den, where past nightmares were
enacted. Nightgale's and Gallagher's acts free the dead, restore balance in
their lives, and reward them with the blessing of love.

Thus once again Sullivan transplants his Native Americans from their
traditional regions to a new environment in which they must nonetheless
draw on their native spiritual heritage to survive or to overcome.

SHERLOCK: SENECAN GUIDE JANE WHITEFIELD

Thomas Perry's fast-paced Jane Whitefield stories, with their tightly interwoven plots, seem like a thoroughly modern crime series involving heists,
mob executions, and corporate scams and complex and ingenious responses
to them. His heroine, petite, blue-eyed Jane Whitefield, is a computer whiz
who stays current with the cutting-edge tools of high technology but who
also has good human instincts. She exploits the possibilities of such new
technologies to access information, manufacture credible credit, education,
and work histories for new identities, create paper trails, set up approved
credit cards and credit ratings, and arrange shifts in identity and crisscross-
ing flights to throw pursuers off the track, mostly via the Internet. Like
Sherlock Holmes, she is perceptive, observant, and knowledgeable about
arcane information, such as how the Seneca turned a 1687 French "surprise" attack into a rout, the history of old growth apple and plum or-
chards, and gruesome details of the Spanish conquest of California.
However, her detection is done on the run, not in a quiet study, though

sometimes she has spent years putting in place the "identities" she has created for herself and for others. Moreover, unlike the traditional detective who exposes secrets and reveals truths, she does the opposite, covering up facts and protecting the weak and the culpable (though not the evil).

Whitefield knows where to buy forged documents and unregistered weapons, and what the going rates are, how to con local computer businesses into letting her access their computer lines, and how to cover her trail electronically. She is not only highly competent but also resourceful with the ins and outs of modern, computerized bureaucracies and with creating paper trails that confirm new identities. She is skilled enough and backed by enough resources to unravel the legal ins and outs of a crime in the making, a multimillion-dollar trust raided by its designated trustees in *Dance for the Dead*. She knows how the court system works and how to use it advantageously for her clients. Furthermore, she runs her own private version of the government's Witness Protection Program for fugitives needing new identities and new lives, ensconcing them far enough out of the way that present threats cannot endanger their future lives. For example, in *The Face-Changers*, a dedicated plastic surgeon has helped the wrong person change his face and now is not only being stalked but also framed for a crime he did not commit, and Whitefield agrees to help him disappear. When her clients are endangered, she has the training and expertise to protect them, as she does in *Vanishing Act*, when she fiercely assaults and debilitates a rather sleazy private detective who is tracking her client for some villainous thugs hired by the woman's abusive husband. Because the greatest danger for her clients comes from their psychological need to retain some elements of their personal identity that might lead their trackers to them, she works actively to analyze their personalities and needs so that their new identities will mesh with their inner selves, thus enabling them to stay out of touch and out of reach. These people may be battered wives trying to escape domineering, destructive husbands, innocent children endangered by something they have witnessed or by their family connections, men and women who know too much about a business swindle or other illegal activities to feel safe around the promulgators, or anyone enmeshed in problems too dangerous for them to extricate themselves safely. The extremes to which some will go to find the people she helps disappear are made clear in *Shadow Woman*, wherein a Las Vegas casino employs a psychotic husband and wife hit team to track down and kill her client.

Why then does Jane Whitefield belong in this series as a Native American detective? The answer is that Perry cleverly depicts the long-term results of successful assimilation: an amalgam of old and new that is essentially different from both. Whitefield's father was Huron, and her mother was a white woman adopted into the Seneca Wolf Clan, so by matriarchal rules, Whitefield too is a member of the Seneca Wolf Clan. She has been raised in modern America to be a highly competent modern woman, but she has also been brought up to believe in Seneca theology, with its stories about Sky Woman and the giant turtle, or about Hawenneyu, the Right-Handed Twin creator, and Hanegoategeh, the Left-Handed Twin destroyer, who together balance the universe. Her genetic heritage and her family connections have instilled in her native values and traditions which guide her life, and she still turns to tribal elders for advice and guidance. Her compromise between the old and the new is to update a traditional Senecan role: that of the guide through hostile territory. Such guides employed knowledge of secret trails and hidden byways to ease the way for those determined to make that dangerous journey. In a viable, modern interpretation of this role, Whitefield smooths the way for her clients' dangerous journeys to the safety of new identities.

The role of guide is not only in keeping with the role of her tribe historically (the Nundawaono, the People of the Hill, took victims away from the Iroquois Confederation and hid them, says she) but it also accords with Seneca belief that this role was approved and aided by *Jo-Ge-Ho*, the Stone Throwers or Little People of the Gorge. Thus after a successful case, Whitefield offers *Jo-Ge-Ho* tobacco as thanks and as a plea for the Stone Throwers to help her client journey to safety. However, unlike the shaman stories discussed above, the supernatural and the shamanistic play little part in her investigations. Whitefield came to this path when, as a college activist traveling the powwow circuit to register voters, she encountered cases of Indian-establishment conflicts based on very different worldviews, for example, the last surviving member of the Beothuk tribe destined for federal prison because of his inability to adjust to the concept of private property (he recorded for posterity the oral traditions and stories of his defunct tribe in exchange for her help fleeing the country).

Sometimes her cases require her to take advantage of the anonymity of Native American life, to leave the marked highways and cut across the countryside following forest trails, to capitalize on the standing treaties that allow Indians to freely cross the Canadian-U.S. border without passports, to bury herself and her client in a way of life that does not involve credit cards, a paper trail, or computer tracking, and to draw on a loose network of distant relatives for hospitality. Her Seneca heritage provides the advantage of secret weapons (a sharpened peg in her hair, water hemlock in her perfume). It also ensures her survival as when, in *Vanishing Act*, she is on foot with only a hunting knife in upstate New York wilderness territory and must draw on traditional skills not simply to survive but to destroy a murderous pursuer. Perry describes the process by which she constructs a Nundawa-style warclub and Seneca-style bow and arrow, sets deadfall traps, and avoids detection until she is ready to strike. In *Dance for the Dead*, Perry vividly captures her fighting skills as she is attacked on her way to the judge's chambers:

The man's eyes shone with triumph and eagerness as he snatched the purse [containing vital evidence] out of the air. The triumph turned to shock as the woman slipped the strap around his forearm and used the momentum of his charge to haul him into the second man, sending them both against the wall to her right. As they caromed off it, she delivered a kick to one and a chop to the other to put them on the floor. This bought her a few heartbeats to devote to the third man, who was moving along the left wall to get behind her.

She leaned back and swung one leg high. The man read her intention, stopped, and held up his hands to clutch her ankle, but her back foot left the ground and she hurled her weight into him. As her foot caught him at thigh level and propelled him into the wall, there was the sickening crack of his knee popping. He crumpled to the floor and began to gasp and clutch at his crippled leg as the woman rolled to the side and sprang up.

The first two men were rising to their feet. Her fist jabbed out at the nearest one and she rocked him back, pivoted to throw an elbow into the bridge of his nose, and brought a knee into the second man's face. (2)

The fact that her client is a child whose life has been repeatedly threatened and whose inheritance is being consumed by shyster lawyers and dishonest trustees makes her fight a righteous one.

When the abnormal behavior of her opponents suggests lunacy, as in *Shadow Woman*, Whitefield turns to Seneca lore about shape-shifters and witches to determine her best plan of attack. As a Seneca, she believes dreams have special significance and pays attention to the modern warnings and clues that appear as historical or mythological events in the dream world, such as her dream of a giant, masked cannibal with a necklace of human teeth in *Dance for the Dead*, a dream Freudians would connect to the modern villain she hunts, one who consumes the wealth of others. This amalgam of Seneca tradition with the modern skills of a seemingly assimilated heroine is a unique and an intriguing contribution to the genre, for Perry makes both Whitefields credible—the native woman with a secure role in the tribal hierarchy and a deep-seated commitment to tribal values, and the highly competent modern professional, who skirts the edge of the law to do good in her community.

CONCLUSION

Of all of the options open to writers employing Native American detectives from the East Coast or Great Lakes regions, the most viable and most innovative is Thomas Perry's creation of a modern Senecan who has adjusted to urban life and to the technology that rules it but has retained a touch of the wilderness in her choice of occupation and lifestyle and in the way she carries out her professional tasks. Perry understands that the survival of a culture lies in preserving its broad values and distinct social roles, not in physical trappings divorced from tribal meaning. Thus Jane Whitefield recreates an ancient role from her Senecan heritage, and does so not for material profit (she accepts gifts rather than charging a fee) but rather as an expression of age-old values, of ending violence and exploitation. When Whitefield does take up the artifacts of her cultural past, they become useful tools or are simply meaningful symbols. Perry's depiction of assimilation might better be called integration, the expression of core native beliefs in thoroughly modern settings.

10

Conclusion: The "Indian" in Detective Fiction—Present Realities and Future Directions

The budget doesn't go too far out here. . . . we can only afford the trade-ins; hell, even our fingerprint equipment is old, . . . cumbersome. . . . The last FBI man . . . asked Skunk if . . . it [w]as part of his junior G-man kit—those FBI men never are the best diplomats around. . . . We won't call them in on our own, though sometimes they force themselves on us. . . . I hated to think what an FBI man would have done in this case—probably gotten in one of those gun-helicopters and shot Charley and Thunder Boy out of the saddle when he'd seen their warpaint . . . , left the Tribe to pay for the horses and probably the buffalo, too. An FBI man probably couldn't tell horses, men, and buffalo apart, couldn't shoot straight enough anyway to hit one without hitting everything.

—Wayne Ude, *Becoming Coyote*, 147

PRESENT REALITIES

Except for Manly Wade Wellman's one short story featuring David Return in 1946, Native Americans in twentieth-century detective fiction up until the early 1970s served as suspects and victims—suspects because of their

Otherness on the fringes of society, and victims when plots required ready-made targets of crime, fodder for mainstream detectives to test their skills with. In Rex Stout's *Red Threads*, the victim's death by warclub immediately made police expect a killer Indian. That conventional role changed dramatically in the 1970s with Hillerman, Garfield, and Stern, all three of whom initially featured Navajo and Apache detectives as hunters/trackers. The 1980s, 1990s, and 2000 have seen a blossoming of over 70 native detectives, some totally assimilated, others bound to their roots, and any number occupying degrees of assimilation in between. Some serve as shamans or engage in shamanistic activities, a role writers perceive as analogous to detective work. The largest numbers (well over 30) have been located in the Southwest and have been Navajo, Apache, Zuñi, or Hopi. For a long time, Hillerman set the standard for the Native American detective and, in fact, writers such as Aimée Thurlo have paid tribute to both the influence of his works and his personal guidance in offering ideas and suggestions for getting the native elements right. Desecration and theft of native graves, relics, and holy items, battles over mineral rights and the pollution produced by stripmining, and historic ill treatment and racism perpetuated into the twenty-first century have become popular, reality-based touchstones for native detective stories.

Of course, as with the ethnic detective story in general, some of the Native American detectives wear their ethnicity as a fashion statement, a faux uniqueness asserted by characters who are actually mainstream in culture, politics, values, and all else. Cecil Dawkins' Ginevre Prettifield, for example, is labeled beautiful, fashionable, and Indian (left undefined); but she is not Native American in any meaningful way. Another instructive case is John Miles' Johnnie Baker; though one-sixteenth Choctaw, local Ute call her an apple, red on the outside, white on the inside. Despite an Oklahoma certificate of tribal heritage, she is a pale-faced blonde; a mainstream coloration protects her from the racism afflicting the dark-skinned Utes in the small Colorado town where she is sheriff. Such ethnic and racial distinctions are part of the background noise in a number of works. The clear trend of the subgenre, however, is to move away from superficial ethnicity that gives comfort that the melting pot works well, and instead to demonstrate the uniqueness of the native investigator. That uniqueness may involve training since childhood in observing the signs of nature as a hunter/tracker; it may involve a different sense of time, obligation, and justice. It should involve a unique worldview, a way of seeing the world quite different from and often at odds with the white way. Naomi Stokes captures that uniqueness in a heroine who is both a tribal officer with Quantico FBI training and a shaman who makes spirit journeys to battle witches with ancient spiritual tools; Muriel Gray likewise depicts spiritual demons that inhabit the native world and that only a strong shaman committed to his culture can overcome. Peter Bowen, in contrast, finds uniqueness in a melting pot that has worked, combining Canadian French, Celt, and Cree with other native groups to form the Métis, a gloriously multi-cultural amalgam. The best stories create credible characters whose degree of assimilation rings true and integrate cultural-ethnic issues into the crime/detection narrative itself.

What general conclusions emerge from these detective works? First, the detective story genre, though pushed in the direction of the horror story and sci-fi fantasy by the incorporation of native mythology (tall tales, oral history) and religion (creation stories), still fulfills some of its traditional mainstream functions as social criticism and an antidote to cultural smugness. As in classic pulp fiction, the seamy underbelly of American life is often on view in these stories, and other lessons are taught as well:

- Heritage can be romantic and exotic but also a millstone that keeps the individual anchored but unmoving.
- Playing Indian is a common American game but has nothing to do with authentic Native American culture; authenticity lies in invisible Ways, not in material trappings.
- True biculturalism is the exception, since it is difficult to exist in two cultures at once; a commitment toward one or the other is inevitable, because the two cultures are often mutually exclusive.
- Identity is the major issue for many Native Americans, as the writers who treat Indian topics demonstrate; in Muriel Gray's *The Trickster*, and in numerous other works, characters who give up their native identities can suffer horribly in ways invisible to whites.

These lessons help lift the Indian detective story above simple entertainment and into the realm of instruction and commentary about U.S. culture. While only the best writers sustain instructive insights, even some simple page-turners provide new ways of seeing some of our closest neighbors.

A final insight, one stressed in the structure and organization of this book, is the importance of regionalism in constructing identity. The late twentieth century brought into existence a number of reconceived and re-formulated identities epitomized in the new literatures that reflected them: African American, women's, Chicano/Mexican American, Asian American, gay and lesbian. Native American and the best of mainstream Indian literature reflects not only its racial and ethnic group but also its region, and perhaps more powerfully than the other literatures creates a unified identity among a people who share similar shaping forces in their environment. Navajo, Hopi, Zuñi, Pueblo—though dramatically different, all are undeniably Southwesterners, enduring the region's common difficulties. A graphic representation of fictional murder by region (see Figure 10.1) illustrates this point.

As the listings show, some methods and motives (bashing skulls, shoot-

Figure 10.1
Regional Murder Chart

Region	Ways of Dying
Alaska and Northwest Territories	Grizzly bear attack; impaling by tree; fall from a height; hypothermia; harpoon; plane crash; stabbing; strangling; drowning at sea; carried under by a sudden, high bore tide; dashed on rocks; gaffing; being taken by the otter gods; drugs (like arsenic); hurtling boulders
Northwest	Grizzly bear attack; eagle talons; moose; elk; avalanche; drowning from sudden incoming tide or at sea; tidal pool quicksand; removal of pituitary gland; mushroom poisoning; shot with gun or arrows; scalped, gutted, and strung up to freeze
Plains and Mountains	Blow gun dart; poison; strangulation; witchcraft; seven black stones flung with a sling; avalanche; shooting; knifing; chemical effluents; evil spirits; poison
Southwest	Dehydration; freezing; snake bite; scorpion sting; bear; Anasazi spirit warriors; corpse dust; *chindi*; skinwalker's curse; "dark wind"; lightning bolt; rising water; falling rocks; noxious/poisonous plants; impaled by tree; fall from a height; loco weed; strangulation; ritual slaying; mysterious illness; vigilantism; cholera; radioactivity; being shot with bone slivers; Apache-style knifing with arm and nose sliced off; face sliced off and preserved as a trophy
East Coast and Great Lakes	Bow and arrow; warclub; water hemlock; deadfall trap; sharpened peg; knife and cannibalism

Figure 10.1 (*continued*)

Motives for Murder	Detectives
Greed; stupidity; cabin fever; oil; drugs; land development; dislike of outsiders; revenge; bad blood	Kate Shugak; Ray Attla; Glen Redfern; Liza Romero and Paul Howard; Mattessee; Kitologitlak; David Talmost
Greed; revenge; conflicts over fishing rights	Jordan Tidewater; Old Man Ahcleet; Sam Hunting Wolf; Angela Biwaban; Diana "Little Crow" Jackman (though the last two originate from East Coast/Great Lakes); Willie Prettybird
Jealousy; desire for power; greed; ambition; witchcraft; revenge; madness	Vicky Holden; Daisy Perika; Charlie Moon; Angela Biwaban; Beneetsee and Gabriel Du Pré; Molly Bearpaw; Mitch Bushyhead; Kyle Old Wolf; Jennifer Talldeer; Tay-bodal; David Return; Morning Tree; Johnelle "Johnnie" Baker
Materialism; ambition; greed for minerals, metals, Native American artifacts; government contracts; racial hatred; drug smuggling; fame; witchcraft; revenge; insanity	Jim Chee; Joseph Leaphorn; Ella Clah; Johnny Ortiz; Connie Barnes (sidekick); Jesús Chuy Leyva; Sheriff Lansing; Gabe Hanna; Tina Martinez; Joseph Payestewa; the Blackhorse brothers (Gabriel, Joshua, Lucas); Belara Fuller; Ashe Redhawk; Cisco Watchman; Benjamin Two Eagle; Ben Naya/Kwikwilyaqa; Trade Ellis; Ginevra Prettifield; Youngblood Duran; Laura Nez; Jasentha Cliffwalker; Emmett Quanah Parker; Anna Turnipseed; Stone Ghost
Lunacy; greed; politics; revenge; eliminate witnesses; prevent family shame	Diana "Little Crow" Jackman; Jane Whitefield; The Ghost of Sarah Many Horses; Charlie Spotted Moon; Old Panther; Bob Eddison; Christine Saksis; Chinachgook

ing; greed, jealousy) are indeed universal, but murder by bear or a sabo-
taged bush plane are typically Alaskan, while being stomped to death by
moose or elk or carried under by a bore tide may be Northwestern or
Alaskan, and the rattlesnake, scorpion, or bone sliver resolutions to social
conflict are recourses for desert dwellers. We have no Indian detectives in
the Deep South or Florida, and no indigenous ones in California, only
transplants from other regions. (This absence is also generally true of the
East Coast.) Removal, urbanization, and simple population pressures have
made true regional native identities unlikely. Perhaps due to Hillerman's
influence, non-Native American writers of detective fiction featuring native
detectives gravitate most toward Southwestern tribes, though the Plains and
Mountains are clearly the second choice, with isolated rural areas more
likely to be settings for Native American detection than urban ones.

Our conclusion that the regional environment creates culture is perhaps
a modest one, but it flies in the face of current wisdom: the culture creates
the environment (why else are malls air-conditioned?). We believe that the
stories examined herein nicely illustrate the first proposition, and that the
debate between the two positions will be ongoing. There is much to learn
from Native American culture, even as depicted in watered-down versions
by mainstream writers; Indians have resisted standardization, conformity,
and the loss of uniqueness—modernism in general—for four centuries, and
they still endure. In a time of ecological crises we would do well to pay
attention to successful alternative models which respect nature.

FUTURE DIRECTIONS

Today's Native American detective stories have laid the groundwork for
some interesting possible future directions.

One direction is a return to nineteenth-century roots: the Indian as pathfinder, scout, guide, hunter, and tracker. Thomas Perry's Seneca Jane Whitefield guides those in need of a justice unattainable within the court
systems, providing them with new identities and new locations far from
the dangers that threaten, and both Whitefield and Mark Sullivan's
Micmac-Penobscot hunter Dorothy "Little Crow" Jackman use all the
hunting skills gleaned from their tribal traditions and family training to
track down and kill serial murderers who stalk them in wilderness settings.
Peter Bowen's Gabriel Du Pré is very much in this school. When observing
a crime scene in *Notches*, he circles the body from about six feet away,
then brings the ground to his eyes, as if he were tracking, noting tiny shards
of green glass shining against the "ocher" earth and paper towels up against
sagebrush: "Been here a while. Yellow stains on them" (7). Later, Du Pré's
friend, Booger Tom, observes that the tracks suggest the man they hunt
"moved wrong," and Bowen confirms that in tracking, "you looked for
what should not be there and was, or what should be there and was not"

(50). De Pré, in this manifestation of his role (he plays several, including avenger), is simply another in the long list of native trackers who astounded Europeans with skills adapted to a demanding natural environment. Such trackers and scouts, as breathless early accounts confirm, could identify faces on distant horizons where Europeans still perceived only riders and could read sign with the ease with which whites read their Bibles. Though no doubt exaggerated as legend, such superhuman abilities often simply reflected lifelong training honed by survival needs. The Native American detective is a perfect venue to celebrate such skill at reading the natural world.

Another literary direction is to return to particular settings in which Native Americans suffered injustice and outrageous exploitation and to use the personal experiences of the amateur detective hero or heroine to win sympathy for the native population of that time. Such settings need not be "historical" in the sense of the nineteenth century and frontier days. Unfortunately, Native Americans suffered injustice in most periods of American history. Fred Grove traces the persecution and framing of Osage Boone Terrell during Oklahoma's oil boom days of the 1920s and 1930s, creating an unforgettable portrait of this largely forgotten time, and Kathleen Eagle, through the murder story of Adam Lone Bull, discloses in dramatic form the lifetime commitment of sane Sioux Indians to the Hiawatha Insane Asylum for Indians in Canton, South Dakota, as part of a land-grab scheme in the 1930s. Some writers, such as Mardi Oakley Medawar and Kathleen and Michael Gear, have established a trend that corresponds to a general movement in detection: the historical detective, in the usual sense of historical. In the case of Native Americans, this means more pre-Columbian or eighteen-or nineteenth-century detectives, investigators possibly anachronistic in their ratiocinative approach to crime but also sleuths who can provide an insider's view of history, archaeology, and culture. Wayne Ude's *Becoming Coyote* suggests another possible direction for the twenty-first century Native American detective: the use of oral storytelling methods to provide a surreal movement between time periods and to interlock past, present, and future in innovative ways in seamless time. Native writers Sherman Alexie and Louis Owens do this in detective fiction that has gained popularity with mainstream readers, and now Rodolfo Anaya has made the form work well to give his Sonny Baca series a historical and cultural depth normally not achieved in the detective format. Such experiments with narrative offer exciting possibilities for cross-cultural amalgams.

Furthermore, the trend has been toward introducing readers to more and more tribes and native identities distanced from mainstream experience. For example, Kirk Mitchell's *Cry Dance* features a Comanche BIA detective and a Modoc FBI investigator but also includes a Rastafarian Havasupai tribal cop with dreadlocks, Pai gamblers, Kaibab (Southern Paiute) witnesses, the last of the Death Valley Chemehuevi (another branch of the Southern Paiute), Shoshone casino dealers, Sioux Sun Dancers, an intertribal shaman, and a Navajo pilot. This very mixed cast promotes discussion about history: million-dollar homes built over Washoe villages, the Pomos' conflicts over casinos, and other such confrontations of past and present. Mitchell works in little-known historical details that, in context, help delineate the character of his heroine:

In 1852, a company of California volunteer militia invited the unarmed Modoc to a peace conference. The soldiers laced their guests' food with strychnine. When the fare was refused, the militia resorted to a more direct method. They shot forty men, women, and children. Twenty years later, Kintpuash—Anna's great-great-grandfather, known to whites as Captain Jack—invited Major General Edward Canby to a parley. Neither side was to come armed. Jack shot Canby dead under a flag of truce. The highest-ranking U.S. officer ever to be killed by an Indian.
     So the key to incomprehensible native behavior was always the past.
     Kintpuash.
     Her own blood. Still, he was an enigma to her. Why had he fought so long and so furiously with no hope of winning? Was the answer in the photograph the army had taken of him in stockade pinstripes hours before his execution? He'd offered the camera a faint, unapologetic smile. Her father's smile. And hers too, she suspected. (188)

Later, as the prisoner of a mad serial killer, her ankle shattered, her body battered, helpless and alone in a dark cave, Anna begins to understand her ancestor's "elation born of rage" as he went down fighting, struggling to save face as she fights literally to keep her face (323); then, at the end, she feels she understands her previously inexplicable ancestor perfectly and acts against her foe as he acted against his, returning deceit with deceit and violence with violence.

     Despite the fact that white, mainstream authors dominate the stories we have discussed, some of them simply exploiting a fad with cardboard Indian figures, Mitchell's mix of tribes and peoples shows how far the subgenre has come from its beginnings in Hillerman's Southwest, and how far, thanks again to Hillerman, we as a culture have come from the figure of the generic Indian defined by Robert Berkhofer in *The White Man's Indian.* Mitchell's passage also reflects another evolving mainstream advance in understanding, a notion alien to ahistorical America—that the past is the key to understanding the present. This is not to say that understanding is complete; on the contrary, we have been at pains to show just how wide the gulf between Native American and mainstream really is, and just how difficult it is to bridge. The intuitive or spiritual—we have used any number of synonyms in our discussion—cannot be reconciled with the rational-material outlook on the world that was the inheritance of the European Enlightenment, the Age of Reason. The older Way accepts human frailty before the forces of fate and nature, endorses accommodation to the human condition, and embraces community and belonging. The more recent Way encourages struggle against nature with the goal of dominance, a continual effort to improve human nature, a rejection of the past, and a celebration of the primacy of the individual. No wonder there is mutual incomprehension in both camps! The very definitions of validity are at odds, with Native Americans, as we saw first with Brian Moore's *Black Robe* and Oliver LaFarge's *Laughing Boy*, regarding dreams and the spiritual world as the ultimate reality, and beauty and harmony as the goals of life, and with European-influenced America putting its trust largely in the empirical and material and regarding all else with suspicion.

Yet some of the better writers that were covered teach positive lessons, and the self-evident curiosity of so many mass readership detective fiction fans about the native way of seeing balances some of the silliness of New Age posturing. There seems to be a gathering unease with standardization and globalization, an emerging desire for a more grounded, spiritual way of life, and an appreciation that materialism does not automatically accord with happiness. If the authors discussed herein pull back the curtains on ways of living with beauty and harmony, their popular fiction genres need no further defense.

Bibliography

PRIMARY SOURCES

Anaya, Rudolfo. *Rio Grande Fall*. New York: Time Warner, 1996.
———. *Shaman Winter*. New York: Time Warner, 1999.
———. *Zia Summer*. New York: Time Warner, 1996.
Babula, William. *According to St. John*. New York: Carol Publishing, 1989.
———. *St. John and the Seven Veils*. New York: Carol Publishing, 1991.
———. *St. John's Baptism*. New York: Citadel Press, 1988.
———. *St. John's Bestiary*. Aurora, Colo.: Write Way, 1994.
Barker, Rodney. *The Broken Circle: A True Story of Murder and Magic in Indian Country*. New York: Ballantine Books, 1992.
Bowen, Peter. *Coyote Wind*. New York: St. Martin's Press, 1994.
———. *Long Son*. New York: St. Martin's Press, 1999.
———. *Notches*. New York: St. Martin's Press, 1997.
———. *Specimen Song*. New York: St. Martin's Press, 1995.
———. *The Stick Game*. New York: St. Martin's Press, 2000.
———. *Thunder Horse*. New York: St. Martin's Press, 1998.
———. *Wolf, No Wolf*. New York: St. Martin's Press, 1996.
Browning, Sinclair. *The Last Song Dogs*. New York: Bantam, 1999.
———. *Rode Hard, Put Away Dead*. New York: Bantam, 2001.

———. *The Sporting Club*. New York: Bantam, 2000.

Chandler, Raymond. *The Long Goodbye*. Boston: Houghton, Mifflin, 1953.

Charlevoix, Pierre de. *Journal of a Voyage to North-America*. 1761.

Childers, Erskine. *The Riddle of the Sands: A Record of Secret Service Recently Achieved*. London: Smith, Elder, 1903.

Cody, Buffalo Bill. *Red Renard, the Indian Detective or, The Gold Buzzards of Colorado: A Romance of the Mines and Dead Trails*. 1886.

Coel, Margaret. *The Dream Stalker*. New York: Berkley, 1997.

———. *The Eagle Catcher*. New York: Berkley, 1995.

———. *The Ghost Walker*. New York: Berkley, 1996.

———. *The Lost Bird*. New York: Berkley, 1999.

———. *The Spirit Woman*. New York: Berkley, 2000.

———. *The Story Teller*. New York: Berkley, 1998.

Cole, David. *Butterfly Lost*. New York: HarperCollins, 1999.

Connell, Richard. "The Most Dangerous Game." In *The Norton Introduction to Fiction*, ed. Jerome Beatty. New York: W. W. Norton and Co., 1997.

Davis, Val. *Track of the Scorpion*. New York: St. Martin's Press, 1996.

Dawkins, Cecil. *Clay Dancers*. New York: Random House, 1994.

———. *Rare Earth*. New York: Random House, 1995.

———. *The Santa Fe Rembrandt*. New York: Random House, 1993.

Delving, Michael. *The Devil Finds Work*. New York: Scribner's, 1960.

———. *A Shadow of Himself*. New York: Scribner's, 1972.

———. *Smiling the Boy Fell Dead*. New York: Scribner's, 1968.

Doss, James D. *The Night Visitor: A Shaman Mystery*. New York: St. Martin's Press, 1999.

———. *The Shaman Laughs*. New York: St. Martin's Press, 1994.

———. *The Shaman Sings*. New York: St. Martin's Press, 1993.

———. *The Shaman's Bones*. New York: St. Martin's Press, 1997.

———. *The Shaman's Game*. New York: St. Martin's Press, 1998.

Duquette, Anne Marie. *In the Arms of the Law*. New York: Harlequin, 1997.

Eagle, Kathleen. *The Night Remembers*. New York: Avon, 1997.

———. *Sunrise Song*. New York: Avon, 1996.

Estleman, Loren. *The Stranglers*. New York: Doubleday, 1984.

Froetschel, Susan. *Alaska Gray*. New York: St. Martin's Press, 1994.

Garfield, Brian. *Relentless*. New York: World, 1972.

———. *The Threepersons Hunt*. New York: Evans, 1974.

Gear, Kathleen O'Neal and W. Michael Gear. *People of the Mist*. New York: Tom Doherty, 1997.

———. *People of the Silence*. New York: Tom Doherty, 1996.

———. *The Summoning God*. New York: Tom Doherty, 2000.

———. *The Visitant*. New York: Tom Doherty, 1999.

Gorman, Ed. *Hawk Moon*. London: Headline, 1995.

Gray, Muriel. *The Trickster*. New York: St. Martin's Press, 1995.

Grove, Fred. *Warrior Road*. New York: Doubleday, 1974.

Guthrie, A. B., Jr. *The Genuine Article*. Boston: Houghton Mifflin, 1977.

Hackler, Micah S. *Coyote Returns*. New York: Bantam Doubleday, 1996.

———. *The Dark Canyon*. New York: Bantam Doubleday, 1997.

———. *Legend of the Dead*. New York: Bantam Doubleday, 1995.

————. *The Shadow Catcher*. New York: Bantam Doubleday, 1997.

Hager, Jean. *The Fire Carrier*. New York: Warner Books, 1996.

————. *Ghostland*. New York: Warner Books, 1992.

————. *The Grandfather Medicine*. New York: Warner Books, 1989.

————. *Masked Dancers*. New York: Warner Books, 1998.

————. *Night Walker*. New York: Warner Books, 1990.

————. *Ravenmocker*. New York: Warner Books, 1994.

————. *The Redbird's Cry*. New York: Warner Books, 1994.

————. *Seven Black Stones*. New York: Warner Books, 1995.

————. *The Spirit Caller*. New York: Warner Books, 1997.

Halsey, Harlan Page (Old Sleuth). *Pawnee Tom, or Adrift in New York: A Story of an Indian Boy Detective*. New York: J. S. Ogilvie, 1896.

Hamilton, Steve. *Winter of the Wolf Moon*. New York: St. Martin's Press, 2000.

Harbaugh, T. *Velvet Foot, the Indian Detective, or, The Taos Tiger*. 1884.

Henry, Sue. *Deadfall*. New York: Avon, 1998.

————. *Murder on the Iditarod Trail*. New York: William Morrow & Co., 1993.

Herbert, Frank. *Soul Catcher*. New York: Putnam's, 1973.

Hillerman, Tony. *The Blessing Way*. New York: Harper & Row, 1970.

————. *Coyote Waits*. New York: Harper & Row, 1990.

————. *Dance Hall of the Dead*. New York: Harper & Row, 1973.

————. *The Dark Wind*. New York: Harper & Row, 1982.

————. *The Fallen Man*. New York: Harper & Row, 1996.

————. *The First Eagle*. New York: Harper & Row, 1998.

————. *Fly on the Wall*. New York: Harper & Row, 1983.

————. *The Ghostway*. New York: Harper & Row, 1984.

————. *Hunting Badger*. New York: Harper & Row, 2000.

————. *Listening Woman*. New York: Harper & Row, 1978.

————. *People of Darkness*. New York: Harper & Row, 1980.

————. *Sacred Clowns*. New York: Harper & Row, 1993.

————. *Skinwalkers*. New York: Harper & Row, 1986.

————. *Talking God*. New York: Harper & Row, 1989.

————. *A Thief of Time*. New York: Harper & Row, 1988.

Hirsh, M. E. *Dreaming Back*. New York: St. Martin's Press, 1993.

Hoeg, Peter. *Smilla's Sense of Snow*. New York: Farrar Straus Giroux, 1993.

Holmes, Sherlock. "The Adventure of The Copper Beeches." *Strand*, June 1892.

Household, Geoffry. *Rogue Male*. New York: Viking, 1977.

Hoyt, Richard. *Fish Story*. New York: Viking, 1985.

Jance, J. A. *Kiss of The Bees*. New York: Avon, 2000.

Kelman, Judith. *Where Shadows Fall*. New York: Berkley, 1987.

Lackey, Mercedes. *Sacred Ground*. New York: Tom Doherty Associates, 1994.

LaFarge, Oliver. *Laughing Boy*. Boston: Houghton Mifflin, 1929.

L'Amour, Louis. *The Haunted Mesa*. New York: Bantam, 1987.

Lane, Christopher. *Elements of a Kill*. New York: Avon, 1998.

————. *Season of Death*. New York: Avon, 1999.

————. *A Shroud of Midnight Sun*. New York: Avon, 2000.

MacDonald, William Colt. *The Comanche Scalp*. New York: Thorndike, 1998.

MacGregor, Rob. *Hawk Moon*. New York: Simon and Schuster, 1996.

————. *Prophecy Rock*. New York: Simon and Schuster, 1995.

Maddison, Lauren. *Deceptions*. New York: Alyson Books, 1999.

Matheson, Richard. *Shadow on the Sun*. New York: Evans, 1994.

Matteson, Stefanie. *Murder on High*. New York: Berkley, 1994.

McClendon, Lise. *The Bluejay Shaman*. New York: Walker, 1996.

Miles, John. *Tenoclock Scholar*. New York: Walker, 1995.

———, as Arthur Williams. *Missing at Tenoclock*. New York: Walker, 1994.

Mitchell, Kirk. *Cry Dance*. New York: Bantam, 1999.

———. *Deep Valley Malice*. New York: Avon, 1996.

———. *Spirit Sickness*. New York: Bantam, 2000.

Moody, Skye Kathleen. *Rain Dance*. New York: St. Martin's Press, 1998.

———. *Wildcrafters*. New York: St. Martin's Press, 1999.

Moore, Brian. *Black Robe*. New York: Fawcett, 1985.

Padgett, Abigail. *Child of Silence*. New York: Time Warner, 1993.

———. *The Dollmaker's Daughters*. New York: Time Warner, 1997.

———. *Moonbird Boy*. New York: Time Warner, 1997.

———. *Strawgirl*. New York: Time Warner, 1994.

———. *Turtle Baby*. New York: Time Warner, 1995.

Page, Jake. *The Deadly Canyon*. New York: Random House, 1994.

———. *The Knotted Strings*. New York: Random House, 1995.

———. *The Lethal Partner*. New York: Random House, 1996.

———. *Shoot the Moon*. New York: Hobbs, 1979.

———. *The Stolen Gods*. New York: Random House, 1993.

Parrish, Richard. *Abandoned Heart*. New York: Dutton, 1997.

———. *The Dividing Line*. New York: Dutton, 1993.

———. *Nothing but the Truth*. New York: Dutton, 1995.

———. *Our Choice of Gods*. New York: Dutton, 1997.

———. *Versions of the Truth*. New York: Dutton, 1994.

———. *Wind and Lies*. New York: Dutton, 1996.

Patten, Lewis B. *Death Stalks Yellowhorse*. New York: G. K. Hall, 1997.

Perry, Thomas. *Blood Money*. New York: Random House, 2000.

———. *Dance for the Dead*. New York: Random House, 1996.

———. *The Face-Changers*. New York: Random House, 1998.

———. *Shadow Woman*. New York: Random House, 1997.

———. *Vanishing Act*. New York: Random House, 1995.

Peterson, Geoff. *Medicine Dog*. New York: St. Martin's Press, 1989.

Prowell, Sandra West. *By Evil Means*. New York: Walker, 1993.

———. *The Killing of Monday Brown*. New York: Walker, 1994.

———. *When Wallflowers Die*. New York: Walker, 1996.

Reynolds, Brad, S.J. *A Ritual Death*. New York: Avon, 1997.

———. *The Story Knife*. New York: Avon, 1996.

Roberts, James Hall. *The Burning Sky*. New York: William Morrow & Co., 1966.

Rust, Megan Mallory. *Dead Stick*. New York: Berkley Crime, 1998.

———. *Red Line*. New York: Berkley Crime, 1999.

Sanders, William. *Blood Autumn*. New York: St. Martin's Press, 1995.

Sands, Marella. *Serpent and Storm*. New York: Forge, 1999.

———. *Sky Knife*. New York: Forge, 1997.

Satterthwait, Walter. *At Ease with the Dead*. New York: St. Martin's Press, 1990.

———. *Wall of Glass*. New York: St. Martin's Press, 1987.

Sayers, Dorothy. *Have His Carcase*. New York: Harper & Row, 1932.

Seals, David. *Powwow Highway*. New York: Plume Press, 1990.

Sibley, Celestine. *Dire Happenings at Scratch Ankle*. New York: HarperCollins, 1993.

Simpson, Marcia. *Crow in Stolen Colors*. New York: Berkley Crime, 2000.

Smith, Martin Cruz. *The Indians Won*. New York: Norton, 1962.

———. *Nightwing*. New York: Random House, 1977.

Stabenow, Dana. *Blood Will Tell*. New York: Putnam's, 1996.

———. *Breakup*. New York: Putnam's, 1997.

———. *A Cold Day for Murder*. New York: Berkley, 1992.

———. *A Cold-blooded Business*. New York: Berkley, 1994.

———. *Dead in the Water*. New York: Berkley, 1993.

———. *A Fatal Thaw*. New York: Berkley, 1993.

———. *Hunter's Moon*. New York: Berkley, 1999.

———. *Killing Grounds*. New York: Berkley, 1998.

———. *Midnight Come Again*. New York: Berkley, 2000.

———. *Play with Fire*. New York: Berkley, 1995.

———. *So Sure of Death*. New York: Dutton, 1999.

Stein, Garth. *Raven Stole the Moon*. New York: Simon and Schuster, 1988.

Steinberg, Janice. *Death-Fires Dance*. New York: Berkley, 1996.

Stern, Richard Martin. *Death in the Snow*. New York: Simon and Schuster, 1973.

———. *Missing Man*. New York: Simon and Schuster, 1990.

———. *Murder in the Walls*. New York: Simon and Schuster, 1971.

———. *Tangled Murders*. New York: Simon and Schuster, 1988.

Stokes, Naomi M. *The Listening Ones*. New York: Tom Doherty Associates, 1997.

———. *The Tree People*. New York: Tom Doherty Associates, 1995.

Stout, Rex. *Red Threads*. New York: Farrar, 1939.

Straley, John. *The Curious Eat Themselves*. New York: Bantam, 1993.

———. *Death and the Language of Happiness*. New York: Bantam, 1997.

———. *The Music of What Happens*. New York: Bantam, 1996.

———. *The Woman Who Married a Bear*. New York: Bantam, 1994.

Sullivan, Mark T. *Ghost Dance*. New York: Avon, 1999.

———. *The Purification Ceremony*. New York: Avon, 1997.

Taylor, Judson R. *Phil Scott, the Indian Detective: A Tale of Startling Mysteries*. 1882.

Thurlo, Aimée. *Black Mesa*. New York: Harlequin, 1990.

———. *Black Raven's Pride*. New York: Harlequin, 2000.

———. *Breach of Faith*. New York: Harlequin, 1992.

———. *Cisco's Woman*. New York: Harlequin, 1996.

———. *Four Winds* trilogy. *Her Destiny*. New York: Harlequin, 1997; *Her Hero*. New York: Harlequin, 1996; *Her Shadow*. New York: Harlequin, 1998.

———. *Redhawk's Heart*. New York: Harlequin, 1999.

———. *Second Shadow*. New York: Harlequin, 1993.

———. *Shadow of the Wolf*. New York: Harlequin, 1993.

———. *Spirit Warrior*. New York: Harlequin, 1993.

———. *Timewalker*. New York: Harlequin, 1994.

Thurlo, Aimée and David Thurlo. *Bad Medicine*. New York: Tom Doherty Associates, 1997.

————. *Blackening Song*. New York: Tom Doherty Associates, 1995.

————. *Death Walker*. New York: Tom Doherty Associates, 1996.

————. *Enemy Way*. New York: Tom Doherty Associates, 1998.

————. *Shooting Chant*. New York: Tom Doherty Associates, 2000.

Trainor, J. F. *Corona Blue*. New York: Kensington, 1994.

————. *Dynamite Pass*. New York: Kensington, 1993.

————. *High Country Murder*. New York: Kensington, 1995.

————. *Target for Murder*. New York: Kensington, 1991.

————. *Whiskey Jack*. New York: Kensington, 1994.

Truman, Margaret. *Murder at the FBI*. New York: Arbor House, 1985.

Ude, Wayne Richard. *Becoming Coyote*. Amherst, Mass.: Lynx House Press, 1981.

Wellman, Manly Wade. "A Star for a Warrior." *Ellery Queen's Mystery Magazine* (April 1946).

Westbrook, Robert. *Ancient Enemy*. New York: Signet, 2001.

————. *Ghost Dancer*. New York: Signet, 1998.

————. *Red Moon*. New York: Signet, 1999.

————. *Warrior Circle*. New York: Signet, 2000.

White, Robb. *Deathwatch*. New York: Doubleday, 1972.

Yarbro, C(helsea). Q. *Blood Games*. New York: Berkley, 1992.

————. *Cat's Claw*. New York: Berkley, 1992.

————. *Music When Sweet Voices Die*. New York: Putnam's, 1979; reprint (as *False Notes*). New York: Berkley, 1991.

————. *Ogilvie, Tallant & Moon*. New York: Putnam's, 1976; reprint (as *Bad Medicine*). New York: Berkley, 1991.

————. *Poison Fruit*. New York: Putnam's, 1991.

Young, Scott. *Murder in a Cold Climate*. New York: Penguin, 1988.

————. *The Shaman's Knife*. New York: Viking Press, 1993.

Juvenile Detective Fiction

Abbott, Kate. *Mystery at Echo Cliffs*. Santa Fe, N.M.: Red Crane Books, 1994.

Bibee, John. *The Mystery of the Vanishing Cave*. Downers Grove, Ill.: InterVarsity Press, 1996.

Brouwer, Sigmund. *The Mystery Tribe of Camp Blackeagle* (The Accidental Detectives, No. 2). Colorado Springs, Colo.: Chariot Victor Publishing, 1995.

————. *Sunrise at the Mayan Temple* (The Accidental Detectives, No. 10). Colorado Springs, Colo.: Chariot Victor Publishing, 1995.

Farber, Erica. *Golden Eagle: An Adventure on a Native American Desert Preserve*. Racine, Wis.: Western Publishing, 1995.

Green, Timothy. *Mystery of Coyote Canyon*. Wauconda, Ill.: Ancient City Press, 1994.

————. *Twilight Boy*. Flagstaff, Ariz.: Rising Moon. 1998.

Hale, Anna. *Mystery on Mackinac Island*. Boulder, Colo.: Harbinger House, 1989.

Hobbs, Will. *Ghost Canoe*. New York: Avon Camelot, 1998.

Lasky, Kathryn. *A Voice in the Wind*. San Diego: Harcourt Brace, 1993.

MacGregor, Rob. *Hawk Moon*. New York: Laurel-Leaf Books, 1996.

————. *Prophecy Rock*. New York: Laurel-Leaf Books, 1995.

Martin, Nora. *The Eagle's Shadow*. Scholastic, 1997.

Murphy, Elspeth Campbell. *The Mystery of the Eagle Feather*. Minneapolis, Minn.: Bethany House Publishers, 1995.

Reed, Nat. *Thunderbird Gold*. Greenville, S.C.: Bob Jones University Press, 1997.

Thoene, Jake, Luke Thoene, et al. *Mystery Lights of Navajo Mesa* (*The Last Chance Detectives*, Book 1). Wheaton, Ill.: Tyndale House Publishing, 1994.

Warner, Gertrude Chandler. *The Mystery of the Lost Village* (*Boxcar Children*, No. 37). Morton Grove, Ill.: Albert Whitman and Co., 1994.

Native American Detective Fiction and Mythologies

Alexie, Sherman. *Indian Killer*. New York: Warner Books, 1998.

———. *The Lone Ranger and Tonto Fistfight in Heaven*. New York: Atlantic Monthly Press, 1993.

———. *Reservation Blues*. New York: Warner Books, 1995.

Allen, Paula Gunn. *Grandmothers of the Light*. Boston: Beacon Press, 1991.

Armstrong, Jeanette. *Slash*. Penticton, B.C.: Theytus Books, 1985.

Barrett, S. M. *Geronimo: His Own Story*. New York: Dutton, 1970.

Beck, Peggy, Anna Lee Walters, and Nia Francisco. *The Sacred: Ways of Knowledge, Sources of Life*. Tsaile, Ariz.: Navaho Community College Press, 1996.

Bierhorst, John, ed. and trans. *The Red Swan: Myths and Tales of the American Indians*. New York: Farrar, 1976; reprint, Albuquerque: University of New Mexico Press, 1992.

Bruchac, Joseph, ed. *Aniyunwiya/Real Human Beings: An Anthology of Contemporary Cherokee Prose*. Greenfield Center, N.Y.: Greenfield Review Press, 1995.

———, ed. *New Voices from the Longhouse: Anthology of Contemporary Iroquois Writing*. Greenfield Center, N.Y.: Greenfield Review Press, 1989.

———, ed. *Smoke Rising: The Native North American Literary Companion*. Detroit: Visible Ink Press, 1995.

——— and James Bruchac, eds. *When the Chenoo Howls: Native American Tales of Terror*. New York: Walker, 1999.

Conley, Robert. *Go-Ahead Rider*. New York: Pocket Books, 1990.

———. *Outside the Law*. New York: Pocket Books, 1995.

———. *The Peace Chief*. New York: Pocket Books, 1999.

———. *To Make a Killing*. New York: Pocket Books, 1994.

———. *Zeke Proctor: Cherokee Outlaw*. New York: Pocket Books, 1994.

Curtin, Jeremiah. *Creation Myths of Primitive America*. Boston: Little, Brown, 1898; reprint, New York: B. Blom, 1969.

Downing, [George] Todd. *The Case of the Unconquered Sisters*. Garden City, N.Y.: Doubleday, 1936.

———. *The Cat Screams*. Garden City, N.Y.: Doubleday, 1934.

———. *Death under the Moonflower*. Garden City, N.Y.: Doubleday, 1938.

———. *The Last Trumpet: Murder in a Mexican Bull Ring*. Garden City, N.Y.: Doubleday, 1937.

———. *The Lazy Lawrence Murders*. Garden City, N.Y.: Doubleday, 1941.

———. *The Mexican Earth*. Garden City, N.Y.: Doubleday, 1940.

————. *Murder on Tour.* New York: Putnam's, 1933.

————. *Murder the Tropic.* Garden City, N.Y.: Doubleday, 1935.

————. *Night over Mexico.* Garden City, N.Y.: Doubleday, 1937.

————. *Vultures in the Sky.* Garden City, N.Y.: Doubleday, 1935.

Edmonds, Margot and Ella E. Clark, eds. *Voices of the Winds: Native American Legends.* New York: Facts on File, 1989.

Erdoes, Richard, ed. *American Indian Trickster Tales.* New York: Viking Penguin Publications, 1998.

Erdoes, Richard and Alfonso Ortiz, eds. *American Indian Myths and Legends.* New York: Pantheon Books, 1984.

Haile, Berard. *Navaho Coyote Tales.* Lincoln: University of Nebraska Press, 1984.

Hale, Janet Campbell. *The Jailing of Cecelia Capture.* Albuquerque: University of New Mexico Press, 1987.

Hazen-Hammond, Susan. *Spider Woman's Web: Traditional Native American Tales about Women's Power.* New York: Berkley, 1999.

Hogan, Linda. *Mean Spirit.* New York: Ivy Books, 1992.

Leland, Charles. *Algonquin Legends.* New York: Dover Publications, 1992.

Lopez, Barry. *Giving Birth to Thunder, Sleeping with His Daughter.* New York: Avon Books, 1977.

Malotki, Ekkehard and Michael Lomatuway'ma. *Hopi Coyote Tales.* Lincoln: University of Nebraska Press, 1984.

Mayo, Gretchen Will. *North American Indian Stories—Star Tales.* New York: Walker & Co., 1990.

Medawar, Mardi Oakley. *Death at Rainy Mountain.* New York: St. Martin's Press, 1996.

————. *Murder at Medicine Lodge.* New York: St. Martin's Press, 1999.

————. *People of the Whistling Waters.* Encampment, Wyo.: Affiliated Writers of America, 1993; reprint, New York: Doubleday, 1997.

————. *The Witch of the Palo Duro.* New York: St. Martin's Press, 1997.

Owens, Louis. *The Bone Game: A Novel.* Norman: University of Oklahoma Press, 1994.

————. *Dark River: A Novel.* Norman: University of Oklahoma Press, 1999.

————. *Nightland.* New York: Dutton NAL, 1996.

————. *Other Destinies: Understanding the American Indian Novel.* Norman: University of Oklahoma Press, 1994.

————. *The Sharpest Sight: A Novel.* Norman: University of Oklahoma Press, 1992.

————. *Wolfsong.* Norman: University of Oklahoma Press, 1995.

————, ed. *American Indian Novelists: An Annotated Critical Bibliography.* New York: Garland, 1985.

Pijoan, Teresa. *White Wolf Woman.* Little Rock, Ark.: August House Publications, 1992.

Querry, Ron. *The Death of Bernadette Lefthand.* Santa Fe, N.M.: Red Crane Books, 1993.

Rockwell, David. *Giving Voice to Bear.* Niwat, Colo.: Roberts Rinehart Publishing, 1991.

Seals, David. *Powwow Highway.* Sturgis, S.D.: Sky and Sage Books, 1979; reprint, New York: Plume Press, 1990.

Trafzer, Clifford E., ed. *Blue Dawn, Red Earth: New Native American Storytellers.* New York: Anchor Books, 1996.

———, ed. *Earth Song, Sky Spirit: Short Stories of the Contemporary Native American Experience.* New York: Doubleday, 1992.

Trout, Lawana, ed. *Native American Literature: An Anthology.* Lincolnwood, Ill.: NTC Publishing Group, 1999.

Walters, Anna Lee. *Ghost Singer.* Albuquerque: University of New Mexico Press, 1988.

———, ed. *Neon Powwow: New Native American Voices of the Southwest.* Flagstaff, Ariz.: Northland, 1993.

Welch, James. *The Death of Jim Loney.* New York: Harper & Row, 1979.

———. *Fool's Crow.* New York: Harper & Row, 1986.

———. *The Indian Lawyer.* New York: W. W. Norton, 1990.

———. *Winter in the Blood.* New York: Harper & Row, 1974.

SECONDARY SOURCES

Allen, Paula Gunn. "The Sacred Hoop: A Contemporary Perspective." In *Studies in American Indian Literature*, ed. Paula Gunn Allen. New York: The Modern Language Association, 1983, pp. 3–22.

Anderson, Eric Gary. *American Indian Literature and the Southwest: Contexts and Dispositions.* Austin: University of Texas Press, 1999.

Armstrong, Virginia. *I Have Spoken: American History through the Voices of Indians.* Chicago: Sage Books, 1971.

Bahti, Tom. *Southwestern Indian Ceremonials.* Las Vegas: KC Publications, 1982.

Barrett, S. M. *Geronimo: His Own Story.* New York: Dutton, 1970.

Beam, John, Barbara Brenstad, and Jack Marden. *The Native American in Long Fiction: An Annotated Bibliography.* New York: Scarecrow Press, 1996.

Beck, Peggy, Anna Lee Walters, and Nia Francisco. *The Sacred: Ways of Knowledge, Sources of Life.* Tsaile, Ariz.: Navaho Community College Press, 1996.

Beidler, Peter G. "Indians in Martin Cruz Smith's *Nightwing*: A Review Article." *Albuquerque Quarterly* 5 (1979): 155–59.

Berkhofer, Robert. *The White Man's Indian: Images of the American Indian from Columbus to the Present.* New York: Knopf, 1978.

Bird, Elizabeth, ed. *Dressing in Feathers: The Construction of the Indian in American Popular Culture.* Boulder, Colo.: Westview Press, 1996.

Cawelti, John G. *Adventure, Mystery, and Romance: Formula Stories as Art and Popular Culture.* Chicago: University of Chicago Press, 1976.

Chief Seattle. "Address." In *80 Readings*, ed. David Munger. New York: HarperCollins, 1992, pp. 52–55.

Churchill, Ward. *Fantasies of the Master Race: Literature, Cinema, the Colonization of American Indians*, ed. M. Annette Jaimes. Monroe, Me.: Common Courage Press, 1992; reprint, San Francisco: City Lights Books, 1998.

Crider, Bill. "Rural Milieu." In *The Oxford Companion to Crime and Mystery Fiction*, ed. Rosemary Herbert. London: Oxford University Press, 1999.

Davis, Mary, ed. *Native America in the Twentieth Century: An Encyclopedia.* Hamden, Conn.: Garland, 1994, 1996.

Deloria, Philip J. *Playing Indian.* New Haven, Conn.: Yale University Press, 1998.

DeMarr, Mary Jean. "Dana Stabenow's Alaska Mysteries." In *Diversity and Detective Fiction: Race, Gender, Ethnicity,* ed. Kathleen Klein. Bowling Green, Ohio: Bowling Green State University Popular Press, 2000.

Dunn, Susan. *Sister Revolutions: French Lightning, American Light.* New York: Faber and Faber, 2000.

Farb, Peter. *Man's Rise to Civilization.* New York: E. P. Dutton, 1968.

Fukuyama, Francis. *The End of History and the Last Man.* New York: Avon, 1993.

———. "Will Socialism Make a Comeback?" *Time* (May 22, 2000): 110–12.

Gill, Sam and Irene F. Sullivan. *Dictionary of Native American Mythology.* New York: Oxford University Press, 1992.

Greer, Allen, ed. *The Jesuit Relations: Natives and Missionaries in Seventeenth-Century North America.* New York: St. Martin's Press, 2000.

Haile, Berard and Leland C. Wyman. *Beautyway: A Navajo Ceremonial.* New York: Pantheon, 1957.

Hall, Edward T. *The Silent Language.* New York: Doubleday/Anchor, 1973.

Holt, Patricia. "Tony Hillerman." *Publishers Weekly* (October 24, 1980): 6–7.

Hultkrantz, Ake. *Native Religions of North America: The Power of Visions and Fertility.* San Francisco: Harper & Row, 1987.

Jilek, Wolfgang G. *Indian Healing: Shamanic Ceremonialism in the Pacific Northwest Today.* Blaine, Wash.: Hancock House Publishers, 1981.

Klein, Kathleen, ed. *Diversity and Detective Fiction: Race, Gender, Ethnicity.* Bowling Green, Ohio: Bowling Green State University Popular Press, 2000.

Kluckhohn, Clyde. *Navaho Witchcraft.* Boston: Beacon Press, 1944.

Kroeber, Karl. *Artistry in Native American Myths.* Lincoln: University of Nebraska Press, 1998.

Macdonald, Andrew and Gina Macdonald. "Ethnic Detectives in Popular Fiction: New Directions for an American Genre." In *Diversity and Detective Fiction: Race, Gender, Ethnicity,* ed. Kathleen Klein. Bowling Green, Ohio: Bowling Green State University Popular Press, 2000.

Macdonald, Andrew, Gina Macdonald and MaryAnn Sheridan. *Shape-Shifting: Images of the Native American in Recent Popular Fiction.* Westport, Conn.: Greenwood Press, 2000.

Macdonald, Ross. "The Writer as Detective Hero." In *On Crime Writing.* Santa Barbara, Calif.: Capra Press, 1973.

McCleary, Timothy P. *The Stars We Know: Crow Indian Astronomy and Lifeways.* Prospect Heights, Ill.: Waveland Press, 1997.

McFarland, Ron, ed. *James Welch.* Lewiston, Idaho: Confluence, 1986.

Mihesuah, Devon A. *American Indians: Stereotypes and Realities.* Atlanta: Clarity Press, 1996.

Paravisini-Gerbert, Lisbeth. "Native American Sleuth." In *The Oxford Companion to Crime and Mystery Writing,* ed. Rosemary Herbert. London: Oxford University Press, 1999.

Parkman, Francis. *The Jesuits in North America.* Gansevoort, N.Y.: Comer House Historical Publications, 1970.

Pronzini, Bill and Martin H. Greenberg, eds. *The Ethnic Detectives: Masterpieces of Mystery Fiction.* New York: Dodd, Mead, 1985.

Riley, John. *Tony Hillerman: A Critical Companion*. Westport, Conn.: Greenwood Press, 1994.

Ruoff, A. LaVonne Brown. *American Indian Literature: An Introduction, Review, and Selected Bibliography*. New York: Modern Language Association, 1990.

Simmons, Marc. *Witchcraft in the Southwest: Spanish and Indian Supernaturalism on the Rio Grande*. Omaha: University of Nebraska Press, 1980.

Taylor, Colin, ed. *North American Indians: A Pictorial History of the Indian Tribes of North America*. Bristol, Eng.: Parragon, 1997.

Tedlock, Barbara. *The Beautiful and the Dangerous*. New York: Viking Penguin, 1992.

Tedlock, Dennis and Barbara Tedlock, eds. *Teachings from the American Earth: Indian Religion and Philosophy*. New York: Liveright, 1975.

Thompson, Jon. *Fiction, Crime, and Empire*. Chicago: University of Chicago Press, 1993.

Wa'na'nee'che (Dennis Renault) and Timothy Frere. *Native American Spirituality*. New York: Thorsons, 1996.

Wild, Peter. *James Welch*. Boise, Idaho: Boise State University Press, 1983.

Winks, Robin. "Tony Hillerman." *Washington Post Book World* (May 27, 1990): 12.

Index

About the Authors

GINA MACDONALD is Assistant Professor of English at Nicholls State University. Her books include *James Clavell: A Critical Companion* (Greenwood, 1996), *Robert Ludlum: A Critical Companion* (Greenwood, 1997), and, with Andrew Macdonald, *Shape-Shifting: Images of Native Americans in Popular Fiction* (Greenwood, 2000).

ANDREW MACDONALD is Associate Professor of English at Loyola University. He has published widely on popular culture issues. His books include *Howard Fast: A Critical Companion* (Greenwood, 1996) and, with Gina Macdonald, *Shape-Shifting: Images of Native Americans in Popular Fiction* (Greenwood, 2000).

Recent Titles in
Contributions to the Study of Popular Culture

The Use of Arthurian Legend in Hollywood Film: From Connecticut Yankees to
Fisher Kings
Rebecca A. Umland and Samuel J. Umland

Agent of Challenge and Defiance: The Films of Ken Loach
George McKnight, editor

Edison's Kinetoscope and Its Films: A History to 1896
Ray Philips

The Last Modernist: The Films of Theo Angelopolous
Andrew Horton, editor

Theory and Practice of Classic Detective Fiction
Jerome H. Delamater and Ruth Prigozy, editors

The Detective in American Fiction, Film, and Television
Jerome H. Delamater and Ruth Prigozy, editors

Imagining the Worst: Stephen King and the Representation of Women
Kathleen Margaret Lant and Theresa Thompson, editors

Bleep! Censoring Rock and Rap Music
Betty Houchin Winfield and Sandra Davidson, editors

The Cowboy Way: The Western Leader in Film, 1945–1995
Ralph Lamar Turner and Robert J. Higgs

Parody as Film Genre: "Never Give a Saga an Even Break"
Wes D. Gehring

Shape-Shifting: Images of Native Americans in Popular Fiction
Andrew Macdonald, Gina Macdonald, and MaryAnn Sheridan

Noir, Now and Then: Film Noir Originals and Remakes (1944–1999)
Ronald Schwartz